THE MILK
COWS

THE MILK COWS

COWS

U-Boat Tankers at War
1941–1945

JOHN WHITE

Pen & Sword
MARITIME

First published in Great Britain in 2009 by
PEN & SWORD MILITARY
An imprint of
Pen & Sword Books Ltd
47 Church Street
Barnsley
South Yorkshire
S70 2AS

ISBN 978-1-84884-008-9

A CIP catalogue record for this book is
available from the British Library

Typeset by Concept, Huddersfield, West Yorkshire
Printed and bound in England by CPI, UK.

Pen & Sword Books Ltd incorporates the Imprints of Pen & Sword Aviation,
Pen & Sword Maritime, Pen & Sword Military, Wharncliffe Local History,
Pen & Sword Select, Pen & Sword Military Classics, Leo Cooper,
Remember When, Seaforth Publishing and Frontline Publishing

For a complete list of Pen & Sword titles please contact
PEN & SWORD BOOKS LIMITED
47 Church Street, Barnsley, South Yorkshire, S70 2AS, England
E-mail: enquiries@pen-and-sword.co.uk
Website: www.pen-and-sword.co.uk

Contents

List of Maps

Preface

This is the story of Germany's submarine tankers, popularly known as the 'milk cows'. Germany's Kriegsmarine was, in the Second World War, the only navy in history ever to operate submarine tankers, a circumstance forced upon the U-boat Command by the difficulty of refuelling U-boats with conventional tankers in an ocean that would become dominated by Allied air and sea power. Their unique ability to submerge to evade detection provided the submarine tankers, for a while, with the means to continue their hazardous undertaking.

Any account of U-boat fortunes in the Second World War tends to leave the reader feeling stunned. By the end of the war, the Germans had suffered 30,000 dead and 5,000 captured U-boatmen from a deployed U-boat force of 41,000 men (latest German assessment), the worst casualty rate sustained by any armed force over a protracted period in all of history, and the milk cows suffered their full share of this carnage. British Intelligence was able to read most of the cows' numerous radio commands from 1943 to the end of the war, and their appalling casualty rate can be largely attributed to this cause. At times, the British Admiralty knew more about U-boat operations than did the Germans.

One cannot help but wonder why the Germans never understood that their ciphers were insecure. The ciphers were produced by mechanical interlocking devices, with rotating rotors to scramble the message, which the Germans well understood could be captured. The coded messages were then broadcast freely as radio messages in large volumes, so that code-breakers had plenty of material on which to work. The German faith in the machines' security relied on the fact that their settings were altered daily, and new mechanical rotors put in monthly, but clearly one could envisage this system being broken by a chance capture (as did occasionally occur) providing both settings and replacement rotors leading to a series of planned captures. Mostly, however, the British relied on the use of the world's first electronic computers to break the ciphers by trial and error.

The published memoirs of the few surviving U-boat commanders who were at sea after mid-1943 make it clear that the men at sea had realized that any broadcast message brought instant retribution, a problem exacerbated by the accuracy of Allied direction-finding equipment used to pinpoint the position of a transmitting U-boat. The older hands would send each other messages couched in terms that would only be understood by the recipient, if they used the radio at all. Yet BdU (U-boat Command) continued to send out radio commands to boats as soon as they had left port instead of providing 'sealed instructions' to be opened at sea. It is true that many U-boats were sunk fortuitously – for example, boats caught unawares at night by radar-fitted aircraft while travelling on the surface in the Bay of Biscay or even in mid-Atlantic – but constant changes to the U-boat ciphers indicated that the Germans had their suspicions.

It must have become apparent that virtually every U-tanker sent to refuel boats for remote theatres was quickly sunk after mid-1943, despite selection of the most secluded sea areas for the rendezvous. It seems extraordinary now that U-boat Command did not send out U-boats with written orders to head to a remote part of the ocean, then broadcast repeatedly in cipher from France that a refuelling was to take place at this remote area and order the U-boat to report back what happened. Several U-boats ordered to rendezvous with a milk cow in mid-Atlantic did report to base that they found only destroyers at the rendezvous, and the cow was never seen again.

Doubtless part of the problem lay with wishful thinking, for any interference with radio commands negated the whole basis of wolf-pack tactics, by which many boats were directed to a convoy located by one of their number. It is to be hoped that our current naval planners have not put the same unquestioning faith in their machine-operated ciphers as did the German Navy, particularly with the much-publicized advances in computer decryption techniques.

For the benefit of younger readers, accustomed to thinking of modern submarines as capable of remaining underwater for sustained periods (months), it should be mentioned that at the time of the Second World War the average 'submarine' was actually a submersible torpedo carrier. It was intended to operate on the surface in a manner similar to a destroyer armed with torpedoes, but with a much-reduced gun armament and with the priceless ability to submerge to avoid detection.

Conventional diesel engines requiring fuel oil were used when the U-boat cruised on the surface, which it did for most of the time, permitting a speed of 17 to 18 knots, far higher than the speed of most convoys and even of many of the convoy escorts. But once the U-boat dived, it switched to its main electric batteries. These provided it with a top speed of 7 knots for just one hour before running out of power, or with a crawling speed of 1 knot for anything up to forty-eight hours. Thus the U-boat lost all its mobility once it dived and the slowest convoy would leave it behind.

Moreover, it could not move any great distance before the exhaustion of its batteries required the U-boat to return to the surface, when the diesels could be used to drive the boat again and also to recharge the batteries (a task that took a few hours). By and large the milk cows did not need to submerge, except to dodge aircraft while passing between their bases (on the west coast of France) and the North Atlantic Ocean. Thus, most of the actions described in this book occurred on the surface.

In 1944 the Germans introduced the first examples of the 'true submarine', capable of remaining underwater for weeks at a time. These were the Type XXI and Type XXIII 'electric' U-boats, which were to revolutionalize submarine design from 1945 onwards.

But the electric boats do not form part of this story.

Acknowledgements

Many individuals have given me assistance with the compilation of this book.

It is a pleasure to acknowledge especially the huge contribution made by Fritz Vogel, who gave me a detailed written account of his patrol in U 461 and of his part in the German Naval Intelligence Service (B-Dienst), lent me maps and photographs, and assisted with a search for other survivors from the 'milk cows' (German submarine tankers).

Special thanks for an equally generous contribution are likewise due to Wilhelm Kraus, who volunteered a detailed written account of two later patrols in U 461, promptly answered many questions and also supplied me with several photographs.

Another very generous contribution was received from Guenther Paas, who made one patrol as midshipman on U 461 before being promoted to another boat, collated many eyewitness accounts of the sinking of U 461 from other survivors and Allied air crews, and provided a complete list of U-boats refuelled by U 461 with their subsequent fates, as well as adding personal experiences.

Gus Britton, of the British submarine museum at Gosport, lent me summaries of U-boat patrols, plus photographs and other particulars of the submarine war. He also put me in touch with the *Schaltung Kueste* magazine and with Horst Bredow's U-boat museum at Cuxhaven.

Fregattenkapitaen a.D. Guenther Hartmann, president of the *Schaltung Kueste*, very generously placed an advertisement in the magazine appealing for survivors of the milk cows – and made no charge.

Ernie Grayston, a close neighbour and an ex-submariner, reviewed an early copy of this manuscript and made many helpful suggestions, and was also instrumental in putting me in touch with Gus Britton (and thereby with the other helpers mentioned above).

Bob Coppock of the Directorate of Naval Staff Duties (Foreign Documents Section) at the Ministry of Defence, London, kindly permitted me to consult some of the U-boat war diaries in his office, and furnished me with particulars of some recent research into the loss of U 460. He also provided a copy of his unpublished investigation entitled 'The Origins and

Development of the Type XIV U-Boat' (FDS 245/81), as well as many helpful corrections to the text.

Horst Bredow provided me with valuable assistance during my stay at his 'U-Boot Archiv', and also furnished the blueprints of the Type XB and Type XIV U-boats reproduced in this book.

Franz Becker and Walter Cloots made several corrections and granted me an electronic, searchable copy of their enormous private database of U-boat operations from 1939 to 1945.

I am grateful to the following individuals who made small corrections to the original text: Commodore Jan Drent (Canada) who identified HMCS *Assiniboine* as the destroyer that rammed U 119; Fritz Schmidt of U 462, Gerhard Korbjuhn and Helmut Rochinski of U 461, also Dudley Marrows and Peter Jensen of 461 Squadron Coastal Command, for detailed assistance with the last cruises of U 461 and U 462 (my original detailed account of 'The Final Battle', from which large extracts appear in Chapter 12, was prompted by the U 461 survivors' association); Herrn Poetter and Vorstadt of U 487 for an eyewitness account of the sinking of their U-tanker; J.D. Brook for a correction concerning the escort of convoy HX.126; and Georg Hoegel for information about his boat U 30 docking at the *Max Albrecht*.

It has been pointed out by those who compile U-boat photographs that there are no very good pictures of the milk cows. I have discovered this for myself and the photographs appearing in this book have all been computer processed to improve them. My thanks again to Horst Bredow, Fritz Vogel, Wilhelm Kraus, Gert Thater, Fritz Schmidt, Walter Storbeck, the Bundesarchiv (Bonn) and the Trustees of the Imperial War Museum, London.

The charts on pages 16, 28, 114 and 160 are Crown copyright and are reproduced by kind permission of the Controller of The Stationery Office. They have been modified by computer processing to illustrate points made in this book, but the artwork remains as in the originals, which were made by the Air Ministry and are archived as U-boat dispositions in AIR 15.861.

The U-boat insignia on page 184 are reproduced from *Embleme/Wappen/ Malings Deutscher U-Boote 1939–1945* (1st Edition, 1984; Koehler/Mittler, Hamburg) by kind permission of Georg Hoegel, Muenchen, Germany (2nd edition published 1996).

And last, but by no means least, I am indebted to those many friends and colleagues who took the immense trouble of reading through earlier and later manuscripts, and for their comments and suggestions for improvement. Any errors that remain are my own.

John White
Wokingham

Introduction

I first discovered the German Navy at the age of ten, when I had to prepare a project for school work concerning the Second World War. I drew on the experience of a British sailor known to me who gave me an eyewitness account of the Allied landings in Normandy in June 1944. Two years later, now at secondary school, I happened to stumble across my old project notes and became interested in how the German Navy had responded to the Normandy invasion. Thus started a lifelong fascination that had resulted, by my late teens, in the compilation of a huge, handwritten database that contained everything about the Kriegsmarine I had been able to discover.

It was in the course of documenting the fortunes of the U-boat arm, by far the dominant force in the Kriegsmarine during the Second World War, that I came across the scattered references to the Germans' submarine tankers, the 'milk cows'. I collected all these references together for convenience in 1975 and realized that I had discovered a neglected, yet extraordinarily interesting facet of the U-boat war. The release in 1977 of hitherto secret information about British Intelligence in the Second World War gave the story a new twist.

The story of Germany's submarine tankers is one of true horror, the equal of any fictitious account put out by the legendary Hammer Studios. For the German milk cows had to lie with their engines stopped, hatches open and long fuelling hoses snaking out to the boat to be refuelled, in an ocean and under a sky controlled by the Allies. And from 1943 the Allies had decoded their fuelling rendezvous.

My objective in writing this book has therefore been to convey to the lay reader some of the terror and dread inherent in the inevitability of the fate of the milk cows and the extraordinary courage and stoicism of their crews. The book is not intended to be a technical account of refuelling at sea, nor a catalogue of the boats that were refuelled. Rather, we shall see how the German tanker crews started their operations under conditions of almost peacetime normality. But then one or two of the milk cows failed to return to base. And then the missions got worse. And worse.

1

In preparing this book, I have read all the 'official' accounts of the war at sea, of which Roskill's *War at Sea* and Doenitz's *Ten Years and Twenty Days* are central to setting the background. I have consulted Brassey's *Fuehrer Conferences on Naval Affairs* and have digested as many eyewitness accounts of the sinking of the individual milk cows as I have been able to discover. I have browsed the intelligence documents of the British Admiralty and Air Ministry for this period, which are now stored at The National Archives in Kew, London. I have spent very many hours perusing individual British decrypts of German signals, stored on microfilm, to and from U-boats for critical events at sea. These are additionally stored at the National Archives. I have scanned the available war diaries for German milk cows that were also released for public perusal in 1977 and have read the U-boat Command war diaries.

As a researcher, I have visited Horst Bredow's famous 'U-Boot Archiv' in Cuxhaven, Germany. This archive has now become a central clearing house for all information pertaining to the U-boat war and contains much that cannot be found elsewhere, especially in survivors' tales. I have also searched for survivors of the crews of the milk cows. The nature of their deployment and their fate ensures that there could be few such lucky men – an appeal in the magazine for ex-U-boatmen, the *Schaltung Kueste*, in 1995 produced just one eyewitness.

Chapter 1

The Birth of the U-Tanker
1926 to August 1940

After the German fleet had scuttled itself at Scapa Flow shortly after the end of the First World War, in 1919, Britain forbade the Germans to build up a strong fleet again, although they were allowed to replace obsolete warships with new ones up to a permitted tonnage displacement. For seven years, the Kriegsmarine had only a coastal role.

In 1926, the first of their obsolete battleships became due for replacement. In the same year, Vice Admiral Wolfgang Wegener published a book entitled *Strategy of the World War*. In it he wrote that, if Germany were ever to become a major power again, she would sooner or later have to face Britain. In that case she must either weave a pattern of alliances with other European powers to neutralize Britain's domination of the trading routes or, better, she could build a strong balanced fleet and obtain naval bases outflanking the British blockade that had trapped the High Seas fleet between the years 1914 and 1918.

The Wegener thesis was rejected by many high-ranking naval officers who believed that Germany would at no price become entangled in another war with Britain, but nevertheless the pocket battleship *Deutschland* was laid down in 1926. Her displacement of 12,100 tons exceeded the permitted 10,000 tons for German capital ships, although the Germans announced the displacement as 10,000 tons to save controversy, and her powerful armament, designed to enable the ship to outgun any faster opponent and to outrun any more powerful, gave Germany immediate control of the Baltic when the *Deutschland* was completed. With her wide radius of action, she was clearly designed for Atlantic operations against Britain or, as was thought more likely, France.

Hitler became the dictator of the Third Reich in 1933. He assured Grand Admiral Raeder, the C-in-C of the German Navy since 1928, that war with Britain would not come until 1948 at the earliest, by which time it was reckoned that German naval rearmament would be complete. The Navy's 'Z' plan called for the creation of a modern, strong fleet that would pose a

3

serious problem for the Royal Navy. The 'Z' plan was finally given absolute priority over all other military rearmament plans early in 1939. It emphasized gun power in its high proportion of large warships, but provision was also made for 233 U-boats. The majority of these would be of the standard attack Type VII, for use in the North Atlantic, and Type IX, for use further afield. Both carried torpedoes as their main armament.

One component of the 'Z' plan was the construction of long-range submarine minelayers to blockade remote enemy ports. The Construction Office of the U-boat Inspectorate (Marinekonstruktionsamt), known by the designation of 'K', was given the task of designing suitable minelaying types, as developments of those used in the First World War but with a capacity for larger mines. In particular, the new minelayers were required to be able to carry the new 'Sonder-Mine A' (SMA), a mine with 350kg of explosive operated remotely by the magnetic influence of a ship passing overhead.

After a number of false starts, the huge 'Type XB' U-minelayer was approved and construction of a prototype began in October 1938. An important feature of the design was that the mines could be carried 'wet', i.e. the mine compartment was normally flooded during use. This obviated the old problems of buoyancy that had afflicted the earlier 'dry' designs. Since only two stern torpedo tubes would be fitted, much weight could be saved enabling better diesel engines to be employed resulting in a high surface speed. Long-range, high-speed U-cruisers were also planned from 1937, again as a development of First World War designs.

Karl Doenitz, a U-boat commander from the First World War who would be made head of the U-boat arm in 1938, became more and more convinced from 1935 onwards that war with Britain was likely, and soon. He called for the immediate construction of 300 U-boats with which he believed, on the basis of exercises conducted in the Baltic, North Sea and Atlantic, it would be possible to strangle Britain's sea-trade routes. He felt that the lengthy shipbuilding required for the ships of the 'Z' plan would not pass unnoticed by Britain, leading to another arms race that Germany could not win. The competition between the two navies to build new capital ships in the first years of the century had been one of the primary causes of the First World War. Doenitz claimed that only the rapid completion of the relatively easily built U-boats would give Germany a naval force capable of posing a threat to the Atlantic lifeline. But the German naval staff were unwilling to pin all their hopes on one weapon to which Britain boasted that she had the answer: Asdic, an acoustic underwater location device whose performance was unknown to the Germans.

The Anglo-German Naval Treaty of 1935 had restricted Germany's warship tonnage to 35 per cent of that of Britain. The U-boat force could be built up to 45 per cent of Britain's submarine fleet, and could be raised in special circumstances to 100 per cent. This appeared to be of little

4

consequence to Britain, despite her disastrous experience of the U-boat arm in the First World War. Submarines are essentially an offensive weapon, the Royal Navy's task was to defend the sea lanes and it had little need for submarines. Consequently, Germany could not build many either. The fact that Germany was showing off her new U-boats within days of the signing of the agreement, although she had not been allowed to build any U-boats prior to this, should have given the British politicians food for thought, but there is little evidence that they took any notice.

Hitler cited Russian submarine building in 1938 as the excuse to enable the Kriegsmarine to build its U-boat strength up to that of Britain. In April of the following year, Hitler pointlessly abrogated the agreement, alarming the British and with no effect on the slow rate of U-boat construction which still had a low priority relative to other warships being built. In September 1939, therefore, it was purely coincidental that the German U-boat force amounted to fifty-seven boats, exactly the same number as Britain possessed. Of these, only twenty-two were suitable for long-range operations and one was at the bottom of the sea after an accident. This last boat was raised and recommissioned late in 1939.

When Britain declared war in September 1939, the German Navy found itself with a force that was only fractionally completed. All work on the surface ships of the 'Z' plan was halted, with the exception of those already close to completion. Absolute naval priority was now conferred on the construction of U-boats, which were recognized to be the only naval force capable of taking the war to Britain. Doenitz sent a memorandum to the Naval Supreme Command on the 8th, outlining his requirements to pursue the U-boat war. What we need (he said) are: attack boats (Types VII and IX); long-range minelayers (Type XB); U-cruisers (Type IXD2) and 'U-boat tankers'. Thus Doenitz approved the continued construction of those Type XB minelayers and U-cruisers that had already been laid down.

The 'U-boat tanker' – later abbreviated to 'U-tanker' – was an idea that was currently being reconsidered by the German Naval Command, which was obsessed with the danger that Britain could blockade Germany from the sea as it had done in the First World War, and therefore believed that it was necessary to create submersible tankers to provide undetectable bases for U-boats in the Atlantic. The first proposal for a submarine tanker had come from the German General Naval Office in 1934, leading to two possible specifications for a 'submersible depot ship' by the Marinekonstruktionsamt ('K') on 20 September 1934. This was at a time when navies everywhere were experimenting with large artillery armaments on submarines, and both proposed types were expected to bear the ludicrous armament of three 105mm heavy guns, as well as sufficient reserve fuel to supply up to six U-boats. One of the types was also planned to carry two torpedo tubes so that it could be used in an attack role.

5

The proposals had languished for years, but increasing international tension caused re-examination of the principle in 1938 when fears emerged that a British blockade might affect U-boats passing from German ports to the Atlantic. First, Admiral Carls proposed in September 1938 that submersible 'floating bases' could be used to supply and direct U-boats in their attacks, and then Kapitaen zS Fuerbringer, a former First World War U-boat commander and current head of the Kriegsmarine's Statistical Branch, suggested in April 1939 the use of 'U-transports' in a role similar to that proposed by Carls. Fuerbringer was particularly pessimistic about the use of surface tankers to refuel U-boats.

Doenitz had hitherto shown little interest in submarine tankers but, in a memorandum dated 23 May 1939, he stated his view that repair ships (surface vessels) would be of more value to the U-boat arm, since the condition of a U-boat's engines ultimately dictated its actions. On 3 August 1939, the German Naval Command countered with the argument that oil was used up much faster than any other U-boat consumable, and therefore a simple submarine tanker would suffice to extend the patrols of other U-boats. Wireless control from Germany negated the need for such tankers to direct other boats.

Two days after Doenitz's memo of 8 September, the German Naval Command made a request for three submersible tankers based on the 1934 specification. Within a week Doenitz, prompted by Raeder, had supplied a new specification. Doenitz and the Naval Command then agreed at a meeting on 30 November to place orders for a third, smaller design, whose outline specification had been finalized by December and which would be approved by Raeder on 2 January 1940. The new U-tankers were to be fitted with workshops, as well as carrying fuel, lubricating oil, provisions, torpedoes and medical aid. The tankers would carry no guns, except an anti-aircraft armament, and no torpedo tubes, and thus would have no attack capability.

Doenitz's request sparked further design work by the 'K' team. The shape of the putative tanker, named Type XIV, was taken from a Type IX boat, but shortened and widened so as to carry more fuel. Towing tests in February 1940 on the hull resulted in changes to the bow shape, and the type was specified as 'final' on 15 April.

Since the fuel to be carried was light – lighter than munitions and lighter than water – it was possible to use a heavier grade of steel in the construction, so that the U-tanker could dive deeper than the corresponding attack boat. This was clearly an advantage for a craft with no offensive capability. Most of the other components were taken from the existing attack Types VII and IX for continuity of construction of all types. Thus, the U-tanker contained many features common to the Type VII boats, but retained the conning tower of the Type IX boat on which it was based. The excess fuel, the reserve for transfer to other boats, was to be stored in a large 'bulge' constructed around the main hull.

The first contract for four tankers was placed with Deutsche Werke, Kiel, on 14 May 1940, and U 459 was laid down on 23 November of that year. Because of their greater complexity, the U-tankers and U-minelayers took longer to build than the other types – about ten months in the case of the U-tankers.

Doenitz insisted, and was to insist throughout the war, that it was essential to sink as many Allied merchant ships as possible in the shortest possible time. His staff had estimated that Britain could be forced to surrender if sinkings from all causes (including by the Luftwaffe) topped 700,000 tons per month. The average gross tonnage of a freighter at this time was 5,100 tons.

In order to maintain the maximum effectiveness from his limited number of U-boats, it was essential for Doenitz to keep them at sea for as long as possible. He controlled the activity of the boats by wireless transmission (W/T) from his headquarters, directing them to the convoys that had been located by air reconnaissance, wireless interception or by sighting from another U-boat, so that the U-boats at sea did not have to waste time searching for targets on their own. When the French ports on the Biscay coast were opened to the U-boats after the French surrender in August 1940, the distance to the crucial area of operations, the North Atlantic, was greatly reduced compared with the distance from Germany or Norway, and these ports remained the normal operational bases for Atlantic operations until after the Allied invasion in June 1944. The bases were gradually turned into enormous, concrete-covered, bomb-proof, U-boat pens.

One way of maximizing the efficiency of the U-boats was therefore to make their operational areas as close as possible to the U-boats' bases. Another method was to cut down the time that each boat spent in port. At the end of each patrol, a U-boat would spend about three weeks being refitted, during which time the crew would be on leave, followed by a further half week spent in briefing the crews for their next cruise. For this reason, Doenitz fought hard throughout the war to save dockyard workers from conscription into the Army and continually criticized the deployment of so many workers for the maintenance of the surface fleet. Doenitz had wanted 300 U-boats at the beginning of the war. He reckoned that 100 would at any time be in dockyard hands, 100 in transit to their operational area and 100 actually engaged in sinking ships. Time was to demonstrate that his estimation of the percentage of U-boats at their operating zones was about correct.

The third method of increasing the effectiveness of the U-boats was to refuel them at, or near, their operational zones. In effect, this is the logical extension of the first method mentioned, moving the base closer to the operational area instead of making the operational area close to the base.

Refuelling U-boats at sea was to become one of the major preoccupations of U-boat Command.

In the first twelve months of the war, however, the U-boats could find easy pickings close to the British coast where there was no question of being able to refuel at sea owing to the danger of surprise attack. Initially the U-boats were deployed to lay mines off key British harbours, then they attacked unescorted merchant ships with gun and torpedo. The British Asdic device was found to be much less of a threat to U-boats than had originally been supposed, although it was to be improved throughout the war. The Norwegian campaign in early 1940 caused a major redeployment of virtually the entire U-boat arm into the North Sea to protect the ships involved in the landings in Norway, and the fall of France caused another major deployment of the U-boats around the northern coast of Britain into the newly occupied French Biscay ports.

In the autumn of 1940, a period known to U-boat commanders as the 'Happy Time', U-boats operating out of France patrolled an area west of the North Channel, known as the 'North-West Approaches' (see Map 1-1), where targets in the form of unescorted ships, or weakly escorted convoys, came so readily that a U-boat could expect to use up all its torpedoes in the space of a fortnight and return to base. Under these circumstances, there

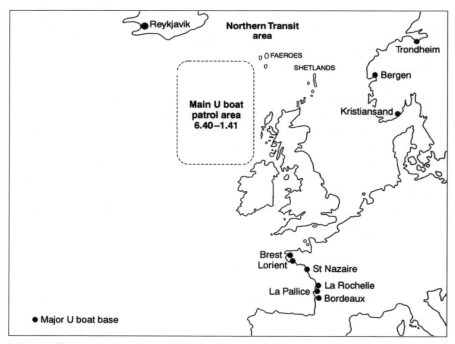

Map 1-1. The North-West Approaches, Autumn 1940.

8

was little need to refuel boats at sea since their bases were so close; moreover, Doenitz considered that it was unnecessary to send U-boats further afield while sinkings in this area came so easily.

Doenitz wanted to send all his U-boats to the North-West Approaches where the critical 'tonnage sunk per U-boat per day at sea' figure was kept to a maximum. But the Naval High Command insisted that some U-boats be sent to other waters in order to stretch the British convoy defences as far as possible. The idea was sound, but Doenitz was very reluctant to implement it. He tried to see the British point of view, asking whether it was better (for the British) if they lost many ships in one area, or lost fewer ships throughout the world, necessitating the introduction of the convoy system worldwide instead of just in the North Atlantic as was the case in 1940. Doenitz reckoned that Britain would prefer not to lose the greater number of ships and so, of course, he felt obliged to try to sink as many as possible.

Post-war analysis has shown that Doenitz was probably wrong. It has been estimated that as much shipping space was lost through the introduction of the worldwide convoy system, when it finally came, as was lost through ships being sunk by U-boats. The convoy system means that all ships must travel at the speed of the slowest, and congestion is caused at ports when the convoys assemble and arrive, while the ports stand empty in between times. Winston Churchill expressed his alarm early in the war at the loss of shipping space caused by the convoy system.

Doenitz compromised with the Naval Command. A large U-boat, which had been built in Germany for Turkey, had been requisitioned and renamed U A. Found in exercises to be rather unwieldy for convoy operations, U A (Kapitaenleutnant Cohausz) was first used to transport highly flammable and explosive materials for the Luftwaffe to the newly captured Norway in May 1940 – a task that was not popular either with her crew or with other vessels moored close to her – and was then sent south in June. She sank two ships in the South Atlantic, refuelled in July from the auxiliary cruiser *Pinguin** (when it was discovered that U A was poorly designed for being resupplied on the open sea, since she lacked equipment to move torpedoes and stores), sank a further four unescorted ships and returned to Germany in September.

In the autumn and winter of 1940, U 65 and U 37 were also sent south singly. They scored spectacular individual successes, but the all-important 'tonnage sunk per U-boat per day at sea' was less than was being obtained by other U-boats in less successful operations in the North Atlantic, a factor due entirely to the long time spent in transit to the South Atlantic.

* Auxiliary cruisers were armed merchant ships sent out from Germany into the remote parts of the oceans to attack unescorted Allied ships. *Pinguin* sank or captured 135,000 tons of Allied shipping, including an entire whaling fleet in the Antarctic, before being herself sunk in the Indian Ocean by the cruiser HMS *Cornwall*.

Chapter 2

The Supply Ships
September 1940 to May 1941

Consider the deployment of a large, Type IXB U-boat in a remote area, such as the mid-Atlantic. The radius of action of this type of U-boat was some 9,000 miles. The distance from a Biscay port to Freetown, a major port in West Africa for British trade from the Far East, was, and is, around 3,000 miles. Therefore, a Type IXB U-boat despatched to Freetown from France could operate for only 3,000 miles before having to return to base to refuel. If, on the other hand, the U-boat could be refuelled at, say, the Cape Verde Islands, its patrol radius would be extended to about 12,000 miles, an enormous increase in effectiveness.

Two surface tankers, the *Charlotte Schliemann* (7,747 tons) and the *Corrientes* (4,565 tons), had been stationed from the outset of war at Las Palmas in the Spanish Canary Islands. These ships had been fitted out for supply operations by the Spanish group of the secret German supply organization known as 'Ettapendienst', whose existence had not been discovered after Germany's defeat in the First World War. The *Charlotte Schliemann* had filled up with oil in the Caribbean, before being diverted before the beginning of the war to Las Palmas where she would remain until February 1942. However, it was the nearby *Corrientes* that was used at this stage to supply oil to the U-boats.

The *Corrientes* frequently refuelled U-boats in the area at night, with the connivance of the Spanish authorities. The boats came to the tanker, took on fuel and stores and then slipped away again before daylight. Most of the U-boats availing themselves of this service had been long-range craft based in Germany and operating west of Portugal, and the subsequent availability of the Biscay bases made this refuelling post less important. Refuelling at sea was soon to come.

The German surface fleet possessed a number of large, fast, purpose-built fleet tankers that were used to refuel major warships at sea. In the autumn of 1940 one, the *Ermland*, was in the Far East and the other three were in the Baltic. On 18 October, the tanker *Nordmark* (10,847 tons,

Kapitaen Grau) put to sea, followed four days later by the pocket battleship *Admiral Scheer*, which the *Nordmark* was intended to supply. Both ships successfully penetrated the British cruiser blockade of the Denmark Strait (between Iceland and Greenland) and headed south. By the end of March 1941, the *Admiral Scheer* was back in German waters after a cruise in the South Atlantic and Indian Ocean that had netted 113,000 tons of Allied shipping. The *Nordmark* remained in the South Atlantic.

It was at this time that Doenitz decided that, since the rate of sinking of Allied ships was falling in the North Atlantic (due to improved convoy defences), and since there was now a sufficient number of the medium-range Type VII U-boats to carry on the battle in this theatre, the time was ripe to redeploy some of the larger Type IX U-boats to the Freetown area.

U 105, U 106 and U 124 achieved considerable success in the South Atlantic in March. They began by refuelling from the *Corrientes* (always called '*Culebra*' in the U-boat Command war diary) between 4 and 6 March, and U 124 subsequently took on fuel far to the south from the auxiliary cruiser *Kormoran* (19 March), while U 105 and U 106 refuelled from the *Nordmark* off Freetown on 30 March and 8 to 9 April. U 124 shortly afterwards returned to base. The other two U-boats of this 'First South Atlantic Wave' were reinforced by five more (including the returned U 124) and also U A, which had sailed from Germany to France in March under the command of Korvettenkapitaen Eckermann and reached the Freetown area in April; the seven U-boats performed a series of double patrols involving refuelling from the *Nordmark* and, in some cases, from the *Egerland* (see below).

Between March and July 1941, no fewer than seventy-nine unescorted ships were sunk and U 107 achieved the war's most successful single patrol, sinking fourteen ships (86,699 tons), earning her commander, Kapitaenleutnant Hessler, the Knight's Cross of the Iron Cross. The British Admiralty diverted all ships from the area and rushed in air and sea reinforcements, thereby achieving the effect predicted by German Naval Command. In addition, U 69 laid mines in the Gulf of Guinea, which sank one ship and caused the ports of Lagos and Takoradi to be closed. Yet, despite these successes, Doenitz still found that the critical 'tonnage sunk per U-boat per day at sea' figure was less than that obtained by U-boats operating in the North Atlantic. By August, there would be no U-boats operating south of the Azores.

The *Nordmark* returned to France in May 1941, having spent six months stationed at 5N 31W ('Point Red') during which time she refuelled forty-five German vessels. She was replaced by the *Egerland*, which had originally been allocated specifically to the support of U-boats and was sent out from France at the beginning of May. By the 21st, the new arrival had refuelled U 38, U 103, U 105, U 106 and U 107, and had run out of spare

11

torpedoes. Doenitz recorded in his war diary that a new supply ship would have to be sent.

The improving effectiveness of Britain's convoy defences led Doenitz to station his U-boats further and further to the west of the Atlantic, where the escorts were at their weakest. Convoy HX.126 was attacked in May 1941 at 40 degrees west while with only a token escort, losing nine ships. Immediately the Admiralty introduced continuous close escort of convoys all the way across the Atlantic.

The increasing distance that the U-boats now had to travel to their operational areas again served to depress the 'tonnage sunk per U-boat per day at sea' figure, and once more steps were taken to refuel the U-boats at isolated areas at sea. This coincided with an increasing number of forays by German surface ships that were also making good use of the availability of the Biscay bases.

Throughout the spring of 1941, a number of surface supply ships had been stationed at remote areas of the ocean for the benefit of German warships that had been running up considerable scores in the North and Central Atlantic. Some of the supply ships were detailed for the support of U-boats in the area. The *Belchen* was positioned just south of Greenland in anticipation of the sortie by the battleship *Bismarck* and the cruiser *Prinz Eugen*; the *Lothringen* was positioned in the Central Atlantic and the *Gedania* north of the Azores. All of these ships were tankers. In addition, a number of other tankers, supply ships and weather ships were sent out in support of the *Bismarck* operation. Moreover, the *Kota Pinang* was ordered from a Biscay port into the South Atlantic in order to support a projected thrust by the U-boats deep into this part of the ocean. The *Kota Pinang* (7,277 tons) was a modern Dutch motorship, formerly used in the run from Holland to the Dutch East Indies before the Germans seized her at Rotterdam.

In the midst of the confusion engendered in the Atlantic by this massive naval effort, the Germans additionally sought to bring home some 'blockade runners'. As the name implies, these were merchant ships, despatched by the Ettapendienst from various neutral countries, with orders to break through the British maritime blockade around Axis Europe with their valuable cargoes of essential war materials, especially rubber and certain metals. What the Germans did not know was that their naval ciphers had been broken.

Chapter 3

The German Ciphers are Broken

May to June 1941

Faced with the problem of having to communicate in cipher with their armed forces around the world, the Germans had adopted an ingenious mechanical device known as Enigma. This was essentially a mechanical typewriter with several rotors at the rear and variable plug connections. Whenever a message was typed into the machine, a series of electrical impulses, following the path set by the rotors, scrambled the message into an unreadable mixture. Enigma required no expertise from the operator, only a knowledge of how to set the rotors. This setting was altered frequently.

There were several versions of Enigma, with different numbers of rotors. The versions operated by the German Navy originally employed three rotors, although there was provision to set a fourth rotor in the issue supplied to the U-boats. The U-boat rotors were changed monthly, or more often if there was reason to suppose that the old cipher was known to the enemy, while the rotor settings were changed daily according to a key transmitted from U-boat Command.

The Germans appreciated from the outset that it might be possible for an enemy to capture a complete Enigma machine, although strict instructions were given that the machine should be destroyed as a matter of priority. However, they assumed that this would lead to decryption of their messages for a month at most, when the rotors were exchanged for new ones. They based their confidence in Enigma on the fact that trillions of combinations were possible from the few rotor settings and that, even if British Intelligence were to attempt to decipher their messages by laborious trial and error, it would take many years to crack the first message, by which time the information would be too late to be of any value and a new cipher would be in force.*

* It is necessary to differentiate ciphers and codes. Ciphers replace letters with different letters, codes replace complete words with different words.

13

Britain received her first Enigma machine from the Polish intelligence service at the outbreak of war, just before that unfortunate country was overrun. It was immediately evaluated and by mid-1940 some very low-grade messages from the Luftwaffe were being intercepted and deciphered. Nevertheless, German naval messages were much more secure and orders were given to Royal Navy ships to make every attempt to seize a working naval Enigma with the then current naval ciphers. It was quickly appreciated that German commanders had orders to scuttle their ships as soon as they were intercepted in order to avoid such seizures, and a special order was sent out by the Admiralty that signals were to be sent to all intercepted German ships saying that if the crew scuttled their vessel, they would be left in the water; if the crew scuttled anyway, they were to be picked up. In practice this idea never came to much, since the German crew had usually scuttled their ship before they understood the message.

As a result, several 'smash-and-grab' operations were planned by the Admiralty. A commando raid on the Lofoten Islands off Norway secured some useful information in February 1941, but the jackpot came in May. First of all, on 7 May the weather ship *Muenchen* was captured intact west of Jutland. Only two days later, U 110 (Kapitaenleutnant Lemp) was abandoned by her crew in a sinking condition after an attack on a convoy. The warship responsible for the damage, knowing the Admiralty's desire to capture documents, at once put across a boarding party. At the last moment, the German captain realized the threat and courageously tried to reboard his command. He was shot dead and numerous important papers, including all the current U-boat ciphers and a complete working Enigma machine, were seized. The German survivors in the water were meanwhile rescued and bundled below where they could not observe the capture of the U-boat. U 110 sank in tow to Iceland shortly afterwards, with the result that none of the German crew knew of the capture of the ciphers.

This valuable capture was followed on 29 May by the seizure of another weather ship, the *August Wriedt*, with the result that from now until the end of the war, British Intelligence was always able to make some attempt at deciphering German messages. Often the decryption came too late to be of any practical value, but it still enabled the Admiralty to form an idea of German tactics. It was necessary to try to manufacture new rotors every month, but this could often be achieved by the acquisition of a few clues.

As early as 18 April, Doenitz had expressed his disquiet about the knowledge that the enemy appeared to have of his U-boat dispositions. There were sharp reductions in the number of personnel who were told current U-boat positions and the Luftwaffe was now kept in the dark, while a request for a special U-boat cipher had been approved by the Naval Supreme Command. The German Navy used several ciphers on its Enigma machines, some of higher security than the others. The rarely used Special Code 100, employed by auxiliary cruisers and blockade runners which normally maintained radio silence, was never broken, but the 'Hydra' cipher used by the U-boats was repeatedly compromised, although there was a long gap during nearly all of 1942, after the U-boats had started to use a new cipher called 'Triton', when little decoding was possible.

The British Admiralty was at first naturally obsessed with the threat posed by the presence of the *Bismarck* at sea, and it appears that none of the information that was shortly to come from code-cracking was yet available. However, the *Bismarck* was sunk on 27 May through a combination of other good intelligence and lucky guesswork, and the cruiser *Prinz Eugen*, which had been detached to hunt merchant shipping in the mid-Atlantic, instead suffered repeated fuelling and engine troubles, wandered from fuelling rendezvous to rendezvous, before being finally ordered back to France, where she arrived on 1 June.

This lifted the curtain on the hunt for her supply ships, whose positions were revealed by code-breaking (see Map 3-1). The first to be caught was the *Belchen*, just south of Greenland on 3 June. She had barely finished refuelling two U-boats when she was attacked by the cruisers *Aurora* and *Kenya*. She was quickly sunk and the cruisers immediately left the vicinity rather than wait for the U-boats to return. U 93 (Kapitaenleutnant Korth) then surfaced and picked up ninety-three survivors. Grossly overcrowded, U 93 made her way directly back to base, curtailing her cruise for which Korth was severely reprimanded. He had declined an offer to pass on his passengers to another supply ship on the grounds that he did not have sufficient fuel should the rendezvous be missed. Next day, the *Esso Hamburg*, *Gonzenheim* and *Gedania* were all intercepted. Two ships scuttled themselves in accordance with instructions, but the *Gedania* was captured intact by HMS *Marsdale*.

The German Navy had prepared grid charts from the outset for all the world's oceans and seas, for the purpose of referring to any specified small sea area (see the quadrant map in Appendix 5), but at this time German refuelling policy at sea called for two ships to meet in a prearranged, labelled area of the sea (such as 'Point White'). The capture of the *Gedania* revealed all to the British, the value of the capture being enhanced by the presence of her cipher books still on board and, if the German account is to be believed, the British signalled all German supply ships to proceed to selected areas where a British warship was waiting. (There is no British evidence for this sequence of events.)

On 5 June, the U-boat supply ship *Egerland* was sunk by two cruisers south of the Cape Verde Islands at the same position previously occupied by the *Nordmark*, and four more tankers and supply ships – the *Lothringen*, *Friedrich Breme*, *Babitonga* and *Alstertor* – were sunk or captured over a wide tract of the Atlantic by the 23rd. The capture of the *Lothringen* divulged to a grateful Admiralty the superior techniques, with collapsible rubber hoses, that the Germans were using for their refuelling. Into the

Map 3-1. Round-up of the Supply Ships, June 1941. (*Reprinted by courtesy of the Controller, The Stationery Office*)

British net fell, too, a blockade runner from Japan (the *Elbe*) and another from South America, the *Lech*. Although their naval ciphers were secure, British Intelligence deduced their presence from orders telling U-boats where to avoid sinking them.

These losses were not known immediately to the Germans. On 7 June, U 38 reported that she could not find the *Egerland* and was low on fuel. The U-boat and others operating off Freetown were advised to return home at once, refuelling if necessary from the *Corrientes* in the Canary Islands. Three days later, Doenitz ordered U-boats in the area to refuel from the *Lothringen* at 'Point White'; however, they had to retain enough fuel to reach the *Corrientes* in case the *Lothringen* had also disappeared. 'The need for our own U-tankers and supplies on land is becoming increasingly

16

urgent in view of the tanker losses,' he wrote. When the *Lothringen* failed (her absence was reported by U 103 on the 22nd), the *Corrientes* was the only remaining tanker close by.

A handful of German ships survived to return to France. After refuelling the *Prinz Eugen*, the *Kota Pinang* had received direct orders to head south to fuel the U-boats sent to operate deep into the South Atlantic (an attack on Cape Town was planned). This change of orders may have saved her as her mission to the South Atlantic was shortly afterwards abandoned and she arrived safely back in France. Another supply ship, the *Spichern*, also made it back to France, and both ships joined the fleet tanker *Ermland* that had arrived from Japan in April. Two blockade runners safely negotiated the short but hazardous journey from the Canary Islands and another blockade runner, the *Regensburg*, arrived from the Far East with her valuable cargo.

At this stage the Admiralty staff belatedly stopped to ask themselves what the Germans would make of the loss of so many ships over so wide an area of sea, and they resolved never again to put their secret knowledge to such obvious use. The Admiralty had intended to leave two surface tankers alone, to lull German suspicions, but both had been discovered through chance by British warships in mid-ocean! In future, all operations that were actually derived from code-breaking were to be so arranged that another explanation would also be possible. For example, if a German convoy was found to be at sea by code-breaking, an aircraft was always sent up to 'discover' it.

The Germans did indeed conduct the most searching enquiry into the cause of the loss of their supply ships, as well as of the *Bismarck*. They deduced that agents could have spotted the sailing of the ships from their ports, while the location of the *Bismarck* was attributed (correctly) to a half-hour message the *Bismarck* sent while she mistakenly believed that her position was known to the British. The loss of the supply ships in the mid- and South Atlantic was, wrongly, attributed to the success of the Freetown U-boats, which must have had a refuelling base somewhere.

An enquiry was convened to determine whether or not the British could have compromised the German ciphers. The enquiry, led by a signals expert, concluded to its satisfaction that this could not be possible, and laid the blame largely on the fabled British Intelligence network in Europe. It further concluded, reasonably, that the capture of one or more of the supply ships would have given away the location of the prearranged, labelled, refuelling squares, and this system was abandoned. On 16 June, Doenitz recorded that 'in order to disguise orders regarding the disposition of U-boats, points of reference will be introduced.' This meant that a position at sea would be defined as, for example, 110 miles at a course of 40 degrees from reference point 'Oscar'. Finally, it was expected that the new July setting of the Enigma rotors would undo any damage that might have been caused if an Enigma machine had been captured.

However, even after the monthly change of the rotors, British Intelligence was still able to read the U-boat and other Enigma ciphers. U-boat Command was never able to introduce radical new changes to its ciphers without informing boats already at sea about the alterations with the existing cipher.

It should be clearly understood that decryption of Enigma consisted largely of trial and error of the ciphered message against likely ('target') meanings. Once a match had been found, then other, unknown ciphered messages could be decrypted with the rotor settings needed to decode the target message. In principle, all messages could be deciphered, but the German confidence in Enigma was based on the fact that there were so many permutations that it would take years to undertake the trial process manually. The Germans overlooked the possibility that an electronic device might be devised to do the pattern searching automatically. Once a fast electronic solution for the trial process was to hand, Enigma was doomed (and Enigma was used by all branches of the German, Italian and Japanese armed forces – the Germans had been good salesmen).

As well as using Enigma to encipher their codes, the Germans also used a 'short signals' book, whereby many common messages could be reduced to groups of four letters, short lists for the numbers of individual U-boats and an 'address book' to encipher U-boat rendezvous positions from 1942. None of these codes was ever broken directly; decryption rested entirely on the seizure of the relevant short signals books from captured U-boats. The Germans proved to be remarkably reluctant to change these short signals once issued, so that captured data remained in force for one to three years before a new capture became necessary. The use of commanders' names to describe the U-boats from mid-1941 (and hence to disguise their types, which might have been obvious from the U-boat numbers) never fooled British Intelligence for long, and was not even applied consistently by U-boat Command, which often resorted to U-numbers when addressing boats at sea. Times to decrypt U-boat transmissions varied through the war, but were typically one to three days. Thus rendezvous information was often deciphered in time for the Allies to anticipate the rendezvous.

However, in February 1942, the Germans introduced the new 'Triton' ciphering system into their U-boats. This machine and its ciphers were much harder to decipher than their predecessors, so for most of 1942 there was insufficient information to enable coded messages to be compared satisfactorily with their supposed meanings. All Allied naval personnel had orders to try to grab a new, working Enigma machine from a sinking U-boat.

The opportunity came on 30 October 1942, when U 559 was forced to the surface with heavy damage in the eastern Mediterranean. Her crew abandoned ship as the U-boat began to settle into the water, but an heroic special boarding party from one of the British destroyers managed to clamber aboard, and seize the cipher and the short signals books. Two British sailors lost their lives as the boat sank while they tried to remove the cipher machine. The documents were rushed to British Intelligence headquarters at an old manorial home called Bletchley Park, where work began on 24 November. The Triton U-boat cipher was finally broken on 13 December.

In order to assist the comparison process between coded messages and likely target meanings, small electro-mechanical devices known as 'bombes' were manufactured which semi-automated the matching process. An important breakthrough was the realization that it was not necessary to have to keep manufacturing replacement rotors with the new settings to fit into the Enigma machines. Instead, the rotors and their settings could all be mimicked electronically. There was always a shortage of these bombes, which by mid-1943 was leading to unacceptable delays in the matching process, and subsequently decoding of 'Triton' U-boat ciphers was transferred to Washington, USA, in November. Thus Bletchley Park was freed for the breaking of the most secure ciphers of all: those used by the Axis military high commands, with its newly built 'Colossus' computer. Since British and US staff involved in decryption always shared any success in breaking German ciphers at once, references to Allied decryption efforts will normally be assigned to 'British Intelligence' in this book, reflecting its dominant role.

How were the target messages to be decoded found? A number of methods were used. One of the most important was to take advantage of the foolish German practice of sending weather reports in low-grade cipher to the Luftwaffe, and then in U-boat cipher to the boats at sea. The Luftwaffe reports were easily decoded, so that the decoded messages formed the target message for which the bombes could search the U-boat ciphers. Indeed, when the Royal Air Force learned that German long-range aircraft were sending weather reports from the north of Scotland, the pilots had to be restrained from shooting the aircraft down without it being possible to furnish any reason! It is now known that the first penetration of 'Triton' in December 1942 was as a direct result of the use of the weather reports.

The Germans also had the difficulty that, when they changed their ciphers, U-boats already at sea had to be informed of the changes – by use of the existing cipher. It would have been much wiser to divide all U-boats into two groups, those with the new ciphers and those without, and to make sure that neither group ever shared common knowledge, but U-boat Command never used this approach.

The author can guess another system for matching coded messages to target meanings. U-boat Command habitually referred to boats at sea by the names of their commanders, many of which were quite distinctive. Thus, if French agents had reported that U 463 (Korvettenkapitaen Wolfbauer) had just put to sea, then British Intelligence needed only to match coded U-boat signals against the name 'Wolfbauer' to find the current cipher settings with the bombes.

Further details about the British 'Colossus' were released in the 1990s. It was the world's first electronic computer and it began operation on 8 December 1943. 'Colossus' was not used to decipher U-boat messages and does not form part of our story. The Duke of Kent opened a full-size working replica on 6 June 1996 in its original room in Bletchley Park, now preserved as a museum. 'Colossus' can be seen in operation every other weekend and, after restoration in 2007, it was used again to decipher some real German wartime messages.

Chapter 4

Remote Areas
July 1941 to February 1942

By the end of June there were several U-boats from the Freetown area that needed refuelling, but only the *Corrientes* was available to them. Three boats availed themselves of the service but this did not pass unnoticed and Britain exerted strong diplomatic pressure on Spain in July 1941, with the result that the U-boats were no longer permitted to refuel in the Canary Islands after the 16th. Consequently, the U-boats now had no satisfactory means of refuelling away from their bases, although sporadic attempts were made to refuel from auxiliary cruisers when these were operating in mid-Atlantic. The Germans also tried to arrange a base with Vichy France, for supply ships at Dakar in Africa, but the negotiations came to nothing.

U 109 and U 331 stole into the Spanish port of Cadiz at the end of July and the beginning of August to refuel from the tanker *Thalia* moored there, but it was understood that this should only be used in emergencies. U-boats were forced to rendezvous with each other to exchange supplies in order that one or two of them could keep up the pressure in the South Atlantic.* By September, a handful of U-boats were making a fresh appearance in this theatre after two months of neglect (Doenitz had been disappointed with the poor results of the last boats in the theatre). German U-boats also made clandestine visits to two German tankers based in Spanish ports, the *Bessel* in Vigo and the *Thalia* at Cadiz, between September and December 1941, by which time *Thalia* had run out of U-boat supplies. A full list of these visits, taken from the U-boat war diaries, is appended at the back of this book.

A rendezvous was arranged for three U-boats – U 67, U 68 and U 111 – at St Antoa, the most northerly tip of the Cape Verde Islands, for the night of 27/28 September. U 111 was to hand over her unused torpedoes to U 68

---

* This was not a new idea. During the closing months of the First World War, SM cruiser-140, returning from the USA, had refuelled the outward-bound U 117 near the Faeroe Islands with 21 tons of oil during the night of 12/13 September 1918. The rendezvous had been arranged with primitive wireless telegraphy.

and refuel from U 67 before returning to France. A sick sailor would be transferred from U 67 to U 111. The rendezvous was decrypted by the British, who diverted the submarine HMS *Clyde*, en route to West Africa, to lie in wait for the U-boats. The *Clyde* fired two torpedoes as U 68 and U 111 lay together at the rendezvous, but both missed (a common fault of British torpedoes early in the war). The explosions of the faulty torpedoes on the beach alerted the U-boats, who were already suspicious of the presence of neutral Portuguese troops on shore.

At that moment, U 67 approached on the surface and, on account of the darkness, accidentally rammed the British submarine that was also on the surface. Both craft were damaged, but neither sank and the *Clyde* fled. U 67 found that the damage was too severe for her to be able to continue operations, with the result that U 68 took over supplies from her too, including lubricating oil, torpedoes and water. U 68 was able to continue operations far into the South Atlantic as a result of this while the other two U-boats headed for France. U 111 was sunk en route after a running gun battle with a British trawler; U 67 arrived safely. The *Clyde* also returned safely to its base in Gibraltar.

Once again, the Germans asked themselves how the St Antoa rendez-vous could have been detected. St Antoa was a deserted island and they had not used it previously. As Doenitz pointed out, the *Clyde* could not possibly have been there by chance and he requested the Naval Command to 'safeguard cipher material' (28 September). Fortunately for the British, U 570 had been captured intact in the North Atlantic in August and U-boat Command assumed, erroneously, when they learned of the capture of the U-boat, that the ciphers must have been seized. These assumptions are recorded in the reconstructed war diary of U 570, by the Naval Staff (SKL) on 18 October and by U-boat Command on 5 November. The Germans believed that the ciphers would then become worthless in one month's time.

As a precautionary measure, from September 1941, all grid-square rendezvous references were double-ciphered, by reference to tables carried by each U-boat when it left port. The wisdom of this approach was utterly undermined by the requirement that non-camouflaged grid references should be signalled in certain circumstances, perhaps before the U-boat had changed position. The number of German staff with a 'need-to-know' had been greatly restricted for U-boat dispositions from the spring.

At this time, U-boat Command had five surface supply ships at its disposal for the replenishment of U-boats. These were the *Bullaren*, *Eurland*, *Kota Pinang* (which was no longer assigned to surface warships, of which not one was then operating in the Atlantic), *Nordvard* (a former Norwegian ship that had been captured by the auxiliary cruiser *Pinguin* and sent to France) and the *Python*.

Increasing British air reconnaissance over all parts of the Atlantic and the ubiquitous presence of Royal Navy patrols was making the use of surface tankers a progressively more dangerous exercise. Refuelling at sea could only take place in deserted sea areas, and U-boats had standing orders not to attack any Allied ships close to a rendezvous with a tanker.

Doenitz never had enough U-boats for his purposes at this stage of the war, and the situation was not eased when Hitler insisted that some be sent into the Mediterranean to help prop up the tottering regime of Mussolini in Italy in the face of gathering British naval power. After Doenitz's angry protests had been overruled (the strong current into the Mediterranean meant that U-boats sent to this sea could never return to the Atlantic), the first boats arrived in October. By the middle of the month, there was not a single U-boat operating against the British North Atlantic convoy routes!

The disappearance of easy targets in the North Atlantic induced Doenitz to consider sending U-boats to Cape Town again. He had been dissatisfied with the results of the last South Atlantic U-boats, due entirely to their inability to refuel, and for this project it was essential that they be fuelled en route if they were to arrive at all. In October, the *Kota Pinang* and *Python* were despatched to the South Atlantic in preparation for the assault on the southern Atlantic by the *Kapstadt* group of U A, U 68, U 124 and U 129.

Once again, decrypting gave the game away and the movement of the *Kota Pinang* from Bordeaux was detected. The cruisers *Kenya* and *Sheffield* were ordered to search from Gibraltar. On 3 October, the *Kota Pinang* was located by the *Kenya* about 300 miles north of the Azores and was quickly sunk. The entire 119-man crew were rescued by her escort, the new Type IXC boat U 129 (Kapitaenleutnant Clausen) on her second patrol (the first had been aborted after highly contagious diphtheria in a crew member had caused Clausen to race back to port). We are going to see a great deal more of U 129, a lucky boat that lived a charmed life in mid-Atlantic on the fringes of treacherous fuelling operations until she was so old and battered that she was decommissioned and scuttled in port in August 1944. In the meantime, U 129 was informed that it would be much too hazardous to try to pass the Bay of Biscay while so overcrowded, and arrangements were made to offload the surplus passengers at El Ferrol on the north coast of Spain. Clausen later reported that he had passed his guests to a Spanish tug, and U 129 arrived safely in France on 8 October. Her next cruise would be into the South Atlantic.

The *Python* (Kapitaen Lueders) survived to reach the South Atlantic. Meanwhile, the auxiliary cruiser *Atlantis* (Kapitaen zS Rogge) was also in the South Atlantic on her way back to France after a cruise covering the Atlantic, Indian and Pacific Oceans that had brought her a score of 144,000 tons of Allied shipping. On 13 November, she refuelled U 68 south of St Helena after rearrangement of an earlier rendezvous that had, to the astonishment of both vessels involved, been fixed by Naval High Command in the middle of a crowded shipping lane between Freetown and Cape Town. The *Atlantis* then received orders to proceed to 'Flower Point Lily 10' to refuel U 126.

Once again the message was intercepted. In the middle of refuelling the U-boat, the British cruiser *Devonshire* arrived. The hoses were cut and U 126 crash-dived, her commander still aboard the auxiliary cruiser. The *Devonshire*'s seaplane was in the air and sighted the U-boat as it submerged; the suspicious warship stayed well outside the gun range of the *Atlantis* as she asked for identification. The latter claimed to be the British *Polyphemus* but the British cruiser was able to establish that the *Polyphemus* could not possibly be in the area and opened fire at long range.

Meanwhile, the inexperienced temporary commanding officer aboard U 126 stayed close to the German vessel, expecting *Devonshire* to close the range. Soon the *Atlantis* was sinking and the *Devonshire* departed. U 126 now resurfaced, was reclaimed by her irate commander, and as many survivors as possible were fished out of the water. The remainder of the lifeboats were towed to a new rendezvous established with the *Python*, which picked up the survivors on the 29th, refuelled U 126, and continued her cruise towards the south and her refuelling mission.

Other U-boats in the area were ordered to take on what supplies they could from *Python* as she was about to be ordered home again. Radio silence and a ban on all U-boat attacks were to be enforced for 400 miles around the rendezvous. U-boat Command had become alarmed about the loss of the *Atlantis*, though decryption was considered 'out of the question'. But once again, the rendezvous signal was intercepted and decrypted. U 124 and U 129 replenished uneventfully from *Python* on 20 November, but on 1 December, while *Python* was in the very act of refuelling U 68 and U A (28S 4W), the British cruiser *Dorsetshire* joined the party. After a couple of salvoes, the *Python*'s crew scuttled their ship and took to the boats, while the ex-crew of the *Atlantis* resigned themselves to a second immersion. The U-boats had not had time to re-establish their trim before diving and performed a series of erratic manoeuvres underwater with little chance of making a successful attack against the *Dorsetshire*, although U A fired a salvo of four torpedoes all of which went well wide. The *Dorsetshire* prudently made off again.

Both U-boats now surfaced to find two ships' companies in the water. Doenitz ordered the other two boats of the *Kapstadt* group, U 124 and U 129, to go to the rescue, and all the survivors were somehow crammed aboard the four U-boats, which turned for home. The Italian Atlantic Submarine Command (Betasom) also ordered out four submarines from Bordeaux to join in the rescue. Both submarine groups met off the Cape Verde Islands, the 'guests' were distributed evenly among the submarines and the entire flotilla returned safely to France, arriving before the last day of 1941. This was the furthest rescue of survivors at sea in history.

The loss of the *Python* meant that 'every possibility of refuelling in the Atlantic has now been eliminated. It will hardly be possible to resume refuelling in the Atlantic on the surface – the time for such undertakings is past' (U-boat Command war diary, 1 December). British surveillance of even remote sea areas was making it more and more difficult for the tankers to escape detection and, once located, the intercepting warship was usually able to penetrate the disguise of the tanker. A system known as 'Checkmate' was shortly to be introduced into the Atlantic, and thereafter to the other oceans. By this system, a British warship could signal the Admiralty in London for the details of any suspicious ship, and for information about the whereabouts of the real ship that the suspicious ship claimed to be. If the details and position matched, the ship under suspicion was allowed to proceed; otherwise, it was captured or sunk.

Doenitz was now pinning his hopes on three new types of U-boat, all of which had been launched for the first time in 1941 and were exercising in the Baltic. These were the Type XIV submarine tanker, unarmed except for anti-aircraft guns, but able to transfer up to 700 tons of fuel to other attack submarines; Type XB, the huge (1,763-ton) long-range minelayer designed for laying mine barrages off Cape Town and other remote, but important, Allied ports; and Type IXD2, U-cruisers that were too unwieldy for attacks on convoys, but whose enormous range of nearly 32,000 miles was sufficient to enable them to operate against unescorted shipping in the Indian Ocean before returning to base. The Japanese were later to allow the Germans the use of the naval base at Penang in what is now Malaysia, but U-boats did not make use of the port until mid-1943.

The advantage of the submarine tankers over their surface brethren was quite simply their ability to submerge to avoid detection by Allied aircraft or ships. A surface tanker that had been located by an aircraft could do little to escape, except to steer away at her best speed, rarely better than 12 knots, or to rely on her disguise. By the end of 1941, neither alternative was possible except by great good fortune. On the other hand, once submerged the submarine tanker was safe from aircraft (until the advent of 'Fido' – see Chapter 11) and only warships fitted with Asdic stood any chance of locating her. The rendezvous areas were selected so as to be as far away as possible from the convoy routes that were the only places where warships fitted with Asdic were likely to be encountered.

Six U-tankers were still on the slips when a second series of four was ordered in late 1941. The first two U-tankers were launched on 13 September, but in trials they were found to have the disastrous defect that they would not steer straight, an unfortunate property for a boat that by its nature would be closely surrounded by others. However, a minor

modification to the stern greatly reduced the problem and the boats proceeded to be commissioned.

Meanwhile, two other surface tankers were prepared for use as supply
ships to U-boats for a projected offensive against Cape Town in February
1942. First out was the *Benno* in December 1941, sailing from a Biscay port.
The *Benno* was the former *Atlantis* prize, the ex-Norwegian tanker *Ole Jacob*
(8,306 tons), which had been sent to Japan to exchange her original cargo of
aviation spirit for diesel oil and brought safely back through the British
blockade to Bordeaux in July 1941. Now renamed as the *Benno* and given
the code identity of 'AQ', Naval Group West despatched her as a supply
ship with a cargo of oil in the short days towards the end of December. The
Benno sailed through the Bay of Biscay close to the Spanish coast before
striking out on a north-westerly course. By the 22nd the tanker steered
towards BE5454 (approximately halfway between south-west Ireland and
the Azores) at a speed of 13 knots while five He115 reconnaissance aircraft
swept her forward path.

A Sunderland on anti-U-boat patrol spotted the *Benno* at 45.15N 12.15W
(BE6983) at about 0900 hrs on 23 December. Asked for identification, the
Benno claimed to be the *Belinder* and the aircraft flew on, while its base
sought to verify the identity. After hearing of the sighting, Group West at
once ordered the *Benno* to 'Turn back. Return passage to limit of Spanish
territorial waters', but it was already too late. The sighting Sunderland was
soon ordered to attack the tanker, wrongly estimated at 12,000 tons, and six
depth-charges and two anti-submarine bombs (all for want of proper
bombs) were dropped onto the *Benno* at 1047 hrs. The explosives straddled
the ship which was obscured by spray. When this had died away, the
tanker was seen to be crippled, losing speed, pouring out smoke and
leaking oil. Return fire from the *Benno* caused slight damage to the aircraft
and a minor injury to an air gunner.

Group West had by now told the *Benno* to expect an escort of three
minesweepers for the following day in BF9677 (just off the north coast
where Spain met occupied France), and to make the return passage off the
Spanish coast disguised first as an iron-ore ship and later as a Sperrbrecher
for passage up the Gironde river. But then the B-Dienst intercepted British
reports of the air attack on the tanker (whose identity was not known to
the British) and U-boats and aircraft were ordered to provide assistance.
U-boat Command directed two U-boats (later a third) to the *Benno*, whose
speed was given as 8 knots. Meanwhile, at midday a second Sunderland
had flown over the *Benno* and taken six photographs, without making an
attack (no reason is given in the British accounts). By 1800 hrs German air
reconnaissance had established that the *Benno* was damaged at BF7199,
about halfway back to the north-west tip of Spain, and making 10 knots on
a course of 160 degrees. Darkness prevented further operations by both

sides, but Group West prepared aerial protection by four Ju88s for first light.

Next day (the 24th) a single Sunderland attempted to attack the *Benno*, but was driven off by a Ju88. The Sunderland tried again twenty-five minutes later, dropping six depth-charges and two anti-submarine bombs; again, the aircraft lacked conventional bombs. All the ordnance missed and the Sunderland had to move smartly into the cloud cover to dodge attacks by the Luftwaffe, before returning safely to base. In the afternoon the *Benno* was attacked by two separate aircraft, apparently without hindrance from the air. The Coastal Command war diary seems to be confused about the timing of the attacks, but probably a Whitley initially made two bombing runs each with three 250lb conventional bombs (all were close misses), followed by a third strafing run. Three machine guns were counted as returning fire. Separately, and probably later, a Beaufighter delivered a single torpedo from 600 yards which struck the *Benno* amidships. Black smoke poured out and the ship was observed settling by the stern.

The weekly intelligence summary for Coastal Command claims modestly that the '12,000 ton' tanker was 'seriously damaged'. Roskill claims in *War at Sea* that the *Benno* was sunk 'in Puerto Carino', north-west Spain. The German coded signals had been intercepted, but were not decrypted until 27 to 30 December, too late to affect the outcome. The Headquarters Operations record book for Coastal Command, which pre-sumably would have seen decrypted information, claims that the tanker (whose name and correct tonnage were still not stated) had been driven aground on the north Spanish coast.

These disasters (see Map 4-1) at the end of 1941 ultimately led U-boat Command to abandon the policy of using surface tankers to refuel their U-boats in the Atlantic Ocean, and the planned sailing of the tanker *Charlotte Schliemann* from Las Palmas in the Canary Islands during the last week of February 1942 for the benefit of U-boats would later be cancelled. The *Schliemann* sailed instead on 20 February to aid German auxiliary cruisers in the South Atlantic.

Three other events influencing the course of U-boat refuelling at sea can be seen, with hindsight, to have occurred during the last three months of this period. First, on 11 December, Germany declared war on the United States of America. For the next six months, easy pickings were to be found for the U-boat arm off the eastern American coast. Second, the first of the new Type XIV submarine tankers (U 459 and U 460) were commissioned respectively on 15 November and 24 December (the first Type XB mine-layer, U 116, had been commissioned on 26 July; her sister minelayers U 117 and U 118 were commissioned in October and December). Third, the introduction of a new U-boat cipher for the North Atlantic in February meant that a long gap of nearly ten months elapsed before the messages could be decrypted again in Britain. It should be noted, however, that the

Map 4-1. End of the Supply Ships, December 1941. (*Reprinted by courtesy of the Controller, The Stationary Office*)

messages of U-boats sailing between Germany and Norway, and of those arriving at French bases, could still be read, so that British Intelligence was at least able to keep up with the general pattern of U-boat movements as they sailed to and from the Atlantic theatre. It was by this decryption of local traffic that the movement of one of the first Type XB minelayers to Norway was detected.

Chapter 5

'Paukenschlag' Against America

January to June 1942

Doenitz had long planned for a campaign against the USA, since there had been many indications that war was coming. U-boats and American destroyers had already fired on each other, and American warships escorted many British convoys from mid-1941 onwards. The assault on American shipping had been code-named Operation Paukenschlag; between 16 and 25 December 1941, six Type IX U-boats put out from Biscay ports and arrived off the American east coast (see Map 5-1) in mid-January. They found shipping followed its normal routing without any convoys or blackout conditions. Sea defences were poorly trained and very weak, despite the fact that the Americans had had a full month in which to prepare. They had even sent a special mission to Britain in 1941 for briefing on anti-submarine measures, but had clearly learned nothing from it.

Now began the 'American Shooting Season'. Zero hour for 'Paukenschlag' was 0000 hrs on 12 January. Between then and the 29th, the 'First Wave' of U-boats sank twenty-five ships of over 150,000 tons. Defences troubled the U-boats so little that they could carefully select the best targets for their precious torpedoes, and tankers were the main victims. News of the easy pickings spread through the whole U-boat arm; everyone wanted to join in the attack.

The range of a Type VII U-boat was reckoned to be insufficient for it to be able to operate successfully off the east coast of the USA, but their enthusiastic crews crammed every available nook and cranny of their boats with fuel, water and provisions to extend their range as far as possible. It was found that, by travelling through the North Atlantic submerged and using their batteries for as long as possible, much fuel could be saved and the underwater speed through calm deep water was almost as great as the surface speed through the storm-tossed surface. The 'Second Wave' of

Map 5-1. Eastern Coast of the USA.

eight Type VII boats operated initially off Newfoundland, but found that shipping was well escorted by the British. They moved south to the waters off Halifax (Canada) but again the British held them off. In March they moved south again to New York, by which time the 'Fourth Wave' of Type VII boats had arrived to join them.

The 'Third Wave' of the larger, Type IX U-boats operated off the east coast of the USA from the outset, from February to March. On 16 February, some boats carried 'Paukenschlag' into the Caribbean, sinking many ships and even bombarding oil installations on some of the islands with their guns. Shipping was massacred everywhere off the east coast of the USA and it was only the shortage of U-boats that saved it from an even worse

30

disaster. The enraged British saw ships that had been closely guarded all the way across the Atlantic sunk outside their destination ports.

It was clear to the German Naval Command that it was essential for the U-tankers to enter service as fast as possible to extend the range of the U-boats, especially the Type VII craft that were expending their fuel in a matter of days before having to make the long trek back to France. The war diary of U-boat Command records a handful of plans to use boats off the American coast to refuel others running low on oil, but all were ultimately cancelled for one reason or another, usually because the supplier was itself low on fuel. Doubts were also expressed about the value of U-boats chasing fast convoys in view of the cost in fuel, requiring the chasers to head straight for base again. In an attempt to relieve some of these problems, the requisitioned ex-Turkish boat, U A (Korvettenkapitaen Cohausz had been newly reappointed), which we last saw returning to France with the survivors from *Atlantis* aboard at the end of 1941, was re-equipped as a supply tanker and sent to sea again (21 February). But the plan was upset when U A developed a defect in her starboard diesel and she returned to Lorient the very next day.

March and April saw the zenith, as the 'Fifth Wave' arrived, although the number of U-boats at any time on patrol never exceeded eight. A total of 119 ships were sunk in American waters in these two months and a whole new generation of U-boat 'aces' sprang up. Most of their victims were sunk between Cape Hatteras and New York, and it was off the Cape that the Americans finally hit their first target, U 85, sunk by the destroyer *Ropey*.

These two months saw two new developments. In April, the Americans belatedly started to put their ships into convoys with an immediate drastic reduction in the number of ships being sunk in the area, while increased American anti-submarine patrols slowly drove the U-boats out of the shallow waters in which they had been lurking, and through which most of the American shipping was being routed.

Secondly, U A had set out again for a fresh attempt in her new role as a supply tanker. The war diary makes it clear that this operation was intended as a trial for submarine resupply by her successors (the new Types XB and XIV). She left Lorient on 14 March, alone, and sailed straight to her first rendezvous off American waters. Between 24 March and 3 April U A supplied the America-bound U 84 and U 203, and the homeward-bound U 202, with food and about 20 to 30 tons of oil each in the first refuelling of U-boats by a purpose-despatched submarine tanker in the war. The rendezvous were arranged to the east and south of Newfoundland and U A was ordered back to Bergen immediately after only her third refuelling. A recurrence of an old oil leak, spillage in heavy seas during oil transfer and her limited fuel capacity (174 tons), coupled with repetition of her previous diesel trouble, forced U A to abandon her mission. Two underwater attacks on lone merchant ships encountered during her home-ward passage failed. After reaching Bergen, U A then returned directly to Germany (arriving on 24 April 1942) and was withdrawn from active service on 1 May, finally winding up in the Baltic as one of the training flotilla craft.

The introduction of convoys off the east coast of America caused the U-boats to turn again to the Caribbean. There was no shortage of un-escorted shipping and by mid-April three U-boats were working in these waters, but only the larger Type IX boats had the range to operate there at first. Then came the arrival of the first purpose-built U-tanker. U 459, a Type XIV U-boat, sailed directly to her fuelling rendezvous some 500 miles north-east of Bermuda, arriving on 18 April.

The trials of U 459 in the Baltic had been expedited, with the normal six months of training for a U-boat crew being reduced to only four months. U 459 had carried out her exercises in the Baltic during the bitterly cold winter of 1941–2 and had had to contend with pack ice at sea. Her first refuelling experiment had been with U 704 as early as 11 December (less than one month after being commissioned), and more trials were con-ducted with U 408 on 7 January. Her commander, Kapitaenleutnant von Wilamowitz-Moellendorf, was at this time forty-nine years old – much older than the average age for the commander of an attack U-boat – and had just previously served for fourteen months as the captain of the coastal boat U 2.

By mid-March, U 459 had been assigned to the 10th U-boat Flotilla. She left Kiel on the 22nd with a Sperrbrecher and a flak escort for Heligoland, but had returned to Kiel by the 26th with a fuel leak.

The day after U 459 had sailed, U-boat Command gave directions for fuelling to all flotilla chiefs, so that at least those boats following the tanker to sea would know the correct refuelling procedures. This belated inform-ation was presumably caused by the general restrictions concerning U-boat dispositions.

U 459 left Kiel again on 29 March, accompanied by U 702, to start the very first refuelling mission of operational U-boats by a U-tanker. She carried aboard a representative of the design team to monitor progress with their creation. Wilamowitz (we have adopted the practice of U-boat Command, who shortened his name thus in signals) was evidently conscious of his place in history or, at any rate, in the eyes of U-boat Command, for his first war diary is exceedingly detailed. This may be tiresome for the historian but was well appreciated by Doenitz who complimented Wilamowitz on his attention to detail and the help that this would provide for the commanders of future milk cows.

By 1 April, U 459 was well into the North Sea, but suffering from a number of minor teething problems. A test dive to 'A+120' (200 metres; this is probably a typing error in the war diary for A+20 = 100 metres) was uneventful, so the tanker pressed on, disdaining a stopover in Norway for repairs. Next day, she dived before an air alarm and dodged the bombs.

The presence at sea of the first true submarine tanker had an immediate effect on U-boat dispositions. Previously, U-boats had been forced to leave their operational areas carrying not only enough fuel for the return journey, but also a sufficient contingency reserve. On 8 April U-boat Command informed boats in American waters that they could use U 459 in emergency, which meant that there was no longer any need to retain the contingency fuel reserve. Consequently, boats could stay longer in their patrol areas. Four days later, Doenitz would write enthusiastically about the prospects of new sea areas in American waters being opened to U-boats after refuelling from U 459.

U-boat Command ordered U 459, U 108 and U 98 (Scholz) to rendezvous east of Cape Hatteras on 10 April, computing that the U-tanker now carried 500 tons of reserve oil and 140 tons that she would need for her own use. Four days later, Scholz and Cremer (U 333) were ordered to make for a revised rendezvous and to take on this many tons of oil and that many tons of provisions. Thus the decisions of the men on the spot were abrogated from the outset by U-boat Command.

Wilamowitz recorded on 18 April that his in-ship bakery had begun work for the boats to be supplied. Meanwhile, slowed in heavy seas, she arrived at her first fuelling rendezvous (*c.* 39N 52W, 500 miles north-east of Bermuda) on the same day and sent out homing signals for U 108. Next day U 108 (Type IXB) was supplied with fuel and lubricating oil, but some difficulties were noted. Contact with U 108 was lost overnight and homing signals had to be transmitted again.

U 98 and U 333 (both Type VIIC) were now in sight and both were provisioned over the next two days. These early fuellings were very slow and Wilamowitz meticulously recorded that the Type VIIC boats were oiled slower than the larger Type IX.

Two brightly lit neutral ships were seen in the early hours of the 22nd and the U-boats moved away a short distance. Here they were joined by U 583 and U 564 (both Type VIIC). It was not until the next day that U 98 and U 333 were free to depart as the weather worsened.

This first refuelling of many U-boats by a special U-tanker has often been passed off by naval historians as a brilliant German success, the first of many subsequent refuelling missions. The common view probably derives from Doenitz's enthusiasm, recorded in his memoirs, since U-boat ciphers were not being broken at this time. The war diary of U-boat Command noted in its summary at the end of April that 'supplying from the first U-tanker has gone excellently', but prudently suggested the need to await the return of U 459 in order to learn full details.

In fact, the war diary of U 459 clearly shows the difficulties that were being experienced. Apart from the breakdowns mentioned earlier, dampness caused an electrical fire in one of the electric engines that had to be put out, and Wilamowitz seriously criticized the lack of power in these motors when he returned to base. Another unforeseen problem had been caused by the bad weather. Since the boats were refuelling so slowly, there was an accumulation of boats in one area, all waiting their turn. On learning of this, Doenitz at once directed that the boats awaiting supply should circle the tanker at the limit of signalling range so as to provide an outer defence, and vowed that this particular problem would be avoided in the future. U 459's war diary suggests that this first series of refuellings was conducted with several U-boats surrounding the tanker, which passed out as many hoses as it could manage while ferrying provisions by dinghy to the other boats. As further U-boats arrived, Wilamowitz recorded further trouble with the starboard electric motor, while U 582 and U 571 were also supplied.

U 459 now moved back to her original fuelling area (26 April) where a further five U-boats were supplied, taking an average per boat of four hours to transfer fuel and two hours to move provisions. The last customers were U 751 and U 107 (the last, Type IXB) on 1/2 May.

U 459 had now 'sold out', having refuelled twelve Type VII U-boats which were thereby enabled to operate in the Caribbean, and two Type IXB boats. The latter had much longer range than the Type VIIs and were being replaced at this time by the Type IXC variant. Type IXC/40 boats were first commissioned in 1942 with a still longer range; they were better suited to remote operations against strong defences than the yet longer-ranged U-cruisers. When Wilamowitz made a lengthy signal to U-boat Command indicating that he had no more spare fuel, U 459 was directed to provide food to U 253, which was accomplished on 5 May, and then she steered towards her new home, St Nazaire on the French west coast. She arrived uneventfully on 15 May, having travelled 7,027 miles at sea, of which only 431 had been underwater.

When he reached France, Wilamowitz reported that refuelling had taken between one and a half and five hours per boat, that the transfer of provisions had taken three to four hours per boat, and that some boats had had to be turned away because of their crews' inexperience with refuelling techniques. Type IX boats had been oiled at 35 tons per hour and Type VII boats at 30 tons per hour. Some 13.1 tons of provisions had been handed over. Spare torpedoes (U 459 carried four) had been transferred only once. Wilamowitz was especially concerned about the number of hours his crewmen had had to work in heavy seas and attributed the absence of serious accidents only to good fortune.

Wilamowitz made a number of technical proposals. He was particularly critical of the electric motors that were too weak in heavy seas, and also of the tanker's sluggish handling when submerged. More positively, the tanker handled well on the surface in bad weather. However, the rubber dinghies used to ferry supplies from boat to boat were overworked and needed superior design. This theme (i.e. the performance of the rubber dinghies) runs through the war diaries of all the cows as they entered service.

Doenitz had two comments to make on the performance of U 459. First, commander and crew had acquitted themselves well and their recorded experiences would be of value to the crews both of milk cows and of the boats being supplied. Second, a clear need had been established to give refuelling training to the crews of attack U-boats before they began their first war cruises.

Meanwhile, another supply boat had followed U 459 into service. U 116 (Type XB, Korvettenkapitaen von Schmidt) was one of the newly built submarine minelayers, whose original function had been temporarily abandoned so that the U-boat could serve as a submarine tanker. The special SMA mines that the U-minelayer had been intended to carry were the subject of various early troubles, including a tendency to detonate prematurely, and U 116 was therefore required to carry out a special minelaying test in the Skagerrak before proceeding with her refuelling mission. Von Schmidt was a highly regarded officer, now thirty-six years old and already with a distinguished career, having been the chief of two U-boat flotillas between 1935 and 1939. However, this was his first U-boat command and he may have felt that he needed some experience at sea to further his career.

U 116 had been commissioned on 26 July 1941. Training took place in Kiel and Danzig up to 1 March 1942 and then she was assigned to the 1st U-boat Flotilla for a 'special mission'. She moved on 3 March 1942 from the Elbe to a bunker in the island of Heligoland, urged on by the impatient Schmidt. The following day she was in the North Sea for further trials, but teething troubles with this new type of minelayer resulted in her transfer back to the builders (Germania Werft, at Kiel) by 17 March, while Schmidt vented his frustration with the delay in his war diary. Some of the crew had been waiting for a year to join their fellows in the successes in the Atlantic.

U 116 was again passed out fit for service on 29 March and took up munitions, but no mines. She departed from Kiel on 5 April with a Sperrbrecher as escort, but again trim dives uncovered further oil leaks. By the 13th she was ready to carry out her delayed minelaying mission dating back to 1 March, but this was prevented by further bad weather (the nature of the special mission is nowhere disclosed in the war diary). Next day, the mission was apparently carried out (U-boat Command recorded on the 15th that U 116 had reported that 'laying an experimental minefield in the Skagerrak' was complete) and U 116 arrived at Kristiansand. A further move to Bergen ensued on the 15th where she arrived next day, docking alongside the homeward-bound U A. There is no further mention of the success of the minelaying, but we may note that there was still an embargo on the use of the SMA mines on 19 May.

On 26 April, U 116 put to sea again with up to 200 tons of reserve oil for supply to other boats. She moved into the North Atlantic, suffering no fewer than five air attacks by the beginning of May, one of which resulted in the U-minelayer leaving a strong oil trail whose cause could not be established. Her crew made repeated, but unsuccessful, attempts to remedy the oil leak and, as a result, von Schmidt decided to abandon his Atlantic refuelling mission and to put into a French base. En route, U 116 detected and reported a convoy west of Cape Finisterre.

U 116 entered the Bay of Biscay on 4 May, enduring another air attack, and arrived the following day in the large U-boat base of Lorient on the west French coast. The commander's war diary stated his views on this first cruise by one of the Type XB U-minelayers: the boat had handled well in seas and manoeuvres, dived well, and the crew was good. Reviewing the war diary, Doenitz remarked only on the termination of the cruise caused by air attack. But several U-boats were now departing from base for operations in the Atlantic and Doenitz had already decided to form the *Hecht* pack, to be supplied by U 116 as soon as the latter had returned to sea.

U 116 put out to sea again less than a fortnight later (16 May) with an escort from Lorient. She carried only five torpedoes, which enabled the boat to carry more provisions (for other boats) than previously. Within three days, a fresh oil leak started, resulting in the loss of 16 tons of fuel, but this time the problem was corrected within twenty-four hours.

Her first fuelling mission was to be some 600 miles south of Cape Race (CC6555). Group *Hecht* was ordered by U-boat Command on 23 May to take on fuel from U 116 on 26 May. Between then and 29 May U 116 refuelled six U-boats (U 106, U 94, U 590, U 96, U 124 and U 569) each with 30 to 45 tons of fuel oil, two weeks' provisions, cigarettes, eggs, fresh bread, fresh meat and chocolate. By 28 May, U 116 had completed the supply with the issue of 215 tons of oil in wind force 5 and a heavy swell. A delighted Doenitz signalled to von Schmidt on 30 May: 'To Schmidt. Refuelling well carried out.'

More boats were refuelled in the first week of June and then U 116, herself out of fuel, returned to Lorient, arriving on 9 June. The commander's war diary contained numerous comments about the supply operation with suggestions for improvement and was commended by Doenitz: 'Patrol short and carried through well.'

Between mid-April and mid-June, twenty of the thirty-seven U-boats operating in the Caribbean were supplied before returning to base, while the boats of the *Hecht* group could continue to operate off Newfoundland. A policy decision was made that Italian U-boats operating in the area should additionally be replenished, although this required an agreement about W/T frequencies and ciphers.

In May and June, sinkings in the Caribbean rose steeply. In these two months alone, 212 ships were sunk in American waters, the great majority in the Caribbean. This had been made possible by the minimal defences afforded to shipping, convoys being entirely absent, and the increase in the number of U-boats made possible by mid-ocean refuelling. But again the Americans at last started to form convoys and unescorted shipping disappeared. The U-boats found themselves patrolling empty stretches of water and the anti-submarine defences pushed them out from the shallow convoy lanes of the Gulf of Mexico. Sinkings fell dramatically in July as a result of these factors.

These spectacular successes (see Table 5-1) had been considerably boosted by the support role of U 459 and U 116. Early indications were that these cows had only added about seven to ten days of extra patrol time to the boats that had been refuelled, with corresponding few extra sinkings, but this crude assessment failed to compensate for the ability of the boats to reach more distant waters, and that the main constraint at this time, when targets were easily found, was shortage of torpedoes. On 14 May, Doenitz was able to report to the Naval High Command that the presence of the supply boats had permitted Type VII boats to patrol for a fortnight as far afield as the Cameroons (Africa) and Bahia (Brazil), while the longer-ranged Type IX boats could now reach the River Plate and Cape Town, if desired. Later, Doenitz was to amplify this account. New U-boats could now proceed directly to the American coast from German waters without the need for a diversion to France to refuel – a saving of two to three weeks on their times to reach operational areas. Even so, Doenitz felt it wise to refuel U-boats on their outward journeys, so that if the supply boat were to fail to turn up the other U-boats could still turn for home.

Both supply boats had returned to France in May and June respectively, each being refitted and 'turned around' as fast as possible – in less than a month. Then both put to sea again. U 459 headed for the North Atlantic air gap to refuel the boats from the packs attacking the North Atlantic convoys – Doenitz's idea in late May that she should again support the boats in

Table 5-1. Operation Paukenschlag (1942).

Month	Sinkings by U-boats in American waters	Sinkings by U-boats in all North Atlantic	Remarks
January	23	48	First strike
February	55	70	
March	62	70	
April	57	60	Convoys off USA
May	108	123	Move to Caribbean
June	104	122	
July	51	59	Convoys in Caribbean

American waters seems to have been abandoned – while another assignment to the south-west awaited U 116 (see Chapter 8).

U 459 left St Nazaire on 6 June, just two weeks after her return from her first mission, in company with U 437. After an uneventful crossing of the Bay of Biscay, she reported a convoy north-east of the Azores, providing an unexpected bonus to her main role. Then U 459 reached her new fuelling zone far north of the Azores on 13 June, but heavy seas hindered the refuelling of U 558.

After that, a succession of U-boats was refuelled – predominantly the Type VII boats used for wolf-pack attacks – as the rendezvous was moved in short hops from one point to another. One of the boats was U 203, commanded by the ace Kapitaenleutnant Muetzelburg, on 18 June. All this was accompanied by a stream of signals from U-boat Command.

A total of sixteen U-boats had been refuelled by 8 July and U 459 returned to France. She experienced three air alarms in the Bay of Biscay, but no attack ensued, and she was docked at St Nazaire on 19 July. In his summary, Wilamowitz expressed contentment with boat and engines (including the electric motors), that all boats to be supplied had been located without the need for homing signals and, significantly, that he had heard the allegedly short-ranged homing signals issued by the new tanker U 460 on 5 July. U 459 was replaced in the West Atlantic by her sister ships U 460 and U 461, both fresh out of Germany on their maiden cruises.

The second tanker of the Type XIV series, U 460 (Kapitaenleutnant Schaefer), had been commissioned at Kiel on 24 December 1941. She carried out the special trials for milk cows in the Baltic for five months, longer than the time allowed for U 459. Apparently U-boat Command wanted to see how her predecessor fared before sending out the next tanker. Schaefer himself was, like Wilamowitz, now forty-nine years old and an old sea dog, having served as a U-boat commander in the First World War, and then moved from office appointments at the beginning of the war to use his experience with service in the newly requisitioned former Dutch boats UD 4 (where he was First Officer) and UD 1 (commander).

U 460 finally started her maiden war cruise from Kiel on 7 June, putting into Kristiansand next day to top up her tanks. Here, a problem arose. The water around the oil pier was only 6 metres deep, insufficient for a Type XIV tanker. Next day (the 9th), U 460 put to sea again with M 1101 as escort and carried out a test-dive to 168 metres before proceeding. She had to submerge repeatedly in the North Sea to avoid approaching aircraft, and during one such dive the U-tanker fell out of control to 146 metres before the dive could be arrested. Troubles with trim were blamed; the rudder was also starting to play up.

Circumstances did not improve over the next week, when first no fewer than twelve drifting mines were passed in the course of a single day, and then a series of minor repairs was needed. Schaefer became so concerned about his poor progress around the north of Britain that he felt it necessary to inform U-boat Command of his position.

Soon after, U 460 received her fuelling orders and headed straight for her rendezvous in mid-ocean (AK6566) far to the south-east of Greenland, where she arrived on 19 June. Two 'customers' appeared and took oil and provisions early on the 20th, but at midday, aircraft and the masts of a convoy were sighted.

All the boats dived to the sound of the alarm and U 460 went down to 120 metres, whereupon the shocked crew discovered that the convoy was about to run right over them. The boat went to silent-running routine and Schaefer took the tanker down to her limit of 210 metres while Asdic impulses pinged all around them. Then four well-placed depth-charges suddenly crashed around the boat and some instruments were damaged. Schaefer fired three 'Bolds' – Asdic decoys that emitted bubbles and strips of metal foil, intended to fool searching ships while the real U-boat slipped away; they had just entered service – and did in fact manage to escape further detection.

The escorts finally departed after four and a quarter hours, but the shaken U 460 prudently stayed deep for a further three hours before surfacing. The other U-boats were again ready for refuelling, but this was postponed while the tanker recharged her batteries and revitalized her air.

A new rendezvous was arranged further south, which the U-boats reached on 21 June. Three U-boats, including the original customers, were refuelled in the next few days, then U 460 moved on again to a new rendezvous deeper south, north of the Azores. En route, her orders were changed, and U 460 arrived at a new rendezvous south-east of Newfoundland on the 29th, where U 576 was waiting – her First Officer was seriously ill and in need of medical attention by the tanker's doctor. The opportunity was also taken to refuel the U-boat.

U-boat Command now made the current position of U 460, south-south-east of St John's, the main rendezvous for other U-boats in the area. But the weather was deteriorating as the other boats arrived, hampering refuelling. On 4 July, the doctor had to be sent to no fewer than seven crew members on U 173, one of the new Type IXC boats. However, Schaefer remarked that in general the health of the U-boat crews was pretty good, although four engine-room ratings on U 584 were sickly owing to the fact that they rarely breathed any fresh air.

Next day, the U-tanker moved briefly again northwards to a new rendezvous where further boats were supplied. It was at this time that U 459, stationed far north of the Azores, overheard the homing signals transmitted by U 460. And now U-boat Command moved U 460 with repeated short stops to meet a string of other U-boats, some requiring homing signals to locate the tanker in poor weather.

By 17 July, U 460 had replenished fourteen U-boats and was down to 10 tons of reserve fuel. Schaefer was uncertain whether he might need this himself for his return journey should the seas worsen. Thus, having taken a sick sailor off U 508, he requested the latter to move off and signal his situation to U-boat Command, pointing out that U 459 was soon expected back in the same area (Schaefer probably confused U 459 with U 461, which was approaching his position).

Next day, U-boat Command responded: U 460 was to return to St Nazaire. Schaefer reached the Bay of Biscay relieved that the good weather experienced en route had drained his fuel less than expected, but on the 29th, he blundered into another convoy with its escorts just off Cape Finisterre. The unarmed U 460 at once went deep and there was no repetition of the previous attack by destroyers.

An aircraft was spotted on 30 July, causing another deep dive, but after an eventful cruise Schaefer was finally able to reach the St Nazaire bunker on the 31st, with an escort of minesweepers. Doenitz was complimentary about this first mission while Kapitaenleutnant Schaefer now left the tanker, to be replaced by the junior Oberleutnant zS Schnoor.

It seems that Schaefer's experience was too valuable to lose, for he now became the captain of U A, where he trained sailors in supply operations until March 1943, and then returned to UD 4, where he had previously been First Officer, as her new captain, in which post he remained until November 1944. A number of shore appointments followed and Schaefer survived the war.

The third U-tanker of the series, U 461 had been commissioned by the experienced Kapitaenleutnant Bernbeck in January 1942, but he was moved on to command the former Dutch UD 4, which was then being evaluated, in April. Bernbeck was replaced with the 35-year-old Kapitaenleutnant Stiebler, who had previously commanded no fewer than four U-boats between 1939 and mid-1940, and then served on a shore appointment.

U 461 had been given a special mission. Before leaving Kiel on her maiden operation (21 June), she had taken on board three radio/B-Dienst (Intelligence) experts and these were now transported to the east coast of the USA, off Maine, where American radio frequencies were monitored for four days (11 to 14 July) in conditions of close secrecy. Apparently these frequencies were not known in Germany. In his book *Walker RN* (Pan, 1956), Terence Robertson has speculated that the mission was a prelude to a commando attack on American radio stations, the idea of which was subsequently abandoned. The source of this information is unknown, since the German ciphers were not at this time being broken, and one of the radio experts, Fritz Vogel, has confirmed to the author (1996) that the principal intention was simply one of collecting information about the frequencies, for which purpose a 'Telefunken' wide-band receiver was employed together with a captured 'SkyRaider' radio receiver.

Stiebler himself knew little of what was going on, although the crew could observe the B-Dienst members at work through the glass window of their radio room. There is only a single mention (15 July) in the entire war diary of U 461 concerning the B-Dienst team, which was communicating directly with Germany, and U-boat commanders who paid subsequent visits to U 461 while their boats were being refuelled were all hurried into the officers' wardroom. Although the Intelligence members were permitted to mingle with the crew, there was little conversation.

After three days the B-Dienst team pronounced that they had finished and U 461 was able to proceed with her refuelling operation. She moved well to the south, replacing U 460 on 18 July at a position south-south-east of St John's (Canada) between 36 and 39N and 48 and 49W.

By the end of July the next two tankers of the series, U 462 and U 463, were well en route to their Atlantic fuelling posts. As had been the intention with all the milk cows, including the damaged U 116, the latest submarine tankers were sent directly from Germany to their first Atlantic fuelling missions via the 'Northern Transit route' around Scotland.

In August, one last wave of U-boats was sent into the Caribbean. They found the confluence of some of the convoy routes near Trinidad and sank many ships, albeit at the cost of three of their own number.

Meanwhile, Operation 'Paukenschlag' had come to an end. In July, Doenitz withdrew most of the Type VII U-boats for operations in the North Atlantic, reasoning that since he now had to face convoys in the Caribbean as well, it was better for the U-boats to attack convoys in a more readily accessible area. U 462 and U 463 were, however, still deployed as tankers to the west of the Atlantic, so that refuelling posts were available to U-boats on both sides of the ocean.

In the space of six months from the sailing of the 'First Wave', 585 Allied ships had been sunk by Axis U-boats (including a small Italian contribution), of which by far the majority had been sunk in American waters.

The Brazilian Problem

The U-boat attack on the USA had raised the difficult problem of relationships with the neutral countries of South America. As early as 16 May 1942, Doenitz had permitted attacks on armed South American merchant ships, except those of countries reckoned to be 'friendly' with Germany (*viz.* Argentina and Chile). Relationships between Germany and Brazil were particularly strained – Brazil had broken off diplomatic relations with Germany on 27 January and would soon allow the USA to operate aircraft from a Brazilian airbase.

Now he went further. Three U-boats (U 126, U 128 and U 161, all Type IX) were directed on 23 May to patrol off the north-east coast of Brazil, while four Italian submarines were stationed to their south-east. But by 1 June the German U-boats had reported a lack of traffic and they were moved much closer to the more promising Caribbean zone. It was planned that they would later refuel from U 459, which was then refitting in dock after her first supply mission. At about the same time, Brazil announced that its aircraft would attack any U-boats found off the Brazilian coast.

On the same day, Doenitz demanded the drafting of contingency plans for a new 'Paukenschlag' against Brazil, with the approval of Hitler, but a submarine tanker was not available to provide the necessary support. However, the prospects for easy success were enticing to Doenitz, who always regarded the sinkings of enemy merchant vessels higher than any consideration of whose, where, or what cargo.

The plans were complete by 6 June. The intended assault envisaged a sudden attack on merchant shipping in Brazilian waters, penetrations by U-boats into Brazilian harbours, and minelaying, but it required a submarine tanker if it was to have any chance of success, owing to the distances involved. U 459 would be sailing the same day from France, but 80 per cent of her reserve fuel was already allocated to boats in American waters. U 460 would sail from Germany next day, but could not reach the equator until mid-July, by which time her own fuel needs would leave only sufficient reserve fuel for ten U-boats (and Doenitz rejected the idea of a stopover in France for U 460 while still en route, owing to the unnecessary hazard of crossing the Bay of Biscay). Besides, U 460 was already assigned to the supply of the boats bound for American waters. U 461 would be a better bet, but she was not expected to leave Germany until near the end of the month. Thus we can see that it was only the non-availability of a Type XIV tanker that saved Brazil from an unprovoked attack in June 1942, and, probably, Doenitz from a fresh indictment at the Nuremberg Trial.

Still Doenitz planned ahead. By 20 June, he could write that U-boat operations against this neutral country were ready to commence, but the Naval High Command caused these plans to be cancelled on the 26th.

Meanwhile, the three U-boats still off Brazil were running low on fuel. Another boat, U 159, had shot off all her torpedoes very quickly in the Caribbean, and she was directed to give up her spare fuel to the Brazil boat U 161 before returning home. This was accomplished on 20 June. All three Brazil boats were then ordered to leave their operational areas in good time to meet a U-tanker far to the east of Bermuda (DE50). But this plan was again cancelled, the boats moved further north and in July all were homeward bound. U 126 would refuel from U 460 on 13 July and U 161 from U 461 on the 23rd, both to the south-east of Newfoundland. Doenitz recorded on 2 July that Operation Brazil had been abandoned, but only two days later attacks on all Brazilian ships were authorized.

Then in August, U 507 (Fregattenkapitaen Schacht) sank five Brazilian ships and a Brazilian sailing ship in quick succession. Brazil promptly declared war on Germany (22 August) and Schacht was ordered to report his actions. According to Doenitz: 'Schacht sank five Brazilian ships and a sailing ship outside Brazilian territorial waters. In so doing he followed the instructions of the OKW and the Foreign Office. The Brazilian government used these sinkings as grounds to declare war on Germany.'

Meanwhile Doenitz seized the opportunity to permit the sinking of ships from neutral Uruguay as well, but he was forced by the Naval Command to countermand the order on the 24th since 'Uruguay was not yet at war'. Moreover, U 507 was not even permitted to penetrate Brazilian harbours for 'political reasons'. It appears that the German Naval Command regretted the entry of Brazil into the war far more than did their overzealous subordinate. Brazil's long coastline afforded the Allies much-needed air and sea bases covering the entire South Atlantic, which was to have important repercussions on rendezvous between U-boats at a later date.

Schacht himself did not suffer from this mission. He received the Knight's Cross on his very next patrol (9 January 1943) and was killed in action when U 507 was sunk just five days later.

South African Waters

The conventional tanker *Doggerbank* (5,154 tons, Kapitaen Schneidewind), another former *Atlantis* prize, the ex-*Speybank*, put to sea from a Biscay port on 21 January 1942, with the Type VIIC U 432 (Kapitaenleutnant H. Schultze) as her escort through the Bay of Biscay. After safe passage, the *Doggerbank* topped up the tanks of her escort with 40 tons of oil in a heavy swell, thereby enabling U 432 to operate with considerable success off Cape Hatteras. The *Doggerbank* headed south. Equipped with mines and U-boat supplies, she was originally intended to support a U-boat attack on Cape Town, but by now the American coast beckoned to all U-boats. She refuelled no U-boats on her cruise south. While off Cape Town, she was intercepted three times by British warships, but in each case her disguise held out and she was able to lay her mines successfully and effectively, sinking two ships and damaging two more.

At first, British Intelligence thought that these sinkings were due to a previously unnoted U-boat pack (decryption of Atlantic U-boat signals was not at this time possible), but then a minefield was discovered and it was realized that a German minelayer had been at work. The three-fold failure of the warships to identify *Doggerbank* led the Admiralty to introduce 'Checkmate' to eastern waters in October.

Subsequently the *Doggerbank* refuelled auxiliary cruisers in the South Atlantic and Indian Ocean before making for Japan. Here she was converted into a blockade runner, but her charmed life, doubtless assisted by the fact that British Intelligence was unable to decipher U-boat signals during most of 1942, ran out when she was inadvertently sunk in the Atlantic by a U-boat on her return. There was only one survivor.

Chapter 6

The U-Tankers

U 459 and U 460 were the first of a series of six Type XIV U-tankers constructed between September and December 1941, and a further four (U 487 to U 490) were later to be built through 1942–3. All these boats were completed by the highly regarded submarine builders Deutsche Werke at Kiel. By September 1942 the general type had been well proven, and a further six were contracted for, followed by an order for a further eight on 17 April 1943. The last fourteen were cancelled in 1944 for reasons that we shall see; only U 491, U 492 and U 493 had been laid down by then and were not completed.

The Type XIV U-tankers were assembled from sections of a standard Type IX attack U-boat, but with the addition of a large bulge around the hull. Consequently, their overall appearance was very similar to that of a Type IX U-boat (for, like an iceberg, much of the structure of a U-boat was invisible underwater), but they were fatter and their decks were somewhat higher above sea level than those of a normal U-boat (see the blueprint page 46 for an exploded view of the U-tanker). The U-tankers actually carried two supplies of fuel, since they retained the fuel tanks of the U-boat from which they had been built, while the bulge around the hull contained further fuel. Their displacement (surfaced) was 1,688 tons compared with the 1,120 tons of a Type IXC boat, and their maximum cruising radius was a nominal 12,350 miles, although this could be extended by the U-tanker living off itself.

The bulge around the hull not only sufficed to carry the extra fuel, but was also used to contain many of the more durable provisions, such as spare torpedoes (typically four were carried) and replacement parts. Since there was no need to carry internal torpedo tubes – the U-tankers lacked any offensive weaponry – internal torpedo reloads, or a supply of shells for a large artillery gun, the U-tankers were much roomier inside than the standard Type IX U-boat from which they were derived.

The U-tankers carried 432 tons of oil that could be made available to other U-boats (700 tons of oil in all, including their own fuel).* Since 50 tons

* The Germans always referred to the fuel supply in 'cbm' (cubic metres); this is equivalent to one metric tonne in the case of water, but is rather less than one tonne for lighter fuel oil. We shall continue to follow convention in referring simply to 'tons' of oil.

of extra fuel enabled a Type VII boat to operate in the furthest reaches of the Caribbean, or to triple the time that a Type IXB boat could remain there, and 90 tons would allow a Type IXC boat to patrol off Cape Town, the importance of these tankers was not lost on either the Germans or the Allies, who made them primary targets for attack where a choice existed. The U-tankers were stationed in remote sea areas, frequently by the Atlantic islands of Bermuda, the Azores or the Cape Verde Islands, and invariably in the air gaps, while these existed, where Allied shore-based aircraft could not penetrate. As the war progressed, the introduction of longer-ranged aircraft caused the air gaps to narrow, but in 1942 the U-tankers were able to carry out their duties without aerial interference in mid-Atlantic.

As well as fuel, the milk cows carried lubricating oil and drinking water (both of which could be transferred by hose), spare torpedoes, food, ammunition, spare parts and a machine shop for repairs. They also carried a doctor and could even exchange some of their own personnel for sick or injured U-boat crew members. Another short-lived role was to take on board as POWs senior merchant officers who had been captured from sunken ships by attack U-boats. There was, for a while, a fond belief in German naval circles that the fear of such capture might deter lower-ranking officers from seeking promotion. The threat of air attack on the boat making the original capture soon ended this notion.

Rendezvous was effected by the U-boat coming to the tanker at a pre-determined area, although after the danger of air attack had greatly increased both U-boat and U-tanker would enter the rendezvous area submerged and then surface for an hour or so before sunset to establish one another's position.

One of the biggest problems was that of locating the U-boat to be replenished. Before the war the German Naval Command had divided all the seas of the world into a large number of quadrants for security and ease of reference (e.g. DE8911 – British Intelligence had no trouble in deciphering these square references after they had captured a map). A U-boat quadrant map is shown in Appendix 5. U-boat Command would have named a grid square as the rendezvous to both supplier and supplied. However, this was 6 sea miles in width, to allow for errors in navigation. Thus both U-boats would enter the appropriate square – more or less – and then cruise around on the surface until they found each other, at any rate until the danger of sudden air attack put paid to casual cruising on the surface.

This simple system failed in bad weather or if the rendezvous was to be conducted after dark. In these cases the milk cow might transmit very weak beacon or homing signals, although that was always an unpopular option. Another solution in the dark was to fire recognition signal flares,

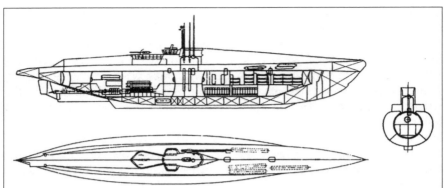

Cross-section of Type XIV U-tanker. Note the conning tower and its typical flak arrangement, and the huge bulge around the central hull that contains the reserve fuel. Four spare torpedoes (like cylinders) are stored forward, on the upper deck. (*Horst Bredow*)

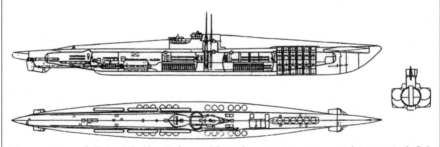

Cross-section of Type XB U-minelayer. Note the conning tower and its typical flak arrangement, and the cylindrical mine shafts that each carry three SMA-type mines in a flooded compartment. Two torpedo tubes can also be seen at the stern. Neither of these representative boats carries a schnorkel. (*Horst Bredow*)

although again the tanker crew could never quite be sure as to who would answer the call.

A characteristic of any submarine is that it has very poor 'reserve buoyancy'; that is, it takes the admission of very little water to cause the craft to sink. While it is evidently desirable that a submarine should be able to submerge quickly, the obverse problem is that it takes very little damage to sink a submarine, especially if it is laden with fuel. The U-tankers were very cumbersome and possessed no offensive armament. Since their major enemy was expected to be aircraft, both on their way to and from operations and actually at the rendezvous, they carried a moderately powerful anti-aircraft armament that was stepped up in 1943. In fact, most of the milk cows were sunk by aircraft.

The mechanics of supplying other U-boats with fuel and provisions were the subject of many appendices to the war diaries of the milk cows, particularly after the early operations. The first to report was the U-tanker

U 459, arriving in France in May 1942. The tanker had used her electric motors for manoeuvring slowly on the surface during fuel transfer, but the inexperienced boats to be supplied constantly snagged, chafed or tangled the fuel hoses, while the electric motors had proved to be too weak to maintain speed into heavy seas. The most serious difficulty concerned the strain on the crew, who had to work for up to sixteen hours per day, lashed to lifelines with the sea swell constantly breaking over them. The rate of fuel transfer had been 30 to 35 tons (cbm) per hour.

Next to relate her experiences was U 116. In an appendix on the role of the Type XB minelayers as milk cows, her commander reported on the supply of fuel, provisions and the time taken for both.

A 20cm strong manila hose could be used for oil transfer up to sea strength five to six. This was attached to a strong steel hawser that actually made the connection. The Type XB craft was found to lie more quietly on the ocean in rough seas than most other U-boat types. In order to make the connection, the milk cow steered at slowest speed for manoeuvrability into the sea, while the U-boat to be replenished remained stationary behind it. Thus the cow was towing the other boat, the strain being taken by the steel connecting hawser and not by the fuel line.

Provisions and other items could be transferred during fuelling. In good weather, a 3-metre rubber dinghy was used to transfer personnel and supplies (a 6-metre boat for some purposes). The dinghies were found by other milk cows to be exceptionally valuable and in later patrols up to three would be carried at a time. In bad weather, the dinghy was too slow (or too dangerous) and transfers were therefore made by a 'dead-man's cradle' drawn with lines between the two U-boats, both lying stopped against the sea at a distance of 80–100 metres. In practice, some three to four loads (each of 100–150kg) could be passed per hour over the cradle.

Provisions had to be passed in watertight containers and their transfer, by whatever route, was found to take twice as long, and be twice as difficult, as the oil transfer. Indeed, there was a constant wastage as sea water managed to break into the 'watertight' receptacles. U 461 made a similar complaint after her first cruise and subsequently other designs were tried.

The boat receiving fuel, after making the connections, would signal 'clear to pump'. The milk cow would then begin pumping and end with 'Forty (or whatever) cbm provided, supply halts with water drawn through, transfer ended'. The cow would now pump water after the oil. When the receiving boat observed the passage of water at its end, it would signal 'water comes' and break the connection. The cow would finally pump air through the hose to clear it for stowage. U 116 observed that the average transfer rate was 13 to 20 tons (cbm) per hour.

The Type XIV U-tankers reported similarly on their experiences, although procedures tended to change slightly with experience. Thus U 459 used hoses for transferring fuel that were made up of several lengths connected together. The internal diameter of the hose was 9cm (a narrower hose was used for the transfer of lubricating oil) and the two ends of the hose were armoured to prevent chafing. The entire hose amounted to some 150 metres. The hose could be passed to the boat receiving fuel by one of three methods: passage across on the rubber dinghy; line dropped by float and the attack U-boat picking up the float; line fired across with a special pistol. The hose was passed around the bollards on both supplier and supplied boats. The original practice of having the milk cow 'tow' the supplied boat was abandoned when it was found that inexperienced commanders of the latter could easily wrap the fuel line around the propellers of the cow. The new practice required the two U-boats to steer slowly ahead together, the smaller boat lying in the lee of the larger, at right angles to it and lagging a little behind (see Figure 6-1). This had the added benefit that more than one U-boat could be supplied at the same time in calm weather, and typical separations of suckler from U-tanker were 50 metres, or up to a 100 metres in very bad weather.

U 461 observed that oil transfer could be carried out up to sea strength six (winds six to seven) and 'middle-high' waves. The biggest difficulty in heavy seas was the loosening of the hose link, which could not be allowed to break. Lubricating oil, of which the U-tankers carried some 15 tons, was transferred in the early days through the main fuel hose, after completion of the fuel transfer, but subsequently was passed through its own hose for speed. Occasionally one U-boat would be fuelled while another was provided with lubricating oil, but this was unusual.

Drinking water could also be passed through its own hose, although this was rarer still and could seriously diminish the milk cow's own supplies. On one occasion, Metz, of U 487, disconnected the water hose to an over-demanding attack boat, on the pretext that the pump had broken.

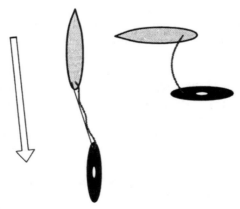

Figure 6-1. Refuelling at sea. The arrow shows the direction of the sea swell. To the left is the older method of refuelling; to the right is the newer.

U 461 had left base on her first supply operation with 735.41 tons of fuel, 18,930 litres of motor oil and 10.4 tons of fresh drinking water, as well as a supply of miscellaneous parts. She supplied thirteen U-boats during the mission with fuel oil (607 tons), received 15 tons of oil from the returning U 43 and experienced pumping rates of 16 to 38 tons per hour. U 461 additionally carried 31 tons of provisions that had taken four days to load at base. Fresh provisions typically lasted fourteen days, but the U-tanker possessed a large cold room. Thus it was quite usual for an attack U-boat to take on fourteen days of fresh supplies, the normal length of time they would keep. U 462 reported after her first fuelling mission that she had supplied twelve U-boats with up to fourteen days of food, but only one had required drinking water.

The on-board bakery of U 462 baked 700 loaves, of which 250 were supplied to other U-boats (the average life of a loaf on a U-boat was only two to three days before it became mouldy; U-boat crews were well accustomed to eating mouldy bread). U 459 had previously recorded that her own bakery had produced excellent bread that kept well and was very popular with receiving U-boat crews. By all accounts, the standard of catering on a U-tanker was superb, since the U-boat crews in any case were awarded the best food of all the armed forces and the U-tanker had the means to preserve it. Chocolate was a luxury enjoyed virtually nowhere outside the U-boat arm – but the U-tanker carried supplies!

The maintenance and repair of other U-boats lay also within the U-tanker's province, provided that the task was not too difficult. U 461 reported that three U-boats had benefited from her expert attention to diving tanks and torpedo tubes, and ready-made spares were handed over to nine U-boats. Her captain complained that the tools laboriously ferried over to a U-boat were never the right ones!

All the U-tankers carried qualified doctors who made their rounds in the rubber dinghy. Minor operations and medical advice could be carried out on the spot; more serious cases would be ferried back to the U-tanker either for more formal attention or, if necessary, transport back to port when the U-tanker had finished its rendezvous. In one or two cases, the patient had to be isolated from the remainder of the crew and again cabins could be allocated for this purpose. In any case, the U-tanker could often furnish one of its own crew members to replace the man taken from the attack U-boat. A common problem was that bad weather might prevent the timely visit of a doctor to his patient on another boat, but there is no recorded instance of threat to life in consequence. The number of cases needing attention was quite surprisingly high, perhaps 10 per cent of the total complement of the U-boat crews, but the number of minor operations was around a tenth of that and the number of crewmen needing to be transferred permanently to the U-tanker was typically two to four per fuelling mission.

The entire transfer operation could be very hazardous, quite apart from the dangers of sudden enemy attack. In rough seas there was a real danger of crew members being washed overboard and there were a number of fatalities. A crewman from U 598 was drowned during a fuelling operation by U 463 near the Caribbean on 5 August 1942, while an officer of U 117 was also drowned when the U-minelayer tried to replenish U 454 on 8 November of the same year. The tanker U 463 reported that three crewmen had been washed overboard from U 706, but all had been rescued safely (27 October 1942).

The hazards of the job also took their toll. U 462 lost one crew member in a fatal accident while in port on 3 October 1942, while U 488 suffered two fatal illnesses (one heart attack) during her second war patrol in autumn 1943 at a time when Allied attacks on the fuelling rendezvous were at their peak.

Many of the milk cows experienced difficulties with balancing the supplies that they took out with them against the needs of their 'customers'. Most reported that they were overladen with foodstuffs in the early missions and frequently had to return to base with their supply of four reserve torpedoes untouched. The biggest problem lay with their overall weight during the cruise, affecting the trim and diving qualities of the tanker. Many of the cows discovered that they were too light on leaving France and too heavy on their return, the reason being that the light fuel oil was replaced with heavier water as the oil was pumped out. The designers had assumed that the donation of foodstuffs to other U-boats would compensate for the increase in weight, but in practice few wanted the foods and Stiebler (U 461) complained that he practically had to throw the stuff at them in order to get it off his boat. U-boat Command transmitted the following order to boats at sea on 15 March 1943: 'To maintain proper trim in the U-boat tanker, all boats on being supplied are to take from the tanker the quantities of victuals appropriate to the fuel allocation. Intend to fit out U-boat tankers accordingly.' In later patrols, the U-tankers would be heavily ballasted with disposable iron as they left port, and carry fewer comestibles.

One important feature of resupply was that the milk cow should remain '*tauchklar*' (ready to dive) at all times, owing to the danger of enemy attack, especially from the air. Refuelling of other U-boats was carried out by way of quick-release hoses, through which ran a telephone cable. Even so, a crash-dive was rarely possible without fuel lines and other impedimenta being stowed away, and in any case this type of craft was much slower to submerge than an ordinary attack U-boat. It was a standing order that, in the event of air attack, no U-boat could submerge until the milk cow had done so. This was planned so that the attack U-boats could defend the cow with their own anti-aircraft guns until the latter was safely submerged. No one, of course, would then be around to protect the attack boats, but these could dive much faster than the cow, and were reckoned to be more expendable. It was better to lose one attack U-boat than to lose the cow and thereby deprive several U-boats of the chance to operate.

This order was extremely unpopular with the attack U-boats, especially as their crews invariably felt that their own boat was more important to the war effort than the inoffensive cow. Perhaps they were right. It is easy to demonstrate mathematically that more sea miles will be travelled by attack craft in aggregate if one milk cow is sunk once, rather than if a steady trickle of U-boats is lost trying to defend the cow. That is, it may be better to have ten U-boats travelling 9,000 miles each without refuelling than to have five U-boats travelling 12,000 miles each after refuelling. This is a very complicated equation that also needs to consider the value of refuelling in the operational area rather than at base, and the life expectancy of an attack boat without refuelling.

It was appreciated by U-boat Command that a U-boat could not keep on being refuelled indefinitely. Even if the U-boat could take it, the crews could not. At this time, the sudden expansion of the U-boat arm had resulted in a large increase in the number of relatively inexperienced U-boatmen at sea, particularly since many of the more experienced crews had been sunk, captured or withdrawn from service to train others. Doenitz reckoned that two months was the average period that a U-boat could keep at sea before the crew's efficiency fell. Many of the Type VII boats, which tended to have the less experienced sailors, found themselves being directed to attack after attack on convoys in accordance with the 'wolf-pack' tactics then in operation. After two or three such attacks, especially if they had been subjected to depth-charging, the crew were exhausted and needed a long rest to recuperate. On the other hand, U-boats proceeding to the relatively quieter South Atlantic were much better able to continue their patrols, and cruises of up to five months were by no means uncommon.

Towards the end of 1942 and the beginning of 1943, the widespread introduction of radar into Allied aircraft scouring the Bay of Biscay for surfaced U-boats (see next chapter) meant that the latter required a primitive radar search receiver (either 'FuMB' or 'Metox') to serve as a warning of impending attack at night. But boats already at sea, perhaps returning from long patrols, did not have the receivers. A major role of the milk cows at this time was to provide such U-boats with Metox (or to repair an existing set that had broken down – the early sets were very unreliable) before the boats returned to their Biscay bases. A similar role in early 1944 was to provide U-boats with the new Naxos and Borkum receivers.

The milk cows were subjected to a barrage of signals from U-boat Command. As soon as they left the Bay of Biscay, they would be directed to the rendezvous quadrant, often at full speed, and would then be required to switch from one area to another. Periodically the cows would be ordered to state their current position and remaining fuel, a policy that defeated the more prudent (and more common) practice of signalling visually to one of the newly supplied U-boats that it should move well away and then announce to U-boat Command how the U-tanker was getting on at the rendezvous. U-boat Command frequently stated explicitly to the cow how much fuel should be assigned to each of its sucklers. Other orders might require a cow to race to take an injured or sick crew member off another U-boat at a mutual rendezvous. Even the final base for the cow would be signalled as it started its journey home.

Considering that all these signals were being decoded by Allied Intelligence after January 1943, the mystery is that any milk cow survived. By and large, after 1943, they did not.

Mention has already been made of the use of a Type XB minelayer, U 116, as a milk cow. These large 1,763 ton (surfaced) U-boats were ready for sea at about the same time as the Type XIV tankers, but the SMA mines developed for them initially proved to be unsatisfactory in use. (The mine was later developed to a state where it could be laid on the sea bed or left floating on a hawser to within a few metres of the sea surface.) Moreover, the U-boats' size precluded their use in the restricted waters around harbours where the mines would have had the greatest effect. Owing to the urgent need for more cows, some of them were pressed into service in this capacity. The minelayers carried 368 tons of fuel, of which around 200 tons could be made available to other boats. Unlike the Type XIV tankers, they carried a small offensive armament, namely two stern torpedo tubes, and a large 105mm gun. They also carried the usual anti-aircraft armament, although in 1942 this was relatively weak, consisting solely of one semi-automatic 37mm on the deck and two 20mm cannon behind the conning tower. Perhaps the most interesting feature of the deployment of these large U-minelayers was that, for every boat built, training during trials would emphasize minelaying and torpedo attacks, but never refuelling.

The Type XB minelayers were the largest U-boats built by the Kriegsmarine and their mine outlets gave them a very distinctive appearance (see the blueprint on page 46 and the photographs). If the mines were removed, then the mineshafts could accommodate a huge quantity of stores, and two of these craft were later to be pressed into service as blockade runners to the Far East. In addition, the U-minelayers carried six containers on the upper deck, principally for the storage of spare torpedoes but they could also be used for cargo. Other boats – but not the Type XIV tankers – also carried some of these containers, and they were found to be easily cracked during depth-charge attacks, permitting an influx of water. The containers were removed from most U-boat types after May 1943; those on the Type XB boats were retained only if special orders were given. The builder of all eight boats of this class that were finally completed was Germania Werft at Kiel.

Two other types of supply U-boat were also built in small numbers. One was the long-range Type IXD1 boat, the predecessor of the attack IXD2 type, and used as a submersible transporter rather than as a U-tanker. Two were built and both were used on cruises between Europe and the Far East; at first neither carried any but defensive armament. The other supply U-boat was the Type VIIF boat. This was built from standard Type VIIC boat sections, but an extra section was added just aft of the forward torpedo room. The extra section housed stores or, more typically, torpedoes, and this class of U-boat was used primarily as a torpedo transport, particularly to the Far East where replacements were hard to come by. A total of thirty-nine torpedoes could be carried.

The class carried the full VIIC offensive armament but, owing to the extra section and the fact that U-boats carried their fuel in tanks outside the hull, had a greater displacement (1,181 tons surfaced) and carried more fuel than the VIIC boats, giving the Type VIIF boats a radius of 14,700 miles. Type VIIF U-boats did not enter trials until June 1943 and were not used operationally until December.

Air Attack – The Battle of the Seconds

The aerial threat was always the greatest menace to a U-boat. It had been observed in the First World War that no submarine could hang around on the surface to satisfy her curiosity as to whether the aircraft had spotted the submarine, nor to discover whether the aircraft carried bombs. If the aircraft was spotted in time the U-boat would always submerge – fast.

First, the bridge watch – which was always kept to the barest minimum against such an eventuality – would scream 'ALAAAAARM' into the conning tower. As alarm bells rang through the U-boat, each member of the watch would instantly jump straight down the conning tower into the control room, into the waiting arms of one of the personnel delegated to catch the falling crewman, and he would then be bodily thrown out of the way in time for the next jumper from the crew watch. Minor injuries were common. During late 1942 and early 1943, when each U-boat carried a metal wire wrapped around a wooden frame as a makeshift aerial for FuMB and Metox, the bulky apparatus would first have to be thrown down the hatch before the watch members jumped. Invariably the 'Biscay Cross', as it was called, would be smashed into splinters and have to be rebuilt before it could be used again.

The last man down would clamber down the ladder, screwing the top hatch and then the lower conning tower hatch securely into place. The ship's commander, if not already part of the watch, would come racing to the control room and be briefed by the bridge watch as to the nature of the threat. Anyone in the boat's lavatories had to come out – at once.

The rate at which any submarine can dive is dependent upon its forward speed at the time of submergence. The diesels would be run up to full

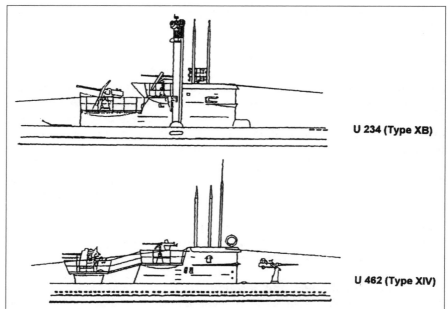

Typical late flak arrangements for U 234 (Type XB) and U 462 (Type XIV). U 234 mounts one of the new automatic 37mm cannon behind two shielded twin 20mm cannon. She also carries a schnorkel, one of only three milk cows to do so (the others were U 219 and U 490). U 462 carries a 'Vierling' quadruple 20mm gun on its own bandstand, an un-shielded single 20mm cannon and, forward, an old-pattern semi-automatic 37mm cannon. The Vierling put up an impressive rate of fire, but was found to be easily damaged in heavy seas. (*Horst Bredow*)

speed, the hydroplanes set to force the submarine underwater, flooding begun and the electric motors would be brought into operation in place of the diesels (which needed air to operate) shortly before the air inlet was submerged. In order to set this sequence in operation, it was essential that every member of the crew did his allotted task correctly. In peacetime, each step of the sequence would await an announcement from the preceding operators that they had done their jobs properly. But under conditions of air attack this policy was, necessarily, accelerated, and this was known as a 'crash-dive'. A quick-diving tank would be filled and each crew member would start his part of the submergence sequence without waiting for confirmation from other crew members that they had done theirs. A few U-boats are believed to have been lost by accident in this way. On at least one occasion a U-boat was well underwater when it noticed that one of the watch was still missing. It came back to the surface, the sailors released the half-drowned crewman from his snagged belt (all members of the watch had to clip themselves to the bridge as a precaution against being washed overboard) and still managed to get down under water again as bombs cascaded around.

Meanwhile, the ship's bosun would be yelling, 'All men forward'. Those crew members not needed at diving stations would run, clamber or be shoved as fast as possible into the bows of the U-boat so as to increase the weight forward, thus ensuring that the U-boat increased its rate of dive at a steeper angle (driven down by the engines). It was important, however, that the angle of dive was not too severe, or the boat's propellers would stick out of the water, denying the U-boat their propulsive power and making an easy target for the approaching aircraft. Once below the surface, the U-boat would normally change course so that it cork-screwed into the depths; if necessary, the engines would be put into reverse so as to slow the descent. It took thirty seconds for one of the smaller Type VII U-boats to dive completely, twenty seconds if the crew were very experienced. A larger Type IX boat took about forty seconds. The time to submergence of a Type XB minelayer or a Type XIV U-tanker was typically fifty to sixty seconds.

An attacking aircraft could cover a lot of sea in fifty seconds and the usual rule of thumb was that the U-boat should not dive if the aircraft was closer than 3,000 metres. In the later years of the war, U-boats had standing orders from U-boat Command not to attempt to dive if they were over-flown by an aircraft that had not dropped its bombs – the aircraft could wheel for a second attack faster than the U-boat could dive.

If the U-boat stayed on the surface, it had to fight. In the early years the anti-aircraft defence was comparatively modest, typically one or two 20mm cannon, but by 1943 much, much heavier armaments were carried by all U-boats. The principal function of the gun crew was to deter an attack, rather than to shoot down the enemy aircraft (a U-boat was far more valuable than an aircraft, so it made no sense to risk the exchange), and armour-piercing shells began to be carried by the boats on the erroneous assumption that the aircraft were armoured (U-boat crews claimed to have seen bullets bouncing off the attacking aircraft). In fact, long-range aircraft were deliberately kept as light as possible in order to extend their ranges. Even so, experience showed that the chances of an aircraft inflicting crippling damage on a surfaced U-boat with bombs or shallow-set depth-charges were very promising. A shoot-out was definitely not a good option for the U-boat.

Given the above facts it is perhaps surprising that the milk cows carried out so few flak drills while at sea. Only one (U 460) records frequent practice in its war diary, while U 461 appears from eyewitnesses to have had only one flak practice at sea in its first three patrols.

Escort

All U-boats were given an escort to the point at which they could safely submerge (usually to the 50-metre line, i.e. the point at which the water first reached a depth of 50 metres) when leaving one of the French west coast ports. Minelaying by Allied aircraft had become a serious problem by 1942 and a submerged U-boat could easily set off a magnetic mine lying on the sea bed in shallow waters.

Thus a typical escort for a U-boat might consist of a Sperrbrecher – a strong boat with a cement-lined bottom that forged ahead of the U-boat, projecting a very strong magnetic beam forward and streaming noise buoys with the intention of setting off any mines before the U-boat arrived – up to three minesweepers (M-boats), one or two small submarine chasers (UJ-boats), armed motor launches (R-boats) but never, to the author's knowledge, with fast torpedo boats (S-boats, commonly known as E-boats). The milk cows were of special importance and might rate an escort of T-boats (light destroyers) or even, late in the war, one or two of the heavy Z-class destroyers based on the French west coast. Generally an air escort was not provided.

Germany's naval building plans had been severely restricted in the 1920s by actual, or anticipated, tonnage restrictions, and this favoured the building of six light (925-ton) *Moewe*-class torpedo boats completed in 1926–8, followed by another six very similar boats of the *Wolf* class in 1928–9. The boats generally carried six 21-inch torpedo tubes at a designed speed of 32 to 33 knots. Their guns amounted to three 105mm in single turrets and four single 20mm cannon for anti-aircraft protection. Germany had continued to construct modern updates of the *Moewe* boats. The un-named 853-ton T-boats, T 1 to T 21, were completed from 1939 to 1942 with a lighter armament (a single 105mm gun) than those of their predecessors. The original plan had been to deploy them for torpedo attacks in stormy waters where the S-boats could not operate, but the Kriegsmarine found that the latter were much more seaworthy than originally supposed. This created the dilemma of what to do with the new T-boats, whose poor armament and experimental engines made them of less value than the older *Moewe*-type boats. Originally used for minelaying or convoy protection along the northern French coast, one by one they were withdrawn to Germany. By July 1943, only two remained on the French west coast. Their replacements at Brest were the first units of a more powerful series of torpedo boats (T 22 to T 36) that carried four single 105mm guns.

By contrast, the fifteen-year-old *Moewe*-type boats were rugged and reliable, although no longer capable of attaining their published maximum speed, and after constant action their crews had reached a high degree of efficiency. Their flak armaments were augmented during 1943 by the addition of a quadruple 20mm flak gun and two more single 20mm cannon on the bridge wings. The ships now also carried radar. By July 1943, the five survivors (*Falke*, *Greif*, *Jaguar*, *Kondor* and *Moewe*) were grouped together as the 5th Torpedo Boat Flotilla, under the overall command of

56

Flag Officer (destroyers), at La Pallice on the west coast of France. The flotilla also had tactical control over a further two boats (T 14 and T 19) that were the remnant of those weakly armed new torpedo boats returning to the Baltic.

The Germans had moved the 8th Destroyer Flotilla with four (Z 23, Z 24, Z 32 and Z 37) of the powerful, 2,600-ton 'Narvik' (Z-class) destroyers to the west of France in February 1943, with a carefully planned operation to get such valuable units through the English Channel. These fast (38-knot) ships carried almost the firepower of a light cruiser with their five 15cm guns, but the weight of the turrets caused their bows to dip far too readily into the lightest of seas which made for poor seaworthiness, while their experimental steam plant had proved to be lamentably unreliable in practice. Every operation by these ships resulted in an anxious calculation of fuel consumption and weather conditions; most of the time, the ships swung at their anchors – except when they were back in dockyard hands for attention to their engines. The original intention had been to use the destroyers to bring blockade runners from the Far East, with their valuable cargoes of metals and rubber, through the Bay of Biscay safely into a French port.

By now the torpedo boats and Narvik destroyers had been called upon to escort U-boats in the Bay, especially those that had been damaged. It was here that their flak armaments counted. Whereas a U-boat was expected to submerge readily, so that the addition of a multiple heavy flak weapon affected the boat's stability and made the gun less accurate, the surface ships made excellent flak platforms. The escort could not proceed too far into the Bay of Biscay for fear of exposing itself to Allied air attack. Typically the U-boats would set out under cover of darkness (in part, to minimize the danger of being reported by French agents) and the escort would depart as day approached.

U-boats returning to France could expect much the same kind of escort on return, except in the case when they were damaged. Then a special effort might be made with air cover also being laid on. A pilot was generally taken on board by those U-boats navigating narrow estuaries, which included those of the cows based at St Nazaire and Bordeaux.

In Harbour
U-boats in general underwent a series of standard maintenance procedures once they had returned to port and the milk cows were no exception. First, the boats were unloaded of torpedoes and remaining provisions; next the boat would be put into dock; then half the crew could go on leave while the remaining half stayed with the boat.

The dockyard workers would overhaul the U-boat, including any necessary maintenance work and repainting, and new technology, if available, would be installed (such as new radar receivers or new guns). There would be a trial cruise ('Probefahrt'). Removal of rust and essential demagnetization, to reduce the chance of triggering a magnetic mine, would be carried out, and finally the boat would be reloaded. By now, the remainder of the crew would be returning to port. The whole procedure typically took one month, although every effort was made to accelerate matters. U-boats, whether tankers or attack boats, could only contribute to the war effort once they were at sea.

The Allies made a big effort to bomb the U-boats while they were moored at their French bases. The risk to the boats was so apparent that the Todt Labour Organization had been commanded to construct huge, concrete, bomb-proof bunkers at the French ports of Brest, Lorient, St Nazaire, La Rochelle and Bordeaux (and subsequently at ports in Norway, Germany and the Mediterranean). Construction of the first pen at St Nazaire began as early as March 1941 and it was handed over within just three months, although further concrete was to be poured onto it and other pens as the Allies increased their bombing raids. The bunkers protected boats and working crews, who were now predominantly rested in the countryside.

When the crew of U 461 returned to St Nazaire in October 1942, they found that half the city had been flattened and their barracks badly damaged by bombs. They took up quarters at La Baule, outside the city, but the subsequent devastation of the French bases by Allied bombers trying to penetrate the bunkers in a series of planned raids in 1943 seems to have left a lasting impression on those who saw it. The last of the attacks was on the night of 2/3 April, by which time most of the French civilian population had fled. Thereafter, there were occasional bombing raids until September.

Doenitz visited one of the French bases to give a speech in mid-1943. He observed that 'the towns of St Nazaire and Lorient have been obliterated as U-boat bases. Not a dog, not a cat, remains in these towns. Nothing remains – except the U-boat shelters. They were built on the far-sighted orders of the Fuehrer.' Not one of the French bunkers was ever destroyed by Allied bombing and some remain intact to this day, when they are used as shelters for fishing boats.

The Crews

The crews of the U-boats were all volunteers and, together with the Luftwaffe bomber crews, were regarded as the élite of the German armed forces. Mention has already been made of the superior rations, including chocolate and pineapples, available to the U-boatmen. However, the sailors could not select the boats on which to serve, and this fact alone renders improbable some claims that the tanker crews suffered from inferior morale to that of the attack-boat crews – all were drawn from the same pool of volunteers.

Individual crew members might be trained for several tasks. For example, Wilhelm Kraus was appointed to U 461 as a radio operator, but also served as a hydrophone listener, a frogman and a paramedic.

In the early years of the war, while the U-boat force was expanding fast, it became common practice to 'rotate' the crews so that half of the crew of a returning U-boat would be transferred to a new U-boat working up in trials in the Baltic. This practice developed a tremendous esprit de corps since everyone on every boat knew one or two crew members on every other boat; however, by 1942 the practice was dying out and it never appears to have applied to the milk cows. Crew lists of the milk cows suggest that only the officers were transferred to new commands as part of their increasing seniority. The other ranks, who had been well trained for their fuelling and minelaying missions, did not get rotated and stuck with their boats to the end.

The skippers of the milk cows tended, in the earlier years, to be highly experienced commanders with commensurate high rank, typically Korvet-tenkapitaen. Again, though, as the war progressed, the seniority of the commanders of the cows declined as the older commanders were killed, captured or promoted to higher positions. Some commanders, such as Schaefer, Wolfbauer and von Wilamowitz-Moellendorf, had served as officers on U-boats in the First World War.

Others had proved their worth as commanders of attack boats in the early days of the war. Stiebler, for example, had served as commander of four Type II U-boats by 1940 and had then served in a training establishment until his appointment to U 461. Yet others received their training as officers on existing milk cows or in captured foreign submarines. But the experience and age of the later commanders were clearly inferior to those of their earlier peers.

As well as being present during the formal training of the crew of their milk cow, all the commanders were expected to attend special classes while their boat was being built. These might last between one and four months.

Once at sea, the freedom of the crew members was necessarily curtailed, although their pay was increased! Smoking was generally permitted only at the foot of the conning tower during darkness (a flame could be seen at night for many miles). Taking photographs was generally not permitted by the crew, for obvious reasons of security. Individual crew members knew roughly where the milk cow was at sea, but were not told the exact position at a rendezvous. Sailors were allowed on deck once the milk cow was out of reach of land-based bombers, and could cheer and wave as a fellow U-boat drew close for resupply. However, they could not cross over to the other boat except as part of their duties.

Missing U-boats

Any U-boat that went missing in action, without clear indication that it had met its end, would be said to have 'missed one star' approximately one month after its last signal. This indicated that it was 'missing' and an asterisk would be placed against its name. The German word for asterisk is 'little star'.

After about six months, the U-boat 'missed two stars', indicating that it was presumed lost. Thus the tanker U 464, sunk by an aircraft on 20 August 1942, missed one star on 23 September and two stars on 8 February 1943, despite contemporary British press reports that it had been sunk by air attack.

Six months might seem an unusually long time to have to wait before assuming that a U-boat had been lost in action, but radio sets could go out of action, U-boats could run out of fuel and there were one or two isolated instances of U-boats returning to port or rendezvous with sails hoisted, long after they had been feared lost.

Name, Rank and Number

Some of the missing U-boats had been sunk and their crews rescued. Allied interrogators went to great lengths to discover what they could about the U-boat operations by questioning survivors from sunken U-boats. The interrogators did not use illegal methods.

The rules of war allow that captured prisoners of war should be required to state only their name, rank and (military) number. This advice is given by all military forces to their personnel against the event of capture: 'Do not state anything more than your name, rank and number. To give away other information may damage our cause.'

The release of secret US Intelligence records in the 1990s (fifty years after the end of the war) reveals clearly how little attention many captured U-boat sailors paid to the rule that had been so sternly drummed into them. Doubtless they were over-relieved at having been picked up from the ocean by Allied ships (they had little other chance of rescue), but the information they gave enabled Allied Intelligence to build up a detailed picture of the U-boat war. The officers tended to be tighter lipped, but some of the rescued seamen from the sunken milk cows gave the most extraordinarily detailed accounts of their operations (parts of which have been used in this chapter). Survivors rescued from U 487 in July 1943 gave away the secret of the German acoustic torpedo, which was just entering into service. Within two months, American groups operating in the Atlantic against U-boats were carrying the antidote: a noise-making device known as 'Foxer'.

British records are also now available for inspection, despite the longstanding policy not to reveal similar interrogation details for seventy-five years in order to protect the sailors who volunteered the information during their lifetimes.

Organization
After commissioning, nearly all the milk cows, U-transporters and U-cruisers underwent training in the Baltic under the 4th (Training) U-boat Flotilla. Exceptions were the Type VIIF U-transporter series U 1059 to U 1062 and the single Type XB minelayer U 234, all of which were assigned to the Kiel-based 5th Flotilla.

The first two Type XB minelayers (U 116 and U 117) were assigned to the 1st and 2nd Flotillas, based respectively at Brest and Lorient, early in 1942, while the 10th Flotilla (Lorient), which had only been formed in January 1942, took the first U-tankers of the XIV series (U 459 to U 464) and the Type XB U 118. The first three U-cruisers also joined this flotilla. Most of these large U-boats sailed from St Nazaire. However, the size of the U-cruisers, U-minelayers and U-tankers was such that they would not fit into the bomb-proof pens at Lorient and St Nazaire, and had to be moored at open quays.

The 12th Flotilla was founded in October 1942 at Bordeaux, under the command of Korvettenkapitaen Scholz, where the concrete bunkers had been designed to accommodate large U-boats. To this flotilla were assigned all the U-tankers, U-minelayers (except U 234), U-transporters and U-cruisers until the disbandment of the flotilla in August 1944, after the Allied invasion of France had jeopardized the safety of the U-boats in the Biscay ports. By this time, all the U-tankers had been sunk, and the handful of remaining U-minelayers and Type IXD1 and IXD2 U-cruisers were assigned to the Flensburg-based 33rd Flotilla which had been founded in September 1944.

The two remaining former Italian U-boats, UIT 24 and UIT 25, used as blockade runners in the Far East, were also assigned to the 33rd Flotilla. Prior to September 1944, these ex-Italian boats, of which there had originally been five, had been with the 12th Flotilla. U-minelayer U 234 was also assigned to the 33rd Flotilla for blockade-running purposes, and her sister ship U 219 was similarly employed, being in the Far East at the end of 1944.

The first milk cow, U A, had belonged to the St Nazaire-based 7th Flotilla until withdrawn from operations in 1942. Subsequently she belonged to the 18th (Training) and 24th (Training) Flotillas in the Baltic.

Operational Deployment
The milk cows used widely different routes to cross the dangerous Bay of Biscay, at any rate in 1942 and early 1943, so as to reduce the danger of several of these valuable units being sunk all at one time. The submarine tankers frequently changed their positions at sea even while still com-

paratively safe from detection. In part this was due to basic security, so as not to compromise the rendezvous by staying too long, and in part due to redeployment to shorten the distance a pack of attack U-boats had to travel to seek replenishment. There were even cases where a milk cow was ordered to follow a convoy at a safe distance so that the besetting wolf pack could be speedily replenished after the attack. Support was always promised to attack U-boats that might run out of fuel as a result of chasing a convoy too far.

Rendezvous were always arranged in the 'air gaps' – the sea areas to which shore-based aircraft could not penetrate with enough fuel to return home – while these existed. A very high proportion of the rendezvous was arranged in the general vicinity of the Azores. Indeed, so many refuellings took place in the sea zone designated as square BD to the north of the Azores that one might think that the Allies had only to send one carrier group to this area to mop up all the U-boats within it. However, the BD sea square extended from roughly 43 to 51 degrees north and 25 to 38 degrees west. This enclosed a sea area of around 350,000 square miles, much more than the limited number of aircraft flown by an escort carrier could be expected to search within one day – and the U-boats might switch areas during the hours of darkness or while submerged. Thus we can see that the fuelling areas north of the Azores could not be properly searched without specific information as to in which part-squares the refuelling would take place.

As the focal point of many U-boats, often arriving from remote areas, the U-tanker served as a centre for the exchange of information. Details of Allied countermeasures and other items of interest accumulated by the milk cow were passed, far too often by W/T (although in cipher), to new visitors. Sometimes sealed orders carried aboard would be transmitted by W/T to the recipient, defeating the purpose of issuing sealed orders.

Careful positioning of a single milk cow in the Atlantic enabled fuel to be supplied to U-boats sent simultaneously to the Caribbean, Brazil and the Freetown areas, and later to the Indian Ocean. Italian U-boats could also be replenished and this was done in the early days of refuelling. However, difficulties with ciphers and wireless frequencies seem to have led to the abandonment of this practice by the beginning of 1943.

U-boat Mines

There were two basic types of German mines: the 'TorpedoMine' (TM), which could be laid by firing from a U-boat's torpedo tube, and the 'SonderMine' (SM, special mine, also known as the 'SchachtMine') which had to be expelled from the shafts of specialized minelayers, the Types XB and VIID. In the early years of the war the U-boats had deployed almost exclusively the TMB and TMC, which lay on a shallow sea bed until operated by the magnetic influence of a ship passing overhead. Much better results were expected from the new SMA, which had an explosive charge of 350kg and was a floating magnetic mine (lacking contact horns) that could be moored by an anchor to the sea bed in such a way that it was just below the surface of the water. The length of the cable could be as long as 300 metres, which made the mine effective in virtually any waters likely to be encountered near a harbour. However, the SMA remained very troublesome. On the one hand, the minefield laid with the SMA could not be allowed to exist indefinitely since it might be necessary for U-boats to enter the same waters at a later stage, even if only to lay another minefield. On the other hand, the premature discovery by the enemy of the minefield would result in it being immediately cleared by minesweepers. Such premature discovery might occur if the mine broke loose from its anchor and floated on the sea surface, when the rocking motion might trigger the sensitive magnetic detector and cause a very noticeable bang. The German solution was to combine a timing mechanism, which would scuttle each mine with a small explosive after a set period of time had elapsed, with another device that would scuttle the mine if it floated free. The difficulty of arranging this combination of desired properties would delay entry of the SMA into operation until well into 1942.

The Type XB minelayer U 117 would place a defensive minefield off Jutland in May 1942, although all but three of the mines suffered premature detonations. When U 118 repeated the operation in the same area, but later in the month, only three mines detonated, and they had been chosen as experiments to test the efficacy of the new anti-wave mechanism. The mines had been laid at a depth of 30 metres, and spaced by 400 metres. U 118 was expected to carry out another test minelaying, but her sister minelayer, U 119, had damaged a torpedo tube in an accident and was therefore assigned the minelaying (see Chapter 8). U 118 instead would lay her mines on active service in enemy waters, since by October 1942 it had become clear that the SMA could be deployed properly. During her trials during November and December 1943, the new minelayer U 233 found that there were no premature detonations at all, as expected.

Chapter 7

New Allied Weapons
1942 to 1943

All the U-boats involved in the Battle of the Atlantic were based in France, in the defended ports of the Bay of Biscay, and all had to traverse the Bay in order to reach the Atlantic. The British realized this and sent up long-range aircraft from Coastal Command to patrol the Bay in the hope of catching a U-boat unawares on the surface as it used its diesel engines to recharge its batteries. The aircraft were virtually undisturbed by the Luftwaffe, which was heavily engaged on the Russian Front, although the German Naval Command was occasionally able to persuade Hitler to order Goering to send a few long-range fighter aircraft to try to drive off the Coastal Command threat.

U-boats acquired the habit of running through the Bay submerged during the day, then coming to the surface at night so that the diesels could be operated under cover of darkness. However, the first part of the journey was through shallow water in which Coastal Command aircraft had strewn numerous mines. U-boats were escorted through this zone on the surface by a variety of small escort craft.

By 1942, the British had equipped many of their Coastal Command aircraft with 150cm radar, so that U-boats could no longer travel safely on the surface across the heavily patrolled Bay at night. Any U-boat foolish enough to try would be located by the aircraft's radar and the aircraft would attack it. On a dark night, the aircraft could not be seen by the U-boat's lookouts, and the sound of the approaching aircraft would be drowned by the boat's engines. When the pilot judged that the moment was right, he would switch on his 'Leigh Light' (an aircraft-mounted searchlight), illuminating the U-boat and dazzling her crew. By the time they had worked out what was going on, the aircraft would have passed overhead, having strafed the U-boat with its guns and attacked it with bombs or shallow-set depth-charges.

The German response to this harassment was to equip their U-boats with a crude radar search receiver known as Metox, first tested operationally by

U 107 in August 1942 while crossing the Bay of Biscay. When Metox picked up the radar impulses of a searching aircraft, it gave an audible warning and the U-boat crash-dived. Since the U-boat needed to stay on the surface for several hours to recharge its batteries, it then had to resurface to complete the job, but the Bay was so heavily patrolled that it might have to crash-dive several times in a single night. During daylight, U-boats stayed submerged while running on their batteries, however they travelled much faster with their diesels than with their electric motors. Consequently the Allied blockade of the Biscay bases meant that U-boats had to spend longer in transit to their operational areas, while the constant threat of surprise attack at night was demoralizing for the crews.

Allied surface ships also carried 150cm radar, which made the old night-surface attack by U-boats against a convoy a dangerous tactic. German radar technology lagged sadly behind that of the British – radar for U-boats was not to come for another year, and even so it was fitted only to a handful of boats. It was found to be too temperamental in operation to have much value.

The arrival of ship-borne radar had little effect on the function of the milk cows, which were only too happy to stay away from convoys and their escorts. Airborne radar, on the other hand, was a much greater menace to the U-tankers as they could not now count on darkness to hide them. While the air gaps were still available for rendezvous with other U-boats, the advent of radar would not affect refuelling operations, but sooner or later the cows themselves had to return to base for replenishment. Their slow diving times made sudden air attacks exceptionally perilous, and even when they had reached France they had still to run the aerial blockade to get out again.

Another Allied development in 1942 was ship-borne High Frequency Direction Finding equipment (H/F D/F), known as 'Huff Duff'. Shore-based H/F D/F had long been available for pinpointing U-boat transmissions, as the Germans knew, but it was not sufficiently accurate to give away the precise position of the broadcasting U-boat. The German B-Dienst had decoded a British message about the position of a transmitting U-boat as far back as February 1941, but the shore-based fix of the boat, whose exact position was known to U-boat Command, was only accurate to 50 miles. Wolf-pack tactics necessitated the passage of a stream of messages between U-boats and their shore command; in particular, the first U-boat to locate a convoy had to wireless its position and details about the convoy, while U-boat Command directed other U-boats in the area to the attack. Sometimes the U-boat even had to emit homing signals, or beacon signals, to enable others of the pack to find the convoy.

Ship-borne H/F D/F was relatively short-ranged, but gave an accurate bearing on any U-boat transmitting within 20 miles of the ship with the equipment. If another ship also took a bearing, the point of intersection of the bearings pinpointed the position of the U-boat. Warships could then be despatched to sink, or at least drive underwater, the U-boat. Once submerged, it would lose contact with the convoy which could then escape from the pack before it had closed in. The effective use of H/F D/F was one of the major reasons for the decline of U-boat successes early in 1943.

Shipborne H/F D/F could also have a potentially important effect on a rendezvous with a milk cow, since the exchange of signals between the cow and the U-boat waiting to be replenished could be pinpointed. However, these rendezvous were usually so far away from the convoy routes that no action could be taken against the U-boats while there remained a shortage of escort ships, although this shortage was not to continue much longer.

Admiralty Appreciation of Submarine Tankers, 1942

The British Admiralty was slow to appreciate that the Germans were operating submarine tankers. This was largely due to their inability to decode the signals of Atlantic U-boats during 1942, while coastal traffic (e.g. around Norway) appears to have made no mention of the role of the U-tankers as they passed through Norwegian waters. Matters were complicated by the fact that it was known that U-boats did occasionally meet with one another to exchange supplies, as had occurred in the mid-Atlantic in 1941.

The following catalogues the sequence of events, as derived from Admiralty Intelligence documents:

March 1942
A supply ship was believed to be operating north-east of George Town, Guyana, South America.

April 1942
Heavy W/T traffic was noted 300 miles to the north to north-east of Bermuda. (This was actually due to the arrival of U 459.)

May 1942
The above W/T traffic was attributed to one of the following explanations:
 (i) Refuelling operations.
 (ii) A wireless ruse (a few U-boats pretending to be present in large numbers).
(iii) Reports of successes by the U-boats.
(iv) U-boats reporting that they had passed a particular longitude of navigation.

It was later concluded that U-boats off the US coast ought to need to return to base owing to a shortage of fuel and torpedoes. Since this did not happen, a later May report suggested that the U-boats must be being turned around very fast in port.

June 1942
Several indications of rendezvous between U-boats at sea were noted.

July 1942
A medium-range (Type VII) U-boat was conclusively sunk by the USAAF off Cape Hatteras. It was deduced that this type of U-boat must have an endurance of at least sixty days.

August 1942
There were 'slight indications' of a supply ship supporting U-boats off Freetown (this was actually U 116).

On 20 August, the milk cow U 464 was sunk in the North Atlantic and the survivors who were rescued reported that they had been serving on a submarine tanker. This was the first definite evidence that such a craft existed. Therefore:

24 August 1942
Accounts from prisoners of war of U-tankers 'between Greenland and Newfoundland' were reported. Photographs of U-boats 'at Lorient' (France) showed that they were very 'beamy'. Similar craft had first been identified at Kiel by air reconnaissance in early April 1942.

Subsequently submersible tankers make sporadic appearances through the Intelligence reports. In October it was estimated that 'about three supply U-boats have been at sea for some time now' – the true figure was six, excluding U 464.

Chapter 8

Onslaught on the Convoy Routes

July to December 1942

The return of the U-boats to pack attacks against the North Atlantic convoys made the function of the milk cows as important as ever. By refuelling the U-boats at sea, the number of boats in a pack could be kept at a high level and the number of hazardous journeys across the Bay of Biscay could be reduced. U-boat wolf-packs were able to attack convoy after convoy in the Atlantic air gaps before being replenished by milk cows in the same gaps, leaving them ready to assail new convoys before returning to base.

U 116 (Korvettenkapitaen von Schmidt) began her second refuelling mission at the end of June from Lorient. She carried a B-Dienst (Intelligence) team aboard that was to prove invaluable for identifying ships encountered at sea. By 8 July she was in mid-Atlantic where she encountered a neutral Swiss ship, the motorship *Saentis*. It was the B-Dienst team that identified the vessel from her W/T calls on the International Short Wave. Moving to the sea area around the Cape Verde Islands, she was able to support the five U-boats of the *Hai* (Shark) pack, the first boats to operate south of the Azores since the 'Paukenschlag' operation. The *Hai* group was met (but not refuelled) on the 8th to the 10th.

Next day U 116 reported a convoy (OS.33) that was attacked by the pack. U 116 took part in that attack, since she carried a torpedo in each of her stern torpedo tubes, together with one or two reloads. While shadowing the convoy she sank an unescorted ship, the SS *Cortona* (7,093 tons), with one of her two ready torpedoes (the ship was identified by her distress call). On the 12th, the SS *Shaftesbury* (4,284 tons) was sunk with another torpedo and her captain taken prisoner. Again the B-Dienst team was able to identify the ship from her distress signals.

Then on the 22nd, U 116 located a 4,000-ton merchant ship and dived to make an underwater attack. The torpedo missed, so U 116 surfaced and raced ahead, before mounting a vigorous assault on her unidentified target with her large (105mm) deck gun and her 37mm heavy flak gun. There is very little humour in the war diaries of the milk cows, but one cannot suppress a little sympathy for the commander's chagrin when, after U 116 had finished blasting away with her guns, the enemy ship steamed calmly into the distance unscathed while von Schmidt remarked ruefully that the fire of both guns was erratic and that the attack had been broken off without success.

The *Hai* boats were now refuelled between 26 July and 4 August and U 116 signalled 'refuelling complete', the boats having received altogether 195 tons of oil and eleven weeks of provisions. The pack then moved in line abreast towards Freetown and further successes, while U 116 headed for home. A further lone merchant ship was sighted on 7 August, but von Schmidt was mindful of the last gun attack and dived until the ship was out of sight, citing 'fifteen hours to darkness' and 'the poor experience of the crew'. U 116 reported a convoy west of Portugal while homeward bound, dodged an air attack on the 19th west of the Bay of Biscay and returned to Lorient on 23 August. Doenitz's only comment on this operation was 'Five U-boats supplied and two ships sunk. Nothing special to remark.'

The new Type XB U-minelayer, U 119 (Kapitaenleutnant Zech), makes her first appearance in the official records at this time. Instead of following on the heels of U 116, she had been reserved for use in German waters, and was now to be employed for the unusual purpose of defensive minelaying (improving the German minefields around home waters that were intended to keep British naval forces out of the Skagerrak). This, the first real minefield laid by one of these craft, must have been a test for the Type XB U-boat and the new SMA magnetic mine (whose use was still embargoed), since there was no other reason why a conventional mine-layer could not extend these minefields so close to German waters.

Zech, at thirty-five years of age, was another experienced officer who had commanded, appropriately enough, the 3rd Minesweeping Flotilla between May 1940 and May 1941. He had then had a variety of office positions until commissioning U 119 on 2 April 1942. Now this 'game-keeper turned poacher' was to lay the first real mine barrage put down by a custom-built U-minelayer.

U 119 took aboard the mines needed on 1 August and moved to Kiel. She then proceeded into the Skagerrak on the 4th, in company with the research vessel *Sundewall* and an escort, and laid a straight line of mines, 350 metres apart on a course of 336 degrees, off the north-west tip of Denmark on the night of 8 August. The operation was successful, and this was to set the minelaying pattern for all future operations with the Type XB U-minelayer and the SMA – typically, the mines were laid in waters

50 to 350 metres deep, spaced 400 metres apart. Generally the period of the new moon would be preferred for maximum darkness.

U 119 had returned to Kiel, with a different escort, by the 10th. Doenitz had no special comments about the minelaying itself, but pointed out to the embarrassed Zech that war diaries were supposed to be updated daily and signed by the commander.

This is the last we hear of U 119 in the official records until her new war patrol in February 1943. She remained in German waters in between times. However, German confidence in the SMA seems to have been established. Although their offensive use was still embargoed in September, plans were being prepared by U-boat Command to lay the first of these mines off the USA. The Germans had also created a development of the Type VII U-boat, the Type VIID, to deploy the mines when it became clear that the Type XB U-minelayers were far too large for many purposes. Six of these 965-ton boats had originally been laid down (U 213 to U 218 inclusive), but two had been sunk during deployment in wolf-pack operations before the SMA had been released. Plans were now drawn up for the four survivors to lay mines around Britain, although a third would be sunk before it could be used.

We left the new U 461 (Kapitaenleutnant Stiebler) at her refuelling zone south-south-east of St John's after her secret B-Dienst mission. Her first 'customer' was U 332 (CC8455; 19 July). Three days later she replenished U 161 before moving east where the *Wolf* group (U 71, U 437, U 43 and U 454) was reprovisioned at the end of July after the pack had attacked convoy ON.113, followed by six further boats, all in the space of four days. One sick seaman was taken off each of five of the U-boats for treatment on the U-tanker.

U 43 must have been thirsty for she was again supplied by U 461 on 5 August at a new rendezvous and then again, further east, in company with U 558 on the 8th, apparently with machinery defects. By now U 461 was well on her way home and, apart from an air alarm just west of the Bay of Biscay, she arrived uneventfully at her new home port of St Nazaire in France on the night of 16/17 August. Here the B-Dienst team departed as secretly as they had arrived (and got two weeks' leave). Stiebler wrote a detailed account of his refuelling experiences, which have been drawn on in Chapter 6.

U 462 had spent the period from her commissioning on 5 March to July in exercises and crew training in the Baltic. She was loaded with provisions at Kiel before sailing on her first refuelling mission on 23 July. U 462 was commanded by Oberleutnant zS Vowe, thirty-eight years old, who had spent most of the war to date in shore posts, although he had had a single three-month stint as the watch officer of the successful U 107. This is the first example of a milk cow commander who lacked considerable experience, and with a commensurate low rank. He was, however, to prove a capable and energetic commander, despite a pedantic and unusually verbose style in the war diary. U 462 arrived at Kristiansand (Norway) on the 24th and put out to sea again with the submarine chaser UJ 1711 as escort.

Numerous aircraft and one destroyer were seen as U 462 headed into the Atlantic through the Iceland–Faeroes gap, but no attack was sustained. A rendezvous was made on 2 August with U 609 south of Iceland in order to take over a sick crew member from the latter, and then the U-tanker headed south-west to her principal refuelling zone. U 558 also received fuel and medical attention en route on 16 August, only eight days after her rendezvous with U 461. Two days later, U 108 was refuelled in mid-Atlantic (DE54; c. 31N 52W) far to the south of Newfoundland.

The *Lohs* group was now ordered to head south after attacks on convoys SC.95 and ONS.122 so that it could refuel from U 462 (six boats) and from the Type IXC attack boat U 174 (three boats) in the same area. These U-boats were replenished between 29 August and 8 September, most of the boats receiving 40 tons of oil, with torpedoes being handed over in one case. A stream of messages from U-boat Command attended these meetings, after which the boats refuelled by U 462 made up a fresh line west of the North Atlantic.

Then came a desperate signal from U 203 (10 September). Her commander, Kapitaenleutnant Rolf Muetzelburg, was seriously injured and needed urgent medical attention. At once U-boat Command ordered U 462 to signal her current position and race at highest speed towards U 203, while U 203 was to rush towards the U-tanker. Soon the Command had calculated the halfway point – the rendezvous was set for CF8455, just to the east of the Azores.

Kapitaenleutnant Muetzelburg was a U-boat 'ace', already awarded the Knight's Cross with Oak Leaves for his successes. On a hot, sunny day in mid-Atlantic, free from the danger of air attack, he had decided to join his crew for a dip in the sea. He jumped off the conning tower head-first onto the part-submerged saddle tank of his U-boat and suffered a severe head injury (one account says that he broke his neck). This was the casualty awaiting the frantic arrival of U 462 and her doctor.

On the 11th, U 203 signalled that Muetzelburg had died in the morning. Was the rendezvous still necessary? U-boat Command ordered both boats to proceed as planned, so that the doctor on U 462 could examine the body. The rendezvous took place the next day and Muetzelburg was buried at sea with a three-shot salute from each of the U-tanker's 37mm cannon. No fuel was supplied to U 203.

U 462 now headed for home, receiving instructions as late as the 18th that her new home port would in future be St Nazaire. She arrived on 21 September. Doenitz congratulated Vowe on a mission 'well carried through'. Vowe appended a huge amount of written material on the subject of his refuelling experience, together with a certain amount of gratuitous moralizing ('the crew must acquire the principle of "one for all and all for one"'). Apparently the conduct of the crew had in fact been good although, while in port, one of the crewmen had the misfortune to die in a dockyard accident.

The fifth U-tanker of the Type XIV series, U 463, had been commissioned on 2 April 1942 by the experienced Korvettenkapitaen Wolfbauer. At forty-seven years of age, Wolfbauer had served on a U-boat in the First World War, had held shore positions since 1940 and was probably deemed to be too elderly for command of an attack U-boat. Trials were conducted in the Baltic until the end of June when U 463 was based at Kiel. Within just three months of being commissioned, she was taken out to sea.

U 463 left Kiel on 11 July in company with U 592 and the conventional tanker *Orion*, arriving at Kristiansand next day. On the 13th, U 463, U 592 and U 607 all departed for the Atlantic together, although it was not intended that they should travel as a group. The U-tanker ploughed through the Iceland–Faeroes gap above and below the surface, with repeated air alarms, and had entered the North Atlantic by the 19th.

The first refuelling by U 463 was on 31 July when U 84 was replenished south of Newfoundland at about 35N 54W. The U-tanker then moved on to her main fuelling zone (28N 60W, south-east of Bermuda) where a stream of U-boats heading into the Caribbean was oiled. These included: U 510, which handed over a Uruguayan ship's captain as a prisoner and received an above-average 85 tons of fuel (most of the U-boats received 40 to 60 tons); U 658, from which a sick sailor was removed and replaced with one of the cow's own crew; and U 598. During refuelling of the latter, one of the U 598's sailors drowned during maintenance work on the hydro-planes and propellers of his own boat, death occurring despite immediate attempts at resuscitation by the tanker's doctor. U 463 took the body on board and committed it to the deep. One of her engine room ratings was assigned to U 598 as a replacement.

U 463 refuelled a total of ten U-boats at this rendezvous. U 600 was 'rapidly refuelled'. The other boats included U 129 and U 505. Then U 463 moved just a little to the south-west where U 164, the Type VIID minelayer U 217, U 511 (from which a sick sailor was removed) and 'U 143' were also supplied. An annotation to the U-boat diary by the British Admiralty correctly reads (for 'U 143') 'probably U 134'. In the course of these operations, conducted between 11 and 13 August, battery room No. 2 on the cow was damaged by heavy seas resulting in a strong release of toxic hydrogen chloride gas. The room had to be evacuated and cleansed.

U 463 had now sold out and headed for home. On 27 August, she met U 594 just north of the Azores in order to donate a spare part and also a little (10 tons) of her remaining fuel. Several air alarms occurred west of, and in, the Bay of Biscay as U 463 continued to France, running mostly on the surface. In one, a single bomb was dropped; in another, four bombs. All missed. U 463 arrived safely at her new home port of St Nazaire on 3 September, receiving a commendation from Doenitz.

The sixth Type XIV U-tanker, U 464, had been commissioned into the 10th U-boat Flotilla on 30 April 1942. She carried out the usual trials in the Baltic until July, but these were cut short so that she could join the other cows out in the Atlantic. U 464 (Kapitaenleutnant Harms) was provisioned at Kiel for her first fuelling mission. Harms, thirty-three years old, had been the commander of three U-boats in 1940, and had subsequently been appointed for a year as a teacher at U-boat school.

U 464 departed from Kiel on 4 August, but had to stop over at Trondheim on the 8th since one of her fuel tanks was leaking, possibly a consequence of her over-hasty departure. This required a transfer to Bergen for repairs, which she reached the following day. U 464 set out again for the North Atlantic on 10 August (according to her reconstructed war diary, on the 14th according to a more realistic British Intelligence report), steering for her Atlantic fuelling rendezvous via the Northern Transit route between Scotland and Iceland. On 20 August, she was sighted by a radar-fitted USN Catalina at 61.25N 14.40W on a south-westerly course. The aircraft attacked and U 464 returned fire but was hit by five shallow-set depth-charges. The U-tanker stopped, discharging fuel. More fire was exchanged and the aircraft directed the Town-class destroyer HMS *Castleton* to the scene of the action. By the time she arrived, U 464 had already sunk. Fifty-three survivors, including the commander, who was the last to leave his boat, were rescued by a small Icelandic fishing vessel. The sailors were held in the forecastle of the tiny ship and covered with a machine gun, together with the stern injunction that anyone who moved forward of the demarcation line would be fired upon.

Subsequently HMS *Castleton* arrived and took the prisoners aboard. There has been some dispute, still unresolved, as to whether the large German contingent had managed to seize control of the Icelandic fishing vessel, but this seems unlikely. The survivors' claim that they were serving on a 'milk cow' was not initially believed, but was subsequently accepted, providing the first confirmation that such vessels were in operation. Ironically, the German Naval Command had suggested as recently as 11 August that 'it must be assumed that the enemy knows of the U-tankers'.

U-boat Command recorded that U 464 had not given any signal since her report that she had left Bergen and had failed to answer their queries about weather, position and fuel status on each of 19, 20 and 21 August, noting British news reports that U 464 had been sunk by a Catalina on 20 August near Iceland. The tanker was declared missing (one star) on 23 September, upgraded to two stars on 8 February 1943.

73

It can be seen from the above that the steady flow of new U-tankers into the Atlantic had resulted in a rapid return of the same cows, now empty, to their Biscay bases. It was not long before the Germans found that they had considerably overestimated the ability of the milk cows to supply all their U-boats, with the result that the cows became greatly overworked, spending only the minimum time needed in harbour. U-boats were therefore ordered to be more economical with their fuel consumption. A number of attack U-boats had to be ordered to 'plug the gaps' in the tanker network by refuelling other attack boats on an opportunistic basis, while the absence of U 464 required the Type IX boat U 174 to refuel U 432 and U 660 of the *Lohs* group north of the Azores on 29 August, aiding U 462 as we have already seen. Moreover, some of the Type XB minelayers still working up in German waters were prepared for use as spare tankers.

U 117 and U 118 (Type XB minelayers) had begun their operational lives on 25 October 1941 and 6 December 1941 respectively, and had been engaged in exercises and training in the Baltic, including gunnery practice and dummy minelaying. Both were subsequently transferred from training flotillas to the 5th Flotilla at Kiel in September 1942. Early in the month, both boats were provisioned together at Swinemuende.

Two senior officers were appointed to these important craft. U 117 was commanded by Korvettenkapitaen Neumann, thirty-six years old and another officer who, after a spell on shore, had been given command of a U-boat (U 72) for operational experience. He was transferred out of U 72 specially to take over U 117. The 38-year-old Korvettenkapitaen Czygan had been to sea on the cruiser *Bluecher* in 1939–40; after that ship was sunk, he had held various shore appointments including an instructional post. Thus he had not served on a single U-boat before joining U 118.

U 118 was first out from Germany, although her departure from Kiel was delayed on 12 September after two of her crew contracted diphtheria. One week later, U 118 set out into the North Sea and by the 27th was off Iceland. She suffered several air attacks to the end of the month and, from one, slight electrical damage was caused by two bombs as she proceeded southwesterly into the Atlantic. Orders were received from U-boat Command on 1 October to commence her fuelling mission and Czygan was also required to report on weather conditions.

U 116 departed for her third refuelling mission with a new commander, von Schmidt having left her on 10 September after two successful cruises in order to resume his flourishing career with increasingly senior shore appointments. He survived the war. Von Schmidt's 35-year-old replacement, Kapitaenleutnant Grimme, joined the following day. He had previously held office appointments, followed by an eight-month period as captain of the attack boat U 146. U 116 left Lorient on 22 September and headed into the mid-Atlantic.

U 117 (Korvettenkapitaen Neumann) was sent out on 6 October when she left Kiel and headed to Kristiansand. Thereafter she made out into the North Atlantic, arriving off the north coast of Iceland on 22 October and moving around the northern part of the island until she was able to begin minelaying on the night of 27/28 October in AE29 (north-east coast of Iceland). Iceland had been occupied by the Allies in July 1941 and was now used as an aircraft base and staging point for convoys, especially those heading around the north of Norway to aid Russia. Thus U 117 had created the first minefield laid with the SMA in enemy waters, although the mines achieved no result. This mission completed, the U-minelayer was appointed as a milk cow on the 29th.

U 460 was now commanded by the 47-year-old Oberleutnant zS Schnoor. The new commander had begun with office appointments, served as watch officer on U 143 and U 108 in 1941 and early 1942, and had been the previous commander of U A for just three months until he had swapped commands with the senior-ranking Schaefer on 9 August. U 460 had been despatched from St Nazaire on 27 August in company with U 590 to replenish the *Iltis* U-boats operating off Freetown in the South Atlantic. Next day, the tanker dived to avoid an approaching aircraft and was found to handle very oddly underwater. A leakage of the bilge water cells was discovered and there was an oil leak. U 460 signalled that she was returning to base. Three more air alarms occurred en route, but by the 29th, U 460 was back at St Nazaire. She set out again on 1 September, dodged an air attack in the Bay of Biscay and had to carry out repairs to a diving vent on the 5th. She was then directed to an opportunistic rendezvous north of the Azores where U 510 required a doctor urgently. U 155 was refuelled on 7 September, after which U 460 headed south-west.

Far to the south-west of the Azores, U 66 (Markworth) made a signal: 'We need medical help urgently.' Within half an hour, U 460, which was fortuitously close, had been ordered to rendezvous with U 66. Next day, the boats met and U 66's stricken Second Officer was ferried to the U-tanker, operated on, and returned to the attack boat in little more than an hour. The two U-boat commanders agreed to a private rendezvous the following day at a different location; this was duly accomplished and U 66 took on 31 tons of fuel and parts.

U 460 now steered for another close rendezvous established by U-boat Command where a further four U-boats were refuelled between 16 and 18 September. Then U 460 headed deeper to the south-east for her meeting with the *Iltis* pack.

U 109 was the first of the *Iltis* boats to be supplied, north-west of the Cape Verde Islands on 20 September, where Schnoor inaugurated a system of sending a team of doctor and Chief Engineer to every boat he met. U 109 received 42 tons of fuel, but needed only five days of provisions.

Still U 460 headed south. She met UD 5 (Mahn) on the 23rd and supplied the former Dutch boat with 50 tons of fuel. Now U 460 moved east to a position north of the Cape Verde Islands, where U 107, U 406 and U 333 (Cremer) were waiting. All of the boats were supplied on the 25th, and U 107 took the tanker's entire complement of four reserve torpedoes, the transfer requiring two and a quarter hours during which other boats were fuelled. A sick sailor was removed from U 406.

Next day, U 87 and U 590 were also supplied before U 460 moved south again to refuel and replenish U 507 and the new U-cruiser U 178 (Ibbecken) on 28 September. U 460 had now refuelled eight U-boats near the Cape Verde Islands after their attack on convoy SL.119; of these, four boats were able to continue their cruise to Freetown.

U-boat Command now decided that U 507 should return to France with the U-tanker. U 507 was provided with a Metox receiver and a sick crew member was replaced by one of the tanker's crew before both boats started for home.

Only three days later, the tanker received an urgent message from U 507, which had become separated – one of her crewmen was very ill. U 460 at once turned to her assistance, but the sailor had died before the tanker arrived a few hours later. Both boats continued together back to France, avoided several air alarms, and U 460 arrived at her new base of Bordeaux on 12 October, where she joined the newly formed 12th U-boat Flotilla. Her entire cruise had taken just six weeks.

Doenitz had adopted a strategy of sending long-range U-boats to seek out weak spots around the Atlantic, where shipping was poorly defended. U-boats were sent to African waters, as in the example above, to Brazil, and to any other sea area that might appear promising. Milk cows were again employed to refuel these long-range attacks; indeed, it was only the availability of the tankers that made this strategy possible. The invariable result was that the U-boats would score a few easy successes, the Allies would strengthen the local defences, and the U-boats would look for another soft spot.

U 461 (Kapitaenleutnant Stiebler) left St Nazaire for her second cruise on 7 September. In the next three days she sustained four attacks from aircraft, the third of which, by a Sunderland flying boat that dropped three bombs, caused minor damage (9 September), most seriously to her FuMB radar receiver (an early and unreliable version that predated Metox). The damage was reported to U-boat Command on the 11th after U 461 had traversed the Bay of Biscay into mid-Atlantic.

After arriving at her North Atlantic refuelling position (c. 40N 45W, east of Newfoundland) on the 16th, U 461 encountered no fewer than ten boats of the *Vorwaerts* group, and also U 594. The boats were refuelled over several days and one of them was able to effect a temporary repair to the radar receiver of U 461.

U 171 and U 164 were refuelled on the 24th after which U 461 moved south-south-west in order to see to the needs of the Type VIID minelayer U 217, where several cases of severe heat-stroke had occurred among the crew during her patrol in the Caribbean in August and September. A doctor was sent and a sick crew member was taken on to the U-tanker. Provisions were provided for eighteen days, the transfer lasting nearly ten hours. U 558 was supplied next day.

By October, U 461 was still seeking suitable repairs for her FuMB receiver before beginning the hazardous crossing of the Bay of Biscay, the parts supplied earlier by a Type IX boat having not worked properly. A rendezvous was arranged with U 160 to the south-west of the Azores for 5 October, and U 461 was thus enabled to return to St Nazaire without being attacked from the air. After her arrival on 17 October, Doenitz complimented Stiebler on his perseverance.

We have already noted that an unexpected bonus for U-boat Command was the ability of the milk cows on their way to and from their refuelling areas to detect and report on convoys. Another example occurred when outward-bound U 118 (which was mentioned above) discovered an ON convoy on 29 September. The *Luchs* pack was ordered to the attack, but instead they located and attacked convoy HX.209. U 116 (now on her third operation) and U 118 were then ordered to refuel four boats each from the *Tiger* group which had made an abortive attack on convoy ON.131, and also the *Sturm* group in BD43, north-west of the Azores. Bad weather interrupted the refuelling by U 118, but two out of five U-boats were oiled (this was achieved on 4 October) while the Type VIID minelayer U 216 was directed to refuel from the U-tanker U 463. The U-boats were able to continue to sweep to the south as the *Wotan* pack, east of Newfoundland.

U 118 (Korvettenkapitaen Czygan) complained to U-boat Command on 12 October that she was having W/T difficulties and was unable to rendezvous with other U-boats. Czygan was ordered home, initially to Brest but redirected to Lorient, where she arrived without being attacked from the air on 16 October.

U 116 (Kapitaenleutnant Grimme) had sold out at her mid-Atlantic rendezvous and was heading home by 4 October. She made a weather report in BD82, north of the Azores, on 6 October but nothing else was ever heard from her again. She was posted missing on 6 November, with the melancholy attachment to her reconstructed last war diary that nothing was known of the fate of her crew.* Allied Intelligence records are also ignorant about the fate of U 116.

---

* This information is taken from the BdU war diary for 16 October, when U 116 was three days overdue at base. The reconstructed war diary of U 116 asserts that her last weather report was from BD82 on 15 October.

U 463 (Korvettenkapitaen Wolfbauer) had left St Nazaire with an escort for her second supply operation on 28 September, having spent fewer than four weeks refitting in port. U 463 had an amazing stroke of luck the following day, when an aircraft was sighted too late to dive. The plane flew over the U-tanker, whose 20mm cannon jammed after the first round. The tanker dived but still no bombs followed her down. Next day, a Hampden bomber caught U 463 at night after the Metox radar receiver had twice given alarms. The tanker went deep but was badly shaken by four very well-placed bombs. The lights went out, there were oil leaks from broken bunkers and much further damage. Nevertheless, Wolfbauer elected to press on.

U 463 had to endure another set of four bombs, which missed by a distance, when attacked from the air on 3 October. She finally reached her fuelling zone (BD27, north of the Azores) and started by re-oiling the Type VIID boat U 216 (Kapitaenleutnant K.O. Schulz) which had previously been unable to refuel from U 118. An injured sailor was also taken off U 216 (7 October). It was his lucky day, for the minelayer was lost south-west of Ireland just thirteen days later. There were no survivors.

U 661 was finally completely refuelled over the next three days in bad weather. Some parts were also handed over and Wolfbauer congratulated his crew on their good work. These two boats were for the *Wotan* pack.

U 463 then moved a short distance to a new rendezvous where she waited for seven days in a storm before the first of a cluster of U-boats of the *Panther* group gathered around the tanker on 14 October. By the 21st, it was still not possible to refuel the pack and the hungry crew of U 620 had to be supplied intermittently with bread. When the storms abated on 22 October, U 620, in dire straits, was first given a huge 76 tons of oil and seven weeks of provisions; eight more U-boats were supplied in the next three days. The weather deteriorated again on the 26th and U 706 could not be replenished. Next day looked promising, but three men were washed overboard from U 706. All were recovered safely but now a merchant ship was seen and both boats submerged to avoid detection. U 706 was at last refuelled on 29 October.

A destroyer was sighted by U 463 the following day but she evaded it on the surface. U 757 and U 575 completed the list of 'customers' before the U-tanker had finally sold out. U 463 was ordered home in company with U 575, the tanker to provide radar detection for the attack boat that lacked Metox. As U 463 began her short, but perilous journey home towards the Bay of Biscay, her Metox cable was damaged. Frantic work restored the radar receiver by the following day. U 463 dodged yet another aircraft in the Bay, recalling her eventful outward voyage, by a timely submergence on 8 November. She was then directed to head for the U-boat base at Brest (U-boats did not steer directly towards the northerly French west coast ports, which were well patrolled by British aircraft, but made towards the general area of St Nazaire, before heading northwards within easy reach of air protection and an escort), arriving with her escort on 11 November. U 463 had refuelled fourteen U-boats.

The Type XB minelayer U 117 (Korvettenkapitaen Neumann) had been newly appointed (29 October, see above) as a reserve tanker after the completion of her minelaying mission off the north-east coast of Iceland. En route to her refuelling area, she encountered two neutral ships (one Swedish, the other Irish) and was forced to ignore them. Then she arrived on 5 November right in the centre of the mid-Atlantic air gap (BD21, *c.* 50N 33W), far to the north of the Azores. Eight U-boats were there by arrangement awaiting the cow, but only two could be replenished on account of the bad weather. By the 11th, though, all had been refuelled and a sick crew member had been taken off U 521. A tragedy occurred on the 8th when Leutnant zS Schwenzel of U 117 was washed overboard whilst manoeuvring with U 454. The cow's medical officer was unable to resuscitate the officer, who apparently died from heart failure. He was buried at sea at 49–30N 31–35W.

U 117 then headed straight for home, arriving at Lorient on 22 November to a strong commendation from Doenitz for Neumann's well-conducted minelaying and refuelling operations. U 117 was now assigned to the 12th U-boat Flotilla based at Bordeaux for her next mission.

U 462 (Oberleutnant zS Vowe) had left St Nazaire on 18 October for her second resupply operation, to aid the U-boats operating off Freetown. For three and a half hours she had an escort of a Sperrbrecher and two small patrol boats before they departed. Just to the west of the Bay of Biscay Vowe spotted a merchant ship and was forced to dive to avoid detection – the disadvantage of lacking offensive weaponry. Doenitz later pointed out to Vowe that he should have sent a sighting report for the benefit of any other U-boats in the area. U 462 subsequently needed a series of submergences in order to avoid a persistent flying boat.

En route to her fuelling area U 462 discovered some flotsam from a sunken merchant ship, which proved to contain American chocolate, corned beef and other items. Her sister tanker, U 459, was sighted on 26 October just south of the Azores and an 'unassigned' fuelling (26 tons) of this boat was carried out. U 506 and U 125 were oiled in the same general area. U 459 and U 506 were returning home together from the South Atlantic, as we shall see in the next chapter, and the U-tanker was itself urgently in need of more fuel.

U 462 was now ordered to meet the ex-Dutch UD 5 which had run short of fuel after a long chase. The latter was encountered on 31 October northwest of the Cape Verde Islands and took on 45 tons of diesel. However, the Freon refrigerator carried by UD 5 ensured that she did not need any provisions. U 516 was also resupplied.

After enquiries from U-boat Command, U 462 was able to report that she still had plenty of fuel and was ordered further south to an area just west of the Cape Verde Islands. No fewer than ten Type IX U-boats operating in the general Freetown area were supplied at this rendezvous between 3 and 16 November. These included Hartenstein's U 156 and Heyse's U 128. The rendezvous with U 128 was three times interrupted. A 'steamer' was seen on the 8th by U 462 that proved on closer inspection to be a destroyer. The tanker dived and was not detected. Next day, a large Allied tanker was sighted. U 128 was informed and chased the nameless tanker (4,000 tons according to U 128, 10,000 according to Vowe; the ship was actually the *Maloja*, 6,400 tons) and sank it with gunfire. The crew of the milk cow gave U 128 three cheers as she returned.

On the 10th, as U 128 was still reloading, another heavily armed tanker was observed. U 128 chased after the new target (claimed as 10,000 tons, but actually the 3,878 ton *Cerinthus*), sank it with a torpedo (the captain went down with his ship, but the First Officer and Engineering Officer were taken prisoner from the lifeboats) and U 128 returned to her cow and another round of 'three cheers'. The prisoners were transferred to the U-tanker.

U 128 and U 462 continued in company for the next two days as four torpedoes and other supplies were transferred. Heyse noted in his war diary that the torpedo transfer had proceeded without difficulty. U 332 and U 552 also arrived for resupply. U 128 remained on patrol in this area and would later be refuelled by U 461 in December.

U 462 signalled to U-boat Command on 16 November that she still had available 140 tons of fuel oil and 3 tons of lubricating oil, together with forty-four days of spare provisions. She was ordered to await the arrival of U 505 (Zschech) and UD 3 (Rigele). Meanwhile, the air inlet fan broke down several times. UD 3 arrived on the 20th and received 55 tons of fuel. U 332 and U 86 took on second helpings of oil and U 505 was also supplied on the 22nd, with an exchange of officers with the last U-boat. U 462 was now sold out and Vowe began the long cruise home. En route, U-boat Command ordered U 462 to change to the U-boat base of St Nazaire. An uneventful passage of the Bay of Biscay followed and U 462 arrived at St Nazaire, in company with U 454, on 7 December, receiving well-merited congratulations from Doenitz.

Meanwhile, the freshly supplied UD 3 had rendezvoused with U 159 (Witte) south-south-west of the Cape Verde Islands and handed over no fewer than eight torpedoes. Rough seas hampered the movement of the torpedoes, but four were ferried across on each of 27 and 28 November. U 159 was one of the most successful U-boats of the war.

July had been a poor month for the U-boats after the successes in the Caribbean, but in August they sank 105 ships, most of them in the North and West Atlantic. In September and October sinkings fell to ninety-seven and ninety-one ships respectively, but in November they rose again to 117 ships and only the onset of winter caused a reduction in December, to fifty-nine ships. At long last, Doenitz's goal of sinking merchant ships faster than they could be built appeared to be reaching fruition. In June, convoy PQ.17 had been massacred in the Arctic, while en route to Russia, by aircraft and U-boats. 'Can you hear the striking of the gong?' asked the German news broadcaster. 'It strikes every second. A ton of goods sinks at every stroke of the gong ... Think of it when you wake up tonight.'

The U-boats' successes had not been achieved without some cost to the U-boat arm. Forty-eight U-boats had been sunk in the Atlantic theatre between July and December, and the milk cows had not escaped. The sinking of U 464 in August and the unexplained loss of U 116 in October have already been described.

Another problem arose after a series of convoy attacks in the North Atlantic in October and November, when the Allies mounted an invasion of North Africa (Operation Torch) in November, and on the 8th Doenitz diverted all U-boats with sufficient fuel to the area west of Gibraltar. Those boats without enough fuel to reach Gibraltar were formed into a pack to attack convoy ONS.144 in the North Atlantic. After sinking five ships and an escort, the U-boats were ordered to operate independently east of Newfoundland before refuelling from U 460 (Oberleutnant zS Schnoor) some 500 miles north-west of the Azores. This provides a good example of how U-boat Command could deploy U-boats short on fuel against an opportunistic target, knowing that fresh supplies were on their way.

U 460 sailed from St Nazaire on 11 November and crossed the Bay of Biscay without being attacked from the air. She reached her rendezvous area north-west of the Azores in the North Atlantic air gap by the 19th to the accompaniment of a stream of messages from U-boat Command, of which one commanded that only the tanker was to emit homing signals. The first of nine boats awaiting the tanker arrived on the 21st and the hoses were connected.

Then a storm broke. Schnoor signalled to U-boat Command on the 22nd that heavy seas had halted refuelling. For five days, the boats were unable to replenish and were in serious trouble owing to their lack of fuel. U 753 (von Mannstein, son of the famous Panzer General), which could not locate the tanker, became increasingly desperate in her signals, and on the 26th U-boat Command ordered Schnoor not to send out any more homing signals for U 753 since they were betraying the rendezvous. Some boats even expected to have to hoist a sail in order to reach the supply area. When the storm died down on the 26th, U 460 found herself almost alone. Only U 84 had managed to remain in contact; this boat was refuelled at once and received a visit from the tanker's doctor. Then two more U-boats appeared, of which one was the errant U 753. U 460 lay with engines stopped on a flat sea as she suckled all nine of the waiting U-boats between 26 and 30 November.

Now U 460 was moved a little to the south-west, where two more U-boats were refuelled. U-boat Command warned on 4 December that there was far too much W/T chatter, and homing signals should only be used after a visual search of many hours by the tanker. In all, six U-boats were fuelled here between 3 and 7 December before Schnoor moved eastwards again.

In his book, *U 977*, Heinz Schaeffer records how his Type VII boat was refuelled underwater in the very first such experiment of the war. The English edition omits to give details of the number of what was then his U-boat (it was U 445), the number of the milk cow, or even the date, but internal evidence from the book and the tanker war diary makes it clear that his U-boat was refuelled underwater by U 460 on 7 December. The experiment was conducted in anticipation of the day when aircraft reconnaissance would make any other course impossible. Other supplies were transferred in the normal way, on the surface; the oil hoses were connected and both boats submerged to a predetermined depth (50 metres). No submarine can hover underwater – it must either sink or rise unless sufficient forward momentum is maintained to enable the hydroplanes to be effective. Both U-boats therefore moved through the water together (in line astern, the tanker towing U 445), keeping in touch with their hydrophones, before resurfacing after three hours, refuelling complete. Underwater refuelling never came to much, owing to the high degree of seamanship required that tended to be lacking in the newly trained crews.

U 460 was now out of reserve fuel, but U 67 and one of the brand-new Type IXC/40 boats, U 183, were provided with foodstuffs on 12 December. U 183 lost a man overboard during the transfer, but he was promptly rescued unharmed. A planned rendezvous between U 460 and her sister tanker U 463, at this time outward bound, was cancelled and U 460 and U 67 set off together for France, losing touch almost immediately. U 460 suffered a failure of rudder power briefly in the Bay of Biscay, submerged quickly when her Metox set gave a radar warning and arrived safely back at St Nazaire on 19 December. Doenitz complimented Schnoor on an operation well carried out.

Meanwhile, all U-boats were withdrawn from the area west of Gibraltar after 26 November, some to return to France and some to be refuelled. U 118 was allocated the latter task. This U-minelayer had spent barely four weeks in dock at Lorient before being sent out on 12 November for her second supply mission, escorted by a Sperrbrecher and three M-boats. While on passage across the Bay of Biscay, U 118 (Korvettenkapitaen Czygan) was attacked at night, without radar warning, by a Whitley bomber (15 November). At first Czygan assumed that the aircraft had been working the area in collaboration with a land radar station; then he expressed doubts about the minelayer's radar receiver. All this was reported to U-boat Command on the 17th.

Next day, U 118 dived to attack a steamer, but found it, and a following ship, to be neutral Portuguese vessels. When she arrived on the 21st at her allocated rendezvous, west of Madeira, two waiting U-boats were refuelled and one was visited by the doctor.

Meanwhile U 461 (Kapitaenleutnant Stiebler) had been despatched from St Nazaire on 19 November, on her third fuelling mission. Diving at dawn and surfacing at night with her ever-watchful radar receiver, she crossed the Bay without suffering any air attack. By the 23rd, U 461 was in the North Atlantic where she received new orders on the 25th to go to assist U 118 with her long list of potential clients. Between 25 and 30 November, the WestWall (sic) pack of Type IX U-boats retiring westwards from Gibraltar, and also U 185, were replenished in an opportunistic single rendezvous along a south-west line running roughly equidistant between the Azores and the Canary Islands for operations off Brazil.

U 118 seems to have become impatient, or possibly Czygan wanted to resume his short home leave. He suggested to U-boat Command that he should dump his nearly full reserve oil into the lap of U 461 as the latter passed by, but was informed that there was so much through traffic that he had to sit tight and wait. Stiebler appeared on the 29th and the two cows reprovisioned the many boats in the area, the contribution of U 118 being to refuel three Type IX U-boats and to refuel and remove a sick crew member from U 653, all on 30 November.

Three well-known 'aces' received fuel shortly afterwards: Lassen (U 160) and Nissen (U 105) were replenished on 2 December, and Mohr (U 124) on the 4th, before U 118 was ordered home on the 7th. She arrived uneventfully at Lorient on the 13th, complaining about the length of time it had taken for the escort to show up. Apparently Czygan was still in a hurry, but he was probably mollified by Doenitz's praise for a well-carried-out refuelling operation.

Meanwhile, the U-tanker U 461 continued to press on into the south for her main refuelling mission. She arrived south-west of the Cape Verde Islands and was able to replenish a further eight U-boats between 8 and 11 December. Visits were made by the doctor to U 172 and U 128 (Heyse), two sick crewmen were taken over for treatment and Captain Lorains of the sunken steamer Teesbank was taken as a prisoner from U 128 (the war diary of U 461 incorrectly gives the name as Lorensen). An unexpected meeting of old friends occurred at this rendezvous when the genial Heyse came across to pay his compliments to his opposite number Stiebler, and brought with him a midshipman. Thus it was that Guenther Paas, a midshipman on U 461, unexpectedly encountered in mid-ocean one of his old classmates from the Naval Academy.

U 176 was provided with three spare torpedoes, Stiebler grumbling that, as on previous cruises, no one else seemed to want any! The last torpedo was later passed to U 128. Heyse departed, and received the Knight's Cross for his sinkings while in company with U 462 (described above), combined with later and earlier successes, when he arrived home.

Now homeward bound, U 461 was given another rendezvous with U 125 (Folkers) to hand over some spare parts. The latter was met, appropriately enough, on Christmas Day, but not before the unarmed U-tanker had run into a small convoy, dived and endured the harrowing experience of having a destroyer pass directly overhead (the U-boat was not detected). U 461 crossed the Bay of Biscay on the surface at night, dived by day and returned safely to St Nazaire without air attack on 3 January 1943.

Experiments with Foreign Submarines

Germany had taken over or seized a handful of foreign submarines by 1942. HMS *Seal* had been captured in the North Sea and renumbered as U B, but was considered to have only propaganda value owing to the anticipated difficulty of getting spare parts. U B was, in fact, paid off in 1943 at Kiel and was not used again. Some French submarines were also unusable. The former Turkish submarine U A, requisitioned while still being built in a German yard, had proved to be unsuccessful in operation (see previous chapters). However, five Dutch submarines had also been captured when Holland was overrun. These were assigned German numbers (UD 1 to UD 5). The most promising were UD 3, UD 4 and UD 5, all 881-ton submarines of the 'O.21' class, with eight 21-inch torpedo tubes, an 88mm cannon and a good turn of speed (19.5 knots). They carried a crew of sixty.

Trials with captured foreign submarines were generally carried out by senior naval officers who had the authority and experience to evaluate the booty comprehensively. UD 3, UD 4 and UD 5 were commissioned at Rotterdam respectively on 8 June 1941, 28 January 1941 and 1 November 1941 and carried out training exercises in the Baltic.

On 27 August 1942, UD 5 (Kapitaen zS Mahn) was the first of the former Dutch boats to be tried out operationally when she cruised directly from Germany (via Norway) to an operational zone off Freetown. Here she was used for combat only in October, but without success. While on the way home, UD 5 encountered and sank the merchant ship *Primrose Hill* (8,000 tons). By November she had berthed in France and Mahn left the boat, commenting on her limited combat worthiness. The main problem was the boat's excruciatingly long diving time – three minutes when attacked by a convoy escort on one occasion. Thus it was that the much more junior Oberleutnant zS Koenig took UD 5 back to Kiel around the north of Britain, arriving on 9 January 1943.

The *Nordmark* refuels U 107 in the South Atlantic during April 1941. (*Bundesarchiv*)

U 459 locked in winter ice during training 1941–2. (*Walter Storbeck private collection*)

U 461 ready to sail from Kiel in July 1942. (*Fritz Vogel*)

U 461 leaving Kiel. (*Fritz Vogel*)

These inflatables were used to ferry personnel and supplies and were always overworked. Crew were often washed overboard in the heavy Atlantic seas. The tanker is U 461. (*Horst Bredow, U-Boo Archiv*)

Transferring supplies onto a Type VII attack boat U 466 in mid-1943. (*Commander U 466, Gert Thater*

Transfer of supplies by a 'dead man's cradle' from U 459. (*Bundesarchiv*)

U 459. The tanker is on the right of the picture; other boats await their turn. (*Bundesarchiv*)

U461. Anti-aircraft practice in mid-Atlantic. (*Wilhelm Kraus*)

Officers of the tanker U 461. Korvkpt Stiebler is on the extreme left. (*Wilhelm Kraus*)

The minelayer U 116 passes the fuel line to U 406, from which this photograph was taken in 1942. The bulge that contains her minelaying shafts is clearly visible. U 116 vanished without trace in the mid-Atlantic at the end of her next cruise. (*Horst Bredow, U-Boot Archiv*)

A 'customer' draws close. The tanker is U 461 and the approaching boat is U 552 commanded by the ace Oblt z.S. Topp, who survived the war to become a NATO admiral. (*Fritz Vogel*)

The Type XIV tanker U 462 with refuelling hose trailing astern to the U-boat from which the photograph was taken. (*Horst Bredow, U-Boot Archiv*)

This Type XB minelayer, U 117, is seen from U 516 whilst receiving supplies on 24 April 1943. The 105mm gun forward and the old-style semi-automatic 37mm anti-aircraft gun can clearly be seen. (*Horst Bredow, U-Boot Archiv*)

A U-boat lying to leeward of the tanker U 460, receiving fuel in heavy weather. Note the fuel line curving across the swell astern of both vessels. (*Horst Bredow, U-Boot Archiv*)

U 462 about to dock in Bordeaux in 1943. (*Horst Bredow, U-Boot Archiv*)

Unloading a torpedo from tanker
U 462. (*Fritz Schmidt*)

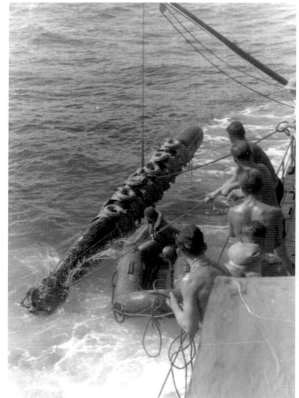

A torpedo is ready to float
across. (*Fritz Schmidt*)

U 461 supplies a torpedo to a Type IX boat. (*Wilhelm Kraus*)

The conning tower of the Type XIV tanker U 462 seen in mid-1943. Note the Vierling four-gun anti-aircraft weapon on its bandstand and also the Octopus symbol on the side of the tower. (*Horst Bredow, U-Boot Archiv*)

The Type XIV tanker U 459 damaged after an air attack by a Wellington bomber in the Bay of Biscay. She sank shortly afterwards. (*Imperial War Museum*)

Tankers U 461 and U 462 being escorted by U 504 whilst crossing the Bay of Biscay in July 1943. The photograph was taken from an Allied bomber. (*Imperial War Museum*)

Tanker U 462 disappears under a cloud of spray from a near miss by a large bomb. (*Fritz Schmidt*)

The last picture of the U-cruiser U 847 *(left)* as she refuels U 172 on 27 August 1943. U 847 was sunk by *Fido* within 24 hours. (*Horst Bredow, U-Boot Archiv*)

The crew of U 461 enjoy a dip in the ocean from the partially submerged stern of the U-tanker. (*Fritz Vogel*)

Bridge watch aboard U 461 in the North Atlantic. (*Fritz Vogel*)

Tanker U 462 oils two U-boats simultaneously. (*Fritz Schmidt*)

Survivors of sunk tanker U 462 are rescued by HMS *Wild Goose*. (*Fritz Schmidt*)

Burial of crewmember at sea after an air attack. (*Fritz Schmidt*)

UD 3 (Fregattenkapitaen Rigele) followed UD 5 into service on 3 October 1942, operating around the Cape Verde Islands. At this time U-boat Command had become concerned about the speed with which some U-boats were shooting off all their torpedoes and then having to return to France for fresh supplies, and it had been decided to use UD 3 as a torpedo transport. She took on fuel from U 462 on 20 November, as we have seen, sank the Norwegian *Indra* (5,041 tons) that she stumbled upon while waiting (26 November) and gave up eight torpedoes to U 159 one week later near Freetown (6N 25W). UD 3 remained on station as a supplier of torpedoes until 26 December, but there were no further calls for her services and she returned to France on 6 January 1943. Again Rigele's report was unfavourable – there was insufficient space on deck for her role as a torpedo transport and he took UD 3 back to German waters in February 1943, arriving on 3 March.

These deployments were not considered as successes. UD 4 had been commanded by the experienced Kapitaenleutnant Bernbeck from April 1942 after reassignment from being the commander of U 461 during the latter's working-up exercises in the Baltic. He was transferred to command an attack U-boat (U 638, Type VIIC) in December 1942, probably as a result of the experiences with UD 3 and UD 5. None of these, nor any other foreign submarine, was used again operationally, other than Italian U-boats used for freight-carrying after Italy surrendered to the Allies in 1943.

However, all the foreign submarines now in the Baltic did find an unexpected role: training officers and crews for subsequent deployment in milk cows. Thus Schaefer, of U 460, served in UD 4 and UD 1 in 1941, before becoming commander of U 460. Subsequently he served on U A and UD 4 as the training captain. Metz (U 487) and Schnoor (U 460) trained on U A before taking over their U-tankers. Mahn trained on U B before taking UD 5 into operations; von Kameke (U 119) was the next commander of UD 5 before taking his U-minelayer out to sea. Schmandt (U 489) served on both U B and UD 5, the latter during her one war cruise, before joining his U-tanker.

UD 4 (Kapitaenleutnant Schaefer) had an important role in September/October 1943 when she was used to conduct fresh trials with underwater refuelling. UD 4 sailed ahead of the boat to be supplied, both on the surface at 2 to 3 knots, and passed back an air-filled (floating) hose, with telephone cable and steel hawser attached. The receiving boat took up the hose and made fast the hawser, both boats submerged to periscope depth and contact was retained through the telephone line (which was found to be much more reliable than underwater signalling). Then both boats went deeper to around 30 metres, with UD 4 towing the other boat. Oil was forced through by water pressure and, when transfer was complete, both boats surfaced together. These experiments were abandoned when it

85

became clear, firstly that newly trained U-boat crews lacked the skills to carry out the operation, and secondly that the new Type XXI 'electric' boats could patrol off Cape Town without the need to refuel. By mid-1944, equipment had been installed in some U-boats, including Type XXI, for underwater refuelling, but it was not used operationally.

Most of the foreign boats were taken out of service in October 1944. U A, U B, UD 1, UD 2, UD 3 and UD 4 were all scuttled at Kiel in the last days of the war (3 May 1945). UD 5 was returned to the Royal Netherlands Navy in 1945.

Chapter 9

Attack on Cape Town
October 1942

The convoy battles in the North Atlantic were becoming so fierce that Doenitz continued to look for other areas where U-boats might attack Allied shipping without serious risk. Thus it was that he revived the old idea of attacking the waters around Cape Town. This was now a focal point for all of Britain's shipping from the East, since the entry of Italy into the war on Germany's side in June 1940 had caused Britain to stop sending ships through the Suez Canal into the Mediterranean. As a result, U-boats sent by Hitler's direct order into the Mediterranean found it very hard to find any targets, while suffering heavy losses themselves.

Doenitz hoped to find plenty of unescorted ships so far south while the defences were expected to be weak. He made it plain, once again, in the U-boat Command war diary that he was only interested in sinkings, with no nonsense about 'strategic value', 'stretching defences' or other concepts – to him, nebulous – expounded by the Naval High Command. In mid-August, the *Eisbaer* U-boat group put out from its base at Lorient. The group consisted of four Type IXC U-boats – U 156 (Hartenstein), U 172 (Emmerman), U 68 (Merten) and U 505 (Poske) – together with the tanker U 459 without which the operation would not have been possible, since the IXC boats did not have sufficient range for the journey without refuelling.

U 459 (Kapitaenleutnant von Wilamowitz-Moellendorf) had left St Nazaire on 18 August for her third mission, avoided an air attack in the Bay of Biscay and then started on the long, long journey south. The U-boat group had strict orders to maintain W/T silence, since a series of transmissions sent from deeper and deeper to the south could hardly have failed to alarm the British. For the same reason, neither boats nor tanker were to emit beacon signals to locate each other, unless they could not find one another within three days at the rendezvous. However, it was intended that the boats should explore W/T conditions after the operation had begun and it had also been necessary to issue the U-boats with long-dated ciphers.

Orders were wirelessed to the group once out of the Bay of Biscay, on 25 August, and the group headed south independently (although they appear to have proceeded in close formation for most of the journey). Wilamowitz was warned specifically that he was to be only the 'eyes' of the group. At first sight of an enemy ship he was to break contact at once without closer investigation.

As a result of this series of orders being intercepted (but at this time they could not be decoded), the British were forewarned of a major assault on a distant sea area, and they had little difficulty in guessing that the target was Cape Town. The Admiralty was able to do little except reroute shipping as far as possible; the shortage of escorts, which were urgently needed in the North Atlantic, meant that none could be transferred to this new theatre.

The U-boats were allowed to attack ships on their way south although, owing to the expected glut of tempting victims at Cape Town, they were not willing to fire at any except exceptional targets on their journey. Such a chance came to U 156 (Hartenstein) on 12 September at a position about halfway between Freetown and the Ascension Islands. The U-boat torpedoed and sank the troopship *Laconia* (19,965 tons) and, on surfacing, Hartenstein found himself surrounded by the survivors of some 1,800 Italian prisoners of war and 800 British and Polish guards, crew and passengers. As U 156 drew close, the *Laconia* finally disappeared with the loss of over 1,000 lives. Hartenstein immediately began to load his U-boat with survivors, reported to base, and broadcast on an international wavelength a promise of immunity to any ship, regardless of nationality, that came to the rescue.

Meanwhile, Doenitz ordered the other four U-boats of the *Eisbaer* group to join the rescue, along with two other U-boats that had been working off Freetown, and an Italian submarine that was in the vicinity. Grand Admiral Raeder was informed, as was Hitler, and arrangements were made with Vichy France to send some ships to take over the survivors from the U-boats. U 156 now took in tow some of the lifeboats from the *Laconia* and displayed a large Red Cross flag prominently on the U-boat's deck.

Next day, Doenitz ordered the rest of the *Eisbaer* group to carry on to Cape Town, since they could not reach Hartenstein before the French ships. On the third day U 506 arrived, closely followed the next day by U 507 and the Italian submarine *Cappellini*, all from the Freetown area. Also on that day came the first sign of the Allies, who had so far done nothing to help, despite the fact that it was their ship that had been sunk. An American long-range bomber appeared over U 156. Hartenstein made sure the Red Cross flag could clearly be seen, kept his crew well away from the anti-aircraft guns and signalled that rescue work was in progress. The perplexed pilot radioed to his base on Ascension Island for instructions.

The American commander there knew of the critical state of the Battle of the Atlantic, had received no orders to respect a Red Cross flag and ordered the plane to attack. The aircraft dropped three depth-charges that narrowly missed U 156 – one hit a lifeboat – and Hartenstein cut the lifeboats free as another attack did considerable damage to periscopes, communications and engines. Survivors on board were ordered to jump clear as U 156 performed a crash-dive. She later surfaced, reported the incident to Doenitz, and made back to France. The aircraft, meanwhile, had reported that it had sunk the U-boat, mistaking survivors in the water for the U-boat crew.

Doenitz took no action until the other U-boats had handed over their survivors to the French (in all, 1,091 survivors ended up in these ships, while a further twenty reached the African coast in a lifeboat), by which time U 506 had also been attacked from the air. He then issued the notorious 'Laconia Order', stating that in future U-boats were not to attempt to rescue survivors from ships they had sunk (he turned a blind eye to commanders who contravened this rule). After the war, the prosecution alleged at the Nuremberg trial that this amounted to an order to 'kill survivors', but many U-boat commanders testified that they had never interpreted the order in this way and Doenitz was eventually acquitted of the charge.

The other four U-boats of the *Eisbaer* group continued south. U 459 passed St Helena on 17 September and finally reached her remote fuelling rendezvous to the south of the island on the 22nd. Here already waiting were U 172, which received 107 tons of oil and 3 tons of provisions, U 68, from whom the captured captain and Chief Engineer of the sunken ship *Trevilley* were removed as well as receiving supplies, and U 505, which was also supplied. In addition three sick seamen were taken onto the tanker from U 172, which had scooped in one each from UD 5 and U 506 as she headed south.

Two days later, U 459 was able to refuel U 159 in the same area. This last boat took on two replacement torpedoes, taking one hour for the transfer. The tanker then returned to a mid-Atlantic station, loitering south of the equator for a while in October. It was intended that U 459 should give up some of her remaining fuel to the *Iltis* boats still in the area, which had previously been refuelled in September by U 460 (see previous chapter).

One of the *Iltis* boats was U 333 (Cremer). U 333 had suffered repeated machinery defects caused by sabotage, a constant problem for boats based in France. After being rammed and severely damaged by a corvette in the middle of a convoy attack, she sent an urgent message to U-boat Command: 'Commander and First Officer wounded. Bring medical aid' (6 October). U 459 was ordered to the assistance of U 333 the following day, once U-boat Command had plotted a suitable rendezvous between the two

89

boats. The tanker's doctor was ordered to stay with Cremer, who was critically injured, on whichever boat Cremer remained.

Other ears heard the rendezvous point. When U 459 arrived on the 8th, U 107 was waiting and was fuelled. Next day, U 333 arrived. Cremer was transferred to the U-tanker, whose doctor was undoubtedly responsible for saving his life. Two dead crew members were replaced by the tanker's specialists, some replacement parts were handed over and Kapitaenleutnant Kasch, an unusually senior First Officer serving aboard U 107, took command of the battered U 333 before sailing it straight back to France, with Cremer as a passenger. Cremer survived the war to write his eventful memoirs. Still at the rendezvous, U 459 was able to provide U 552 and U 125 with small amounts of fuel between 10 and 11 October, and then headed for France via the Azores area.

U 506 and U 174 were encountered south of the Azores on 21 October. The latter provided a much-needed FuMB radar warning receiver to the tanker for her trip across the Bay of Biscay. U 506 received provisions, but not oil.

U 459 was herself now running low on fuel and she left with U 506 for a new rendezvous just south of the Azores with the outgoing U-tanker U 462 (Vowe) – such were the complications of the U-boat supply chain in late 1942. Vowe was met on 26 October and U 459 received 25 tons of fuel, while U 506 was also supplied. This was a timely fuel transfer, for worsening weather conditions caused both homeward-bound U-boats (U 459, U 506) to start to guzzle oil.

As the two boats crossed the Bay of Biscay, there was a momentary alarm as an Allied submarine was spotted. An air alarm followed (2 November). U 459 reached her home port of St Nazaire on 4 November having travelled 11,855 miles, of which only 379 had been submerged. Doenitz's only comment was 'Well carried through supply operation'.

Meanwhile, the first of the huge, new Type IXD2 U-cruisers, U 179, had been sent south after the *Eisbaer* boats. Not needing to refuel and with a superior speed, she finally caught them up, being the first to start operations off Cape Town. She sank one ship, but was sighted on the surface the following day (8 October) by a British destroyer and sunk.

After this inauspicious start, the remainder of the group commenced operations. Expecting to find unescorted ships everywhere, instead they found seas empty of any activity owing to the rerouting of shipping. Nevertheless, the British could not hide all their ships indefinitely and the U-boats soon began to locate targets.

Zero hour for the attack was 0000 hrs on 9 October, when U 172 penetrated the minefield around Cape Town harbour and attacked shipping there. By the end of October, when all the U-boats had to return to France for want of fuel, the three remaining boats of the *Eisbaer* group and an Italian submarine had between them sunk twenty-one ships of some

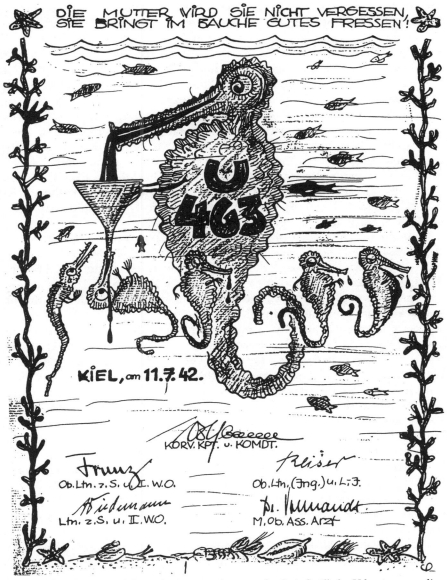

This type of picture was left as a 'going away' present for their flotilla by U-boats proceeding on their first patrols. (*Horst Bredow*)

160,000 tons, reminiscent of the 'Paukenschlag' against America. Included in the tally were four large troopships, the *Oronsay* (24,043 tons), *Orcades* (23,456 tons), *Duchess of Atholl* (20,119 tons) and *City of Cairo* (8,034 tons). Even so, Doenitz recorded his unease with the fact that the U-boats had at first found only empty seas. U 459 had reported that she had sighted a German auxiliary cruiser in the South Atlantic, where unescorted shipping had once been prevalent, and he wondered whether the British had responded to the activities of the cruiser by re-routing shipping.

Three more U-cruisers arrived between October and December. They sank many ships between Cape Town and Mozambique and so badly disrupted shipping that the port of Lourenço Marques had to be closed with a subsequent effect on the flow of oil to the Middle East. Convoys were introduced to the area in December and the U-cruisers withdrew to France for want of fuel. By the end of the year, forty-nine ships had been sunk by U-boats in this highly productive theatre.

Keeping up the pressure in other parts of the South Atlantic, U 461 supported nine U-boats in November for operations off Brazil. They sank only seven ships, but caused the local defences to be strengthened before departing. Doenitz continued to send U-boats into areas like this where easy pickings could be found, and at this time the Allies still lacked the air and sea escorts to cover them all.

One other point is worthy of mention in connection with the attack on Cape Town. The fleet tanker *Uckermark* (the renamed ex-*Altmark*; 12,000 tons) was despatched from France on 9 September, equipped both as a blockade runner and a supply ship. Although she refuelled an auxiliary cruiser in the South Atlantic at this time, it was apparently not thought worthwhile to risk her to refuel the U-boats. The *Uckermark* carried on to Japan where she was accidentally destroyed by an internal explosion on 30 November. The flames also destroyed the adjoining German auxiliary cruiser *Thor*. The official report blamed a fire caused while careless dock-yard workers were cleaning empty fuel tanks. The surface tanker *Brake* (9,225 tons) also broke the British blockade when she sailed from a Biscay port on 27 September under the code name 'U 907' (the real U 907 had not yet been commissioned), but the *Brake* too made for Japan without refuelling any U-boats.

The *Charlotte Schliemann* (7,747 tons) had left the Canary Islands on 20 February 1942. During the night of the 20th, Kapitaen Rothe received orders to depart on a special Atlantic refuelling mission and sailed so secretly that several sailors with shore leave had to be left behind. They were replaced at the last moment by sailors from the *Corrientes*, which had previously refuelled U-boats at Las Palmas. Equally, two U-boats in the area, U 68 and U 505, had to be informed abruptly by U-boat Command that they could no longer rely on the availability of the tanker. The *Charlotte Schliemann* remained in the South Atlantic at various refuelling posts for six months, intermittently supplying the auxiliary cruisers *Michel* and *Stier* and taking on prisoners from both. Apparently her first refuelling in June was so inept (doubtless due to lack of practice at sea fuelling other ships) that the incensed commander of the *Stier* fined the *Schliemann's* chief officer a small sum in Deutsche Marks. However, later refuellings by the *Schliemann* proved to be trouble free. After a last rendezvous with *Michel* the reserve fuel capacity of the *Schliemann* was exhausted, and the ship was ordered on 1 September to move along a deserted route ordained by the Naval High Command past Cape Town, across the Indian Ocean and finally into the Sunda Strait. Not a single ship was sighted during the entire passage, but more worrying for the crew was the complete absence of any visible Japanese patrol activity off Malaya. It was only when the *Charlotte Schliemann* reached Singapore that a Japanese patrol craft was amazed to see it and arranged for a pilot into the harbour where the *Schliemann* docked after a cruise of eight months. Even so, the crew were not allowed to disembark. The tanker was filled with petrol and directed to Yokohama in Japan, arriving on 20 October 1942. Here the *Schliemann* would receive a long refit, during which time she was fitted with a heavy gun (a Japanese 75mm cannon), anti-aircraft armament (1 × 37mm, 4 × 20mm) and a naval contingent of forty-eight men led by an ex-officer of the *Michel*. The total crew was now ninety men.

During her stay in Yokohama the *Charlotte Schliemann* was moored close to the *Uckermark* when the latter exploded, but rapid action by Japanese firefighters saved the nearby *Schliemann* from damage. It was not until March 1943 that the *Schliemann* was ready to sail. We shall meet the *Brake* and *Charlotte Schliemann* again in due course.

Chapter 10

The Problems Mount
January to April 1943

At the end of December 1942, British Intelligence again managed to break into the new Triton cipher of the Atlantic U-boats. Decryption was now possible for the remainder of the war, although the information was not always available at once. Despite its profession of confidence in the Enigma machines, U-boat Command seems to have had its doubts since the Germans slowly equipped all their U-boats with a new Enigma machine with four rotors (instead of three, as previously). On 1 March, all U-boats were ordered to make the changeover to the new machine. Brilliant work by British Intelligence meant that this change – which they called the 'Shark' cipher – had virtually no effect on their ability to decipher the new messages.

Another innovation by U-boat Command was to start disguising their map references, a prudent precaution but one that was negated by the way it was applied. Grid references were rearranged according to pre-planned schedules, although on some occasions these changes caused more difficulty to the U-boats, which went to the wrong sea areas, than to the decoders who were often able to untangle the disguises. Moreover, the Germans were not even consistent. Signals in the war diary of U 117 show that it, and other U-boats, were ordered to meet together in mid-1943 at square 'XY ...', a position that did not exist as such in the North Atlantic. Then the refuelled U-boats were requested to move a little way from the milk cow and report to U-boat Command the situation with the tanker: how much fuel it still had, and so on.

So far, so sensible. But the refuelled U-boats now transmitted their current positions to U-boat Command without special disguise of the map reference, as 'DG ...' The Allied decryptors had only to find the centre of the squares named to locate the milk cow!

U 459 (Kapitaenleutnant von Wilamowitz-Moellendorf) had set off, in company with U 442, on her fourth supply mission on 19 December. As previously, her operational area was to be the South Atlantic, this time in support of the *Seehund* group. U 459 crossed the Bay of Biscay without difficulty and ploughed on into mid-Atlantic. Here, far to the west of Cape Finisterre, U 564 was supplied with food and parts on the 26th, while U 459 dumped 2.4 tons of ballast.

Mention has already been made of the problems that the U-tankers were experiencing with trim. U 459 appears to have been particularly badly affected, and the new idea of providing disposable ballast does not appear to have placated her commander, judging by his comments in the war diary.

U 459 now moved north-west of the Azores where U 185 was provided with a FuMB radar receiver on 27 December. Two days later, U 381 approached to demand parts that the tanker could not supply. U 381 dogged the tanker hopefully for a while before moving off. U 459 then headed south for her main fuelling mission. But the first decryptions of U-boat messages were now beginning to bear fruit for British Intelligence. U 333 (Schaff, temporary commander while Cremer was still in hospital) was sent to refuel from U 459 on 1 January at what was described as a 'remote mid-Atlantic rendezvous'. Schaff reported that he had found 'only destroyers'. The tanker had meanwhile moved on.

At this time, only U 459 (west of Madeira), U 463 (far to the south-west of the Azores) and U 117 (north-west of the Azores) were actually posted at their fuelling rendezvous.

U 459 was then ordered by U-boat Command to refuel the Italian submarine *Cagni* south of the equator, where the Italian was supposedly waiting. When the tanker arrived on 12 January, she found only a destroyer. Within twenty-four hours the U-tanker had recorded the presence of two destroyers and a long-range bomber over the rendezvous, but seems to have regarded all this activity as coincidence. U-boat Command, by contrast, was alarmed at U 459's report.

Cagni was located on the 13th. She had already been at sea for 100 days, having slipped out of the Mediterranean into the Atlantic on 21 September, and expected to remain so for a further fifty days, with a wide radius of operations (25,000 miles) and an extraordinary number (forty-two) of torpedoes. There were two German speakers aboard, but despite this *Cagni* infuriated Wilamowitz by continuing to manoeuvre after being told to stop for the pumping of oil. It took ninety minutes to transfer 50 tons of oil, a feat achieved without any further difficulty. When the Italian departed, U 459 seized the opportunity to offload a further 4 tons of ballast. Wilamowitz recorded that the U-tanker now seemed to have acquired normal stability.

U 459 continued her march south, passing Ascension Island on 19 January. Her South Atlantic rendezvous will be described in the appropriate place.

U 117 (Korvettenkapitaen Neumann), now assigned to the 12th U-boat Flotilla, had been overhauled and provided with a new anti-aircraft armament plus a new radar warning detector during her stay at Lorient. She put out to sea again on 24 December 1942 and on the first day of 1943 she was in position north of the Azores. Five boats of the *Spitz* group were re-fuelled, during which U 117 was twice forced to dive by British corvettes. She was then directed to a different rendezvous to the north-west of the Azores accompanied by a stream of complicated messages from U-boat Command. The suckling U-boats were ordered not to signal but to await directions from the U-minelayer. In each case, Neumann was directed to report when refuelling was complete.

U 117 refuelled the *Ungestuem* pack at 44N 30W from 8 January. This operation was detected by British Intelligence, who reported that five U-boats had refuelled from the milk cow followed by a 'complicated series of minor exchanges' between individual boats before most of the latter (some fresh out of Germany) had returned to France. In fact U 117 had replenished U 440, U 662 and U 123, endured a tropical storm, then dealt with U 455 and U 706 (a doctor was sent to U 455 to attend to two sick crewmen). U 117 and U 455 set off together to France on 14 January.

Having been redirected back to a new area north-west of the Azores to refuel U 260, U 117 was ordered to report fuel supplies to U-boat Command on the 25th, sent to a second rendezvous with U 662 and, after weathering a three-day storm, the latter U-boat was finally supplied on 30 January.

By 7 February, U 117 was back in Lorient after an unmolested passage above and below the waters of the Bay of Biscay. After a job well done, in which twelve U-boats had been resupplied, Neumann must have been a little disappointed to read Doenitz's comment in his war diary: 'Nothing special to remark.' Next day, U 117 departed from Lorient with an escort for the short move to the French U-boat base of Brest, arriving the same night.

The U-tanker U 463 (Korvettenkapitaen Wolfbauer) had left Brest late on 6 December 1942, escorted by two M-boats, for her third fuelling mission. Travelling surfaced by night and diving by day, she made poor progress across the waters of the Bay of Biscay in stormy weather and finally made the remainder of the journey submerged. This at any rate enabled U 463 to avoid the air attacks that had so plagued her in the past in the Bay.

By 15 December, U 463 had reached her first rendezvous with U 183 north-east of the Azores, but the continued poor weather delayed the refuelling until the 18th. Then homing signals failed to draw in U 91 and U 155 until the following day. Both received Metox equipment and cable, but no oil, for their short run home.

U 463 now travelled on to her principal fuelling zone just north of the Azores. Arriving on 22 December, four boats were supplied with oil and

Metox; U 86 was similarly treated on the 24th. Again U 463 moved off to a new rendezvous west of the Azores. En route a small convoy was located and a sighting report sent. U 129, U 163, U 154 and U 508 (all Type IX boats of the *Delphin* group) were each given 30 to 45 tons of fuel and provisions on 27 December. The boats made a sweep to the south and then planned to move on further south.

Tanker convoy TM.1, consisting of nine ships protected by four escorts, left Trinidad in late December 1942 for Gibraltar with fuel for the Allied armies in North Africa. The convoy was first sighted on the 29th by U 124 and again on 3 January while just east of Trinidad by U 514, which torpedoed and damaged a single tanker while reporting contact. Again British Intelligence decoded the signals and reported that a U-boat group (i.e. *Delphin*) had been ordered to sweep the likely convoy route. However, no support could be given to the threatened convoy.

The *Delphin* group, now of ten U-boats, proceeded south with U 463 which reported, in response to a query by U-boat Command on 2 January, that she had 300 tons of fuel available after reaching latitude 12N. Her signal – 'In Qu. EG90, 300 cbm abgabebereit. Stehe Qu. DF 2550' (weather report) 'Wolfbauer' – was decoded by British Intelligence. Two days later, U-boat Command ordered Wolfbauer to stop and hold his position, now south of the Azores.

The convoy was located, the group attacked (8–11 January), along with another single U-boat in the area, and the defence of one destroyer and three corvettes was swamped. The result was a catastrophe: seven tankers were sunk at no cost to the U-boats. Some of the tankers were hit by up to six torpedoes! Only two tankers reached Gibraltar and the German C-in-C in Africa sent his congratulations to Doenitz – the *Delphin* pack had undoubtedly eased the burden on the Afrika Korps by denying the Allied armies their fuel. But the German Naval Intelligence service, B-Dienst, capable of reading many Allied codes at this stage of the war, reported that Allied convoys had been rerouted around the *Delphin* pack.

Seven U-boats of the *Delphin* group were then refuelled between 11 and 15 January by U 463 at her rendezvous south of the Azores, allowing them to sink a further three freighters from convoy UGS.4 before returning to base. U 463 was herself now sold out and set out for home. During the return passage she stopped to give U 258 a spare part and to take on board a sailor with a broken arm.

Returning through the Bay of Biscay, U 463 was twice given warning by her Metox equipment of impending night attack by aircraft and twice submerged in good time. She reached St Nazaire on 26 January. Doenitz was pleased with this operation in which eighteen U-boats had had their patrols extended.

U 462 (Oberleutnant zS Vowe) left St Nazaire for her third refuelling mission in company with U 608 and a Sperrbrecher as dusk fell in the afternoon of 20 January. The intention was that U 462 should replace U 463, refuelling boats, including those dispersing from *Delphin*, in mid-Atlantic. Next day she suffered from diesel trouble which was cleared within one hour, but then water was found in the fuel oil. Vowe reckoned that there had been damage to the bilge water tanks. After that, a test dive revealed other difficulties. A U-tanker ran on fuel, not water. Vowe signalled to U-boat Command on the 22nd that U 462 was abandoning her cruise. Her escort soon arrived and the U-tanker was back in port the same evening. Oil bunker 6 was found to have leaked, and U 462 required another four weeks in dock.

This move was detected by British Intelligence and cited (wrongly) as part of a general increase in U-boats seizing on excuses to return to port. However, the absence of U 462 and the subsequent failure of U 460 to reach the Atlantic (see below) at the end of January caused a certain amount of rethinking at U-boat Command, which described the supply situation as 'poor'. U 504 (Type IXC) was given instructions to act as a temporary cow south-west of the Azores, while other attack boats on their way back had to provide small quantities of fuel when needed. U 504 supplied U 124 and U 105 on 2/3 February, but a planned rendezvous with the Type VIID U 217 had to be called off because of the poor weather. U 504 herself was now to be replenished by U 118 (see below).

Grand Admiral Raeder resigned in January 1943 after a disagreement with Hitler over the deployment of the Kriegsmarine's large surface ships. Hitler wanted to scrap all ships larger than a destroyer, after a particularly poor performance by two heavy cruisers in the Arctic, so that all the effort devoted to these ships could be expended on the U-boat arm. Not surprisingly, Hitler appointed Doenitz as the new Grand Admiral. Doenitz soon appreciated the wisdom of Raeder's view and managed to persuade Hitler to retain the capital ships of the German Navy. Doenitz continued to take an active and dominating interest in the U-boat campaign, but day-to-day operations were now conducted by the new head of U-boat Command, Admiral Godt.

U-boats were being sent to the Atlantic front at an ever-increasing rate and, as the storms prevalent in the Atlantic in January died away, the stage was set for a new onslaught on the North Atlantic convoy routes.

At long last, the Germans felt able to lift the embargo on offensive deployment of the new SMA mines and some of the Type XB U-minelayers could be used for their original function, although they would then be pressed back into service as milk cows after minelaying was complete.

U 118 (Type XB, Korvettenkapitaen Czygan) left Lorient briefly on 7 January with three 'new' M-boats, arriving in Brest later that night. Here she received further dock work and, more significantly, mines were taken on board on 23 January. Czygan commented in his war diary that there was difficulty in loading the mines owing to the lack of suitable cranes at

Brest. He received written orders for the minelaying operation, which was common practice for minelaying missions, although written orders remained very rare for normal patrols.

U 118 sailed from Brest at midnight on the 26th and crossed the Bay of Biscay submerged during daylight. During the surfaced night passage she suffered several air attacks and a few bombs were heard far off. She surfaced again on the 28th to give her position and received orders to carry out her special mission.

On 1 February U 118 was tangled up in fishing boats close to the Straits of Gibraltar and dived to avoid them. After resurfacing at 2310 hrs, minelaying began. Most of the mines were laid from the surface, but two air alarms caused some to be deposited from the submerged U-boat. The last (fiftieth) mine was dropped at 0421 hrs. After withdrawing to a safe distance, U 118 signalled to U-boat Command that the special operation had been completed (3 February). She was ordered to make for the Central Atlantic, in the area around the Canary Islands, for her refuelling mission. The mines laid by U 118 in the Straits of Gibraltar scored spectacular successes, sinking a corvette and three merchant ships (14,064 tons), and damaging a destroyer and a further two merchant ships (11,269 tons). However, one of the ships sunk was the Spanish *Duere* and the Spanish government protested vigorously. Since Spain was a neutral country friendly to Germany, the Naval High Command directed that no further mines should be laid in that area.

While proceeding to her rendezvous, U 118 encountered an unnamed Italian submarine. Greetings were exchanged, but no fuel was supplied. Between 8 and 14 February, U 118 resupplied three individual U-boats (U 176, U 730 and the Type VIID minelayer U 214), five boats from the *Rochen* group (30 tons each) and finally the remaining fuel (71 tons) was handed over to U 504 together with three weeks' provisions. It may be recalled that U 504 had herself served as an emergency tanker one week previously. In addition, three sick crew members were taken aboard from the above boats. The *Rochen* pack was thus enabled to search the US–Gibraltar convoy route south of the Azores.

U 118 now signalled to U-boat Command that refuelling was complete and that she was on the way home. She received orders on the 20th to return to Bordeaux, not Brest, and arrived with an escort on 27 February. In his appraisal of Czygan's mission, Doenitz joked: 'The B-Dienst and Press have detected mining successes. Nine U-boats were refuelled. This was an important operation! But nothing special to remark!'

Another U-minelayer, U 119 (Kapitaenleutnant Zech), whose six-month absence from the record books after August 1942 has already been noted, was sent out from Germany. She left Kiel on 6 February in company with two other U-boats and a minesweeper and the group was later joined by a Sperrbrecher for the passage through the Belts. The U-boats arrived in

Kristiansand on the 8th, where U 119 was made fast to the destroyer *Richard Beitzen*.

Next day, U 119 was escorted to sea again for a combined minelaying and resupply mission. She received her operational orders to begin mine-laying off Iceland directly from Naval Group North on 11 February. While proceeding through the Atlantic, she was able to dodge a number of air attacks by timely warning from her Metox receiver.

By 16 February, U 119 was in the Denmark Strait having problems with icing in the winter seas. When storms began Zech decided to dive to conserve fuel. U 119 now laid her 'eggs' off the south-west coast of Iceland, near Reykjavik, on 20 February, but Zech restricted the original mining area so as to avoid excessive thinning of the minefield. Next day, further mines were laid in bad weather in a new field just to the west of the previous one. There was no Allied interference and U 119 started the long trek to her refuelling zone north of the Azores. During the same day, Zech gleefully recorded in his war diary that he had heard no fewer than thirteen detonations in the mined area. In fact, no mine had been set off, and the bangs must have had another origin – perhaps the old problem of premature explosions remained.

U 119 now avoided two further air attacks with warnings from her Metox equipment and, having moved a fair distance from Iceland, sig-nalled on 25 February that the mines had been successfully planted. How-ever, this message was intercepted by British Intelligence, who instigated minesweeping almost at once so that the mines achieved no result. U 119 was warned by Metox of a fast-approaching aircraft shortly after trans-mitting her signal, the signal having perhaps provoked the attack, and dived. Meanwhile, U-boat Command ordered U 119 to surrender her remaining fuel to U-boats north of the Azores.

Running confidently at night on the surface of the Atlantic to her fuelling zone, relying on Metox for radar detection, on 2 March, U 119 suddenly blundered into what she later described as a British V- or W-class destroyer when close to her destination. There was no warning given from Metox (which could detect radar only of around 150cm wavelength). The destroyer was actually the Canadian destroyer HMCS *Assiniboine*, which had located U 119 with 10cm radar. It was pitch black just before midnight and the U-minelayer was battened down ready to dive when the destroyer was sighted just 800 metres away, and closing fast. Zech dived hurriedly but the *Assiniboine* rammed the U-boat causing 'severe shaking' (the destroyer reported later that she had achieved only a glancing blow on the U-boat and then dropped six shallow-set depth-charges). Frantically the U-boat crew blew its tanks, fearing that the boat must be mortally wounded. On arrival at the surface, Zech saw the destroyer stopped just 500 metres away. He ordered all guns to be set and the U-boat turned stern-on towards the enemy. At this point he was told, 'Boat makes no water' – the pressure hull had apparently not been breached. U 119 then ran off on the surface into the night, while the *Assiniboine*, whose engines had been knocked out by the explosions of the depth-charges, made no effort to follow. Repairs to the *Assiniboine* would take four months.

About an hour later, U 119 carried out a test-dive, which proved to be uneventful. Her crew discovered twenty-one minor gun hits on her conning tower and deck when daylight came, and the 37mm cannon had been shot through. Zech now carried on the short distance to his main refuelling area, as we shall see later.

Owing to the large number of U-boats engaged in 'wolf-pack' operations against the North Atlantic convoys at this time, there was a constant need for tankers to be in position in the air gap far to the north of the Azores. U 119 was intended to aid in these refuelling operations, but other tankers had arrived first.

British Intelligence had correctly predicted that U 461 (Kapitaenleutnant Stiebler) would make for 46N 27W to provide fuel for U-boats now short after an attack on convoy SC.118. The tanker left St Nazaire for her fourth supply operation on 13 February with the usual escort. The most important part of her cargo was a supply of the new Metox radar search receivers, for transfer to U-boats out in the Atlantic that had not yet received one. She crossed the Bay of Biscay uneventfully and reported safe passage to U-boat Command on the 17th. As with her previous mission, U 461 had only a short run to refuel her customers waiting close in east and south of the Azores.

U 461 refuelled four U-boats in individual meetings, while U-boat Command continually ordered Stiebler from one boat to another, with short 'meeting done' signals to signify success. The *Rochen* group was replenished on 28 February (U 118 had previously supplied *Rochen*, see above). U 558 and U 202 each took on two torpedoes, so that Stiebler could no longer complain about having to take them home again. One of the torpedoes crashed into the sea 'despite new lines' while being transferred to U 558, hitting the U-tanker and driving two holes into the diving cells above the waterline. Metox equipment was supplied to both U 202 and U 569.

Another stream of signals from U-boat Command gave explicit details about the *Rochen* rendezvous, but required only the briefest responses from the boats at sea. U-boat Command was clearly worried about the threat of radio direction-finding equipment pinpointing the rendezvous, but not of cipher-breaking.

U 460 (Oberleutnant zS Schnoor) departed from St Nazaire on 26 January as part of the solution to the continuing demand for more fuel in the North Atlantic air gap. During a test-dive on the 28th, the U-tanker suddenly handled much heavier (more problems with trim) and U 460 returned to

101

port with her escort, protected overhead with an unusual guard of two Arado seaplanes. She was back at St Nazaire by the 29th.

Two days later, U 460 emerged again with a Sperrbrecher as escort. Crossing the Bay of Biscay in the conventional manner, U 460 was forced to dive before approaching aircraft four times in two days after warnings from her Metox equipment.

Two U-boats were given opportunistic supplies of fuel north-east of the Azores as U 460 headed for her main fuelling zone (7 to 8 February). The *Taifun* group of U-boats was awaiting replenishment as the U-tanker arrived 400 miles north of the Azores in the air gap on 11 February. Nine boats of the pack were refuelled between the 11th and the 18th, with numerous short moves by the tanker; some of the newly supplied boats headed for home, while others joined the new *Wildfang* pack.

U-boat Command now ordered U 460 to move another short step to the south-west, putting her in position far to the north-west of the Azores. During the transition, Schnoor learned that he had earned a well-merited promotion to Kapitaenleutnant. Another nine U-boats were refuelled in the new area between 21 and 24 February, but a momentary panic ensued when a British submarine was sighted while U 303 was actually in the middle of being oiled. Refuelling was at once ended and U 460 ran off at full speed, warning U-boat Command that the rendezvous was known to the enemy. The fuelling zone was changed again on the 22nd while U-boat Command advised that U 462 would be sent with all possible speed to the assistance of U 460.

U 460 had now refuelled eighteen U-boats, predominantly of the Type VII class, although one or two Type IX boats were oiled as they passed through to remote waters. For example, U 525 (Drewitz, Type IXC/40) received 40 tons of fuel. With no reserve fuel left, U 460 was ordered back to France. She arrived at Bordeaux on 5 March, having had an uneventful passage of the Bay of Biscay.

U 462 left again from St Nazaire with an escort on 19 February, after her failed attempt to reach the Atlantic in January. Like the other U-tankers at this time, she carried several stocks of the Metox radar search receiver for supply to boats already at sea. A test dive to 'A+30' (110 metres) was satisfactory and U 462 proceeded across the Bay of Biscay but, resurfacing after an air alarm (in which she had not been attacked), Vowe discovered that the U-tanker was leaving a bad oil leak from the same bunker as previously. Contrary to the views of British Intelligence, the intrepid Vowe signalled to U-boat Command: 'Despite damaged oil bunker, will complete mission.' An oil leak was a serious danger to a submarine of any type, since it left a trail that an enemy could easily follow. Vowe was ordered to proceed at increased speed to his fuelling zone north-north-east of the Azores (BD81), where U 462 would replace U 460.

A series of complicated orders for rendezvous was now transmitted by U-boat Command to U 462. U 358, U 707 and U 303 all received substantial quantities of fuel on 26 February. Bad weather hampered the supply operation and initially prevented the tanker's doctor and two sick sailors from returning from U 707 to U 462.

Between 27 February and 2 March, a stream of U-boats was refuelled and provisioned by U 462, and supplied with radar search receivers (*Burggraf* group). Two more U-boats were replenished on 3 March after a slight shift of rendezvous, and the supplied U-boats were asked to signal to U-boat Command 'refuelling complete' once they had moved well away from the rendezvous area. One of the boats resupplied on 3 March was the U-transporter U 180 heading for the Indian Ocean.

Between 11 February and 5 March, twenty-seven U-boats of the *Taifun* and *Burggraf* packs were replenished by U 460 and U 462. This enabled the boats to switch from convoy to convoy as the opportunity arose and three successive convoys – ONS.165, ON.166 and ONS.167 – were attacked in the North Atlantic ('ONS' designated slow convoys, 7 knots, from Britain to America; 'ON' convoys were the faster, 9-knot, equivalent). In the productive month of February, there were only three U-boats on patrol off the entire American coast (north and south)!

U 462 now set off for base, being ordered to return to Bordeaux on 5 March. The Bay of Biscay was traversed mostly submerged and without air attack, and U 462 joined the 12th U-boat Flotilla on her arrival in Bordeaux on 11 March. She had supplied sixteen U-boats in all.

Her place was taken by the U-minelayer U 119, newly arrived from minelaying off Iceland (see above). U 119 now assisted with replenishment of the *Burggraf* pack (March) and helped U 463 to refuel the *Raubgraf* boats (see below). U 119 had arrived safely at the rendezvous area (48.46N 30.11W) north of the Azores on 5 March, where she cruised in circles awaiting her first customers. But by the time U 608 appeared, the sea was so rough that refuelling could not take place (7 March). Next day, U 608 was supplied and homing signals attracted U 377. Again re-oiling had to be postponed to the following day.

The sounds of a local convoy battle were heard all through the night, after which more U-boats arrived in search of replenishment.

Between 8 and 19 March, no fewer than thirteen U-boats, predominantly Type VII, were intermittently refuelled in atrocious weather, typically receiving 20 tons of oil each. A medical visit was made to U 638, which also received a Metox cable, as did U 603. One man fell overboard from the rubber dinghy as he tried to reach U 566, but was safely rescued. U 757 was particularly unhappy, since she could not be oiled for two days, nor could crewmen in need of medical attention be taken onto the cow. U 119 was now sold out, but she made one further move to a fresh rendezvous where

U 590 was encountered, a sick sailor was taken off the newcomer and a spare part handed over (22 March).

U 119 then set off for home. On 24 March she dived into the still depths of the ocean to permit the doctor to operate on the patient removed from U 590. U 119 crossed the Bay of Biscay without difficulty and on 1 April was escorted into her new home base, Bordeaux.

Zech had performed an outstanding mission with U 119, having carried out a minelaying (which he believed to have produced results), survived being rammed, and then refuelled a wolf-pack in terrible weather – all on his first Atlantic cruise in a U-minelayer. He was duly congratulated for his achievement by Doenitz, and would soon be moved on to a higher command.

U 461 replenished five boats of the *Tuemmler* group – operating between Gibraltar and the Canary Islands in the Central Atlantic – early in March. Of these, U 504 and U 66 were refuelled by U 461 on 1 March, and provided with Metox gear. Captain Davies of the sunken steamer *St Margaret* was taken over as a prisoner from U 66 (Markworth). Much later, rescued survivors from U 461 were to misconstrue this incident, and told their interrogators that Davies was handed over by U 558, a myth that has long been perpetuated.

For want of any new orders, Stiebler elected to stay in the area while the damage caused to the U-tanker by the falling torpedo was repaired. U-boat Command ordered U 461 to show position and fuel stocks on 4 March, resulting in the further transfer of fuel and Metox to U 106 and U 521 on the 5th, south-west of the Azores.

A heavy storm shook U 461 severely on 8 March, but the bad weather had subsided by the 13th, albeit with considerable expenditure of fuel by the tanker. Stiebler declined further orders to make rendezvous owing to lack of fuel and the weather, preferring to return home, for which permission was granted. While homeward bound, U 461 encountered two destroyers which departed after a two-hour search and U 461 subsequently was able to cross the Bay of Biscay uneventfully, reaching St Nazaire in the late afternoon of 22 March. She had returned within six weeks of leaving port. Doenitz was generous in his praise for a well-carried-out supply of twelve U-boats in difficult weather conditions.

In March, the best results of the war against convoys were achieved when combined Atlantic convoys SC.121/HX.228, and then SC.122/HX.229, were beset by wolf-packs, between them losing thirty-eight ships of over 225,000 tons. The SC and HX convoys were the slow and fast convoys to Britain from America, and their cargoes were particularly important. The British Admiralty was forced seriously to consider whether convoys across the North Atlantic should continue, although there appeared to be no alternative. 'The Germans never came so near to disrupting communication between the New World and the Old as in the first twenty days of March 1943,' admitted a later Admiralty report. U-boat Command, speaking of the attack on convoys SC.122/HX.229 which they believed to have been a single convoy, boasted with exaggeration: 'In all thirty-two ships of 186,000 tons and one destroyer were sunk and hits were scored on nine other ships. This is the greatest success ever achieved in a single convoy battle and is all the more creditable in that nearly half of the U-boats scored at least one hit.'

Sinkings of Allied merchantmen in the two months of February and March amounted to 173 ships in all theatres, of which 114 had been sunk in the North Atlantic. However, British Intelligence was able to detect growing signs of strain in the whole U-boat arm as more and more U-boats were being sunk.

At this stage of the war, the German Intelligence service B-Dienst had reached the pinnacle of its war achievements. Able to decipher many of the British signals, U-boat Command became alarmed over the evident fact that the Allies knew much more about U-boat dispositions than they had done three months previously. Had the German ciphers been broken? Or was there a traitor at headquarters? They engaged the Abwehr security organization to conduct a search through U-boat Command for possible explanations. The Abwehr found no signs of any leaks from the Command and it must have been with relief that Doenitz noted in his war diary (5 March) that the great bulk of the knowledge of U-boat movements could have been deduced from a multiplicity of other factors, of which one was location by aircraft fitted with radar. A number of changes were made to U-boat tactics, not least of them the requirement to submerge for half an hour as soon as Metox picked up a radar signal. Thus, the Germans remained in blissful ignorance of the existence of shipborne H/F D/F and the fact that the British could decipher the German ciphers.

We left U 459 heading south for her appointment with the U-boats of the *Seehund* group, which was making its way towards southern Africa. Now began the first of a series of problems with her magnetic compass. For three hours on 22 January, U 459 had to steer by the stars after the compass temporarily failed. A similar problem occurred on the 26th, but the tanker still managed to make her rendezvous on 28 January to the south of St Helena, where she signalled to other boats that she had arrived. British Intelligence detected the exchange of W/T signals near 25S 1W, but could do nothing about it.

Next day, the boats of the *Seehund* group began to show up. U 516 (Wiebe), U 159 (Witte) and U 506 (Wuerdemann) arrived and received sub- stantial resupplies of fuel, more than 100 tons in each case, as well as 2 tons of provisions for each boat. Two sick sailors were taken onto the tanker from U 506 and one replacement crew member was provided in return.

U 459 now turned northwards and by 3 February St Helena was again close by. Here she transferred another 100 tons of fuel to U 160 (Lassen) and an incredible 8 tons of provisions. Lassen also took on one extra torpedo and Wilamowitz boasted to his war diary that the transfer of the torpedo from deck to deck had taken just eighteen minutes. U 459 had now disposed of 450 tons of fuel to just five U-boats (including *Cagni*), leaving little fuel in reserve. She set off homewards but the compass broke down again.

Ascension Island was passed on 9 February as U 459 steered north and three days later the compass broke down once more. U 459 navigated by the stars for the Cape Verde Islands and as she left them astern, she was asked for her position by U-boat Command on 20 February, but could only provide an estimate. Nevertheless, U 459 was directed to a last rendezvous south-west of the Azores where, on the 27th, she met up with U 513, provided her with food, Metox and a heater and, most importantly, a sick crewman was removed from the attack boat.

Headed for France, U 459 crossed the Bay of Biscay, diving by day to avoid air attack, and surfacing at night. A last alarm occurred on 7 March as U 459 headed for Bordeaux with an escorting Sperrbrecher which detonated a mine so close to the U-tanker that the latter was covered with flotsam, but she docked safely at her new base with the 12th U-boat Flotilla. Eight U-boats had been supplied by U 459 (although only five received fuel) in an operation that had lasted a little more than six weeks. Doenitz congratulated Wilamowitz on a well-carried-out operation.

Between February and April the *Seehund* group sank fifteen ships of 92,837 tons in the waters off southern Africa, the best result being obtained by 'Gunner' Lassen in U 160 who sank three independents (19,353 tons) and four ships (25,852 tons) from convoy DN.21, as well as damaging another two ships from the same convoy. The U-cruiser U 182, which was operating independently in the same area, sank a further 30,000 tons of shipping, but was herself sunk during her return to France.

The overworking of the available milk cows meant that returning members of the *Seeraeuber* group near the Canary Islands had to provide fuel so that seven boats could remain for a short while on station. This occurred at the end of March, when U 106 refuelled U 159 and U 155 south-east of the Azores, while U 109 refuelled three boats north-east of the same island group.

U 463 (Korvettenkapitaen Wolfbauer) had left St Nazaire for her fourth refuelling mission on 4 March, with the usual escort. Next day she was attacked without radar warning at night by an aircraft in the Bay of Biscay. The U-tanker was illuminated with a Leigh Light, but the bombs missed and U 463 dived. Wolfbauer must have been getting sick of sudden air attacks without warning. He wrote in his war diary: 'In future I shall only surface to recharge the batteries.'

By 11 March, U 463 was in the North Atlantic, but the weather was deteriorating. The supply area was close to that of U 119 in BD24, but no

U-boat could be replenished from the 16th (when U 409 was encountered) until the 19th. Then seven boats were supplied, followed by U 91 next day and U 230 (Siegmann) the day after that. U 230 took two and a half hours to refuel with just 15 tons of oil; her First Officer, Herbert Werner, was later to write his grim memoir, *Iron Coffins*, of life aboard an attack U-boat during 1943.

A slight muddle arose on 23 March. The homeward-bound U 190 was ordered to give 80 tons of unwanted fuel to U 463. U 463 was then to give oil to U 84. All three boats met on the same day, together with U 415, and U 190 pumped oil directly into U 84. 'U 190 is my delivery boat,' joked Wolfbauer.

Boats for the *Raubgraf* and *Loewenherz* groups, stationed south-east of Greenland, were refuelled by U 463, aided by U 119, at this time. A typical example was the refuelling, by U 463, of the badly damaged U 89, which had survived engine trouble and depth-charges from a convoy escort. The U-boat returned to La Pallice on 28 March, but was sunk on her next (fifth) patrol.

U 463 had moved a short distance to a new rendezvous by the 28th, but U 642 could not be supplied until the 31st owing to more bad weather. Other boats arrived and the whole circus moved again in search of a better fuelling zone. Then, still with heavy seas running, U 463 was able to replenish no fewer than nine U-boats from 0916 to 2350 on 3 April, an easy record for a single day's supply by any milk cow. Wolfbauer commented only that 'the crew worked hard'. Between 5 and 8 April, a further six U-boats were resupplied, although U 610 caused anxiety with her delayed arrival. These U-boats were part of the twenty-two boats of the *Seeteufel* and *Seewolf* packs which had expended much fuel in a fruitless chase after convoy HX.230. The newly replenished boats were added to the thirteen-strong *Loewenherz* group south-east of Greenland, intending to operate against the forth-coming SC.126 convoy. Other boats, refuelled by U 463 (and later by U 462), were assembled as the *Meise* group to the east of Newfoundland.

U 463 was now sold out and Wolfbauer set off for home, crossing the Bay of Biscay without incident, reaching St Nazaire on 17 April. In his review of the tanker's war diary, Doenitz remarked: 'Very well carried out. Twenty-six boats had their operations extended.'

The Type XB minelayer U 117 (Korvettenkapitaen Neumann) had taken on mines at Brest, from where she sailed with an escort on 31 March. She was bombed unsuccessfully by an aircraft close to the north-west coast of Spain just after receiving her special orders – 'Carry out mission. Use high speed.' – on 4 April. By the 9th, U 117 was in position off Casablanca, dodging the many fishing boats with their lights.

Minelaying began off Casablanca, just to the south-west of Gibraltar, on 10 April, initially being laid from the surface and then all through the following day after the U-minelayer had submerged. U 117 finally withdrew to a safe distance and on 12 April signalled the success of her minelaying mission. She was ordered to proceed to square DG85 (*c*. 28N 28W, far west of the Canary Islands) to begin her refuelling assignment. U 455 (Type VIIC, Kapitaenleutnant Scheibe) also laid mines off Casablanca on 10 and 11 April. Taken altogether, the mines sank one ship (3,777 tons) and damaged two others (14,269 tons).

The *Seehund* group was refuelled on its return by U 117 west of the Canaries (29N 30W) between 16 and 28 April, one boat requiring attention by a doctor. In all, eight U-boats were supplied (U 68, U 159, U 160, U 185, U 506, U 509, U 516 and U 518). U 117 was additionally ordered to replenish the Italian submarine *Archimede* that had also been operating in the South Atlantic, off Brazil. A special signal was required and U 117 was told to wait even if the Italian did not show up.

On 29 April, U 117 dived to attack a solitary steamer, but found that it was a neutral Spanish ship. By 2 May, the *Archimede* had still not turned up (unknown to the Germans, she had been sunk by air attack on 16 April) and U 117 signalled that she would return home. A fast Allied tanker was sighted the following day, but it escaped U 117's underwater attack.

U 117 was then ordered to hand over her remaining supplies of fuel to the U-tanker U 460. The minelayer arrived two days early, U 460 showed up on 5 May and there was an exchange of meats. Finally U 117 arrived safely at Bordeaux, her new home, on 14 May having evaded all Allied aircraft in the Bay of Biscay, thus becoming one of the lucky boats to escape the carnage in the North Atlantic that month. In his appreciation of Neumann's war diary, Doenitz criticized the minelaying operation for the fact that the mines had been laid too close together. However, the refuelling operation was commended.

Meanwhile, U-boat pack attacks on the North Atlantic convoys were reaching their climax, principally supported by U 462 and U 463. U 462 (Oberleutnant zS Vowe) had been refitted in port very quickly (just three weeks) and left Bordeaux on 1 April, which proved to be a fool's day – when Vowe carried out a trim-dive in shallow water U 462 set off an air-laid magnetic ground mine. The blast badly rocked the boat and when it resurfaced Vowe found that oil covered the upper deck and bridge. For the third time in succession, he was commanding a U-boat that left a trail of oil. A pilot was taken on board and the outgoing U-cruiser U 177 provided the tanker with an escort into deep water in the Bay of Biscay.

U-boat Command ordered U 462 to make good speed ('with all due care') to her refuelling zone far north of the Azores in the mid-Atlantic air gap. Later, after the U-tanker's return to France, Doenitz was to admonish Vowe for his failure to adhere to standing instructions that no U-boat was to dive in waters with fewer than 50 metres under its hull, except in the case of air attack, the reason being precisely to counter the threat from ground-lying magnetic mines.

While en route, U-boat Command transmitted another detailed and complex series of rendezvous instructions to the boats at sea awaiting the arrival of U 462. Refuelling of the first boats began on 8 April. U 462 had to give repeated weak call signals in order to advertise her presence to incoming U-boats, so next day the rendezvous was shifted a short way to the west. A stream of U-boats was refuelled between 10 and 17 April for the *Meise* group, despite difficulties with the rubber dinghy and also accidental flooding of the U-tanker on the 13th. There were so many customers that the brand-new tanker U 487, fresh out of Germany, was ordered to go to the assistance of U 462.

U 487 was the first of the short second series of four Type XIV U-tankers to be built. She was commissioned at Kiel on 21 December 1942 and, after only three months of training in the Baltic, she returned to Kiel to load up with provisions. Her commander was the 37-year-old Oberleutnant zS Metz, his first command, although he had previously served as watch officer on three U-boats (including U A) between 1939 and October 1942. It would appear that U-boat Command was still seeking age and experience in its tanker commanders, although high rank or a long shore appointment was no longer a prerequisite. As it transpired, Metz was to acquit himself well.

U 487 departed from Kiel with a minesweeper and two flak escorts on 27 March. She stopped in Kristiansand on the 29th for fresh provisions and a test-dive before putting to sea again. Nothing noteworthy occurred as U 487 passed around the north of Britain into the Atlantic, finally reaching her fuelling zone, once again in the giant BD box to the north of the Azores.

Between 11 and 30 April, U 487 supplied no fewer than fourteen U-boats with 534 tons of oil, 13.7 tons of lubricating oil and 17 tons of provisions at three main rendezvous. Among the boats was the outward-bound U 188 (Luedden, Type IXC/40), the others being predominantly Type VIIs from the *Seeteufel* and *Seewolf* groups.

The two U-tankers were reported by British Intelligence together at 49.30N 31.30W on 12 April. As it happened, two American submarines had been assigned to cross the Atlantic for deployment in European waters and it was agreed that the submarines should, for the first time, make a deliberate attack on U-tankers at a fuelling zone. Nothing more appears in British records and the Germans seemingly never knew of the attack (if any) as neither U-tanker was harmed at this time.

U-boat Command directed either that both tankers remain on station, or that U 462 should give up her remaining fuel to U 487. The latter option was chosen, U 462 and U 487 met together on 18 April, and the new arrival was supplied with fuel, Metox equipment and other parts.

U 462 then set off back to France. The war diary records that the punctilious Vowe mustered his crew for the Fuehrer's birthday on 20 April; more prosaically, U-boat Command demanded a weather report from him.

Next day, Vowe had the bright idea of crossing the Bay of Biscay on the surface, confiding to the war diary that the Bay 'is not overly watched by enemy aircraft'. Three and a half hours later, U 462 crash-dived before an approaching Sunderland could reach him. Reverting to the conventional pattern for Bay passage (surfaced at night, dived by day), a bomber fitted with a Leigh Light dropped four bombs on her in a night attack – and without any warning from the Metox detector – with a further four bombs being dropped just five hours later, both on 23 April. The previous day, Vowe had radioed simply: 'To Bordeaux?' It took nine hours to receive the answer: 'Ja, ja, BdU West.'

It must have been a relieved (and somewhat giddy – they had been in and out within twenty-four days) crew that collected its escort and rare air cover on 24 April, before reaching Bordeaux. U 462 had supplied fourteen U-boats with 627 tons of fuel oil and 122 days of provisions. No torpedoes had been handed over. Doenitz commented that the supply operation had been very well carried out.

In April, the number of ship sinkings fell because many of the U-boats had had to return to base after the March convoy battles. U 487 remained on station north of the Azores until the end of the month.

The tanker *Corrientes* had remained in the Canary Islands after the departure of the *Charlotte Schliemann* in February 1942. She played host to the survivors of U 167 (Fregattenkapitaen Sturm) after this Type IXC boat had been severely damaged by air attack and forced to put in to the Canaries, where she was scuttled by her crew on 6 April. The sailors remained briefly on the islands, where they were playfully photographed by British agents while sightseeing, and were smuggled out at night to the waiting U 455. They were then split among three further U-boats for the journey back to France. Within two months of being sunk, virtually the entire crew of U 167 was at sea again in a brand-new Type IXC boat, U 547!

U-boat Command had a new worry. In March, U 333 (still commanded by Schaff) reported to base that she had been attacked at night, without radar warning, by an aircraft that she had managed to shoot down. U-boat Command then received sporadic reports throughout March and April that U-boats had been attacked by aircraft in the Bay of Biscay without receiving any warning from their radar receivers. One of these boats was the tanker U 463 (5 March), another was U 462 (23 April). The explanation was that Britain had secretly equipped a handful of Coastal Command aircraft, and many of the surface escorts, with a new, short-wave (10cm) radar that could not be detected by the German radar receiver Metox. The latter was designed to detect transmissions around the 150cm wavelength only. The Germans had no idea that such short wavelengths were feasible as research into radar had fallen way behind that of Britain owing to Hitler's cancellation of all long-term research work in 1940 – he had expected a short war – and experts claimed that centimetric radar wavelengths were impossible.

U-boat Command did consider the possibility that, notwithstanding the opinions of the 'experts', centimetric radar was being used, but could find no concrete evidence. British Intelligence reported towards the end of March that the first complaint from a U-boat (probably U 156) of a night attack without warning by a bomber fitted with 10cm radar had occurred on 7 March off Trinidad. The U-boat was sunk the following day, the report noted, so it could tell no tales when it got home to base.

U 461 (Kapitaenleutnant Stiebler) had departed from St Nazaire on 20 April and crossed the Bay of Biscay in the conventional manner, surfaced at night and submerged by day. Her Metox apparatus gave constant warnings of aircraft in the vicinity during the hours of darkness. Then, at 0247 hrs on the 23rd, she was attacked without radar warning by a twin-engined bomber fitted with a Leigh Light. Three bombs and two smoke bombs were dropped as the aircraft flew past, the bombs exploding on the starboard side apparently causing only minor damage. The attack was so sudden that the 20mm cannon on the bridge could not be used and Stiebler dived at once. Some leaks were quickly repaired. Stiebler considered that 'the aircraft must have sighted the boat in the full moon. No [radar] warning was received.' On surfacing, the damage was found to be much more serious than had first been supposed, the tanker leaving a massive oil slick from a ruptured tank.

After consultation, U-boat Command ordered U 461 to steer, with care, but with all possible speed, to her refuelling zone (far north of the Azores, c. 51N 31W). U 461 smashed her way through seas so heavy that the 20mm cannon became inoperable and machine guns had to be brought up to the bridge from below, at one stage diving to avoid a four-engined bomber. The remainder of her patrol will be told in the next chapter.

The situation with the radar was confused by the fact that most British aircraft still employed the older 150cm radar, a deliberate policy by Coastal Command designed to cause the Germans to believe that Metox remained effective. Recalling that U 333 had shot down her assailant, and noting that the U-boats could no longer rely on detecting an aircraft during the dark, on 27 April Doenitz ordered the U-boats to cross the Bay surfaced during the day and submerged at night, thereby reversing the normal procedure. Initially boats were ordered to submerge when their lookouts sighted an approaching aircraft, but within a week three U-boats were sunk and three badly damaged. After Coastal Command aircraft had made a further thirty-seven attacks on U-boats, Doenitz ordered that the latter shoot it out on the surface if they could not safely submerge.

At this critical stage, Goebbels, the German propaganda minister, gloated: 'Thanks to our U-boats, we have at last grabbed Britain by the throat.'

Chapter 11

Black May

May 1943

After the wind-down in U-boat operations during April, a flood of them entered the Atlantic from their Biscay bases and from Germany towards the end of the month. In May there were well over a hundred U-boats at sea and full-scale attacks on the North Atlantic convoys were set to resume. However, British Intelligence had noted during April that their morale was not what it was. The intensity of the Battle of the Atlantic, increasing losses, and the strain of being switched from one convoy battle to another with short intercessions for more fuel instead of an extended shore leave had weakened the resolve of some of the U-boatmen.

The milk cows were mostly in port at the beginning of the month, with the result that the South Atlantic specialist, U 459, had to be deployed in mid-May north of the Azores. The positions of the milk cows on 1 May 1943 can be seen in Map 11-1. In its summary of 10 May, British Intelligence described the presence of three milk cows (these must have been U 459, U 461 and U 487; U 487 had just started for home) and over thirty U-boats in the region of 50.55N and 30.40W (far to the north-north-west of the Azores). Most were fuelling and repairing. The new tanker U 487 (Oberleutnant zS Metz) had remained north of the Azores until 30 April, and had then started for her new base in France. On 4 May she went deep to 160 metres as a convoy battle could be heard in which, naturally, she could not participate. There were two air alarms in the Bay of Biscay, but no attack chased the diving U-tanker. By 12 May, U 487 was safely docked in her new home base at Bordeaux. Metz had acquitted himself well on his first war patrol and was appropriately congratulated by Admiral Godt.

U 459 (Kapitaenleutnant von Wilamowitz-Moellendorf) had set out from Bordeaux for her fifth supply operation on 20 April (U 461, it may be recalled, had set out independently from St Nazaire on the same day). After leaving her escort of a Sperrbrecher and two minesweepers behind, U 459 carried out a test-dive to 150 metres, resulting in yet another complaint from Wilamowitz about the loading and distribution of ballast about the U-tanker. Unlike U 461, U 459 was able to cross the Bay of Biscay with only one air alarm, when her Metox set gave plenty of advance warning.

U 459 was diverted on her march across the ocean briefly to aid U 306 with a medical visit, far, far to the north of the Azores. Then she cruised south to her main refuelling zone in the usual area north of the Azores. On 3 May, en route, she was surprised by an attack from a British destroyer. The U-tanker dived steeply, but was rocked by eleven single, well-placed depth-charges as she passed a depth of 40 to 60 metres. Wilamowitz took the tanker down to 160 metres and sat tight while the destroyer made many more overruns of the submerged cow. Although the first attack caused minor damage, the destroyer finally departed, U 459 came to the surface some ninety minutes later and fled quickly on the surface. The war diary records that the Metox apparatus was later found to be defective, which might explain how the destroyer was able to get so close. U 459 arrived at her fuelling zone in the air gap north of the Azores on 5 May. U 258 was supplied.

Next day, U-boat Command sent this message to all U-tankers: '(Change in standing orders.) Use least possible W/T communication with which to inform U-boat Command in full detail on the situation of the supply boat and for other messages.' U-boat Command was getting increasingly concerned about the number of rendezvous that appeared to have been discovered by the Allies.

Five more U-boats were supplied in the original area between 7 and 9 May, and then U 459 moved south, stopping to refill a latecomer en route. By 15 May, U 459 had reached her new rendezvous where she and the other cows received new general orders from U-boat Command: 'To all suppliers. If possible, do not use homing signals. At earliest, transmit twenty-four hours after arrival. Retiring boats first send on confirmation through W/T. Especial care: reckon with carrier aircraft and search groups.' Two days later, U-boat Command sent out a further warning: 'To all supply groups in BD [i.e., north of the Azores]. Beware of enemy aircraft and destroyers.'

U 459 refuelled eight U-boats in quick succession between 15 and 17 May, giving Metox sets to those boats that required it (U-boats fresh from Germany lacked the French-made Metox), then moved on again for fear that her W/T signals had betrayed her position. The tanker was in any case nearly 'sold out'. U 262 was encountered on the 18th, and then U 129 two days later. U 129 lost a man overboard briefly from the rubber dinghy, but he was soon rescued.

U-boat Command ordered U 459 to meet U 403 (Clausen) and then both boats were to return to France together. U 403 was duly met on 24 May and oiled with the tanker's residual fuel. Next day, two further U-boats were provided with Metox and U 459 received 52 tons of oil from the

113

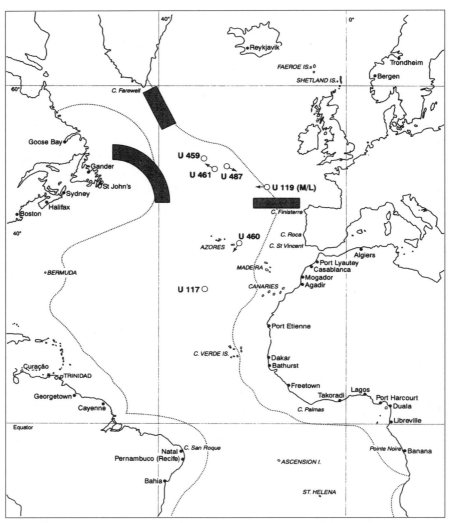

Map 11-1. Milk Cows at Sea, 1 May 1943. The shaded areas denote U-boat groups. The milk cows are labelled. U 119 is en route to a minelaying operation. The map does not indicate the large number of individual U-boats in transit to and from their operational areas. The broken lines denote the limit of land-based air patrols. (*Reprinted by courtesy of the Controller, The Stationery Office*)

homeward-bound Type VIID U-minelayer U 218. The oil was passed onto U 92 on the following day.

U 459 then turned for home. She had been rather fortunate in her crossings of the Bay of Biscay hitherto, but now her luck ran out when she was surprised on the surface on 30 May, just after midday, by a Whitley bomber. U 459 blazed away with her semi-automatic 37mm and 20mm

C/38 cannon as the aircraft passed by, dropping two depth-charges and four bombs. A strong explosion was seen in the aircraft as it flew over the tanker, but the detonation of the bombs caused the tanker to slew to a halt in the water.

The first aircraft had disappeared from view, and Wilamowitz and his delighted crew claimed to have shot it down (this was confirmed by Allied sources; the Whitley's last message was 'engine trouble', presumably as a result of the return fire. The crew was never heard from again.) But meanwhile a second aircraft, a Liberator, flew in through what it described as intense and accurate flak and dropped a total of nine bombs in two runs, some of which were uncomfortably close to the U-tanker. The Liberator suffered only slight damage. The gun crews of U 459 scrambled below as the bomber overflew the tanker, which promptly dived. The only damage sustained had been to the long-suffering compass. Six hours later, U 459 resurfaced to the sounds of a distant battle between aircraft and U-boats. She dived again and ran straight for home.

U 459 met her arranged escort of U 564 on 3 June and arrived safely back at Bordeaux on the same evening. Admiral Godt was forthright in his praise: 'An especially well carried out and seamanlike supply operation. The successful air fight on 30 May is especially notable. Credited: one aircraft shot down.'

An interesting feature of the deployment of the submarine tankers at this time was that the U-minelayers were temporarily not being used as milk cows. U 117 had returned from her Canary Islands fuelling rendez-vous by mid-May.

The tanker U 460 (Kapitaenleutnant Schnoor) was also sent out into the Central Atlantic for her fifth cruise on 24 April. The operational orders for the U-tanker required her to support six U-boats that had been cruising during April off Freetown. Her escort exploded a magnetic mine before departing and U 460 crossed the Bay of Biscay without difficulty, although her prudent commander insisted on numerous practice dives. Before heading south, U 460 was diverted to assist other boats with immediate difficulties. U 185 was encountered just outside the Bay of Biscay and provided with a 'Dora' active radar set. (Dora was a radar transmitter; German radar technology, however, lagged far behind that of the Allies and Dora was never of much use in active service in U-boats.)

U 183 (H. Schaefer, not the former commander of U 460) was provided with food and a medical visit south of the Azores on 3 May, but no oil was handed over (U 183 had been refuelled by U 117 just one day previously). Two days later, as we saw in the previous chapter, U 117 was encountered, provided with meats and battery parts for her journey home, and the U-minelayer handed over 45 tons of reserve fuel to the U-tanker. The two milk cows parted to go their separate ways and Schnoor carried out a full

115

anti-aircraft drill, the only reference to such an event in all the war diaries of the milk cows.

By 15 May, U 460 was west of Freetown and had to submerge to avoid a four-engined bomber, probably, Schnoor thought, considering its altitude, nothing more than a transport crossing the Atlantic at its narrowest point between Freetown and Brazil. But the rendezvous was now very close and the bomber might have been searching for the milk cow.

This was the area where so many ships had been sunk in 1941. The current U-boat group had found few single targets and many convoys. During an attack on one of them in April, U 124, commanded by one of the most experienced commanders, Kapitaenleutnant Mohr, was lost after she had sunk two ships. However, U 515 (Kapitaenleutnant Henke, another experienced commander) had sunk seven ships from convoy TS.37.

U 460 lay at her rendezvous between 17 and 26 May, during which time six Type IX U-boats were supplied. A sick sailor was taken off U 154. Henke had an interesting problem. One of his engine-room ratings had been confined to quarters for 'allowing sabotage on board', and was trans-ferred as a prisoner to the tanker.

U 460 then moved north-west to a position west of the Cape Verde Islands, where U 513 (Guggenberger) was waiting on 2 June, having arrived after operations off Brazil. Next day, U 460 started her long trek back to France. Her story will be continued in Chapter 13.

We left U 461 (Kapitaenleutnant Stiebler) proceeding into the North Atlantic with a trail of oil from a bomb-damaged bunker. The oil finally ran out on 28 April – U 461 had lost 20 tons of fuel – and on the following day she received orders to refuel many U-boats from various packs. Her sister tanker, U 487 (Oberleutnant zS Metz), handed over new Metox equipment as U 461 arrived in the North Atlantic air gap well to the north of the Azores (BD36).

Three U-boats (U 631, U 267 and U 610) were refuelled on 1 May, more slowly than usual, in heavy seas. None needed provisions and Stiebler remarked on the need to revise again the levels of food provisions carried on board. Foodstuffs were nevertheless handed over to U 267 and U 610, while U 108 and U 706 were also supplied.

The bad weather resulted in poor navigational fixes and subsequent difficulties in locating other 'customers'. After a string of signals, U 532 (Junker) and U 598 (Holtorf) were finally encountered and issued with Metox (5 May). Two days later, U 528 (Rabenau) was supplied after U 461 had been forced to emit beacon homing signals. An alarmed U-boat Command transmitted: 'Stiebler. Care. Because of today's beacon signals, rendezvous may be harassed.' (The commander of a U-boat nearby had signalled that two destroyers were in the area.)

Between 9 and 14 May, U 461 refuelled a further eight U-boats, including the Type VIID minelayer U 218 (Kapitaenleutnant Becker). She was then redirected to a new rendezvous close by before heading home. Six further U-boats, including the Type VIID minelayer U 217 (Oberleutnant zS Reichenberg-Klinke), were replenished in the new area (16 to 19 May). U 461 took one sick seaman off U 228. A number of parts were also handed over. By now, the U-tanker had adopted a policy of 'dived at night, surfaced during the day'. U 217 and U 218 had been engaged in minelaying with the new SMA mine in May around the coast of Britain – the former in the waters off Land's End, and the latter in the North Channel – and were then diverted to the Central Atlantic where U 217 would be sunk on 13 June.

U-boat Command then (21 May) ordered Stiebler to give U 463 a Metox apparatus at a fresh rendezvous north-east of the Azores, but Stiebler failed to locate U 463 after arrival and reported this to U-boat Command. Then U 461 turned for home, arriving with her escort at Bordeaux on 30 May. Surprisingly, she suffered only one air alert and no actual attack, while crossing the Bay of Biscay. Godt was highly complimentary about this mission, in which no fewer than twenty-six U-boats had been supplied after the U-tanker had sustained initial damage.

What had happened to the U-tanker U 463 (Korvettenkapitaen Wolfbauer)? U 463 left Bordeaux on 12 May for her fifth refuelling mission. Two days later she reported to U-boat Command that she was steering to her refuelling zone to the north of the Azores. But on 16 May the outwardbound U 463 was stalked by a Coastal Command Halifax bomber. The aircraft remained up-sun of the U-boat as the latter steered due west at 10 knots, then swooped to make its attack. The U-tanker started to dive, too late, and an accurate straddle of ten depth-charges was delivered while the conning tower was still visible, sending U 463 straight to the bottom. As the aircraft and its companion circled over the spot only bluish oil could be seen at the point of impact – and bodies. There were no survivors.

Wolfbauer and his crew had suffered repeated air attacks in the Bay of Biscay during previous patrols and he must have been unenthusiastic about the order of 27 April to traverse the Bay in daylight, especially if it was cloudy with good shelter for lurking aircraft. U 463 had been sunk so fast that she had no time to signal. Thus, on 18 May, U-boat Command asked U 463 to show her passage past the Bay. By the 20th there had been no reply, nor did the U-tanker give her position on the 21st. It was finally assumed that she had been lost with all her crew during the passage of the Bay. She missed one star on 20 May and the second star on 13 January 1944.

The second of the new series of U-tankers, U 488 (Oberleutnant zS Bartke), departed from Kiel on 18 May for her first war cruise. Unlike Metz of U 487, the 34-year-old Bartke had had only a seventeen-month stint as Second Officer on the attack boat U 403 before receiving his command. It is hard to see what qualification this gave him to command a U-tanker, but heavy losses among potential candidates had doubtless reduced the number of options for U-boat Command, while certainly Bartke could claim the wisdom and perhaps caution of greater age than most attack commanders. Fortunately for the Germans, he was to prove himself as able and capable as Metz.

U 488 docked at Kristiansand on 20 May, then put to sea again, reaching the North Atlantic without incident. Here she paused briefly north of the Azores for some repair work on her batteries, before marching on to her refuelling zone far to the west of the Azores, where she was to replenish the *Trutz* group. Her further story is also taken up again in Chapter 13.

The Allies had not been idle at sea. Some of their escort ships were equipped with the new 10cm radar, and generally they were converting wide experience into proficiency, unlike the U-boat crews of whom many had come from Germany on their first patrols. Moreover the convoys had one particularly unpleasant surprise for any approaching U-boats, for some of them were defended by the new escort carriers.

Escort carriers were essentially aircraft carriers built by laying a flight deck onto the hull of a converted merchant ship. They differed from the older merchant aircraft carriers, which were ordinary merchant ships to which a short flight deck had been added for a handful of aircraft, and which carried ordinary cargo; escort carriers had to be specially constructed. The escort carrier was by no means a new innovation. As early as 1941, HMS *Audacity* had protected convoys on the dangerous run, past Luftwaffe-controlled skies, taken by convoys between Gibraltar and Britain, but until 1943 there had never been enough of them and the few available had been used in support of the Arctic convoys, which were threatened by the Luftwaffe, surface warships and U-boats, and for Operation Torch. Both the British and Americans had quickly seen their worth and each built a large number, although the massive American shipbuilding industry manufactured the great majority. Between 1942 and 1945 they constructed 115 escort carriers, with an average time between being laid down and commissioned of only twelve months. By July 1943, the Americans were already operating twenty-nine of these carriers.

The use of the escort carrier to accompany convoys in the North Atlantic finally bridged the air gap between the American continent and Britain. No U-boat could feel safe on the surface within range of a convoy, and this effectively meant that, once a U-boat had been forced to submerge, it could never catch a convoy up again as even the slowest convoy was faster than the underwater speed of a U-boat; at the same time the U-boat could no longer surface and race to a position ahead of the convoy when the immediate threat had disappeared.

The aircraft sent aloft by the escort carriers were fitted with two new anti-submarine weapons, in addition to the well-tried bombs and shallow-set depth-charges. First was the air-to-surface rocket, which was designed to hit a U-boat below the waterline, practically guaranteeing that it would sink. Second was the top secret 'Mark 24 Mine', which was actually an acoustic torpedo. Once dropped into the water, it steered itself to the nearest source of sound, the U-boat's propellers, and then exploded on contact. The Mark 24 Mine was more commonly referred to as 'Fido', since it 'sniffed out' the enemy.

Fido was relatively insensitive to noise and was most likely to succeed if the propellers were 'cavitating', the name given to the popping of bubbles produced when propellers turn at high speed. Normally a U-boat would be cavitating in the effort to get as far away as possible, but if she submerged slowly then Fido would be ineffective. Consequently it was very important to the Allies that the Germans should not discover the secret, and orders were given that under no circumstances was Fido to be used when a U-boat was in a position to see the effect. In practice, this meant that Fido was used exclusively against U-boats in the process of submerging, and the secret of the 'Mine' was not discovered by the Germans throughout the war, despite the fact that they developed their own acoustic torpedo at virtually the same time and all U-boats carried acoustic torpedoes after September 1943. A spy in the USA would report to U-boat Command in 1944 that an American plant was manufacturing acoustic homing torpedoes. The account was not believed for the extraordinary 'reasoning' that if homing torpedoes were being used by the Allies, there could be no survivors, and it was known that survivors were being taken from some sinking U-boats. The possibility that homing torpedoes might be in use at the same time as other anti-submarine weapons was beyond the imagination of U-boat Command.

The Allies were fortunate that Fido was not found out after its very first use against a submerging U-boat. U456 was hit in the region of the propellers (13 May), but miraculously survived to return to the surface, severely damaged. She reported to base that she had been hit by a bomb in the stern and was later sunk by warships sent after her without having any inkling that she had been the first victim of Fido.

The U-boats were taken completely by surprise by aircraft from the escort carriers, and many were sunk. What was worse from the German view was that the U-boats were having great difficulty in sinking any ships at all, while the toll of sunken U-boats was increased still further by the convoy escorts. Hysteria reigned in U-boat Command as the staff tried to discover the cause of this sudden reversal, resulting in a torrent of messages and warnings to the boats at sea, and it was noted that losses of the large Type IX boats had been out of all proportion to their numbers. Moreover, the air patrols over the Bay of Biscay had become such a menace to the boats trying to make the passage on their way to and from operations, that the U-boats returning to France were ordered to band together in groups of three to six to provide one another with anti-aircraft cover.

On 24 May, Doenitz decided that he could not sustain such a rate of loss in the North Atlantic any longer. He ordered all U-boats out of the theatre, some to regroup near the Azores where he hoped that the convoys would be less well protected, and the remainder to return to France. 'We had lost the Battle of the Atlantic', he later wrote. At the time, though, Doenitz was less pessimistic, attributing U-boat losses to the superiority of enemy location methods that could be defeated with improved radar-detection equipment and superior anti-aircraft guns.

By the end of May, forty-one U-boats had been sunk, over one third of those at sea, of which twenty-nine boats had been destroyed in the North Atlantic alone. In exchange, sinkings of Allied ships by the U-boats in the North Atlantic came to only twenty ships, just two more than those sunk by a group of seven long-range U-boats, including six U-cruisers, working (unsupported by cows) in the South Atlantic and off Cape Town. Even here they now found convoys but sank 200,000 tons of shipping before withdrawing.

The milk cows did not at first suffer directly from the catastrophe that had overtaken the rest of the U-boat arm, since they were still reasonably safe in their secluded refuelling areas. However, U-tankers crossing the Bay could expect serious trouble from Allied aircraft owing to their slow diving time and the fact that they had to make the passage on the surface during daylight. It was soon to become apparent, too, that the absence of massive U-boat attacks on the convoys would free Allied naval forces to the extent that they could start to hunt down the milk cows in their own territories.

Meanwhile, the withdrawal of U-boats from the North Atlantic and the heavy demands made on their services between March and May meant that many of the cows had 'sold out', or were otherwise no longer useful in the Atlantic, and could be called home again.

Zech had been moved from his command of U 119 (Type XB) on 14 April, shortly after the boat's return from her last Atlantic operation, being given a series of subsequent shore appointments, and he survived the war. His place was taken by Kapitaenleutnant von Kameke, a rapidly rising 27-year-old who had first served on the heavy cruiser *Admiral Hipper*, taken a shore position for five months, served as First Officer on U 119's sister ship, U 116, leaving at the same time as von Schmidt just before the boat was sunk, and briefly as First Officer on the attack boat U 84, before receiving commander's training and the captaincy of UD 5 for just one month. Von Kameke could clearly claim to be highly experienced, which was perhaps as well since he had only ten days to prepare himself for his new command.

U 119 had been sent out from Bordeaux on 25 April to lay a mine barrage off Halifax, Canada, little more than three weeks after her return from her previous mission. She was attacked by two RAAF Sunderlands during passage of the Bay of Biscay and in the ensuing gunfight one sailor was killed. The boat was also straddled by depth-charges, but these caused little damage. The aircraft dropped smoke bombs to mark the diving point and U 119 fled as fast as she could into the Atlantic.

The temporary shortage of milk cows in the North Atlantic resulted in her deployment, unusually, for refuelling purposes to the north of the Azores before she had laid her mines. U-boat Command first ordered U 119 to meet U 92 far to the south of Greenland for a huge fuel transfer of 90 tons on 6 May. Such a drain on her supplies must have severely reduced the U-minelayer's effectiveness (she carried only 320 tons of fuel in all, and needed a large part for herself), but U 119 reported that she had found only two British destroyers at the rendezvous. The rendezvous was moved further south, where U 92 and U 954 received their fuel and a spare part. Three further U-boats were given 23 tons of oil each by U 119 between 15 and 16 May, and U 119 reported that she had 157 tons left.

U-boat Command now made the bizarre decision to employ U 119 as a weather boat (a U-boat whose purpose was to send Atlantic weather reports to Germany, enabling long-range predictions to be made for a variety of military purposes) until she should start her minelaying mission. This occupied U 119 for about a week, before she moved off to the east coast of the USA to begin her minelaying mission with the new moon. The task was accomplished on 1 June, and the fifty-five mines subsequently sank one ship (2,937 tons) and damaged one other (7,176 tons). U 119 signalled to U-boat Command on 3 June that her mission was completed successfully and was ordered to head to the area west of the Azores to assist U 488 with her refuelling operation. Her fate will be described in the next chapter and her attempts at refuelling in Chapter 13.

U 515 (Type IXC) was employed as an auxiliary tanker, stationed off St Paul Rocks (mid-Atlantic, east of Brazil) throughout May, and a similar cow (U 530, Kapitaenleutnant Lange) was still there in July.

Doenitz and Hitler spent most of a long naval conference on 31 May discussing the U-boat situation. Doenitz assured the Fuehrer that the U-boats would return to the Atlantic just as soon as new weapons were available to counter the threats of aircraft, radar and sea escorts (respectively improved anti-aircraft guns, a new radar search receiver and the new German acoustic torpedo). Meanwhile U-boats would be sent to quieter areas to stretch the Allied defences and to keep in touch with new Allied countermeasures. 'There can be no talk of a let-up in the U-boat war', declared Hitler. 'The Atlantic is my first line of defence in the west. And even if I have to fight a defensive battle there, that is preferable to waiting to defend myself on the coast of Europe. The enemy forces tied down by our U-boats are tremendous, even though the losses inflicted by us are no longer great.'

Chapter 12

Disaster in the Bay

June to August 1943

Doenitz ordered that the anti-aircraft armament of the U-boats be strengthened, in an attempt to deal with the threat of attacking Coastal Command aircraft. The relative quiet in the Atlantic after the withdrawal of the U-boats had enabled Britain to reinforce the air patrols over the Bay of Biscay, and the Luftwaffe, which had become overstretched as a result of the number of fronts on which it was fighting, was no longer able to control the skies in the area. It was not long before British escort groups, no longer needed in the Atlantic, began to appear in the waters just to the west of the Bay, and the ships were moved to locations reported by aircraft as containing a newly submerged U-boat. Once detected, the U-boat stood little chance against these highly trained escorts.

Doenitz further ordered the U-boats to sail in groups for mutual protection, which increased their firepower towards attacking aircraft. Meanwhile, the gun platform behind the U-boat conning tower was widened (and later armoured against aircraft gunfire) and a second platform was fitted just aft of the original. The large deck gun was dismantled, since opportunities to use it had always been rare and the threat of the air menace was such as to make it completely useless. The original 20mm cannon on the old gun platform was replaced by two twin 20mm cannon, and the new aft gun platform mounted either a 37mm cannon or, more commonly, a quadruple 20mm gun known as a 'Vierling'. The Vierling possessed a primitive optical ranging sight, but there was no sighting mechanism on the weapon itself. The three gunners were expected to follow its tracer shells visually for aiming purposes. The centre of the cone of fire, where the cannon shells from all four gun muzzles converged, was about 1,500 metres.

Doenitz also fitted out a number of U-boats as 'aircraft traps'. They possessed yet another gun platform, this time in front of the conning tower, and mounted a total of eight 20mm cannon in two quadruple mounts plus a new, automatic, fast-firing 37mm gun with a heavier explosive charge than the older semi-automatic 37mm. U 441 was the first to be used in this capacity towards the end of May. Her orders were to shoot down any aircraft she encountered, in the hope of deterring aircraft from attacking U-boats that were less well protected. U 441 shot down her assailant in her first engagement, but was so badly damaged by bombs that she had to return straight to base. However her experience with the automatic 37mm cannon was later to encourage its widespread adoption, while her experiments with rockets were ruled out as far too dangerous.

The attempts to deter Coastal Command were entirely unsuccessful as orders were passed to the aircraft to attack at all costs, a bomber being worth much less than a U-boat (see map 12-1). But the heavily armed U-boats achieved some surprise at first. U 758 (Kapitaenleutnant Manseck) was one of the first to be fitted with the new, standard, anti-aircraft armament. On 8 June, she blasted her way across the mid-Atlantic, until the aircraft modified their tactics with a series of simultaneous attacks that caused U 758 to submerge with a long line of casualties and three guns damaged. 'Well done. Long live your Vierling', signalled Doenitz to Manseck before he learned of the casualties.

More U-boats crossed the Bay and suffered under continuous air attack; the luckless crews found that some aircraft mounted 40mm cannon, whereas the U-boats generally had only 20mm with its shorter range. If the U-boats tried to fight it out on the surface, the aircraft simply sprayed them with gunfire at long range until the gun crews were out of action, whereupon the aircraft could close to bombing range with impunity. If, on the other hand, the U-boats tried to submerge, the aircraft could attack them at the moment of submergence when they were again defenceless. In the first weeks of June no U-boats were actually sunk by air attack as they crossed the Bay, but several were forced to return to base with damage or heavy casualties, and doctors had to be carried aboard them to deal with gunshot wounds.

The Luftwaffe had been persuaded by U-boat Command to supply long-range fighters to try to drive off the Coastal Command bombers. Units of Ju88C twin-engined fighter-bombers of KG40 (V Group) were based at Brest, Lorient and Bordeaux, while single-engined FW190 fighters provided short-range cover from Brest. The aircraft hunted in packs, so that lone British aircraft caught unawares had little chance unless they could find cloud cover. The British therefore detailed groups of Beaufighter and Mosquito fighters to attack the Ju88s. They were superior fighters to the German aircraft but had first to find their quarry, who held the advantage of the initiative and surprise. Doenitz became so anxious about the aerial combat that ensued that he pressed Hitler to authorize patrols by the latest Me410 fighters over the Bay. The Fuehrer agreed, but the new aircraft made only a handful of sorties over that sea before being called back to

Germany to defend her industries against the daily pulverization by the RAF and USAAF.

It is not surprising that U-boat crews became increasingly nervous and would seize any realistic excuse to return to base. On 17 June, Doenitz ordered the U-boats to traverse the Bay entirely submerged, surfacing only for the minimum time needed to recharge batteries. The boats were still to sail in groups, however, and if the group was surprised at sea, it was still to fight back.

Each group of three or more U-boats was led by a 'senior officer afloat' who had to decide whether or not the U-boats all had time to submerge after an aircraft had been sighted. It took twenty seconds for a medium-size Type VII boat to crash-dive if the crew were very experienced (longer if they were not), and the attack time of the aircraft after sighting the U-boat was around forty to fifty seconds. A system of flag waving was developed. If the commanding U-boat thought that all the boats could safely submerge, then a yellow flag was waved; if, however, there was not sufficient time, a red flag was waved and the gun crews closed up to their action stations. Flag waving suffered from one extremely serious defect that the U-boats only found out by experience. It assumed that the aircraft would attack at once, when it was thought, reasonably, that there was a good chance of shooting it down. But British aircraft soon adopted the tactic of circling the group out of gun range while calling up reinforcements of other aircraft, or even of warships. Soon the U-boat group would be beset by overwhelming force. If the boats tried to submerge before the reinforcements arrived, the encircling aircraft immediately swooped onto the defenceless U-boats as they were in the act of submerging.

At the same time, the British Admiralty also agreed to make available a hunter-killer group of warships highly experienced in anti-U-boat warfare, with a view to chasing up sightings of U-boats reported by aircraft, and to provide the aircrews with the morale-boosting knowledge that they would soon be rescued if they were shot down over the Bay. On 16 June, the famous 2nd Support Group of five sloops, under the command of Captain 'Johnny' Walker, left Liverpool to provide the killer group. Walker, a resolute, imaginative and innovative commander with a reputation for doing things his own way, was already famous as Britain's leading anti-submarine ace.

British aerial minelaying outside the U-boat bases also caused the boats to stay on the surface until they had reached deep water in the Bay. Doenitz reported to Hitler that 'the only outward route for U-boats is a narrow lane in the Bay of Biscay. This passage is so difficult that it now takes a U-boat ten days to get through.' Coinciding with this effort, British Bomber Command made repeated air raids over the U-boat bases, but the boats remained safe within their concrete-covered pens.

One of the boats that ventured out was the U-tanker U462 (Oberleutnant zS Vowe), with orders to refuel long-range U-boats steering towards the Indian Ocean. U462 had returned to Bordeaux from her previous mission on 24 April and, after dockyard work, had been moved to the U-boat base of La Pallice on 17 June, where she made fast to the heavy destroyer Z24. Leaving again on the 19th with an escort of a Sperrbrecher, U462 proceeded into the open sea with all non-essential crew members on deck wearing lifejackets. After carrying out a trim-dive – this time with 70 metres of water under the hull – U462 set out into the Bay of Biscay with two M-boats and with U382 (Koch) as the other member of the group. The 'flag-waving' sequence was agreed with Koch.

Both boats lost contact with each other after the very first air alert, when both dived. On the 20th, U462 manned her anti-aircraft guns and asked U-boat Command for a rendezvous with U382, still within the Bay. The Command proposed BF8327, a point that U462 had already passed. Vowe amended the rendezvous to BF7366. Meanwhile, Koch was also complaining that he could not find U462. U-boat Command had the last word – meet in BF8241.

U462 had already endured many eventful actions, but her hardest trial yet was to come on 21 June, en route to regroup with U382. U462 was caught on the surface at 1215 hrs by four Mosquito fighter-bombers (the war diary claims five) that were making a sweep against Ju88 aircraft supposed to be in the area. The Mosquitoes at once attacked at low level. U462 retaliated with a massive amount of fire from her Vierling and Flak 38 (single 20mm) guns, but the bridge watch were severely wounded. The attack was warded off as the sailors replaced the injured gunners. One aircraft was claimed shot down, confirmed by British sources. Of many bombs dropped, none caused damage.

At last U462 managed to submerge and went deep. The ship's doctor tended to the four badly injured sailors and Vowe complained bitterly in the war diary that the casualties could have been avoided if the anti-aircraft guns had been fully enclosed within turrets. One seaman died of his wounds. Meanwhile, the U-tanker handled so badly underwater that it was supposed that the oil bunkers must have been damaged.

U462 surfaced nearly seven hours after the original action to discover that oil bunker 7 and the deck had been damaged. She dived again but had to resurface at dusk as her batteries were exhausted. During what must have been a long night, U462 deployed the new Aphrodite radar decoy balloons, with long, dangling, metal strips intended to lure away any lurking enemy ships or aircraft. Vowe was unhappy with the results, since the balloons tended to drift close to, or snag around, the U-boat (other U-boats reported similar difficulties, although Doenitz was to praise its effectiveness in September, after special trials). Early next morning, after the dead sailor had been buried at sea (45.14N 27.22W), U462 signalled her predicament to U-boat Command and that she was abandoning her mission.

The alarmed FdU West (U-boat Command in the west), fully aware of the value of a U-tanker, ordered Koch to continue alone into the Atlantic and prepared a massive escort to aid the stricken cow. Meanwhile, Allied aircraft swept the Bay and early on the 22nd U 462 was forced to dive quickly to dodge three fighter aircraft. She surfaced again for the homeward run at 0925, and was told to expect two T-boats (light destroyers) and air cover close to her home port.

U 462 was able to report at 1320 that she had sighted the two T-boats and nine Ju88 long-range fighter aircraft. The T-boats followed in her wake as she returned on the surface towards Bordeaux. As darkness fell the air cover departed and U 462 was attacked, unsuccessfully, again from the air in the early hours of 23 June. She reached Bordeaux with an escort of a Sperrbrecher, two M-boats and two UJ-boats. Doenitz complimented the crew on its resolution and bearing.

In the month of June, four U-boats were sunk, and six severely damaged, in the Bay. One of these boats was the U-minelayer U 119 (Kapitaenleutnant von Kameke), which was returning from her minelaying operation off the USA, followed by a subsequent mid-Atlantic fuelling mission described in the next chapter. U-boat Command had ordered U 119 to join with U 449 and U 650 north-east of the Azores in order to form a group with which to cross the Bay of Biscay. Von Kameke reported that he had found U 650 but not U 449. Revised orders were sent, requesting the returning U-tanker U 460 to join the group later on, and the three boats headed for their French bases.

The exchange of signals and the enforced loitering of the U-boat group while they collected themselves together were to have disastrous consequences. British Intelligence alerted Walker's 2nd Support Group so that his hunter-killer group of experienced escorts barred the path of the homeward-bound U-boats. The group was sighted by aircraft, leading to a search by the support group. Early in the morning of 24 June, Walker's sloop *Starling* detected U 119 with her Asdic, accompanied by loud, unexplained whistling noises. A single depth-charge pattern of ten charges sufficed to cause U 119 to surface, where she was immediately attacked with gunfire by all the ships of the support group. *Starling* then turned to ram the U-boat, but was simultaneously struck by a stray shell from one of the other ships, which exploded against her bows, luckily without doing much damage. She then increased speed towards the U-boat.

U 119 had smoke pouring out of her conning tower and appeared to be settling in the water, but the *Starling*'s crew noticed that she was still battened down with no attempt being made to abandon ship. Apparently her commander thought that he could still escape. *Starling* struck her abreast the conning tower, bows crashing down onto the U-boat which

126

slowly rolled over underneath the sloop. As the latter came off her, having completely overrun the unfortunate U-boat, depth-charges were dropped straight onto her. The sloop *Woodpecker* then rushed in to deliver a final pattern 'to make sure'. There were no survivors from the U-boat.

Starling was badly damaged as a result of the ramming, the shell strike and the close explosion of the depth-charges, and had to be sent back to port for repairs. Shortly afterwards, the other ships of the support group sank U 449 with a 'creeping attack', the name given to the procedure whereby one ship kept Asdic contact with the U-boat while another escort crept above the unsuspecting victim dropping depth-charges. The submerged U-boat could not hear the attack until the depth-charges were exploding all around.

The forlorn U 650 reported that she had lost touch with the other boats, and was ordered to wait at a precise rendezvous on the 27th, while FdU West arranged massive air and naval protection for the missing boats. But U 119 made no signal, gave no response to a direct order on the 29th to report her position, and was assumed lost as of 24 June. U 119 missed one star on 3 July and two stars on 9 March 1944. U 460 had meanwhile made her own way back to base in company with the badly shot-up U 758, the U-tanker arriving at Bordeaux on 25 June.

Those of the milk cows that had returned to base by June were fitted out with heavier anti-aircraft guns, which were typically stepped up to two semi-automatic 37mm guns on the deck and four 20mm cannon in the gun platforms in the case of the Type XIV U-tankers. The Type XB minelayers based in Biscay ports also received better anti-aircraft protection, but the later ships of the class, still in German waters, continued to bear a more conventional armament.

The slow diving times of both types of cow, worse than fifty seconds, made their crews poor insurance risks while crossing the Bay on the surface. The available German fleet torpedo boats (small destroyers) in the area – T 5, T 19, T 22, T 24, T 25, *Falke*, *Greif*, *Moewe*, *Jaguar* and *Kondor* – together with the powerful Z-class destroyers based on the Biscay coast (Z 23, Z 24 and Z 32) were employed to escort the cows on their way to and from missions. The escort generally comprised up to four destroyers and torpedo boats at a time. The warships were also used to escort damaged U-boats trying to cross the Bay and to rescue survivors from other boats that had been sunk.

The shortage of fuel at sea among the U-boats still operating in the Central Atlantic induced U-boat Command to send out more U-tankers. U 487 (Oberleutnant zS Metz) slipped out from Bordeaux on 15 June. On the 25th she reported to U-boat Command that she had safely passed the perilous waters of the Bay but needed some parts. She was ordered on to a refuelling zone south-west of the Azores with a stream of messages. It was her second cruise.

U 462 again tried to get out through the Bay of Biscay, again with orders to refuel boats heading into the Indian Ocean (the rendezvous zone was to be grid FD20). She left Bordeaux on 29 June with an escort of a Sperrbrecher and two M-boats, together with U 160 and an Italian U-boat at which to wave flags. The Sperrbrecher detonated one mine before departing.

In the afternoon, the U-boat group continued with an escort of six Ju88 long-range fighters overhead. The latter departed as night fell, while the two U-boats soon lost contact with the Italian boat in the darkness.

Next day, U 462 surfaced at first light to find herself alone, but after searching for a while, she relocated U 160 (together with another group of three U-boats). Both boats continued into the Bay of Biscay. An air attack as darkness fell caused a hasty dive by the U-boats, but contact was quickly established when they resurfaced early on 1 July.

All through the day the thunder of far-off depth-charges and bombs could be heard, and a new version of Aphrodite was released on several occasions during the evening, U 462 surfacing each time.

Then came disaster. While still on the surface at 1544 on 2 July, a 'Catalina flying boat' approached fast (according to the war diary). The aircraft was in fact a Liberator long-range bomber that had first obtained, then lost, a radar contact around 1420 and regained contact at 1530 at a range of 18 miles. It emerged from cloud at just 2 miles. U 462 waved the red flag and manned her guns. The aircraft, which had closed in on U 160, turned towards U 462, upon which U 160 seized the opportunity to dive. U 462 also tried to submerge, but discovered that two men were still on deck. Vowe screamed at them to get in as the aircraft flew over the U-tanker's bows without attacking. The boat dived very badly despite 'all men forward', and five bombs fell around the tanker as it reached a depth of 40 metres. U 462 was badly hit and electrical sparks flew. Emergency power was restored and the boat levelled off at 100 metres, while she moved as far away as possible from the danger area at high underwater speed. In the air, the pilots saw air bubbles, an oil streak and little else. Yet Vowe had been lucky, for a misunderstanding had caused the bombs to be dropped incorrectly.

Later, U 462 surfaced to inspect the damage, which proved to be severe. Both gun shields had been broken, while diving tanks and the bows were damaged. U 160 was now in view and U 462 signalled with her Aldis lamp: 'Hit on forecastle, diving tanks 3, 7, 8 ruptured, able to dive. Returning to base.'

U 462 was lightened by dumping drinking water. Then another radar warning was received. U 462 was unable to dive at once, since men were repairing damage on her deck, and so she manned the guns as a Sunderland flying boat closed in. U 160 also stayed on the surface, mainly to defend the milk cow. Both boats manoeuvred so as to turn their sterns

128

towards the attacking aircraft, with their formidable anti-aircraft guns at the back of their conning towers. The Sunderland made two approach runs while U 462 and U 160 fired a barrage back. The following signals were exchanged with U-boat Command, where all eyes were on the fate of the U-tanker and its ill-starred commander. U 462: 'Attacked by two or more aircraft. Fighting back.' U 160: 'Enemy aircraft shadowing.' U-boat Command: 'Give position.' U 160: 'BF7791'. (Just to the west of Vigo, Spain. This was followed by a transmission by U 160 on the condition of U 462 as previously reported by the tanker to U 160.)

As dusk darkened the sky, Vowe again ordered Aphrodite to be deployed. As another air attack came in, U 160 recommended diving, but U 462 remained on the surface since the crew was still working on deck and the water was shallow. The boats opened fire and the tanker's external crew was reduced to a minimum. Early on 3 July both boats were finally able to submerge (badly, in the case of U 462), and they crept back towards France.

The two U-boats resurfaced in daylight, still in contact with one another, but were soon attacked by aircraft. After a short shoot-out, U 462 again dived very slowly and badly in a crash-dive. Vowe resurfaced to receive orders from the worried FdU West, who must now have had plenty of practice at rescuing his boat. But U 462 had to dive again and was forced to sit on the bottom, in 90 metres of water, as her battery had overheated.

Upon coming to the surface again, FdU West had further instructions: 'U 160 immediately report position – expect rendezvous for 5 July 0700 hrs. Destroyers or T-boats, Ju88s – Rendezvous at BF8596' (just off the north coast of Spain).

Both U-boats now made the best progress they could to the rendezvous with the escort, to the accompaniment of a barrage of orders from U-boat Command, which was additionally trying to arrange fighter protection for another boat, the stricken U 386. The rendezvous was finally reached on 5 July, when the relieved crews of U 462 and U 160 met up with the torpedo boats *Jaguar* and *Moewe*, with five Ju88s circling overhead. The air cover departed as the weather deteriorated, but U 462 arrived safely back at Bordeaux, with a pilot aboard, on the 6th. Meanwhile, U 160 had headed back into the Atlantic.

Doenitz's 'U-boat group' plans had gone sadly awry, but he still complained to Vowe that the handling of U 462 had been all wrong, despite standing orders. Thus, according to Doenitz, the U-boat always had to be ready to dive, but it should not dive after an overflight by an aircraft that had not dropped bombs, especially if the U-boat lacked forward momentum; the bombs could probably have been avoided if the U-tanker had not dived. However, Doenitz did concede that the attack by the Sunderland had been correctly handled.

By the beginning of July, U-boats were hugging the Spanish coast, where airborne radar could not easily distinguish them against the backdrop of mountains, all the way to Cape Finisterre in their efforts to reach the Atlantic. This was known in the U-boat arm as the 'Piening Route', after the commander of U 155, the first boat to attempt the route in July. Further confusion was caused by the arrival of the Naxos-U radar search receiver in some U-boats, which swept the low centimetric radar wavelengths. But the device was so crude that it had a very short range and most British aircraft still employed the 150cm radar. Consequently, U-boats were still often surprised on the surface without warning and U-boat Command decided that there must be some other reason for their location. They feared that the old Metox search receiver must be giving off unsuspected radiation that a sensitive airborne receiver could detect.

Another worry was that German aircraft patrolling the Bay had reported that U-boats in general dived as soon as they had seen the aircraft, but the stern was still sticking out of the water as the aircraft flew overhead. U-boat Command reminded all U-boats on the 9th of the dangers of diving too late, and that there should always be deep water (100 metres or more) before the boat dived at all. Two days later, all sailings by U-boats that had not been fitted with the Vierling were cancelled.

On 12 July, U 441 set out on her second aircraft decoy mission. She had the misfortune to fall in with a flight of fighters instead of the expected lumbering bomber and again gunfire caused a shambles on her upper decks. Her return to base was covered by another sortie by the overworked Ju88 long-range fighter-bombers, which shot down two shadowing British aircraft. Meanwhile, air attacks on U-boats in the Bay continued unabated.

Faced with an increasing lack of enthusiasm by the U-boat crews for fighting on the surface, Doenitz felt moved to issue a cautionary warning on 20 July to the U-boats crossing the Bay of Biscay: 'Of three U-boats in a group, the one that dived first got bombed. Moral: if caught on the surface, remain there and shoot. To dive is death.'

The surviving tankers had all returned to their French base at Bordeaux for more fuel by mid-July, so that there was now not a single U-tanker at its refuelling zone. Again U-boat Command had to send out U-tankers to the aid of the boats requiring fuel in mid-Atlantic. Their plans called for the despatch of the minelayer U 117 to Gibraltar for a mining mission, the tanker U 459 to refuel boats bound for the Caribbean far to the south-west of the Azores, the tanker U 462 to refuel all U-boats in mid-Atlantic between Natal and Trinidad, stationed west of the Cape Verde Islands, and U 461 to act as a reserve. The old idea of sending these precious craft out singly was temporarily abandoned, possibly owing to the difficulty of providing individual craft with a sufficient escort.

But U 462 was not yet repaired from her last, aborted foray through the Bay of Biscay, while U 461 grazed against a large ship in port while manoeuvring in a choppy sea on the 22nd, just as she was preparing to join the other two milk cows. This caused a leak in diving tank No. 6 (a split external fuel tank, according to the U-boat Command war diary) and she had to return for repairs. Thus it was that U 459 (Type XIV) was despatched from Bordeaux with U 117 (Type XB) on 22 July, together with an escort of three of the heavily armed 'Z'-class destroyers based on the Biscay coast. The destroyers turned back at 46N 10W on the morning of the 24th.

Eight hours after the departure of the destroyers, U 459 was forced to remain on the surface for repair work on her exhaust gas valve and lost contact with U 117, which proceeded independently out of the Bay. While U 117 survived to reach her refuelling zone, U 459 travelled underwater until it became necessary to recharge her batteries, surfacing at about 45.45N 10.30W.

Suddenly, without any warning from her radar receiver, U 459 was surprised by a Wellington bomber. The aircraft had tracked the U-tanker by radar contact at 6 miles, broken cloud at 5 miles, sighted the boat and immediately attacked, at 100 feet, having first sent a W/T message to say that it looked as though the U-boat would fight it out on the surface. The milk cow opened up at 1,000 metres with a massive barrage from its augmented AA armament (one 37mm, one quadruple 20mm, two single 20mm cannon and two heavy machine guns). Accurate gunfire fatally hit the bomber, which crashed into the starboard side of the U-boat, sweeping away the single and quadruple anti-aircraft guns. The sailors cleared away as much of the wreckage as they could and fished the sole survivor of the aircraft out of the water.

Then they found that two depth-charges from the aircraft remained on board the boat. Clearly they could not stay there, since they would explode when the U-boat dived to their shallow-set depth (25 feet). The cow's commander, the newly promoted Korvettenkapitaen von Wilamowitz-Moellendorf, decided to pick up speed and have the depth-charges pushed overboard in the hope that the U-boat could get clear before they exploded. But U 459 did not have sufficient speed to save herself and the resulting explosions wrecked her steering gear, caused a fire in the electric motor room and disabled her diesel engines. Water poured in through a breach in the pressure hull. In this sorry state she was unable to dive and at that moment another Wellington bomber approached. With most of her anti-aircraft guns overboard, U 459 was doomed. Although the air attack missed, Allied warships were directed to the scene. Von Wilamowitz-Moellendorf ordered the cow to be scuttled and went down with her. Five officers and thirty-seven men, together with the aircrew member, were rescued by the Polish destroyer *Orkan* after ten hours in the water.

For some reason, U 459 had failed to inform U-boat Command that she was being abandoned. Thus the latter only knew that she had failed to give progress reports on 27, 28 and 29 July. U 459 missed one star on 26 August, the second star on 26 April 1944. Later, a repatriated prisoner was able to give U-boat Command a full account of the loss of the tanker. Meanwhile, U-boat Command recorded grimly that the supposed loss of U 459 had resulted in the recall to France of some U-boats that she had been intended to supply.

There was nothing else for it, U-boat Command had to send out another U-tanker. It was decided to despatch U 461 and U 462 together, to make respectively for the Brazilian and central African coasts, with U 460 in reserve.

It is necessary here to understand how Germany's Naval Group West had organized the despatch of the U-tankers U 459 and U 117 (and the intended U 461, which had to abort the mission with minor collision damage in the River Gironde) on 22 July. The escort of the boats by three heavily armed Z-class destroyers was treated as a major naval operation, while their gun-power and flak capability meant that the destroyers could be expected to guard the U-boats all through the night, *all through daylight on the next day*, and well into the next night before the destroyers could bolt back to France at high speed (35 knots) during daylight the following day.

U-boat Command and Naval Group West had transmitted a large number of signals before U 459, U 117 and their destroyer escort had departed Bordeaux, and further messages (weather, enemy sightings, radio frequencies) had been sent when the U-boat group was at sea. All these signals had been decrypted by British Intelligence, which organized an air-and-sea search, but it is unlikely that the Admiralty knew the destroyers planned to escort the tankers on the surface as far as 10W, so the U-boats would have passed through the threatened area faster than the British anticipated. This was in spite of delays caused by machinery defects with U 459 (the French Resistance had cleverly sabotaged an air inlet duct by wrapping copper wire around it), which required some hours to fix followed by a test dive in mid-ocean.

But when U 459 was sunk alone on the surface (while running in broad daylight to recharge her batteries, as per standing orders) in the Bay of Biscay on the 24th – probably after a chance sighting by the aircraft which dealt the fatal blow – the German naval staff seem to have considered that it was the volume of signals alone which gave away their plans. The movement of U 460, U 461 and U 462 would be accompanied by the transmission of far fewer signals, both before and after the boats sailed. However, British Intelligence had interrogated survivors from U 459 and knew that the tanker had been escorted across the Bay on the surface. Now they understood the significance of the earlier decrypted signals to the destroyers and the '4th Defence Division': to escort the tankers across the Bay and to provide minesweeping for tankers and escort.

The key signal to alert British Intelligence for the movement of the tankers U 460, U 461 and U 462 was transmitted on 25 July. It was decrypted on the following day:

From: Group West. To: 8th Destroyer Flotilla.
Decision will be taken today as to whether U-boat escort on 27 July will be carried out by four T-boats or two destroyers. Agree to begin work on Z 24. 8th Destroyer Flotilla is to decide whether Z 32 and Z 37 are to remain at Royan. Starting time for U-boat escort will be 11.00 27 July.

After that, British Intelligence could easily follow the signs that the U-tankers were preparing for sea and that minesweepers were moving into action.

It appears that the decision was made *not* to use the heavy Narvik (Z-class) destroyers on this occasion, notwithstanding the belief of the U-tanker crews when interrogated as POWs, and the statements in many U-boat histories. The war diaries of Z 23, Z 24, Z 32 and Z 37 show that the first two were in dockyard hands at this time, while the other two remained moored in the Gironde river prior to degaussing treatment. Therefore the escort for tankers U 460, U 461 (after repair from her collision) and U 462 would be four of the lighter-armed torpedo boats of the 5th Torpedo-boat Flotilla.

This change was to have important consequences. The U-tankers would be escorted across the Bay, as previously, at 12 knots, their cruising speed. This slow rate of progress would allow the British plenty of time in which they might locate the tankers and their escorts by reconnaissance and organize a counter-attack. Unlike the Narvik destroyers, the torpedo boats could not be expected to risk exposure to assault by British aircraft or destroyers in the Bay of Biscay. Moreover, they were significantly slower than the destroyers. Despite their nominal top speed of 33 knots, these ageing craft could now only manage about 30 knots during their return voyage. Thus the U-tankers could not expect to be escorted as far west as 10W, but only to a point some 100 sea miles further to the east (see Map 12-1). Then the torpedo boats would have to race back to France.

U 460 (Kapitaenleutnant Schnoor), U 461 (Korvettenkapitaen Stiebler) and U 462 (Kapitaenleutnant Vowe) emerged blinking into the sunlight from their bomb-proof bunkers at Bordeaux at about noon on 27 July, as planned. The three tankers made their way down the long River Gironde towards Royan at the head of the river. But U 460 had to drop out early on with a faulty clutch control and her place was taken by the Type IX attack boat U 504 (Kapitaenleutnant Luis). Most accounts state that U 504 was intended to provide an escort for the tankers across the Bay, but there is no documentary evidence for this; it appears to have been a piece of opportunism to slip a boat that was ready for sea into a prearranged escort operation. U 461 had some unusual supernumeraries aboard – the camera crew from a German propaganda company wanted to film some action pictures at a refuelling zone. At Royan, the group's escort of minesweepers was waiting.

The flak carried by the U-tankers had been newly strengthened. U 461 and U 462 had formerly possessed a heavy semi-automatic 37mm cannon forward of the conning tower, and another 37mm cannon aft. There was, however, only a single 20mm cannon on the conning tower, wholly in-sufficient for easy anti-aircraft protection when the boat was under way. Before this, their last cruises, the weaponry was changed. U 461 replaced the forward 37mm cannon with a single, lighter, 20mm cannon (intended for use only while the tanker was stationery at a fuelling rendezvous), the aft 37mm cannon with a Vierling cannon on a bandstand aft of the conning tower, and there were now two single 20mm cannon (one each side) on the tower itself. U 462 had been only partly re-equipped. She retained the 37mm cannon forward of the conning tower and the single 20mm cannon in the conning tower, but possessed the new Vierling cannon on its own bandstand aft. Both tankers also had mounts for two heavy MG81 machine guns, but these were little used (they did not travel well in sea water).

Meanwhile, the three torpedo boats *Moewe* (Kapitaenleutnant Bastian), *Kondor* (Kapitaenleutnant Peter-Pirkham) and T 19 (Kapitaenleutnant Weinlig), with U 231 (Kapitaenleutnant Wenzel), a type VIIC boat that was hitching a ride with the escort, and a Sperrbrecher escort comprising elements of the 4th Defence Division, had departed from La Pallice at 1800 hrs. The chief of the 5th Flotilla, Korvettenkapitaen Koppenhagen, was aboard *Moewe*, as was also a small team of specialists from the B-Dienst. Group West wanted to establish the extent of Allied air activity (numbers, tactics, operational areas) over the Bay of Biscay during their naval operation. They would be joined by the torpedo boat *Jaguar* (Kapitaen-leutnant von Luedde-Neurath) at Royan.

Alerted by their code-breakers, the British Admiralty was ready, ordered Coastal Command to step up its air patrols and moved the 2nd Support Group to the likely line of march. Naturally, the aircrews were not told of the special intelligence – they were told only to search various sectors in the Bay of Biscay. The 2nd Support Group had had to return previously to the port of Plymouth on Britain's south coast, but the ships returned to sea on 23 July.

At 0615 hrs on 28 July, with dawn close, the U-tanker formation reached the 200-metre line, where U 231 demanded another test-dive. The whole group stopped while this was carried out, but resumed at 12 knots after 0700 hrs. But U 231 was clearly suffering from mechanical difficulties and at 0915 hrs she reported a problem with her diesel engines that restricted her speed to 9 knots. The tanker group and its escort proceeded at 9 knots for half an hour, before Wenzel (U 231) decided to throw in the towel. The perplexed Koppenhagen, who had not anticipated such an eventuality, decided his best plan was to send *Jaguar* back as escort for U 231, and the two vessels parted from the remainder of the flotilla at 1020 hrs, Koppenhagen sending a signal to Group West to announce the change of plan.

Visibility in broad daylight was good and sea strength two to three. A fishing fleet, presumably Spanish, was sighted just after midday, and at about 1330 the radar receiver on *Moewe* gave a clear warning. The other boats were warned, flak guns were manned, but by 1400 the all-clear was given. Speed of the group was still 10 to 12 knots. By now the flotilla had passed the Allied line of submarine patrols stationed at about 5 degrees west. They had not been sighted. Group West announced to the flotilla at 1712 hrs that they could expect protection from seven Ju88s, but these were never seen. Indeed, the commander of *Moewe* later mentioned in his war diary that he never saw a single German aircraft, despite constant announcements from Group West about Luftwaffe patrols in the Bay. Darkness returned at about 2145.

The B-Dienst team on *Moewe* was also keeping its ear to the airwaves. They had already noted that the British were making a big aerial effort, but their report at 2200 was particularly ominous. No fewer than thirty-two Allied aircraft had been ordered for reconnaissance during that afternoon and night – this was evidently part of the Admiralty's efforts to find the U-tankers. Faced with such alarming news and the imminent threat of air attack, Koppenhagen ordered (by light signals) that double watches should be maintained on the torpedo boats. He also advised his commanders that he planned to drop off the U-boats during the early hours of the coming morning and that the torpedo boats should be ready for full speed at ten minutes' notice.

Midnight came and went without disturbance. It was now 29 July. At 0200 hrs the flotilla reached the pre-planned drop-off point (BF4981), the torpedo boats wheeled to starboard and departed. It was a clear, starlit night, which had allowed very precise navigation and visibility was about 2 kilometres. Sea strength was three, with 'middle-high' waves. The three torpedo boats, now unencumbered by the slower U-boats, enjoyed a leisurely cruise at 24 knots back to La Pallice. The B-Dienst on *Moewe* reported at 0800 that there remained a high level of British aerial activity, but it appeared to have no special focus. The U-tankers could not yet have been discovered. Indeed, when they got home the B-Dienst reported their belief that there was no Allied air activity to the east of 9 degrees west.

The torpedo boats had maintained W/T silence until they were well clear of the point where they had detached the U-boat group, but at 0922 on the 29th they had signalled: 'From 5th Torpedo-boat Flotilla to Group West. Detached three U-boats at 02.00 in BF4981, top left, as planned. Shall be at "444" at 18.00.' This signal was decrypted by British Intelligence, who within hours had moved their best piece, Walker's 2nd Support Group, to an interception point with the U-boats on their giant chess board. At 1300 hrs on the same day, Walker's group was ordered north to position 46.15N 11W.

We have to this point been following documentary evidence established from warship war diaries. It is now, at 0200 hrs on the 29th, that the sequence of events, which can only be put together from survivors of the U-tankers, becomes confused until we pick up documentary evidence from Allied aircraft and warships in the morning of the 30th. Today, survivors of U 462 are quite certain that the boats crossed the Bay of Biscay mostly submerged, but on the surface to recharge their batteries during daylight, in accordance with current standing orders. The same story was recounted by one of their wounded officers, the repatriated Oberleutnant zS Jarolin, to U-boat Command when he returned to Germany. Then the three U-boats made a submerged passage during the night of 29/30 July, planning to regroup at an agreed rendezvous further west in the Bay. This depleted all the boats' batteries, but especially those of U 462, whose batteries had been weakened for months. However, Stiebler himself stated emphatically after the war that he had planned that all the U-boats should travel on the surface during the night to recharge their batteries. This account has received wide circulation, requires Stiebler to have flagrantly disobeyed standing orders for passage though the Bay of Biscay and is almost certainly wrong.

The boats joined together at the rendezvous in daylight and Stiebler later claimed that he had planned for the group to continue submerged (against orders). But U 462 reported that her batteries were not recharging at a sufficient rate, so the boats started to make the daylight passage of the Bay on the surface and continued in line abreast formation relying on their new anti-aircraft guns for their safety.

One cannot help but wonder what effect his last attempts, ended by air attack, to get into the Atlantic must have had on the mind of Vowe, who, like von Wilamowitz-Moellendorf of U 459 and Stiebler of U 461, had been newly promoted. He had proved himself to be courageous and determined, albeit unlucky and twice criticized by Doenitz for failure to follow standing orders. Was he prepared this time to go on at all costs?

The boats proceeded on a south-westerly course with all crew members wearing uninflated lifejackets (another standing order while in the danger area of the Bay of Biscay). The gun crews were at their stations. Seven tons of flak ammunition were available to each boat. Below decks, the tankers' resident doctors made sure that all was in order, in case bullet wounds needed to be treated. U 461 was in the front as the command boat. To the left and behind cruised U 504. To the right and behind ran the errant U 462. The boats cut a pretty V-formation as they traversed the surface of the Bay of Biscay under a sky that was almost clear – there was straggling cloud, visibility was about 6 miles with fog patches at 800 feet. The wind was 240 degrees at 17 knots, while the sea strength was moderate.

To the north-west of the U-boats, Walker's 2nd Support Group had arrived at its Admiralty appointed position at about 0100 hrs and was now sweeping slowly to the south-east, course 149 degrees. It is puzzling to note that the support group obtained an H/F D/F fix at 0914, since the reconstructed war diaries do not record any messages transmitted by the U-boat group. It is possible that Walker picked up another U-boat, transmitting coincidentally on about the same bearing as the U-tankers. Whatever the explanation, the support group headed towards the bearing.

It was at 0957 that Liberator 'O' (Pilot Officer Irving) of British Coastal Command Squadron 53 sighted the U-boats as they proceeded across the surface. The Liberator had already been airborne for over five hours. Irving sent a sighting report to headquarters, but the position given was 80 miles too far south. U 461 issued her first signal to base: '10.00. Aircraft shadowing.' The message was pinpointed by the 2nd Support Group with H/F D/F, and the ships changed course to 225 degrees. The south-westward movement of the U-boats had left the support group a little behind as they closed from the north.

At 1010 hrs Sunderland 'R' (Pilot Officer White) of 228 Squadron, which had been flying for seven hours, also sighted the U-boats and signalled the correct position to its base. At headquarters, Coastal Command believed that two U-boat groups had been located, but the confusion would soon become clarified. The gun crews of the U-tankers could reach White's plane and opened fire on it. White dodged quickly out of gun range and circled at about 3,000 metres range, transmitting homing signals.

Korvettenkapitaen Stiebler had not been unduly worried when the first aircraft appeared. His boats could summon a huge amount of anti-aircraft fire and he had no doubt that a single lumbering bomber posed little threat. But when White's Sunderland circled, sending out homing signals (detected by U-boat Command in France and by the tanker's own radio room), Stiebler sent a second message at 1015: 'Two aircraft shadowing.' These messages were transmitted on the frequency reserved for Atlantic U-boats, and were not decrypted until as late as 15 August. There were presently Irving's Liberator and White's Sunderland in the vicinity. It would now be very difficult for the U-boats to dive without facing an attack while they were at their most vulnerable, at the moment of submergence when the guns were not manned and the aircraft had an easy point at which to aim. Moreover, the 2nd Support Group got an excellent H/F D/F fix on the transmission and changed course again in order to intercept.

Did Stiebler miss a chance for the U-boats to dive after they had been located by aircraft? We have already shown that U 504 was not intended as an escort for the U-tankers, but there is no reason why she should not now have been appointed as such. U 462 could dive, covered by the flak of U 461 and U 504. Then U 461 could dive, covered by U 504. This might have been tough on U 504, but there were already standing orders that an attack boat could not submerge until a U-tanker had reached a safe depth. Why did Stiebler not take this option? The slow diving time of a U-tanker (sixty seconds to 30 metres) must have acted as a deterrent. Moreover, to take the gun crews below would require a further minute, while the submergence of the U-tanker would be marked by the passage of air bubbles blown from the diving tanks. After the war, Stiebler wrote that he considered that the U-tankers lacked sufficient time to dive, but he did not allow for a surface defence by U 504. Another explanation might be a survivor's complaint that the U-tankers were so slow underwater that they could not escape hunting warships. Yet U-tankers managed this on several other occasions. The only alternative was to continue on the surface as more Allied aircraft appeared, while hoping that the Luftwaffe would ride to the rescue, like the US cavalry in the best cowboy films. But this would take time to organize in France, as we shall see. After a third aircraft approached the U-boat group, it was probably too late to dive.

Shortly afterwards, a Catalina flying boat 'K' of 210 Squadron, which had been operating in close conjunction with Captain Walker and the 2nd Support Group in the Bay of Biscay, and was engaged in making a systematic sweep of the local area, also came upon the U-boat group. It too gave a sighting report (1049 hrs) and after ten minutes rushed back towards Walker's ships, guiding them towards the scene of the beleaguered U-boats. The Admiralty had stationed the support group wisely. When the first sighting report was given, the ships must have been within 50 miles of the U-boats. The German lookouts had seen the Catalina and Stiebler sent another message: '10.52. Stand in fight with three enemy aircraft.' Ominously, his radio room now reported that warships could be heard closing fast.

A stray Ju88 had approached and chased off White's Sunderland at about 1045, which jettisoned its depth-charges as it raced for the nearest cloud cover. But an American Liberator 'A' (Pilot Officer Leal) of 19 Squadron had been guided in by White's homing signals, and White's Sunderland itself returned after shaking off its aerial predator. Both reached the U-boat group at about 1115, more or less coinciding with reassuring news from FdU West: '11.19. Nine Ju88 long-range fighters arriving over U-boats at about 14.00, while conducting fighter-sweep.' Well, fairly reassuring. The boats had nearly three hours to wait for their air protection and the Allied air pressure was building up all the time. The same message told the U-boats that they should split up if naval forces came into view. Above the U-boats the three circling aircraft, a British Liberator, an American Liberator and a British Sunderland, tried unsuccessfully to contact one another with a view to mounting a co-ordinated assault. White's weaponless Sunderland, low on fuel, gave up the attempt and headed for base at about 1133.

At 1125, a British Halifax 'B' (Pilot Officer Biggar) of Coastal Command 502 Squadron was vectored in, prompting U 462 to inform U-boat Command: '11.33. Four aircraft shadowing.' Walker's ships got a fix on the transmission and turned course to 243 degrees. The sloops were now less than 30 miles away from the encircled U-boat group. Again, attempts to establish radio contact between aircraft proved to be fruitless and the impatient Biggar decided to try his luck with the new 600lb anti-submarine bombs that his Halifax carried. The bombs were designed to be dropped from a great altitude with the equally new Mark XIV bombsight. As Biggar made his decision, the circling aircraft were joined by another Halifax, 'S', from 502 Squadron (the pilot was a Dutchman, van Rossum), also bearing the 600lb bombs. Van Rossum had been another to respond to White's homing signals. A new note of desperation crept into Stiebler's messages to U-boat Command. No longer were the U-boats being 'shadowed'. Instead: '11.40. Group stands in fight with five enemy aircraft. Please send air cover.' The circling aircraft were joined by Sunderland 'U' of 461 Squadron, piloted by an Australian, Marrows, at 1148. The latter Sunderland was short of fuel after a prolonged patrol off the west coast of Spain, but had been diverted to the U-boat group. The U-boats were now surrounded by Irving's Liberator, Leal's Liberator, Biggar's Halifax, van Rossum's Halifax and Marrows' Sunderland. The aircrews all observed the tremendous flak barrage that was put up whenever any aircraft strayed too close to the U-boats.

Biggar's Halifax then (1148 hrs) bore in at 1,600 feet, much higher than conventional depth-charge attacks on a U-boat, but was met by withering fire from the U-boats, which were zigzagging at high speed. U 462 had manned her forward 37mm cannon, a clear sign that the crew had no immediate plan to submerge. He dropped all three of his 600lb bombs onto a U-boat that had become slightly separated from the others (it is not clear which, probably U 462), but all overshot by some 70–100 metres. The Halifax survived with only slight damage to the starboard elevator. The other aircraft continued to circle as they watched for the spray to fall away. The U-boats were making high-speed, clockwise circling turns, as can be seen from surviving photographs taken from the air.

The crews of the U-boats could make out the distinct sight of smoke on the horizon as Walker's 2nd Support Group ploughed in at full speed. Walker, too, had seen the explosions on the horizon and his ships were now making their maximum 18.5 knots. After the war, German survivors supposed that the aircraft immediately all attacked to prevent the boats from diving, but there is no indication of this in Coastal Command records and, as already stated, communications between the aircraft were close to non-existent. Van Rossum estimated, from his elevated position, that the sloops of the support group were less than 20 miles from the U-boats and he decided to attack at once. However, he would drop only one bomb at a time, in case the U-boats then cleared their gun decks and tried to submerge – he did not want to be short of bombs if this happened. He chose as his target the unfortunate U 462, which had become a little separated from the other boats, and flew in at 150 knots at the high altitude of 3,000 feet from which he could drop his 600lb bombs singly with little disturbance from flak. At about 1158, van Rossum's Halifax dropped one bomb onto U 462 that landed close to the tanker's stern. Smoke was observed pouring out of the conning tower.

This single bomb, dropped with uncanny accuracy, had actually landed just alongside the starboard side of the rear of the U-tanker, where the explosion caused a mortal wound. The rudder was damaged and the boat was forced to travel in circles. The aft torpedo hatch was buckled by the force of the blast and therefore U 462 could no longer submerge. As her stern slowly flooded and water crept into the engine room, her crew prepared to abandon ship.

The five sloops of the 2nd Support Group sighted the U-boats at 1200 hrs and at 1204 Walker characteristically and memorably gave the order 'Hoist General Chase', a command (by flags) for each ship to try to chase any target of a retiring enemy. The order had only rarely been given before in the history of the Royal Navy: for example, when Admiral Drake pursued the ships of the Spanish Armada through the English Channel in the sixteenth century, and again when Admiral Nelson defeated Napoleon's fleet at the Battle of the Nile early in the nineteenth century. Walker's fame was assured even if he never sank another enemy vessel.

Although van Rossum's crew had sighted Walker's ships from his greater altitude, he was unable to communicate the fact to the other circling aircraft. If they had known, they might have continued their watch, shepherding the U-boats into the eager hands of Walker's sloops (the U-boats could not dive without first clearing their gun decks, when the aircraft could have attacked without facing any counter fire), but some of the aircraft were already very low on fuel, especially Marrows' Sunderland. All feared the imminent arrival of Ju88s. Van Rossum's result motivated the remaining aircrews to take their turns. Without any coordination, or agreed plan, Irving, Leal and Marrows attacked at once at about 1200 hrs.

Irving's Liberator led the charge, concentrating on the starboard boat, U 462. Leal's American Liberator homed in on the lead boat, U 461, both aircraft at low level. Marrow's Sunderland began a run in but was driven back by the terrific flak barrage. Marrows reported later that the shrapnel rattled like hail off the fuselage of his Sunderland; the 20mm cannon shells were set to explode at a predetermined range. To counter this defensive fire, his Sunderland mounted forward only a single light machine gun that had a magazine of precisely 100 rounds. Marrows made a circle, then bore in again on U 461 at just 50 feet, hoping not to be noticed while wave-hopping – a flying boat was particularly suited to this tactic.

Irving's depth-charges all missed their target and the aircraft was heavily damaged by the defensive fire from U 462. Irving decided at once that he had to make for the nearest safe landing place, which happened to be neutral Portugal (Spain was closer, but was too pro-German. The aircrew might not be repatriated.) Leal's aircraft now attracted all the fire from the gunners of U 461, whose Vierling and 20mm cannon followed the giant Liberator round. The other pilots later credited Leal with deliberately trying to draw off the flak from their aircraft.

Meanwhile, Marrows' Sunderland was still unobserved, skimming above the waves at 50 feet towards U 461. The pilot had carefully chosen an approach angle such that the other U-boats could not fire upon his aircraft owing to the intervening bulk of his target, U 461. At the very last moment, the latter's gun crews observed the threat and began to turn their weapons. According to survivors' accounts, Stiebler also wanted to turn the boat, but was hemmed in by the proximity of the uncontrollable U 462. In any case, it was all too late. At a range of just 400 metres, the front gunner of the Sunderland, a crack shot, sprayed his 100 rounds at the U-boat crew.

The unfortunate exposed members of U 461 were swept by a murderous hail of lead as their weapons rotated. The mount of the Vierling was hit and the multiple guns would no longer turn. Gun director Alex cranked the foot pedal frantically, while his loader was killed beside him. Alex ran to the conning tower to get a replacement pedal part, but found that blood was coming out of his left side. He got permission from Stiebler to go below for attention and started back to the tower. Another gunner, Momper, found that the supply of ammunition to the Vierling had suddenly ceased. On the conning tower the steering officer, Obersteurmann Klimaszewski, was hit in the chest and head and stumbled into the tower. He was attended by medical orderly Hoeffken, but died in the arms of the battle-steersman Rochinski, who briefly left the rudder to place his jacket under Klimaszewski's head before returning to steer the boat. It was at about this time that Stiebler seems to have shouted down a new, desperate appeal for air protection. The order was passed through to the radio room, but does not appear to have been received by U-boat Command. Signalman Korbjuhn was firing the single 20mm cannon from the conning tower, but his weapon ran out of ammunition as the Sunderland reached 100 metres. Bullets whined all around him as he shouted for reloads, but his No. 2 had, like that of the Vierling, collapsed dead by his side.

As the Sunderland overflew U 461, Marrows released seven of the eight shallow-set Mark XI Torpex depth-charges that the aircraft carried (the eighth was kept as a reserve). It was an excellent straddle, with the depth-charges spaced at 20 metres apart. Three of the depth-charges fell far enough away not to be noticed, but two fell just to the port of the conning tower, and the other two just to the starboard side. It was the last that did the damage, for the U-tanker was turning to starboard as they sank to their pre-set depth and ran right over them as they exploded. From above, a crew member of Marrows' Sunderland calmly pointed his camera backwards out of the galley window and took a picture as U 461 disappeared under a cloud of spray.

U 461 shook with the explosions and was then lifted bodily out of the water. As she settled again, Stiebler shouted into the boat: 'Damages to boat?' At once gunner Alex, still on deck and moving to the conning tower for treatment to his wound, yelled: 'Boat is cutting [sliding] under!' Stiebler shouted immediately 'Everyone out!', but the boat sank like a stone still at full speed. Marrows' stern gunner reported that the tanker had broken in half as the aircraft zigzagged wildly to dodge the flak from the other boats. Later, Coastal Command would log that U 461 had sunk at 1155 (the fascinated spectator, Walker, recorded 1206 hrs).

The stricken tanker sank so fast that not one of the crew on deck was able to jump clear, before being either washed overboard or half-submerged as water poured into the conning tower. The fact that all the survivors were wearing lifejackets from the outset undoubtedly saved their lives. The lifejackets were inflated and crew members found themselves spread over a distance of some 50 metres. Rochinski had clambered out from the conning tower against an inrush of water, preceded by one of the camera team, but the latter probably could not operate his lifejacket and later disappeared. No one else had the time to follow Rochinski out of U 461.

Van Rossum had gone round again and dropped a second large bomb from 2,000 feet at 1205. Again U 462 was the target. Despite terrific flak at the lower altitude, none damaged the Halifax and the target disappeared beneath spray as the bomb exploded some 80-100 metres astern. U 462 continued in a wild circle.

Leal's Liberator attacked again, this time at low level, onto the un-damaged U 504. But accurate shooting by one of the surviving boats (U 462 later took the credit) hit the bomber's depth-charge release gear so that the charges would not drop. At about the same time van Rossum's Halifax dropped its third and last 600lb bomb onto U 462 from 2,000 feet. It missed narrowly by some 40 metres, but the earlier attacks had already wrecked the boat. U 462 came to a standstill and her crew began to abandon ship. Leal's Liberator tried a third time to attack, but this time the depth-charges could not even be jettisoned from the damaged release gear. The aircrew concentrated instead on taking photographs of the scene below.

By now the oncoming sloops of the 2nd Support Group were less than 5 miles away and began firing (1205 hrs) on the remaining U-boats. The encircling aircraft were momentarily confused as shell splashes rose around the targets. When they realized what was happening, they abandoned their attacks and left the vicinity with alacrity. U 504 immediately dived, still covered by protective fire from U 462, and reached temporary safety beneath the waves. Van Rossum had initiated the aerial assault and he had also dropped the last bomb. It was all over in just sixteen minutes.

The situation on U 462 was desperate. Her flak gunners remained at their posts but had almost run out of ammunition. The 37mm cannon was down to its last forty-eight shells. The control room (beneath the conning tower) was knee-deep in spent 20mm cartridges and the boat could not be dived. Vowe ordered the diving vents to be opened – it was essential that the British should not be able to board the damaged boat and perhaps steal its secrets or its Enigma codes – but then two shells landed. Walker later claimed hits on U 462 at 1213 from a range of just 1,350 metres. The hits determined Vowe to abandon ship. One gunner had been killed by aircraft fire, two seriously wounded crewmen were transferred into rubber dinghies and the remainder of the crew jumped into the dinghies as their tanker sank. U 462 sank on an even keel with smoke still issuing from the conning tower. Deep underwater there was a loud detonation, leading the survivors to speculate that the batteries had exploded. Wreckage rose to the surface. Coastal Command logged the sinking at 1210, Walker recorded 1214, while the survivors of U 462 observed that their wristwatches had suddenly stopped at 1212–1214 hrs.

From the air, Marrows and his crew watched the struggling survivors of U 461 with sudden compassion. The Sunderland flew low over the U-boatmen and dropped a rubber dinghy. Stiebler at once swam over to it, managed to find the compressed air cylinder underwater and inflated the boat. The wounded survivors of his U-tanker were placed within the dinghy, while Stiebler and the remaining crew clung on to the ropes at the sides. There were only fifteen of them in all.

Meanwhile, Walker and the 2nd Support Group had arrived (1230 hrs) having expended in total 121 rounds of 4-inch ammunition. Van Rossum had signalled to the sloops that one U-boat had managed to submerge and the group at once deployed an appropriate search pattern, a 'square patrol', to find the escapee. U 504 was first located by Asdic at 1234 when *Kite* dropped ten depth-charges at settings of 90 metres and 45 metres. *Wren* fired another pattern six minutes later, but contact was lost in the underwater disturbances. When Asdic contact was re-established, it proved to be difficult to maintain. It became clear, firstly that the escaped U-boat was too agile to be a tanker, and secondly that it had gone very deep. Walker deployed his ships again to start a more systematic search. When contact was finally firmly re-established at 1332, Walker's own ship, *Kite*, first dropped another ten depth-charges set for 105 and 165 metres,

Woodpecker repeated the treatment at 1403 and then *Kite* directed 'creeping attacks' on the submerged U-boat. First, the sloop *Woodpecker* attacked (1458 hrs) with twenty-two depth-charges set for 150 metres and 230 metres. When the boiling sea had settled, oil was seen on the surface. At 1542 Walker directed *Wild Goose* to drop more deep-set depth-charges. After this, Asdic contact with U 504 was lost.

The 'creeping attack', deep depth-charges were dropped at a distance of only some 500 metres from the survivors of U 461 and U 462, some of whom were still immersed in the water clinging to the side of Marrows' dinghy. This was apparent to Walker and his crew, but the Germans would just have to take their chances. When the first explosives went off 200 metres below, the shock waves severely affected the men in the water. Stiebler later recounted how his eyes had started from their sockets with every explosion and his chest was crushed by the pressure; he would never fully recover from these shock-induced injuries. Fortunately for the floating survivors of U 461 and U 462, the second creeping attack sufficed to destroy the submerged U 504. Oil, wreckage and human remains came bubbling to the surface and the depth-charge attacks were halted while boats were lowered (1640 hrs) to examine the evidence. Walker supposed, correctly, that U 504 had been sunk and recorded the sinking at 1543 hrs. There were no survivors.

The sloops now returned to pick up Stiebler, Vowe and the other survivors from the U-tankers at about 1800, consistent with the survivors' estimate that they spent five to eight hours in the water before rescue; no doubt it felt much longer. HMS *Woodpecker* took on board the survivors from U 461, while the sloops *Kite* and *Wren* picked up the former crew of U 462. All would be landed in England.

At 1310 hrs FdU West asked U 461 to transmit homing signals for air protection but this and further requests went unanswered. After the war, Hessler of the U-boat Command staff, who wrote an annotated commentary on the U-boat Command war diary for the British Admiralty, reckoned that the nine Ju88s promised as protection had possessed insufficient fuel to arrive. However this does not fit with signals from FdU West. The aircraft had had enough time to fly out from France and remain overhead for at least one hour, but navigation by dead reckoning over the featureless sea was difficult, and without homing signals from U 461 the Ju88s probably flew to the wrong area. On 1 August, Doenitz ordered the U-boats to show a passage signal (that they had got through the Bay of Biscay) at the earliest opportunity. Two days later, U-boat Command ordered the boats to show their positions at once. No reply was received.

The Allied aircraft also turned for home, except Irving's Liberator that had had to divert to Portugal, where it was written off after a crash-landing. This was the only loss that the U-boats had managed to inflict on their opponents. In all, 109 men lost their lives from the U-boat group, whose last messages spelled disaster to U-boats in the Atlantic urgently in need of refuelling:

Attacked by aircraft. Sinking 46N 10W. U 461
Aircraft bombs. Sinking 46N 10W. U 462
Attacked. Depth-charges. Sinking at 46N 10W. U 504*

The tragic outcome of this one-sided contest fascinated U-boat Command for many months to come. A long account of the action from foreign sources was appended to the last war diary of U 461, as was the report of a repatriated crewman. Many years later, Dudley Marrows, who had sunk U 461 (by coincidence he was flying aircraft 'U' of 461 Squadron), took pains to look up his former adversary and Stiebler made a number of trips to Australia. Stiebler died in 1991.

British Intelligence must have been grateful for the opportunity to question no fewer than three important U-tanker crews captured within a week. Their one previous opportunity had been with U 464, sunk eleven months previously. All the crews were reckoned to be of good quality and Stiebler (U 461) particularly impressed with his intelligence and security consciousness. Vowe (U 462) was adjudged worthy, but dull, while von Wilamowitz-Moellendorf (U 459) was not available since he had deliberately gone down with his ship.

As a result of this disaster and the loss of a large number of other U-boats crossing the Bay in groups, Doenitz cancelled all group sailings on 2 August, and ordered that all inward-bound U-boats should hug the Spanish coast (within Spanish territorial waters) all the way in to base. In the month of July and the first two days of August, no fewer than sixteen U-boats had been sunk in the Bay.

On the same day, Doenitz ordered all U-boats to turn off their Metox radar search receivers. His specialists had demonstrated that Metox did indeed give off a radio emanation that could be detected by a suitable receiver at a range of up to 50 miles, and U-boat Command jumped understandably to the conclusion that Metox was responsible for the previously unexplained sudden attacks on U-boats by aircraft at night. A new, non-radiating radar search receiver for the 150cm wavelengths, called W. Anz (also known as 'Hagenuk', after the name of the manufacturer), was ordered for earliest delivery. Meanwhile, U-boats at sea had to rely on their lookouts' eyes to detect an incoming aircraft. This may have been a blessing in disguise, since they could no longer be caught unawares by aircraft fitted with 10cm radar.

---

*This information is given in Werner's *Iron Coffins* (1972, Pan Books). It does not appear in original documents, but is retained here to illustrate the stunning impact that news of the tanker sinkings had on the men at sea.

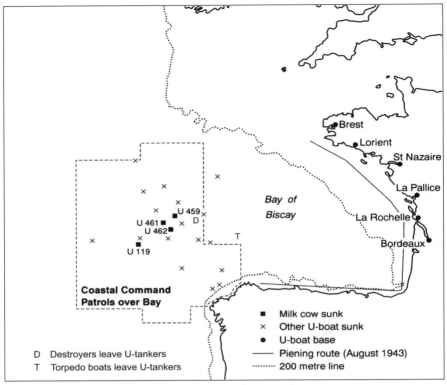

Map 12-1. Sinkings of U-boats in the Bay of Biscay, 1 June–2 August 1943.

The loss of so many U-tankers between May and August caused U-boat Command to order all U-boats leaving Germany to refuel at Norway before heading into the Atlantic. The few U-boats leaving on patrol from France in August crept out along the edge of the Spanish coast, travelling individually and with strict orders to come to the surface for the minimum time each night for recharging batteries. Meanwhile Doenitz kept most of the U-boats in their Biscay pens, awaiting the arrival of W. Anz.

Chapter 13

Disaster in the Atlantic

June to August 1943

In June, Doenitz despatched U-boats to a variety of different theatres, in an effort to maintain the volume of sinkings of merchant ships while the convoys in the North Atlantic remained unmolested. Each U-boat was given a large segment of the ocean in which to operate, in the hope that the Allies would not be tempted to reinforce their defences in that area. Moreover, the Type VIID U-minelayer U 214 laid mines off Dakar, sinking one ship (6,507 tons). The *Trutz* group was also formed at the beginning of June south of the Azores, where it was hoped that only weakly defended convoys would be found. The group was to be refuelled by U 488.

We left the brand-new tanker U 488 (Oberleutnant zS Bartke) heading from Germany towards her first fuelling rendezvous (Chapter 11). By 7 June she was at her fuelling zone west of the Azores, and was at that time the only milk cow on station. U 170, U 535 and U 536 were ordered to give up their fuel to U 488 and then to return home.

The U-minelayer U 119 (Kapitaenleutnant von Kameke) was also heading for the same fuelling rendezvous after her successful mining mission off Halifax in May. U-boat Command evidently had hopes of repeating the earlier successes of her sister ship U 116 against enemy shipping. Two messages told U 119 to expect named British ships along her line of march – a credit to the decryption skills of B-Dienst – but neither seems to have been located (7 and 10 June). U 119 had previously transferred 160 tons of fuel to four U-boats in May, see Chapter 11.

U 488 supplied a total of fourteen U-boats, predominantly of the *Trutz* group, between the 7th and the 15th, including some medical visits by her doctor, and she moved from position to position to accommodate her 'clients'. There were no untoward incidents and the U-boats formed three patrol lines from the 16th.

U 119 appeared on the 11th and von Kameke was asked by Bartke, the junior officer, if he would kindly help with the refuelling of other U-boats in this area. But U 119 had been ordered by U-boat Command to dump her

147

remaining oil onto one of the other boats and return home at best speed. U 119 actually refuelled U 603 before departing and von Kameke reported to U-boat Command that he was homeward-bound on 14 June. The subsequent fate of U 119 was described in the previous chapter.

Some of the new encryptions of U-boat rendezvous areas were giving trouble to supplier and supplied alike, and Bartke at one point was forced to play a hunch about the intended new rendezvous square. His choice was vindicated with further orders from U-boat Command. Eight more U-boats were refuelled by U 488 at the new rendezvous close in to the west of the Azores between 23 and 30 June. In addition, two Type IX boats, U 536 (Schauenberg) and U 170 (Pfeffer), aided in the refuelling, which included the transfer of some spare parts.

Despite the high hopes of U-boat Command, the *Trutz* group's strength was slowly chiselled away by the escort carrier groups in the area without the U-boats achieving any reasonable success. The pack was ordered east on 21 June, dissolved on the 29th, and the survivors patrolled west of Gibraltar.

U 488 started for her French base, having sold out on 1 July. She crossed the Bay of Biscay submerged, surfacing only long enough to recharge her batteries, and thus avoided all air attacks. She arrived at Bordeaux on 10 July to hearty congratulations from Admiral Godt, since Bartke had refuelled no fewer than twenty-one U-boats and provided aid to a further five.

The fact that U-boats were now being forced to operate further and further afield to try to avoid the Allied defences naturally meant that more fuel was required. The longer-ranged Type IX boats could operate as far away as Brazil without too much difficulty, but the shorter-ranged Type VII boats, hitherto the 'workhorses' of the Atlantic, needed guaranteed supplies even to reach the Caribbean if they were not to be hopelessly stranded. On 6 July, Doenitz reminded all U-boats heading into the South Atlantic of the need to save fuel by economical cruising when out of reach of shore-based aircraft – they had to retain as much fuel as possible for operations in their patrol areas. Moreover, the lack of tankers meant that only a few of the boats could expect to be refuelled on their homeward passage.

Owing to the shortage of tankers at sea in June and July, Doenitz decided to make more use of the Type XB minelayers in a refuelling capacity, after first deploying them as part of a larger minelaying effort. The first to depart was U 119 at the end of May. Her deployment was described in Chapter 11 and her homecoming fate in Chapter 12. She would be followed by U 118 (end of May) and U 117 (July).

Many U-boats of the ordinary attack types were also used for minelaying at this time, since it was a relatively safe way of disrupting Allied shipping. In all, only three minelaying operations were successfully carried out in

June and July (U 119, fifty-five mines off Halifax, Canada; U 230 and U 566 (Type VIIC), together twenty mines off Chesapeake. The latter were laid too deep to be effective and were not, indeed, ever discovered), while some of the other U-boats concerned were sunk while engaged in refuelling others, or receiving fuel, in the vicinity of the Azores. Thus U 607 (Type VIIC) was sunk in the Bay of Biscay shortly after starting her mission to lay mines off Kingston, Jamaica (13 July), while her sister ship U 613 was sunk by a US destroyer on her fourth war cruise south of the Azores on the 23rd, en route to lay mines off Jacksonville, USA. U 373 (Type VIIC) was damaged on 24 July by aircraft from the *Santee* carrier group while en route to mine Port Lyautey (north of Casablanca). U 107 (Type IXB) then laid twelve mines off Charleston Harbour on the night of 26/27 August before attacking shipping with torpedoes that turned out to be defective. The mines were laid outside the main shipping channel and were found only by a routine sweep on 20 September. U 107 returned safely to base. The results of this minelaying effort may have been disappointing to the Germans, who considered the mines to have been defective or wrongly placed, but it caused the Allies to concentrate considerable forces to the east coast of the USA.

On the Allied side, the surplus of warships enabled them to form 'hunting groups' of several destroyers centred on an escort carrier. Using intelligence based on the interception of wireless signals by H/F D/F or decryption, the hunting groups were able to scour the approximate replenishment areas of the U-boats. The Americans, who supplied the majority of the carrier groups, were all for sinking the milk cows at once, but Slessor, the Chief of British Coastal Command, managed to persuade them to sink the tankers over a period of months so as not to reveal the source of their information to the Germans. The Americans had formed an unusual shore-based command in May, called the '10th Fleet' for reasons of secrecy, under the command of Admiral Ernest J. King. Its purpose was to direct the carrier groups against the North Atlantic U-boats with information from cipher decryption.

U 118 (Korvettenkapitaen Czygan), a Type XB minelayer, had started her fourth war operation on 27 May. She carried mines aboard to be laid off Halifax, Canada, as part of the larger minelaying strategy then being pursued by U-boat Command. By June she was safely in the Atlantic and was, like U 460 (Kapitaenleutnant Schnoor), conveniently close to the badly shot-up U 758 (Kapitaenleutnant Manseck) that had been attacked from the air on the 8th shortly after reporting convoy UGS.9 – see previous chapter. On 9 June, both cows were ordered by U-boat Command to go to the assistance of Manseck, who was met by U 118 on the same day. These orders were deciphered by the '10th Fleet' on 11 June, complete with the rendezvous square. On the 10th, U 460 joined the other two U-boats at the rendezvous.

U-boat Command now exchanged another torrent of signals, many of which were deciphered by Allied Intelligence or intercepted by H/F D/F, ordering U 460 to provide U 118 with fuel and then to make for yet another rendezvous. U 758 was to tag along. U 460 therefore provided U 118 with 50 tons of oil and U 118 then steered for her principal fuelling rendezvous (30.45N 33.45W) in mid-Atlantic, where it was intended that she should replenish the outward-bound U 530, U 172, U 572 and U 759 between 12 and 16 June. The rendezvous was selected with special care by U-boat Command, well away from any shipping routes and well out of the reach of land-based bombers. But the carrier *Bogue* and three destroyers were closing fast.

On 12 June, U 118 was surprised by eight aircraft from the *Bogue*. She dived, was straddled by four depth-charges, returned at once to the surface and her crew manned the guns. Lacking the new heavy anti-aircraft guns being fitted to other U-boats at this time, she mounted only four machine guns and a twin 20mm cannon. Seven aircraft became involved in the attack and the U-boat was so damaged by bombs that it was deemed to be unfit to dive. The planes strafed the guns and chased the crew round and round the conning tower; one aircraft suffered flak damage, but managed to return to the carrier. The crew finally abandoned ship, but a few sailors continued to fire the anti-aircraft weapons. Further depth-charges were dropped and one detonated the U-boat's own mines. There were only seventeen survivors from the several unlucky wounded personnel from U 758 aboard and the 55-man crew, one of whom later died. Another of the cow's survivors was subsequently repatriated to Germany where he reported the gist of the above facts to U-boat Command. Not one of the cow's officers survived. Subsequent interrogation of the survivors by the Americans gave the usual unreliable mixture of ill-remembered truths about the U-minelayer's past history. However, the most interesting conclusion was that the boat was a happy one, the commander (Czygan) was well liked, the crew were efficient and all the prisoners were too security conscious to divulge much. The crew had spent too long bathing and catching turtles, and had been taken unawares by the air attack.

U 172, commanded by the very experienced Kapitaenleutnant Emmerman, heard the bombs and reported to U-boat Command in the evening. She was ordered to search for a further twenty-four hours. On the evening of 14 June, the prudent Emmerman transmitted just one word: 'Negative.' U-boat Command issued a warning on the 13th that U-boats even in the most remote areas could expect to be hunted by carrier aircraft.

This loss considerably inconvenienced the U-boats sent into remote waters – some Type VII craft were even operating off Brazil – and a number of Type IX attack boats had to be sent to refuel them, much to the annoyance of their commanders who had not expected to brave the hazards of the Biscay crossing just to serve as a cow. The attack U-boats were ordered to transfer fuel through their fire hoses and this proved to be reasonably successful.

U 530 (Type IXC/40) was forced to serve briefly as an emergency tanker far west of the Cape Verde Islands in mid-June, after the loss of U 118. U 530 had been commissioned by Kapitaenleutnant Lange on 14 October 1942 and after joining in several wolf-pack attacks in the North Atlantic for her first cruise, the U-boat had returned to Lorient. She departed again on 29 May 1943 for a patrol planned to go deep into the South Atlantic, for which she was to be refuelled by U 118, together with U 592, U 172, U 572, U 333 and U 510, in square DG75. However, by 13 June the loss of the refueller had been assumed by U-boat Command and U 530 was appointed as the replacement next day. The rendezvous were moved in short steps in a general area some 900 miles south-west of the Azores.

U 530 supplied U 572 with 30 tons of oil and two weeks of provisions on 15 June, U 172 with 27 tons and two weeks on the 16th, U 759 with 30 tons and two weeks on the 18th, and U-transporter U 180, coming from the Indian Ocean with an important cargo, with 38 tons and two weeks of provisions on the 19th. U 572 was also given extra supplies on the same day. U-boat Command had directed that U 530 should now return to France in company with U 180, to provide an escort against aircraft. On the 30th, U 530 therefore provided flak defence for U 180 against an Allied bomber in the Bay of Biscay, and then both boats arrived safely at Bordeaux. Lange would survive two more lengthy patrols with U 530 before being appointed to an office post just two years after he had first joined his boat. The U-boat would also survive the war under a new commander, finally surrendering in Argentina.

U 460 arrived at her new rendezvous south-south-west of the Azores on 11 June, where she sighted a submarine and dived. Finally, though, she managed to meet with U 92 and the battered U 758 as prearranged. Both boats had dived and resurfaced at the rendezvous all day without being aware of each other's presence, as part of the new precautions against enemy attack. As Schnoor said: 'It's a real pig when you can't tell if a sub-marine is friend or foe as it pops up and down at the rendezvous.'

It may be recalled that U 92 had received a massive 92 tons of oil south of Greenland from U 119 only one month previously. She now needed more fuel to be sure of getting back to France and was oiled on the 12th. All three U-boats then set off together on the long journey home. Next day, U 460 decided to provide U 758 with a Metox apparatus and also made another medical visit. There appears to have been a serious medical emergency, since both boats lay stopped together for all the next day and two injured sailors were transferred to the U-tanker. This unexpected loitering in mid-Atlantic may have saved both boats from the forces being assembled against supply boats around the Azores.

U 460 had to dive suddenly on the 15th as her Metox set gave a radar warning. She was now ordered to meet the Type VIID minelayer U 214 (Kapitaenleutnant Stock) south of the Azores. U-boat Command had become very concerned about the dangers of Allied direction-finding capabilities. Although the Germans remained ignorant of Huff-Duff, they knew that the Allies had built many shore-based direction-finding stations all around the North and South Atlantic. It seemed reasonable to suppose that together these stations could provide a reasonably accurate fix on any transmitting U-boat. Each boat was ordered to respond to another deluge of commands with the single word 'Ja'.

U 214 was supplied only with food on the 16th, the 'lost' U 92 was found again and all four U-boats were ordered to return to France together (U 460: 'Ja').

More air alarms occurred east of the Azores and the boats proceeded underwater during the hours of darkness. The air warnings worsened as the Bay of Biscay was reached, but on 22 June U 460 noted the outward passage of U 382 (Koch) which, it may be recalled, had been forced to desert the damaged tanker U 462 in the Bay at this time. U 460 met up with her escort of Sperrbrecher, two M-boats and two escort ships on 25 June, and arrived safely at Bordeaux in the evening. She had refuelled twelve other U-boats and Schnoor had proved himself to be a prudent, but able commander. U-boat Command evidently shared this view, for Admiral Godt had these words to say: 'The undertaking was, as previously, carried through with proven caution and noteworthy energy.'

On 9 June, Doenitz ordered nine U-boats supported by U 462 to head to the Indian Ocean. This was known as the 'First *Monsun* Group'. Since these U-boats were predominantly the IXC or IXC/40 types starting from France, the first boat would expect to arrive in mid-Atlantic by July. The early loss of two tankers (U 461 and U 462), described in the preceding chapter, meant that U 487 and the attack boat U 160 had to be ordered to refuel the *Monsun* group as it passed through mid-Atlantic. U 160 had previously accompanied tanker U 462 during the latter's unsuccessful June attempt to break into the Atlantic, but had herself arrived safely in mid-ocean.

U 487 (Oberleutnant zS Metz) had arrived safely in mid-Atlantic from the Bay of Biscay and by early July she was in position south of the Azores. Between July and August there were up to sixteen U-boats off the Azores, of which U 487 was able to replenish nine 600 miles south-west of the islands between 6 and 12 July. One of them was the Type IXD1 U-transporter, U 195 (Korvettenkapitaen Buchholz), returning from her patrol off Cape Town (see next chapter) and provided with just enough fuel for the most economical journey home.

U 487 had been ordered to a single rendezvous and U-boat Command further directed that no homing signals should be transmitted. Her canny commander was disinclined moreover to reveal his position with too many signals and kept W/T silence for so long that U-boat Command finally ordered U 487 to show her position at once on 10 July, doubtless fearing that she had been sunk. Her report came as a relief to U-boat Command, who had decided that U 487 should refuel the *Monsun* boats as they passed through. Their thinking was that by so doing, the *Monsun* boats would no longer have to rely on a second refuelling from surface tankers stationed in the Indian Ocean. This meant that there would now be insufficient fuel for the ordinary attack boats in mid-Atlantic, and Doenitz gloomily recorded on the 11th that the tanker situation was 'bad', that very few independently routed merchant ships were now to be found as soft targets and that the *Trutz* operation appeared to have failed. As a temporary measure, Doenitz switched refuelled U-boats to remote areas, while outward-bound boats, still not refuelled, were diverted to the closer operational zone of Freetown.

British Intelligence suffered a three-week blackout on cipher decryption early in July, but the presence of the cow had already been detected and no fewer than four American carrier groups (*Bogue, Card, Core* and *Santee*) searched the waters around 27N 37W (600 miles south-west of the Azores) for the U-tanker and its dependants. Fido was now available and the aircraft were sent out in pairs – one to force the U-boat to dive, the other to plant Fido on her tail.

On 13 July, two aircraft from the carrier *Core* surprised U 487 on the surface 720 miles south-south-west of the Azores, while the crew were amusing themselves. The bridge watch had observed a wooden box floating ahead of the tanker and Metz gave the order to bring all available empty sacks on deck in order to fill them with a strange type of cotton wool (actually gun-cotton!). This was despite the standing order of U-boat Command that no flotsam should be fished out, since it could bring about the loss of the U-boat by distraction of the watch – an order that proved to be prophetic. At about 1430 hrs U 487 was unexpectedly shot at by the fast-closing aircraft, causing the sacks loaded with gun-cotton to erupt into balls of fire all over the deck. An immediate attack with depth-charges straddled the U-tanker, causing her to make a sharp right-hand circle, losing speed and leaking oil. The main rudder was badly damaged by a bomb so that the boat was no longer manoeuvrable. The tanker was also no longer submersible due to leaks. A fire started internally and, although it was soon put out, dense smoke made repairs impossible. A leak of chlorine from damaged batteries caused the death of one of the crewmen; the remainder of the crew manned the guns and returned fire.

The 'Vierling' of U 487 was actually only a twin flak gun. Two additional dummy barrels had been fitted underneath, to deter attacking aircraft. *Core* sent four more aircraft but one was shot down, although some of the gun crew also fell at their station. When the ammunition finally failed to reach the twin gun due to flooding below, Metz gave the order 'abandon ship'. The Vierling gun crew were the last to jump into the water while Metz remained absentmindedly on the bridge and failed to observe an aircraft closing with guns firing. He was hit by several bullets and fell dead. Another straddle by four depth-charges next to the U-boat caused it to sink within five seconds, prompting the crew to give two 'Heils' from their dinghies in the water. Thirty-three survivors were rescued out of a crew of sixty-two. U 487 missed one star on 17 August and the second star on 26 April 1944. Later, U-boat Command got the full story from a repatriated prisoner of war.

U-boat Command was again behind the times in the war at sea. The *Monsun* boats received their instructions on 15 July: 'Refuel from U 462.' (U 462 had returned with damage from her aborted mission to the Azores on 6 July and would depart again with U 461 on 27 July, as we saw in the previous chapter. The timing of this message is very curious.) 'If U 462 is sunk, use U 487. Each boat is to take on forty tons of fuel and ten days of provisions. No homing signals. Every third boat is to signal the situation with the tanker after the rendezvous. U 160 is to give up its fuel to U 487.' By 18 July, U 487 had failed to answer the repeated calls from U-boat Command and was assumed missing. At once U-boat Command directed that two outward-bound boats not of the *Monsun* group, U 160 and U 155, should each provide fuel to three *Monsun* boats at separate rendezvous far west of the Cape Verde Islands, then they were to return home together. On the same day, Doenitz noted that other outward-bound U-boats could no longer be refuelled, since boats already at sea were in desperate need of replenishment.

Between the 13th and the 16th, the *Core* and *Santee* carriers between them sank a further three U-boats, mostly with Fido, including U 160. U 160 (Type IXC, Oberleutnant zS Pommer-Esche), on her sixth patrol but her commander's first, was attacked by carrier aircraft the very day after receiving her initial orders to aid U 487 with the *Monsun* boats. She dived in good time and was promptly sunk by Fido. It was not until the 20th that U-boat Command learned that U 160 had not turned up at her rendezvous.

These losses at first mystified U-boat Command until a Spanish merchant ship returned from the vicinity of the Azores stating that she had observed a large aircraft carrier in the region. The rendezvous area was consequently moved well to the west of the Azores.

U 155 was commanded by the highly experienced Kapitaenleutnant Piening – he of the Piening route from France into the Atlantic – and she surrendered her fuel to the three *Monsun* boats U 183, U 188 and U 168 between 21 and 23 July, supplying more than 200 tons of oil. The alert Piening reported to U-boat Command on 2 August that there was excessive U-boat W/T traffic before returning safely to France alone. Both U-boat and commander survived the war. The importance of experience at this time for U-boats at sea could scarcely be overstated.

154

By now, the outward-bound U516, which had been planned to refuel as one of the three *Monsun* boats from U160, had had to be ordered herself to transfer fuel to the other two boats, but only U532 arrived at the rendezvous on 26 July, U509 having been sunk two weeks previously by carrier aircraft from the *Santee*. U516 was now directed to a rendezvous with U662 (Type VII) to hand over ammunition before returning to base, but again the other boat was missing (she had been sunk on the 21st). Further losses to the *Monsun* group, in the Bay or at sea, meant that it was down to five U-boats by the time they arrived in the Indian Ocean.

There was now temporarily not a single cow available to replenish the fifty to sixty U-boats bound to or from remote theatres, so other attack boats newly out of France were assigned refuelling duties. U648, a Type VII boat, handed over some fuel on the 23rd to enable U527 (from the Gulf of Mexico) to reach France – the original plan had been for the latter boat to refuel from U487 – but the boats were surprised by *Bogue*'s aircraft. U648 managed to dive, but U527 was sunk by bombs. U648 made a long and fruitless search for U527 before reporting that the latter had disappeared. U648 had also been detailed to supply the returning U67 with fuel, but this boat too had already been sunk by carrier aircraft on the 16th. U648 managed to struggle home. Then on 30 July, U43 (Type IXB), which was returning from minelaying off Lagos and had been pressed into service as another emergency tanker, was sunk by Fido from *Santee* aircraft, just after she had refuelled U403.

By the end of July sinkings in all theatres were relatively high – forty-six ships – of which by far the majority had been sunk in the South Atlantic or Indian Ocean, but this had been achieved at a cost of thirty-eight U-boats, nearly as many as in 'Black May'. Aircraft had accounted for the majority of these and July was the last month in which OKW (German High Command of all Armed Forces) announced U-boat successes until after the Normandy invasion.

At the beginning of August British Intelligence suffered another ten-day blackout and then there were several gaps of seven to fourteen days owing to the lack of sufficient high-speed bombes for decoding Enigma. Deliveries from the USA were rushed in from August, but the entire decryption of the U-boat ciphers was finally moved to Washington, USA, in November. Since both Allies shared results as soon as they had them, there was no noticeable difference in operation. However, the rate of sinkings of the milk cows by the Americans again caused severe anxiety to British Intelligence, who feared that the Germans might guess the ciphers had been broken.

Meanwhile, many U-boats were in danger of being stranded at sea owing to lack of fuel. All attempts to get U-tankers into the Atlantic from France had failed (see preceding chapter) and the position was not eased when, on 4 August, the brand-new tanker U489 was sunk by an air patrol west of the Faeroe Islands while still on her way from Germany to her first refuelling in the Atlantic.

U 489 had been commissioned on 8 March 1943 by Oberleutnant zS Schmandt, a 34-year-old officer who had enjoyed the benefit of previous experience as an officer on U B and UD 5. After the usual working-up exercises, U 489 had departed from Kiel with the attack boat U 647 on 22 July – the same day that the ill-fated U 459 and U 117 had sailed from Bordeaux – and entered the Northern Transit area, with orders to refuel U-boats returning from the South Atlantic. But on 3 August the U-tanker was sighted on the surface by three aircraft. Intense flak kept the aircraft at bay, although the U-boat was slightly damaged by a close miss from a 100lb bomb. Then U 489 managed to dive unobserved in heavy rain. The boat remained submerged all night, while her crew listened to the propeller sounds of hunting destroyers.

Air patrols scoured her likely forward route and were rewarded at 0810 hrs the following day when a RCAF Sunderland located the U-tanker, which had been forced to surface to recharge batteries and revitalize her air. Attacking through heavy anti-aircraft fire, the aircraft's shallow-set depth-charges severely damaged the cow, which slowed and settled by the stern, just as the aircraft was shot down. HMS *Castleton* and accompanying destroyers arrived quickly and Schmandt scuttled his command. Schmandt and almost his entire crew of fifty-four, as well as three German fliers who had been rescued from their dinghy after their plane had ditched north-east of the Faeroes on 29 July, were saved (the Chief Engineer of U 489 did not survive). Of the eleven-man Sunderland crew, five failed to get out of the aircraft. The remaining six, all wounded, were rescued. U 489 had been sunk just fourteen days into her first war patrol, ironically on the same day that she had received her first refuelling instruction, with U 664. The entire operation was uncannily similar to the destruction of her sister ship U 464 one year earlier; even the latitude and longitude were virtually the same.

Attempts to maintain the U-boat pressure in remote sea theatres came to an abrupt halt at the end of July because U-boats could no longer be refuelled. The Type IXC boats could still operate for a short period before having to return to base, but use of the Type VII boats in remote waters had to be discontinued. Boats at sea had to be prematurely recalled.

On 4 August, Doenitz had noted that supplies were still available for U-boats short of fuel returning from their operational area. Next day, this had to be amended: there were 'no more reserve tankers left; only the most essential supply operations can be carried out, and then only on the outward passage.' Refuelling U-boats on the outward passage meant that they could still return at once to base if the rendezvous failed, although there inevitably had to be a reduction in long-range U-boat operations. Next day, Doenitz ordered his commanders at sea not to report too much bad news –

156

if necessary, such information should be sent by officers' cipher only. A further order required U-boats to make aircraft carriers their primary targets.

Werner, the first officer of the Type VIIC boat U 230, which had been minelaying in Chesapeake Bay, USA, has described the difficulties facing U-boats stranded at sea at this time. In the first fortnight of August, U 230 was moved repeatedly to different refuelling rendezvous with different milk cows, but each time the cow failed to turn up. The new German practice of banning wireless transmissions near to a refuelling zone meant that U-boat Command frequently no longer knew that a tanker had been sunk until it failed to answer their repeated calls. In the end, U 230 had to accept the little fuel that a sister ship, U 634, could provide, in order to reach her last refuelling rendezvous when, as we shall see, the cow finally did arrive.

The loss of U 489 had been confirmed by 11 August and Doenitz recorded that 'with the loss of U 489, the last fuel reserves for boats coming from the south are exhausted.' U 117 (Korvettenkapitaen Neumann), a Type XB minelayer, had been despatched with U 459 from France for a mining operation off Gibraltar (see previous chapter). But her mission was changed on 24 July, only two days after she had left Bordeaux, to carry out her alternative mining orders off New York so that she would be available to refuel U-boats near the Azores. U 117 arrived west of the Azores at the end of July where she was ordered to replenish, in the first instance, the U-cruiser U 177 and the much-travelled U 66 (Type IXB, Kapitaenleutnant Markworth) in CD64, about 39N 37W, well west of the Azores.

After an air attack, U 66 had suffered three dead and eight wounded, including her commander. Her inexperienced First Officer was temporarily in charge and U 66 requested assistance from a doctor.

The order from U-boat Command, on 30 July, was decoded on 1 August, although the rendezvous square could not be accurately assigned. On the same day U 117 explained the exact rendezvous point to other U-boats over the W/T, and this was also intercepted by the carrier groups. Later in the day, U-boat Command informed U 117 that U 66 was waiting for the cow at the rendezvous. On 4 August, U-boat Command transmitted the single word 'Vorsicht' ('Caution!') to U 117, but the carrier *Card* and her killer group were already patrolling the area. Early on 6 August, U 66 signalled that she had not been able to find U 117 and a new rendezvous was ordered. Oberleutnant zS Frerks of U 117 was to replace the injured commander of U 66. U 117 met U 66 later that night and the exchange of officers took place. Allied Intelligence had not yet been able to decipher the position of the revised rendezvous, but they knew enough to conduct a general search of the immediate area.

The following day, as both U-boats lay 50 metres apart, rubber dinghies paddling in the sea and oil hoses connecting both craft – in short, at the worst possible moment – aircraft from *Card* made a surprise attack, not being detected until they were within 400 metres of the boats. With orders always to sink the cow where a choice existed, the aircraft went for U 117 (visibly the larger U-boat) and dropped two depth-charges. U 66 promptly dived, while the damaged U 117 (she had been hit astern) manoeuvred erratically, pouring out dense, black smoke. U 117 had been fitted out with the new, powerful, anti-aircraft armament and her gunners returned fire vigorously but inaccurately, while several aircraft now came in to the attack. Severely damaged further by depth-charges, U 117 submerged, came back to the surface and went down again. At this point Fido was dropped onto her stern. A shockwave was seen in the water, air bubbled to the surface and U 117 was never seen again.

U 66 was still not refuelled and a new rendezvous was ordered between cow and attack boat for the 8th. W/T silence was to be maintained for a radius of 400 miles around the rendezvous. U-boat Command followed this with another stream of detailed instructions up to the 13th (after the loss of U 489, U 117 was expected to replenish fourteen U-boats, all in the same sea area south-west of the Azores), then U 117 was given one star. On the 14th, U 66, now very low on fuel, reported that she had waited two days for U 117 at a new rendezvous; furthermore, after diving at the original rendezvous she had heard two detonations, then three detonations followed by sinking noises. U 117 received her second star the same day.

The sinking of U 117 finally precipitated the fuel crisis in the Atlantic. It was clear to U-boat Command that only by using U-boats on the way out to refuel those already at sea could the latter return to base. Some U-boats had to rig sails in order to reach their rendezvous with outward-bound boats, while others were attacked from the air while wallowing helplessly on the surface. A strange by-product of these sinkings was that, as U-boat Command sought frantically for the clue to all these losses, they arrived at the conclusion that shore-based H/F D/F was giving away the approximate position of the boats, and then radar-fitted aircraft scouring the area were locating the radio aerials of U-boats transmitting at periscope depth. All boats were given warnings about this possibility on 9 August, together with instructions to keep changing W/T frequencies.

The long-range attack boats U 525 (Kapitaenleutnant Drewitz, Type IXC/40) and U 129 (Oberleutnant zS von Harpe, Type IXC) were ordered to break off their patrols and refuel other U-boats (10 August). But emergency tanker U 525 was sunk 376 miles west-north-west off the Azores on 11 August by more aircraft from the *Card* group, which strafed her forcing her to submerge, attacked her with aerial depth-charges and finally despatched her with the help of Fido. In this instance, the aircraft that had dropped the Fido was actually in a position to observe the homing torpedo as it chased the U-boat, submerged in clear water at a depth of only 10 metres, and struck the boat halfway between conning tower and stern.

There were no survivors. Only the previous day, Doenitz had warned his U-boat commanders to beware of 'new, more dangerous bombs' – the devastating effect of Fido had been observed at long range by some of his commanders. As previously, the loss of the cow was not appreciated by U-boat Command until a week after the event.

Doenitz – still unaware of the loss of U 525 – wrote on the 14th that about 400 tons of fuel would be needed to replenish boats at sea, and that U 525 and U 129 might not be able to manage it between them. U-cruiser U 847, coming from Germany, was ordered to be ready to assist, while U 760 was to take on fuel from the attack boat U 84. But U 760 reported that she had been attacked by two destroyers at the rendezvous; she crept back to Spain with severe damage and was interned early in September, while U 84 was sunk by aircraft from the carrier *Core* on 26 August.

U 129 was able to replenish four U-boats in mid-August before being ordered home on 20 August. She returned safely to France. One of these four boats was U 333, again under the command of the recuperated Kapitaenleutnant Cremer, who had volunteered as one of three 'old hands' to give a first-hand account to Doenitz of conditions at sea (the others were Kuppisch and Guggenberger). Cremer was the only one of the three to return to port. His tour was a nightmare of aircraft attacks, breakdowns and sabotage, necessitating a rendezvous with U 618 for some parts, with U 600 for others and with U 571 for a compressor. U 333 witnessed the sinking of U 487 from afar. The rendezvous with U 129 took place after U 333 had had to wait for four days and had run out of food. She finally reached France on 30 August.

The U-cruiser U 847, which had sailed from Bergen outward-bound to the Indian Ocean as the last member of the *Monsun* group, was diverted to refuel some of the stranded U-boats on 19 August. Her commander, Kapitaenleutnant Kuppisch, who had commanded attack U-boats success-fully early in the war but had then held a long, 21-month, shore appoint-ment, had been earmarked to take command of the *Monsun* group when it reached the Indian Ocean, but this had to be abandoned. As Kuppisch agreed, with a signal to U-boat Command: 'There is no other choice.'

U 847 had acquired a reputation as an unlucky boat. Commanded briefly by Kapitaenleutnant Guggenberger, then by Kapitaenleutnant Metzler, and finally by the 44-year-old Kuppisch (who had had to give up his brand-new command of U 516 after just six days), she had had three commanders, and had suffered two deaths and two injuries to her crew while still in training. She had sailed from Kiel on 5 July as an early *Monsun* boat, planning to enter the North Atlantic via the Denmark Strait between Greenland and Iceland, but had hit an unexpected iceberg on the 17th. This had caused damage, necessitating a return to Bergen for repairs and the cancellation of a planned rendezvous with another U-cruiser (U 198) near

159

the equator. U 847 sailed again early in August on her first war patrol. It would also be her last.

The course of U 847 out from Norway and into the North Atlantic had been plotted by British Intelligence throughout her cruise. This last-chance tanker acted as a magnet to every U-boat within a 1,000-mile radius as she approached her fuelling rendezvous, by far the most worthwhile target to Allied carrier groups, as can clearly be seen on the sea maps attached to contemporary U-boat reports prepared for the Admiralty (see also Map 13-1). Ten U-boats closed in on the U-cruiser!

The signals from U-boat Command were decoded on 21 August. On the same day, orders were given for seven U-boats to make for the rendezvous

Map 13-1. Late August 1943. U 847 (Type IXD2) is the last-chance tanker in the Atlantic. Most of the other U-boats are returning home. Note the complete absence of U-boats in the North Atlantic. (*Reprinted by courtesy of the Controller, The Stationery Office*)

and the message was decoded almost at once. Two carrier groups (*Card* and *Core*) were ordered by the American '10th Fleet' to converge on the rendezvous.

U 847 was able to resupply three boats without interference on the 23rd in the Sargasso Sea, west of the Azores, at about 40N 38.30W. W/T silence was ordered to be maintained for a 400-mile radius. However, U 508 reported that she had been attacked from the air just before refuelling and was in fact extremely fortunate to dodge bombs and (unbeknown to her) a Fido.

Then a rendezvous was arranged by U-boat Command for the 27th, south of the original location, between U 847, U 172 (Emmerman again, from Brazil), U 230, U 634 and U 415 (all from mid-Atlantic). Most of the U-boats had acquired a healthy respect for unannounced aircraft and, when the boats assembled together, the attack craft all had anti-aircraft gunners standing by throughout the exchange of fuel and supplies.

Not so the U-cruiser, whose commander had not been to sea since the air threat had become so deadly and who claimed not to have seen any aircraft since leaving the Denmark Strait. All four U-boats managed to replenish themselves safely from the U-cruiser and at once turned for France since they had only enough fuel for the direct homeward trip; the U-cruiser had only been able to spare them 15 to 20 tons each. U 508 was also resupplied on the same day.

U 847 then signalled to U-boat Command that refuelling was complete. Immediately Allied H/F D/F equipment pinpointed her position and within only hours of the refuelling rendezvous she was located by three aircraft from *Card* that had been hunting for the escaped U 508.

U 847 was heading at her cruising speed of 12 knots on a south-easterly course as the aircraft swept in. She put up a heavy flak barrage as the two fighters strafed her in an attempt to cause her to dive. This was successful and U 847 submerged. Now it was the turn of the third aircraft, which closed in and dropped Fido into the diving swirl. The torpedo was seen to change course onto the track of the U-boat, then there was silence. Suddenly, a mass of water blew into the sky and bubbles rose to the surface. Twenty seconds later, a 'terrific flash', 100 metres long, was seen underwater by the observers in the sky. The explosion was so loud that it was overheard by the submerged U 508, which reported the loss of U 847 (at 28.19N 37.58W) to U-boat Command. There were no survivors.

According to Cremer, U 847 sent no final signal to U-boat Command so that her loss was not immediately known. One of the refuelled U-boats, U 634, was also sunk while homeward-bound. She had what was now considered to be the misfortune of finding an Allied convoy, whose escorts soon located her with fatal consequences. The other three boats and U 508 returned safely to France.

161

Shortage of fuel effectively wound down the curtain temporarily on operations in all remote theatres, except the Indian Ocean. Doenitz noted in his war diary that the operational objective for July and August – 'the momentary use of U-boat forces for defence purposes' by tying down enemy shipping – had been achieved only at great cost. All boats had had to return home early for want of fuel, and had spent only three weeks in their operational areas, far below that known to be required for reasonable successes.

In September, there were only six U-boats on patrol in remote theatres, and the U-cruiser U 198, which was returning from the Indian Ocean and had been tasked to refuel U 847 before reaching home, instead gave up her surplus oil to U 161 so that the latter could patrol off Brazil. Up to May 1943, the Germans had lost just one U-tanker and one U-minelayer, with nearly 400 U-boats refuelled south and north of the Azores alone. By the end of August of the same year, they had lost a further six U-tankers and three U-minelayers.

Chapter 14

Refuelling in Other Theatres
1942 to 1945

U-boats were deployed at one time or another in every ocean and sea of the world, from the Arctic to the Pacific, from the Caribbean to the Black Sea. Although the North Atlantic was always the principal operational theatre, and accordingly where the biggest refuelling effort was made, refuelling was also attempted in some other areas. These are described below.

Indian Ocean, 1943–5
This operational area was the furthest of the lesser theatres from a German-controlled base and required by far the greatest effort.

The Germans had been sending blockade runners (surface ships) from Japan to France from 1940 onwards. Some 40 per cent of the world's rubber, for example, was shipped from Malaya at this time while Japan was still neutral, but Malaya was held by the British. After the Japanese had overrun Malaya, Java and surrounding areas, the Germans hoped that the Japanese would provide a shorter run for surface blockade runners directly from Malaya to Europe. However the Japanese had different ideas, insisting that the German ships should still sail from Japan with war materials to Malaya before picking up their rubber, tin and other strategic materials for Europe. The Japanese had renamed several of the ports that came under their control; thus the old Dutch Batavia in Java was renamed Djakarta, while the occupied British port of Singapore became Shonan. The Germans also used these new names.

Shortly before the German U-boat attack on Cape Town in September 1942, the Italians had proposed that their light cruiser *Eritrea*, at that time in Japanese waters, could usefully be employed to refuel Italian submarines in the Indian Ocean. This ship was really little more than a motor yacht, armed with two gun turrets, designed for the use of an Italian ambassador. However, the Japanese were unenthusiastic, reckoning that their submarines would shortly be working the same waters.

This did not transpire and early in 1943 the port of Penang, Malaya, was made available to the Germans by the Japanese as a base for U-boat operations. In March the surface tankers *Charlotte Schliemann* and *Brake* were assigned to support the U-boats, both ships having arrived in the Far East from the Atlantic in 1942 (see Table 14-2).

In April 1943, seven U-cruisers operated off South Africa and around the large island of Madagascar, running up a score of 200,000 tons between then and August. The two prototype U-cruisers, the torpedo-less Type IXD1 U-transporters (U 180 had been commissioned on 16 May 1942, U 195 on 5 September of that year) had been refitted to provide them with a similar armament to the U-cruisers, and had been used in this operation. Both had experimental engines, based on those used in motor torpedo boats, but they caused numerous teething problems resulting in eight months of trials. One, U 180 (Korvettenkapitaen Musenberg), left Germany on 9 February for a rendezvous in the Indian Ocean with the Japanese submarine I.29. She carried the Indian Nationalist leader, Chandra Bose, together with the Arab Nationalist leader Abid Hasan, goods and documents.

U 180 received 60 tons of fuel from tanker U 462 on 3 March north of the Azores before proceeding into the South Atlantic. She was diverted on the 18th to a rendezvous with an Italian submarine about halfway between Freetown (Africa) and Natal (Brazil) in order to provide medical assistance, but she was unable to locate the Italian and by the 21st was heading south again. In a short patrol off southern Africa between 5 and 20 April, U 180 sank the tanker *Corbis* (8,132 tons), but her commander was less than enthusiastic about the U-transporter's experimental engines that, apparently, 'smoked like an old coal boat'. The rendezvous with the Japanese submarine was delayed due to bad weather, but the transfer was effected on the 26th. I.29 then returned to Penang with Chandra Bose, while U 180 set course for France with 2 tons of gold aboard as well as specimens of the deadly Japanese 'Long Lance' torpedoes. Japanese torpedoes at this time were the fastest, and possessed the longest range, in the world. En route she sank a Greek ship (5,166 tons, 2 June), refuelled from the emergency tanker U 530 in mid-Atlantic in mid-June, before arriving at Bordeaux on 2 July after evading a massive British sea-and-air search and a submarine attack in the Bay of Biscay.

According to a television documentary in 1995, Chandra Bose was sent by the Japanese to foment rebellion in what was then the British colony of India, where he recruited a number of Indians for fighting on the Japanese side in Burma and other theatres. After the surrender of Japan, most of the Indians involved were pardoned. Chandra Bose himself was mysteriously killed in a Japanese air crash right at the end of the war.

U 180's position off Cape Town was taken by the other Type IXD1 U-transporter U 195 (Kapitaenleutnant Buchholz), which had sailed from Germany on 20 March 1943. U 195 managed to contribute two ships sunk (14,391 tons) and a further ship damaged to the total toll exacted by the

U-cruisers, but again her commander complained about the engines and U 195 was forced to discontinue her patrol. She met U 177 (Gysae) south of Cape Town in June in order to exchange parts and to donate a sea map, and then set off for home. After refuelling from U 487 south of the Azores in mid-July, she too returned safely to France on 23 July. On return, Buchholz wrote a detailed account of the (non-) potentialities of this type of U-cruiser.

Both U 180 and U 195 were decommissioned at Bordeaux on 30 September, partly owing to their poor condition after their long cruises, and partly because of their comparative uselessness, since they could not carry the fuel of a U-tanker or the mines of a U-minelayer, while their experimental engines lacked the long range of a Type IXD2 U-cruiser. Moreover, as Doenitz pointed out in the U-boat Command war diary, U 195 had taken a large number of torpedoes all the way to the South Atlantic and then had had to bring most of them home again after just a few days in the operational area, owing to the unreliability of her engines.

Meanwhile, the deteriorating situation in the Mediterranean had induced Italy to call most of her smaller submarines back from west France into that sea. A handful of large submarines were reckoned to be too large and unwieldy for profitable deployment there, and they remained at Bordeaux. At a conference between Hitler and Doenitz on 13 February 1943, the Fuehrer had remarked that it was essential to get more rubber by blockade running. Doenitz replied that he had planned to ask for Italy's approval to use their Atlantic submarines, which were poorly suited to operations against convoys, as blockade runners to and from the Far East. The original plan called for the Italian submarines to be loaded 'if possible' from surface ships near Madagascar in order to shorten the route. By 18 March, the Italians had agreed to the plan in principle, and they were offered a German Type VIIC U-boat for every submarine blockade runner. The Italian commander of Betasom (the organization for the Italian Atlantic submarines) turned to the task energetically and by the end of May Doenitz was able to congratulate him for his efforts. The Italian submarines had been adapted by the removal of all their deck guns, their attack periscopes and some batteries, while the torpedo tubes and ammunition lockers had been converted to store fuel to extend the boats' ranges. This inevitably meant that the submarines lacked any offensive capability, but they could carry some 150 tons of cargo each. Between 11 May and 26 August 1943 five such Italian submarines set out with cargoes of spare German torpedoes, high-grade steel, aluminium and mercury, and radar equipment for the Japanese. The *Tazzoli* and *Barbarigo* were sunk by air attack in the Bay of Biscay, but the *Giuliani*, *Cappellini* and *Torelli* survived to reach Singapore, where we shall meet them again. One had been refuelled by U 178 south-east of Madagascar in mid-August. By now, the risky original idea of loading the submarines near Madagascar had been dropped.

We left the tanker *Charlotte Schliemann* (Kapitaen Rothe) in Japan. At the end of April 1943 the *Schliemann* was given preliminary instructions to attempt a breakthrough from Japan to France with a full cargo of strategic materials, but these were soon rescinded owing to the difficulty of penetrating the Allied blockade. Instead the ship sailed to Malaya for a load of coconut oil which was taken back to Kobe (Japan). After offloading, the crew were startled to discover that the *Schliemann* was receiving supplies and diesel fuel that could only be intended for submarines. When she sailed for Singapore, the tanker had not been disturbed thus far by American submarines known to be infesting the route, but during this transition there was an attack marked clearly by the torpedo tracks racing towards the tanker. The torpedoes all missed, one apparently running under the bow without exploding. The *Schliemann* immediately ran off at full speed (12 knots), and safely reached Singapore, where further supplies were taken on board. After a week's sojourn, the tanker moved on to Djakarta.

Finally the *Charlotte Schliemann* was ordered out into the Indian Ocean, in order to make her first rendezvous with the U-cruisers off Madagascar. The *Schliemann* replenished the remaining U-boats between 21 and 26 July some 700 miles south of Mauritius. The U-boats ringed the tanker so as to provide an outer shield while single U-boats approached her for resupply. Each U-boat received some 200 tons of fuel to reach full capacity. The U-boat crews were allowed to stretch their legs on the ship as a welcome change, although the Japanese-sourced food was not much appreciated, especially since it was filled with cockroaches and other insects. British Intelligence had detected the fuelling arrangement, but could not assign the disguised rendezvous position accurately. Two Italian U-boats carrying freight were also recognized as passing through as well as U 511. Six of the U-cruisers then patrolled the sea areas around Madagascar and Cape Town before returning to France. The seventh, U 178, became the first U-boat to use Penang. U 511 also passed through the Indian Ocean at about this time, on her way to Malaya where she would be handed over to the Japanese at Penang on 17 July as a gift.

The *Schliemann* then returned to Kobe by way of Djakarta and Singapore, and docked in August 1943.

Doenitz had previously obtained excellent results in terms of sinking Allied ships by making sudden hard strikes into areas previously unvisited by U-boats. The most successful had been the summer foray with several long-range boats into the Caribbean Sea in 1942, but 'Paukenschlag' on the American east coast and the sudden strike on Cape Town had also been spectacular. So far, it may be said that only the western edge of the

Indian Ocean, around Madagascar, had been exploited by U-boats. The collapse of operations in the North Atlantic in May meant that Doenitz now had an excess of U-boats, the Indian Ocean seemed to be ripe as the next target and on 9 June he ordered the *Monsun* group of U-boats to make a 'blitz attack on enemy shipping and enemy surface forces in the Arabian Sea'. The full plan, outlined as an appendix to the U-boat Command war diary for 30 June 1943, called for the despatch of eight Type IXC/40 boats and two U-cruisers (U 200 and U 847) into that theatre. Most of the boats would sail from France, but the new U-cruisers would emerge from Germany. The shorter-ranged Type IXC boats would receive refuelling in the South Atlantic in square FD20, some 300 miles east of St Paul Rocks, from tanker U 462. All U-boats would then refuel from the surface tanker *Brake* south-east of Madagascar, carry out offensive patrols in the Arabian Sea and off the southern tip of India, then return to the *Brake* for refuelling, patrol off southern Africa, and then return home. Boats in need of mechanical attention would have to head for Penang for replenishment and overhaul. These boats would then load up with strategic goods for delivery to Germany, carry out another offensive patrol in the northern Indian Ocean, refuel near Madagascar again from another surface tanker, then return to France. The boats had all been fitted out with radar search receivers before leaving Europe, and were assigned the special 'India' W/T frequency for communications with Germany.

This was known as the 'First *Monsun* Group', since the U-boats were expected to arrive just after the south-west monsoon in late summer. But two cows (U 461 and U 462) were lost in the Bay of Biscay, the intended replacement tanker U 487, already stationed in mid-Atlantic, was also sunk by aircraft, and some of the India-bound U-boats had to be diverted to refuel each other or U-boats stranded in the Atlantic. Others were sunk and the *Monsun* group had been reduced to just five Type IXC U-boats by the time it reached the South Atlantic. Feeling fairly safe from air attack, the U-boats now deployed *Bachstelze*, a mechanical rotor-powered device rather like a helicopter, to enable their lookouts to search for shipping over a much wider area than was normally possible.

Bachstelze obtained its power by being towed along behind the U-boat travelling at full speed. The lookout, who was actually a pilot and not a sailor, was carried high into the sky and wore a parachute so that in an emergency he could drop straight down again without waiting to be wound in. *Bachstelze* was tricky to land safely and was never much of a success owing to the danger of sudden air attack.

At the beginning of September 1943, the survivors of the *Monsun* group refuelled south of Madagascar from the *Brake*, together with U 177 which was still in the area. Refuelling from surface tankers was more profitable here than in the Atlantic, owing to the paucity of the Allied defences and in particular the decreased probability of surprise attack from the air. But even in the Indian Ocean, this situation was not to last much longer.

The six U-boats went singly alongside the tanker, while the remaining five boats circled at a good distance as lookouts. Oil and foodstuffs were provided only during daylight and took no fewer than three days to complete. A momentary panic occurred at U-boat Command when Italy surrendered to the Allies on 8 September, and on the 11th the Italian warship *Eritrea* escaped from Penang. It was feared that she might betray the rendezvous and the *Brake* was ordered to move away, in a direction dictated by local weather conditions. But next day U-boat Command learned that the boats had completed their refuelling successfully. The *Eritrea* had been in transition between Singapore and Sabang when news of the Italian surrender reached the crew, who at once changed course for Colombo, Ceylon, and arrived safely. British interrogators were disappointed to discover that the crew knew nothing of Axis rendezvous plans.

The U-boats then proceeded into the Straits of Madagascar and the Indian Ocean, where the shortage of sea and air escorts enabled them to find plenty of unescorted shipping. It became apparent only now that the batteries required to operate both the U-boats themselves when submerged, and also their electrically powered torpedoes, had suffered severe deterioration in the heat and humidity of the tropical Indian Ocean. Thus sinkings from the five survivors of the *Monsun* group in the northern Indian Ocean were unexpectedly feeble, despite the opportunities. Furthermore, the very high-grade lubricating oil used by German U-boats was subject to excessive consumption by diesel engines, caused by the tropical heat and the very long cruises required, and could not readily be replaced by the Japanese. It must be said here that consequently results from U-boats in the Indian Ocean were always disappointing, although this would not stop the German propaganda machine from announcing to the public in late 1943 that U-boats were then operating even in the Indian Ocean. U 533 had gone to the Gulf of Aden, U 188 to the Gulf of Oman, U 168 to the Gulf of Cambay, U 532 to the southern tip of India and U 183 to patrol off the oil terminal of Mombasa, East Africa. They maintained radio silence, which made it very hard for British Intelligence to locate them.

The Germans had agreed a rough zone of operations in the Indian Ocean, to separate the activities of German and Japanese submarines. The 'chop zone' was 70 degrees East – U-boats to the west, Japanese to the east. However, neither side adhered very strongly to this formula and U-boats, in particular, could be found well to the east of the demarcation line. Use of the port of Penang for essential maintenance and refuelling inevitably required U-boats to head eastwards towards Malaya. It took about eight weeks to turn around U-boats for sea after they had arrived.

The *Monsun* plan called for Penang and other German bases in the Far East to be well equipped and a succession of transport U-boats, originally

168

supplied by the Italians, was to ferry supplies from France to Penang and back, without, however, carrying out any offensive patrols. Any U-boats that could not return from Penang owing to severe mechanical defects would be used, insofar as possible, for offensive patrols in the north Indian Ocean from Penang.

The surface tankers had to be used with circumspection and this had some restraining effect on the U-boats' operations. Moreover, mechanical defects had been more severe than anticipated, so that the plan to refuel them for a return to Europe after their patrols in the north Indian Ocean was abandoned. The four survivors of the *Monsun* group (U 533 had by now been sunk) were forced to make for Penang and by mid-November there was not a single German U-boat in the Indian Ocean. It was difficult to reinforce the U-boats since the Type VII craft lacked the range to arrive without repeated refuelling, and even the long-range Type IXC boats had to be refuelled before proceeding on cruises to the theatre.

Six further U-boats were sent to the Indian Ocean between September and November 1943. Three were brand-new U-cruisers sailing from Germany at one month intervals as they became available after completing trials; the other three comprised a Type XB minelayer, U 219, a Type IXC boat, U 510, and an older Type IXB boat, U 172, which had first had its fuel tanks specially modified to provide greater range. The latter two boats sailed from France and U 219 from Germany for her first cruise. These boats are often referred to as the 'Second *Monsun* Group', although this name does not appear in German official records. The three U-cruisers saw the return to sea of experienced commanders from easier times, but all would be sunk in the North Atlantic as they headed south, as would U 172, while U 219 would be diverted to refuel boats stranded in the Atlantic and would return to France (see next chapter). Thus there remained only U 510 (Kapitaenleutnant Eick) as sole survivor from the Second *Monsun* Group. Japanese submarines were also active at this time in the north Indian Ocean, as they were spasmodically from mid-1943 to mid-1944, but they were less effective than the U-boats.

The four survivors of the original *Monsun* boats resumed operations from Penang in January 1944 and now enjoyed much greater successes in the north Indian Ocean than during their eastward trip from Europe. Sinkings increased to the point where, in 1944, they amounted to about half of those sunk in all theatres together. All the boats had been loaded with strategic materials to take home to Europe, including tin and other heavy metals installed into their keels. In the same month the British made a search (Operation Canned) for the tanker that they had discovered to be in the area, but this time their intelligence was too good, for the *Charlotte Schliemann* had not yet reached her refuelling rendezvous.

The *Schliemann* (Kapitaen Rothe) had remained at Kobe until despatched again to Singapore, arriving on 24 December just in time for Christmas.

Then she moved on again to Djakarta for more U-boat supplies before being ordered out into the south-western Indian Ocean for another rendezvous. She finally arrived towards the end of January and refuelled U 178 and U 510 on 27 January. U 178 received current cipher materials from the new arrival, U 510, together with 400 tons of fuel for her huge oil tanks, ninety days of provisions and 19 tons of rubber from the *Schliemann* in anticipation of the U-cruiser's home voyage. Consequently, it was possible to use U 178 as an auxiliary tanker in the Indian Ocean for a while.

The refuelling operation was revealed by H/F D/F, leading to a search by aircraft based in Mauritius and also by the destroyer HMS *Relentless*, sailing from Mauritius on 5 (or 8) February. Meanwhile the *Charlotte Schliemann* had rendezvoused with U 532 (Fregattenkapitaen Junker) on 11 February, which had apparently been warned by U-boat Command of the proximity of searching Allied warships. Rothe and Junker therefore agreed to move 600 miles southwards, postponing the refuelling of the U-boat for seventy-two hours. One of the Catalina flying boats searching from Mauritius was sighted by both vessels later that same afternoon and U 532 dived. The aircraft demanded identification from the *Schliemann* and was not fooled. It remained in contact with the tanker for ninety minutes, then disappeared. At once Rothe ordered the *Schliemann* to change course to the east and ran off at full speed, hoping to be saved by the approaching darkness, but it was too late. A 'cruiser' was seen after midnight and, after unsuccessful evasive manoeuvres, the tanker's crew prepared to scuttle and abandon ship. The 'cruiser', actually the *Relentless*, closed at 30 knots to just 2,000 yards and fired a salvo of eight torpedoes, before hitting the tanker with many shells as the crew abandoned ship. The final blow was a torpedo that hit the *Charlotte Schliemann* amidships (a crewman from *Relentless* would claim sixty years later that three torpedoes had struck home), although sinking was expedited by the tanker crew setting off 80 kilograms of dynamite as their last act. The *Relentless* rescued forty men, including Rothe, from the water before departing at full speed, having been notified by the Catalina of U-boats in the vicinity.

This left some forty to fifty survivors in the water. They were distributed among four lifeboats, all fitted with sails. Two of these lifeboats reached the east coast of Madagascar after nightmarish voyages of twenty-six and thirty days, during which food supplies were exhausted and the weather had alternated between fierce sun and tropical storms, saving a further twenty-two men (one had died en route). The other two lifeboats with an estimated twenty men aboard were never seen again. The survivors from the lifeboats were reunited with those rescued by the *Relentless* in the same POW camp in Kenya.

The tanker *Brake* had been informed as recently as December 1943 that her services would be required to refuel the returning *Monsun* boats. However, the availability of the *Charlotte Schliemann* seems to have resulted in the latter being used instead. According to decrypted German signals, the *Brake* remained at Djakarta from 14 October to 25 November, when she sailed for Singapore to load 7,000 tons of oil suitable for U-boats. The *Brake* was reported as remaining at Singapore on 21 December and 13 January 1944. Then she seems to have moved to Penang, receiving orders in February to sail out to replace the now sunken *Charlotte Schliemann*. The *Brake* departed on the 26th.

U 532 (Type IXC/40) took on fuel from the U-cruiser U 178 on 27 February. Three U-boats (U 532, 168 and 188) were then ordered to wait two weeks to replenish from the *Brake*. Again code decrypting gave away the rendezvous and the Allies had knowledge of the new rendezvous even after it was changed on 5 March. The Germans arranged for the U-boats to make a preliminary reconnaissance of the waters around the rendezvous before closing, and the former Italian submarine UIT 24 and the *Monsun* boat U 183 were expected to arrive about 19 March. U 188 (Kapitaen-leutnant Luedden) arrived first at the tanker, but her refuelling was interrupted by bad weather. The commander of the *Brake*, Kapitaen Koehlschenbach, appeared to be very nervous about the possibility of the rendezvous being discovered, the weather was worsening, and, when refuelling of U 188 was complete, the *Brake* moved off to the south-west, taking U 532 and U 168 with her.

An aircraft from the escort carrier HMS *Battler* sighted the fully laden tanker south of Mauritius and east of Madagascar on 12 March, while she was in the act of refuelling the two U-boats. In fact the *Brake* was then in company with U 168 (Pich) and U 532 (Junker), of which the first was only part refuelled, and the second had been refuelled but had not yet received lubricating oil. All three U-boats (including the fully replenished U 188) had departed by the time British warships arrived and the tanker had no option but to scuttle herself when she was shelled by the destroyer HMS *Roebuck*. The warships departed, but aircraft continued to circle the area awaiting the arrival of a U-boat at the rendezvous. Sure enough, U 168 turned up. Forewarned by the survivors of *Brake* whom she picked up, U 168 was caught in the middle of a crash-dive as the aircraft attacked. She was hit by a single bomb that failed to explode and managed to reach Penang safely. U 532 also witnessed the sinking of *Brake* and returned to the surface to pick up other survivors, some of whom were later handed over to U 168. In all, 125 survivors (all but four of the original crew) from the *Brake* returned to Penang.

The next 'filling station' for Indian Ocean U-boats was at this time off the Cape Verde Islands, in mid-Atlantic. U 188 (Type IXC/40) had enough fuel to make the long journey home, where she arrived safely after an eventful journey through the Atlantic (see Chapter 16) in such a state of disrepair that she could not be used again, and was finally scuttled at Bordeaux on

20 August 1944. The other Type IXC/40 boats, U 168 and U 532, together with the newly arrived U 183, were forced to return to Penang. U 532 had claimed that she planned to return to France but, as we shall see, she would soon have to be deployed as an emergency tanker. Thus the interceptions of the two surface tankers had almost completely wrecked the ability of the *Monsun* group to return to Europe, loaded with essential strategic materials such as tin, molybdenum, rubber and raw opium. However, the attacks on secret rendezvous made it clear that the Allies had managed to decrypt the current U-boat signals, and Junker, of U 532, signalled to U-boat Command that 'provisionings have been systematically compromised'. This would have serious implications for subsequent Allied decryptions of German signals (see Chapter 16).

Penang was now the only refuelling area for the Indian Ocean U-boats, which were forced to return prematurely for replenishment. Convoys were to be found in most parts of the Indian Ocean, defences were stiffened and the U-boats' successes fell steeply. The Indian Ocean was always starved of Allied escort ships, but air coverage appears to have been quite good, especially around the focal points of shipping. Convoys were introduced to the Persian Gulf-Aden areas whenever the threat became too severe, but the convoys were withdrawn when there were known to be few U-boats in the Indian Ocean from decryption. Thus convoys were encountered in the Arabian Sea from July to November 1943 and subsequently from February to September 1944. Even so, there was such a shortage of convoy escorts that many fast independents were allowed to sail simply to reduce congestion in the ports. Indian-flagged warships, under British commanders, comprised many of the escorts and patrols.

Penang itself was an unpleasant base for a European, being very hot, riddled with fever and possessing little skilled labour; moreover, the Japanese Navy showed little inclination to assist their allies. Many parts, such as batteries, had to be imported from Japan, while U-boats requiring all their electric batteries to be replaced had to move to the special dry dock facility in Kobe. However, the former crew of U 511 was available to form a nucleus of trained personnel for crew replacements and engineering work, and dockyard work was reckoned to be of good quality, albeit slow. The former commander of the U-cruiser U 178, Korvettenkapitaen Dommes, was appointed 'Chief in the Southern Area' and also became the local flotilla commander in all but title.

Penang was used as the first German base in the Far East. There was a rest home, Penang Hill, formerly a hotel reached by funicular railway, high in the mountains above the steamy port. The main rest home for U-boat crews, however, was in the mountains of Java, near Djakarta, on an old tea plantation which was called Tjikopo. Singapore (renamed by the Japanese as 'Shonan' after they had captured it) had extensive facilities with excellent docks and harbours developed by the British. The Germans were permitted to make use of its facilities after 17 May 1943, but the dockyards were frequently choked with damaged Japanese warships. Therefore Surabaya was made available to German staff for maintenance in July 1944, but again this port became clogged with damaged Japanese ships after December as the Pacific war intensified.

The interaction between Japanese and Germans, supposedly allies although they rarely co-operated, caused some difficulties. The biggest problem was the Japanese insistence on controlling the giant radio transmitter at Penang, and then broadcasting precise details of rendezvous plans for U-boats and ships leaving port or returning. Allied Intelligence, centred principally on the Australian Defense Center, regularly broke all the Japanese codes and Allied submarines were directed to lie in wait for targets in the shallow waters around the Sunda Strait. So good was the intelligence from decryption that the submarines could frequently be stationed on the expected path of a German or Japanese vessel as it entered or left port. This might not have mattered if the Japanese escorts had been up to the job, but there is universal agreement today among German U-boat crews that the vessels were hopelessly inadequate. The escorts comprised mainly fishing cutters or similarly inappropriate vessels with poor armament and inadequate anti-submarine capabilities, while their crews seemed to lack both interest and ability in their task. Indeed, Allied submarines simply ignored them. Thus many U-boats, and sometimes Japanese submarines, were sunk within twenty-four hours of reaching or departing harbour. The shallow waters did, however, allow handfuls of survivors to reach the surface using underwater escape gear. So contemptuous of the escorts were the Allied submarine commanders that they would often surface to interrogate the survivors and take prisoner experienced officers. However, the Germans had access to two Arado seaplanes and a Japanese float plane for escorting U-boats at Penang, and later at Djakarta. By then, one of the Arados had been accidentally burnt out.

U-boats intending to enter one of the German-occupied Far Eastern ports (Penang and Djakarta) for the first time from France or Germany received these instructions from the radio station at Penang:

1. Shave off beards, so as not to betray the long sea cruise.
2. Travel submerged for two days before reaching the Sunda Strait.
3. Show the German war flag on deck to mark the boat as a U-boat.
4. Details of the rendezvous and time to meet a Japanese escort within the Sunda Strait.

The Germans also took over a number of large Italian submarines at Bordeaux and in the Far East after the surrender of Italy on 8 September 1943. Both Germans and Japanese had employed various pretexts to prevent the boats from sailing before the anticipated surrender. They were still to be employed as transport submarines (now known as 'Mercator boats') to ferry supplies between France and Penang. UIT 21 (Oberleutnant zS Steinfeld – according to the war diary, probably Steinfeldt, who would later become commander of U 195; Steiner, according to Herr Kraus, who served on this boat; other sources give other names) was commissioned at Bordeaux on 14 October and trained in French coastal waters. This elderly boat was manned by German sailors but had a conscript Italian crew of engineers (notwithstanding the fact that Italy was now officially fighting for the Allies), supervised by an Italian junior officer who spoke German. It was intended that UIT 21 should transport radio equipment to aid Japan, but the boat was found to require new diesel engines and was decommissioned at Bordeaux on 15 April 1944.

UIT 22 had been commissioned by Kapitaenleutnant Wunderlich on 11 October 1943. Both UIT 21 and UIT 22 reached Brest on 20 November from Bordeaux in order to give both crews familiarization with their boats, before returning to Bordeaux. UIT 22 left Bordeaux again for the Far East on 19 January 1944, returned with engine trouble on the 21st, and departed, this time for good, on the 26th with a cargo that included 18 tons of mercury and 131 tons of special steel. An RAF Liberator bomber caught the U-boat on the surface in the South Atlantic on 12 February and dropped depth-charges causing the boat to submerge with a heavy list. According to Wunderlich, with a signal to U-boat Command after he had resurfaced, the aircraft made three overflights, dropping six depth-charges on the third that caused damage to the periscope and to No. 4 fuel tank, resulting in the loss of 32 tons of fuel. However, Wunderlich claimed that he still had sufficient fuel to reach Penang without refuelling.

A rendezvous between UIT 22 and the U-cruiser U 178, so that UIT 22 could hand over current codes, the new Naxos and Borkum radar receivers, and receive fuel in exchange, was set at a position 600 miles south of Cape Town for 12 March. South African forces intercepted the signals, a Catalina of the SAAF surprised UIT 22 on the surface on 11 March near the rendezvous and dropped depth-charges in two passes. Return fire from the U-boat damaged the aircraft and the U-transporter submerged with a marked list. She returned to the surface within minutes and was attacked by a second Catalina which dropped six depth-charges, straddling the U-boat. UIT 22 disappeared under the water again, oil and wreckage bubbled up, followed shortly after by a much larger oil slick. UIT 22 was presumed lost by U-boat Command on the 12th after she had failed to keep her expected rendezvous with U 178. The U-cruiser reported that she had found only oil and patrolling aircraft at the meeting point.

Three other former Italian submarines – *Giuliani*, *Cappellini* and *Torelli* – which had been sent to the Far East before Italy's surrender, were now taken over by the Germans at Singapore and were renumbered respectively as UIT 23, UIT 24 and UIT 25. These unarmed former blockade runners were given a new German 105mm deck gun and a single 20mm anti-aircraft weapon. New commanders were appointed to all three on 6 December 1943; Schaefer, formerly of U 183, which had been sent to Penang, and who had had to be replaced as her commander owing to illness, was moved to UIT 23. He died in Singapore, apparently of a heart attack, just one month later and the commander's post remained vacant for a while pending arrival of a suitable officer in a U-boat arriving from France. UIT 24 was assigned Kapitaenleutnant Pahls as her new commander. UIT 25 was taken over by Oberleutnant zS Striegler. Striegler had previously been the first officer of U 511 which had earlier been handed over to the Japanese.

UIT 24 was the first of the ex-Italian submarines ready to attempt the return to France. She was loaded with rubber, tin, wolfram, quinine and opium, and left Penang on 8 February. But W/T problems caused UIT 24 to miss her rendezvous with the *Brake* and she informed an incredulous U-boat Command that she had only 20 tons of fuel remaining while close to the rendezvous. U 532 was at once ordered to her aid, the refuelling was completed on 18 March with 80 tons of oil, while U 532 received the lubricating oil that she had failed to obtain from *Brake*, and both boats proceeded in company to Penang where UIT 24 would receive a complete overhaul after she had arrived on 4 April.

Since UIT 25 was not yet ready for operations, Striegler was transferred to the vacant captain's post in UIT 23 on 14 February 1944. By now UIT 23 had been moved to Singapore and filled up, like UIT 24, with rubber, tin, wolfram, quinine and opium, and without further ado Striegler sailed out, destination Penang, then France. But these were dangerous waters and within twenty-four hours, shortly after leaving her base, UIT 23 had been torpedoed and sunk by the British submarine *Tallyho*. Fourteen survivors, including Striegler, were rescued by the Japanese.

To lose one's new command within twenty-four hours could not be called a propitious start to a U-boat career, but Striegler was reappointed as commander of UIT 25 the very next day. He remained with this transport boat until September, carrying out local ferry operations.

There were still shortages of many vital supplies at Penang, and a particular problem was that use of ancient torpedoes, left in store for more than a year at the base by earlier German blockade runners, was now resulting in many torpedo failures. An attempt was made to relieve some of these difficulties by the despatch of the Type VIIF torpedo transport U 1062 (Kapitaenleutnant Albrecht) to Penang. U 1062 sailed from Kiel to Norway in December 1943, but was located on the 22nd by nine Beaufighter aircraft while being escorted by minesweeper M 403. The aircraft attacked with guns and torpedoes, but the presence of the heavily armed minesweeper (the aircraft reported it was a destroyer) saved the U-transporter from serious damage. U 1062 was then sent out to the Far East from Bergen on 3 January 1944, with orders that her mission was urgent; only exceptional targets were to be attacked en route. After passing through the South Atlantic in February, she handed over new cipher material to the returning U 188 (22 March), received 30 tons of oil from the diverted U 532 (which had, as we have seen, received fuel from U 178 on 27 February, failed to get lubricating oil from *Brake* in March, and given oil to UIT 24) on 10 April in the Indian Ocean (or she would never have arrived), and finally reached Penang safely in company with U 532 on 19 April. Refuelling operations in the Indian Ocean were becoming as complicated as those in the Atlantic.

A second Type VIIF boat, U 1059, was sunk in mid-Atlantic while en route with torpedoes to east Asia by the *Block Island* carrier group (19 March 1944). She had been looking for a cow from which to refuel (see Chapter 16).

Throughout 1944 a further sixteen U-boats were ordered into the Indian Ocean. Those which were not U-cruisers would be dangerously short of fuel by the time they arrived, but in fact only six U-boats reached the Indian Ocean and only two were not U-cruisers. U 537 (Type IXC/40) was refuelled in mid-Atlantic by U 488 in mid-April, and then again in the Indian Ocean by the Penang-based U 183 (also Type IXC/40) on 25 June, which allowed a long patrol off southern India before her arrival at Penang. An unusual development in April 1944 was the planned supply of U 843 (Type IXC/40) by a Japanese submarine in the Indian Ocean. But U 843, having been refuelled by U 488 in mid-Atlantic, was badly damaged by bombs en route to her rendezvous and was forced to proceed directly to Djakarta. One stroke of luck for the Indian Ocean-bound U-boats was that as a result of the disaster with U 1059 (see above), Doenitz ordered the mid-Atlantic fuelling rendezvous to be shifted further to the west. As usual, this was intercepted and decrypted, with the twin results that the Allied carrier groups moved west and the long-range U-cruisers could slip through the original area unobserved.

Those U-boats sailing from France or Germany to the Far East after February 1944 were carrying technical supplies not only for their Far Eastern bases, but also for the Japanese (such as medicines, blueprints, mercury, optical glass and disassembled aircraft such as the Me163 and Me262). All boats returning to Europe were expected to accommodate as many strategic materials as possible, especially tin, rubber and opium (for morphine). Heavy materials were most conveniently stored in the U-boat's keel, but this required dry-docking in a suitable port in order to add or remove the commodity. Since dry docks in the area of Penang and Java were rare and were overused by other ships, there were delays in off-loading the U-boats. Owing to difficulties with refuelling and lack of cargo capacity, no more Type IXC boats would be sent to the Indian Ocean after March 1944. U-cruisers and Type XB U-minelayers would be used exclusively.

The Allied invasion of Normandy caused the last reinforcement of the U-boats in the Indian Ocean, when as many boats as possible put to sea in order to avoid becoming caught in Biscay bases by the rapidly advancing Allied armies. Among them were the Type IXD1 U-transporters U 180 and U 195, and the Type XB U-minelayer U 219, whose stories will be told in Chapter 17. After that, no more U-boats would be sent to the Indian Ocean until the despatch of U 864 (sunk off Norway) in February and U 234 in April 1945.

The Type VIIF transporter U 1062 (Kapitaenleutnant Albrecht) twice attempted to leave Penang for France in mid-1944. On 20 June she set out, but was unsuccessfully attacked almost at once by a waiting Allied submarine. By the 30th, U 1062 had sustained damage to a compressor, a planned rendezvous with U 183 was called off, and U 1062 returned to Penang. On 16 July U 1062 tried again, again evaded a submarine attack, and carried on into the Atlantic. Her subsequent attempts to refuel near the Azores for her return to Germany, with the outward-bound Type XB minelayer U 219, will be told in Chapter 17.

There was little activity by the Indian Ocean U-boats between July and October 1944 due to lack of fuel and maintenance, with no fewer than six U-boats being laid up at Penang and Djakarta during this period. The Allies suspended convoys in the Indian Ocean indefinitely and the surviving U-boats were ordered back to Europe from September onwards. The unlucky Striegler handed over UIT 25 to Oberleutnant zS Schrein in September and replaced Kentrat as commander of the newly arrived U 196.

The two surviving ex-Italian boats in the Far East (UIT 24 and UIT 25) were both sent to Japan for overhaul, but were not ready until September 1944. Schrein was replaced on UIT 25 by Meier near the end of the year (records are uncertain), while Pahls remained as commander of UIT 24 until the end of the war. Both boats had been used predominantly as transports between Japanese and Malayan ports after the aborted return of UIT 24 to France. Having reached Djakarta on 24 March 1944, UIT 24 moved to Penang, then to Singapore for a refit, which she reached on 6 April. After a month, the ex-Italian boat moved on to Kobe in Japan, arriving on 6 June just as the Allied invasion of Europe commenced. Here UIT 24 would remain for a major overhaul until 5 September. Equally, UIT 25 (Meier) shuttled between Singapore and Penang, then back again, in February 1944. Subsequently the boat moved to Surabaya where she remained for three months, presumably for a refit. On 10 June 1944, UIT 25 sailed again to Tama and then on to Kobe, arriving in July 1944 where she required a lengthy refit. Since the UIT-boats could not be refuelled to enable them to return to Germany, a decision was made at some point to hand the boats over to the Japanese. Thus not one single ton of cargo was delivered by any of the 'Mercator' (ex-Italian) boats, despite all the dockyard labour and new equipment.

By now an arrangement had been made with the Japanese whereby German transport boats would ferry supplies from Malaya to Japan (for German and other European nationals in Japan), and back again with Japanese military supplies, in exchange for Japanese payments to the Germans for the transportation. Thus UIT 24 served as a reverse transport, moving in stages from Kobe to Penang (arriving 28 September) via Singapore, then back to Kobe where she docked on 18 February 1945. Again major repair work was required for the engines of the ex-Italian submarine, and UIT 24 would be taken over at Kobe by the Japanese in May 1945 after the surrender of Germany.

Records are uncertain as to the fate of UIT 25, although Meier would joke about the number of short transport missions he had undertaken. Decrypted German signals show that UIT 25 was in a dockyard on 18 January 1945, but work would be delayed until 4 March 1945. On 23 March U-boat Command ordered that the boat must be sent urgently to Singapore, where U 862 needed 'ZDM7' before sailing, but on the 26th another signal shows that the boat was still in dock with eleven pistons burned out. On the 29th, U-boat Command enquired whether UIT 25 was still worth repairing. Apparently she was, for the Japanese Navy estimated to Germany that both UIT 24 and UIT 25 would remain in dockyard hands until the middle to end of June. UIT 25 surrendered, like UIT 24, at Kobe in May 1945, and both boats were taken over by the Japanese as I.503 and I.504.

An entry in its war diary for 15 September shows that U-boat Command had arranged for U 537 and U 843 to return to Europe in September 1944. The plan required that the two boats be refuelled in the western Indian Ocean by UIT 24 and an 'IXD' (presumably a U-cruiser, or perhaps the outward-bound U 180 or U 195). However this plan was evidently aborted for unstated reasons, and both U 537 and U 843 appear to have been in dockyard hands during September.

By the end of 1944 there were acute shortages of all kinds, including fuel, in the Indian Ocean. The waters surrounding Penang were blockaded and periodically mined by Allied submarines, but a major aerial minelaying effort by Liberators on 27 October 1944 – which might have been repeated at any time – caused Germans and Japanese to abandon Penang as a naval base in favour of Djakarta in Java, which became the official German headquarters base on 26 November 1944. On 3 December, in response to a request from U-boat Command, the 'Southern Command' reported the following torpedo stocks:

Penang: enough parts for eight T1Fat1, five T2, one T1 torpedoes.
Djakarta: enough parts for nine T1Fat1, one T1, two T2, one T3 and
          one T5 torpedoes.
Surabaya: similar to Penang.

The only other torpedo supplies available in the Far East were those brought by the U-boats themselves, and these were usually in poor condition.

In December 1944, U-boat Command ordered all U-boats that were capable of making the journey to return to Germany, loaded with as many valuable commodities (especially rubber) as they could carry. Since the boats lacked the schnorkel (see Chapter 17), they were required to cross the North Atlantic during the hours of maximum darkness, so that they would have to reach Norway by mid-January 1945 at the latest. The process of using returning U-boats as blockade runners had started with U 178 in mid-1944, and by the end of the war a handful of other such blockade runners had also reached German-occupied ports with their cargoes.* Five Japanese submarines also attempted to carry cargoes from Penang to France and back again between mid-1942 and early 1944. Three completed the round trip, but two of these were sunk with their cargoes while onward bound for Japan from Penang.

Some of the shorter-ranged IXC/40 U-boats would need refuelling en route if they were to reach Norway, since France was now predominantly under Allied control. Thus U 510 was despatched from Djakarta on 26 November for Norway, and U-cruiser U 196 was sent out from the same port on the 30th to refuel U 510 near Madagascar before returning for an Australian operation (below). However, U 510 was forced to return to Djakarta with exhaust defects, arriving on 3 December, and U 196 was recalled from their fuelling arrangement, but she never replied. She was ordered instead to refuel the Europe-bound U 843, which had sailed on 10 December, and had already been refuelled by the east-bound U 195 on the 20th, but still there was no response. U 196 was posted missing on 22 December 1944, but to this day no one knows the reason for her disappearance. U 843 was then directed to take on oil from U-cruiser U 181, which was then to return to Djakarta since neither U 196 nor U 181 were in fit state to return all the way to Norway themselves. U 181 successfully refuelled U 843 on 1 January 1945 before returning uneventfully to Djakarta. U 843 continued safely all the way to Norway, arriving on 3 April 1945 with a cargo that included 100 tons of zinc. By great misfortune, the boat

* Blockade Running. As early as 11 April 1943, Doenitz had proposed the construction of submersible blockade runners, to transport essential war supplies between Germany and Japan. The first of these boats, known as Type XX, were expected to be completed by Deschimag of Bremen in the summer of 1944 and would be able to carry 800 tons of cargo. But delays in the programme caused its cancellation on 27 May 1944. No Type XX boat was ever completed.

A revision of the list of 'essential war materials', also in May 1944, established that no such supplies would really be needed until June 1945, when shortages of rubber and certain metals would arise in Germany. Thus blockade running was assigned a lower priority by U-boat Command.

was sunk by aircraft rockets and cannon in the Kattegat while moving onwards to Germany with her cargo still aboard. Only twelve of the crew were rescued.

In view of the lack of unescorted targets in the north Indian Ocean, and the long journeys required to reach the patrol areas, the commanders of both U 183 and U 862 suggested independently to U-boat Command that a sudden onslaught on Australian waters might be profitable. The commander of U 862 (Korvettenkapitaen Timm) had served in the area before the war as a merchant navy officer. U-boat Command agreed to the proposal, and assigned U 537, U 168 and U 862 to make a simultaneous attack (U 183 was returning from patrol and would not be ready for operations again until January 1945). However U 168 was sunk by an Allied submarine as soon as she left port (5 October 1944). When the fact became known from rescued survivors, U-boat Command assigned U 196 (Striegler) as the replacement boat, but complications with refuelling homeward-bound U-boats required U 196 first to head west to refuel the Europe-bound U 510, then to patrol off Australia, and finally to make for Japan for a full overhaul.

Meanwhile U 537 (Kapitaenleutnant Schrewe) sailed from Surabaya on 9 November for Australian waters. Again the rendezvous and route instructions for the Japanese escort were decrypted and U 537 was sunk without survivors by the US submarine *Flounder* that same day. The loss was not known to U-boat Command until U 537 was overdue for return to harbour in January 1945. U 196 had also disappeared (above).

That left only U-cruiser U 862 of the original four U-boats detailed for the Australian attack. Timm managed to get out of port unobserved, since this time there had been no tell-tale Japanese radio messages, and reached the west coast of Australia safely. Thus it was in December that U 862 carried out the only patrol by a U-boat in the Pacific Ocean. The much-travelled Timm, holder of the Knight's Cross, had started his active U-boat career in the Arctic in 1942. U 862 sank two ships in a long cruise around the south of Australia to New Zealand and back again. U-boat Command recalled all three Australia-bound U-boats on 17 January 1945 to Djakarta, for immediate replenishment and return to Europe. There were (unfounded) fears that a large Allied force was about to invade Java or Malaya, rendering all the German bases in the area inoperable.

The story of U-boat operations in the Indian Ocean for 1945 is continued in Chapter 17, but no further attacks would be made on Allied shipping there during 1945, and only two more U-boats would be ordered to that theatre from Norway. Operations in the Indian Ocean had been reasonably successful in terms of Allied ships sunk at low cost (see Table 14-1). However, the futility of German attempts to bring home strategic war materials by U-boat can be measured by just two statistics: the cargo of the German merchant ship *Weserland*, captured by the Allies in the Atlantic in

Table 14-1. U-boat successes in the Indian Ocean.

Month	Allied ships sunk	U-boats sunk	Month	Allied ships sunk	U-boats sunk
1943			March	5 (17,035)	0
May	7 (36,015 tons)	0	April	1 (5,277)	0
June	5 (23,453)	0	May	0	1
July	14 (76,941)	0	June	3 (15,645)	0
August	7 (46,400)	1	July	4 (23,000)	0
September	4 (27,144)	0	August	9 (57,732)	1
October	8 (10,050)	1	September	1 (5,670)	0
November	0	0	October	0	2
December	1 (7,244)	0	November	1 (10,198)	2
1944			December	1 (7,180)	0
January	6 (38,751)	0	1945		
February	11 (39,234)	0	Jan–May	1 (7,176)	1
			Total	89 (454,145)	9

Table 14-2. Tankers used in the Indian Ocean.

Name	Type	Commander	Remarks
Brake	Surface	Koelschenbach	Sunk Mar 1944
Charlotte Schliemann	Surface	Rothe	Sunk Feb 1944
U 178	IXD2	Spahr	Aug 1943 & Feb/Mar 1944
U 181	IXD2	Freiwald	Dec 1944 & Jan 1945
U 183	IXC/40	Schneewind	June 1944
U 195	IXD1	Buchholz	Dec 1944 & Feb 1945
U 196	IXD2	Striegler	Dec 1944 (sunk)
U 219	XB	Burghagen	Not used
U 532	IXC/40	Junker	Mar/Apr 1944
U 861	IXD2	Oesten	Feb 1945

January 1944 while in transit from Malaya to Europe, amounted to 10,000 tons when offloaded. The total cargo delivered to a German-occupied port by all U-boats combined from 1943 to 1945 was less than 700 tons.

The Arctic, 1942–4

Two flotillas of U-boats were stationed in Norway with the main purpose of attacking convoys between Iceland and Russia (see Map 14-1). Relying on interception of radio signals, reports of agents in Iceland and Luftwaffe reconnaissance, they were able to remain in port until the convoy sailed, then dash out to attack the convoy and return to base. All the U-boats were of the medium-range Type VII craft, but the short distances involved made refuelling unnecessary.

However, the sailing of the convoys was suspended during the summer months since the period of continuous daylight made the passage past the

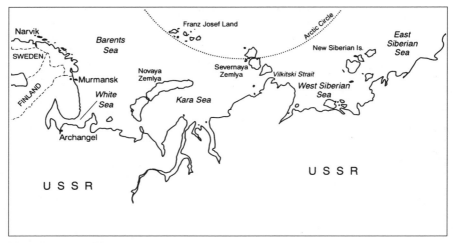

Map 14-1. Arctic Waters.

north of Norway excessively dangerous. Between August and September, therefore, the U-boats could be diverted to attack Russian shipping, raid Russian wireless and weather stations, and minelaying. The shortage of Soviet merchant shipping made most U-boat patrols fruitless without information as to whether ships were at sea, but occasional convoys could be found on the Siberian sea route between the White Sea and the Pacific. The U-boats did not, however, have the range to penetrate far into the Siberian Sea.

In August 1942, U 255 (Reche) arrived in Spitzbergen for the purpose of refuelling a BV-138 flying boat that, fitted with extra fuel tanks, was to reconnoitre the Siberian sea route for use by U-boats and the pocket battleship *Admiral Scheer*. The *Scheer* made a sortie into the sea route (Operation Wunderland) but was only able to sink a single ice breaker.

The following year, U 255 (Harms) again provided a seaplane base but, after four seaplane sorties in August, again no targets were found. This time the pocket battleship *Luetzow* was available (Operation Wunderland II), but did not venture out. By exchanging supplies off Novaya Zemlya, U 255 was able to extend the patrol of U 636 into the Kara Sea. The 'furthest east' in the Arctic was recorded by U 354 and U 302 which sortied into the Vilkitski Strait (West Siberian Sea) in August 1943, where they sank two ships.

In August 1944, there was no pocket battleship available, but the *Greif* group of six U-boats operated in the Kara Sea. U 711 and U 957 both handed over their surplus fuel in mid-August to three other boats before returning to base.

No other opportunities came until the end of the war.

182

The Mediterranean and Black Sea, 1942–4

Type VII attack boats were sent at Hitler's direct order into the Mediterranean from the end of 1941 onwards, to prop up in the first instance the Italian Navy and subsequently to interfere with Allied supply operations to their various invasion forces in North Africa, Sicily and Italy. These orders were extremely unpopular with U-boat Command, who considered that the boats were being diverted away from their main strategic function (interrupting the flow of supplies to Britain) and further that U-boats in the Mediterranean were lost to the main U-boat force forever, since the only way into the sea was past the heavily patrolled Straits of Gibraltar. The U-boats could not return to the Atlantic on the surface and a submerged return was out of the question, since the underwater current into the Mediterranean from the Atlantic was almost exactly equal to the maximum submerged speed of a U-boat trying to move against the current.

Orders to sail into the Mediterranean were also unpopular with the U-boat crews, who had to contend with the immensely hazardous passage of the Straits of Gibraltar. Those that survived to enter the sea were then forced to endure long periods of inactivity interspersed with the occasional massively protected convoy. The waters were shallow, very clear (so that submerged submarines could be seen to a considerable depth) and the entire sea was subject to constant surveillance by land-based bombers. There were no 'air gaps' such as could be found in the Atlantic.

The U-boats made a spectacular start to their new careers in the Mediterranean, sinking several Allied warships including a battleship and two aircraft carriers, but the introduction of radar and the increasing dominance of Allied forces, particularly after Italy capitulated in September 1943, greatly reduced their effectiveness. The last successful attack by a U-boat on a merchant ship was made in May 1944, although they continued to make occasional patrols until 1945.

U-boats in the Mediterranean could be based at La Spezia (a northern port on the west coast of Italy), Toulon (southern coast of France) or Salamis (Greece). Every corner of the Mediterranean was readily accessible even to the shorter-ranged Type VII attack U-boats from these ports, thus there was little need for refuelling. Moreover, the constant threat of air attack made any operation on the surface of the sea excessively dangerous. The U-boats spent most of their time crawling around underwater, powered by their batteries, so that fuel consumption was reduced anyway. The author has been unable to discover any instance of U-boats being refuelled at sea in the Mediterranean.

The advance of the German Army into Russia in 1941–2 meant that the Black Sea fell into its sphere of influence. The Soviet forces were using the Black Sea for naval transport and it was felt that neutral Turkey might be pressured into joining the German cause. Accordingly, six of the tiny Type II U-boats, which had previously been used in coastal operations

183

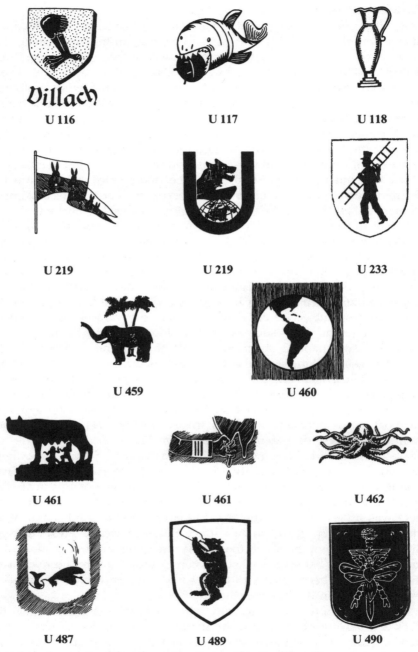

U 116

U 117

U 118

U 219

U 219

U 233

U 459

U 460

U 461

U 461

U 462

U 487

U 489

U 490

These insignia were carried on the conning towers of some of the milk cows. (*Georg Hoegel; Horst Bredow U 233, U 489 and U 490*) against Britain, were decommissioned, transported by huge road transporters and then by barge down the Danube, and finally recommissioned at the Romanian port of Constanza. From here they made many patrols against Soviet ships on the far (eastern) side of the Black Sea.

Again, though, worries about sudden air attack by Russian aircraft made all movement on the surface very dangerous (although refuelling at night might have been feasible, given the Russian lack of radar). The 'canoes', as the tiny U-boats were called, made short crossings of the Black Sea and then sat on the bottom for extended periods, waiting for something to turn up. The shortage of worthwhile targets ensured that no greater effort was ever required.

Turkey remained neutral until March 1945, when it declared war on the Allied side. By then, Russian forces had recaptured occupied Russia, Poland and Romania, and the six canoes had been sunk by air attack at Constanza or scuttled to prevent them from falling into Soviet hands (August and September 1944).

Chapter 15

Return to the North Atlantic

September to December 1943

At the end of August 1943, Doenitz felt able to resume wolf-pack attacks against convoys in the North Atlantic. The U-boats had by now been fitted out with increased anti-aircraft armaments, the new W. Anz non-radiating radar receiver (which was useless, but he did not know that) and each carried four of the new acoustic T-5 torpedoes, the German equivalent of Fido. The Germans had sacrificed naval production elsewhere in order to have eighty T-5 torpedoes ready by the beginning of August.

But first, there was some urgent business to which to attend in the Bay of Biscay. The increasingly daring British escort groups were advancing deeper and deeper into the waters of the Bay, posing a severe threat to U-boats trying to traverse it. The Luftwaffe increased its air patrols over the Bay and, on 25 August, the new Hs293 radio-controlled glider bombs were deployed for the first time against Allied ships. Fourteen Do217 and seven Ju88 bombers attacked the British escorts, steering the gliders onto the ships from a safe distance. This first attack caused only minor damage.

Two days later, a second glider bomb attack launched from eighteen Do217 bombers sank one ship and severely damaged another. The British response was to pull the escort groups much further to the west of the Bay, making life for the U-boats a great deal safer, particularly as the Allies had now discovered the Piening route. Now Doenitz could send his new pack into the North Atlantic.

In the last week of the month and the first week of September, twenty-two U-boats and U-tanker U 460 left Biscay ports. Hugging the Spanish coastline and surfacing at night only for the minimum time needed to recharge their batteries, they lost only one of their number in the passage of the Bay of Biscay.

Another six U-boats also reached the North Atlantic safely from German waters, but this did not prevent anxiety about the effectiveness of their new radar receivers. Thus Doenitz could boast on 8 September that scarcely a single U-boat had been attacked in the Bay of Biscay since W. Anz had been installed, although U 386 had reported that she had been attacked at night on the 2nd, without warning, while crossing the Bay. A further innovation was the stationing of the heavily armed aircraft trap U 621 just to the west of the Bay of Biscay. She spent her time sending dummy messages in the hope of provoking an air attack, while boats at sea were told that they could avail themselves of her defensive services should they run into trouble.

Twenty of the U-boats now in the Atlantic were formed into the *Leuthen* group, with orders to blast their way through the convoys' defences before attacking the merchant ships. Doenitz must have been hoping for some speedy results – his war diary's list of reported successes had been empty for weeks.

U-boat Command's stocks of milk cows were by now beginning to run low, but they could still muster three Type XIV U-tankers and a further three Type XB U-minelayers, although by no means all of these were ready for sea. One cow in the Biscay bases had already accompanied the *Leuthen* boats to sea, and the only other U-tanker in France, U 488 (Oberleutnant zS Bartke), was sent out after her with instructions to refuel U-boats for the remote theatres. U 488 had been ready for sea since 18 August, but had had to wait for W. Anz to be fitted. This had been accomplished by 7 September. Next day, U 488 put out to sea with an escort of two M-boats. All the cows carried the new powerful anti-aircraft weapons; in the case of the Type XB boats this now amounted to one automatic quick-fire 37mm gun and four 20mm cannon. The large old 105mm gun had been dismantled, as it had also from all the other U-boats, transporters and U-cruisers.

The *Leuthen* boats were also massively armed against air attack and Doenitz had ordered specifically that U-boats running on the surface, in order to get ahead of convoys, should shoot it out with an approaching aircraft rather than submerge and let the convoy escape. This tactic had not worked so well in the Bay in July, but their anti-aircraft guns had not been so powerful then and aircraft in mid-ocean were reckoned to be an easier proposition. The policy of surfaced *Leuthen* U-boats shooting it out with attacking aircraft was ordered by Doenitz against his own better judgement, and on the advice of U-boat commanders newly returned from sea. The order would soon be rescinded.

U 460 (Kapitaenleutnant Schnoor) had been refitting at Bordeaux since 25 June. She had been unable to join U 461 and U 462 for their failed breakout through the Bay in July due to a mechanical defect. During trials on 23 and 24 August with an escort, she sprang a leak in one of her batteries and had to return to base.

Now U 460 began her sixth and last patrol. She left Bordeaux (La Pallice according to her reconstructed war diary) on 30 August and was ordered to steer towards the Azores for yet another fuelling rendezvous to the north of these islands. This was presumably deemed to be the most appropriate area for refuelling the boats being lined up against the North Atlantic convoys. Her initial task was to refuel two boats west of the Azores, but the detailed instructions sent to Schnoor at sea were continually decoded, albeit often too late, so that British Intelligence was able to track U 460 all the way across the Atlantic.

First of all, U-boat Command sent orders on 7 September to U 460 to cancel the first rendezvous with the outward-bound U 536 and U 170. Instead, U 460 was ordered to move north to refuel some of the *Leuthen* boats between 10 and 12 September. These orders were not decoded by British Intelligence until the 13th. U 460 supplied five U-boats (U 260, U 305, U 338, U 386 and U 645) on 11 September and took a sick engineer off U 645. The reason such a detailed account is available will become apparent shortly.

On 13 September, U-boat Command ordered U 460 to loiter in her refuelling area, north of the Azores. A new rendezvous was arranged between U 460, U 170 and U 536 for the 15th. The last had been sent out with the task of picking up escaped German POWs from the east coast of Canada, a laboriously arranged exercise intended as a morale booster. The special operation was cancelled, luckily for the POWs, since U 536 was herself sunk on 20 November. U 170 was also provided with oil and food.

The British Admiralty was so alarmed at the prospect of renewed wolf-pack attacks in the North Atlantic that it asked the Americans to use their carrier groups to hunt down and sink U 460, whose position was known from decryption. The Americans were happy to oblige and the *Bogue* carrier group was ordered to the rendezvous area, but arrived after the U-boats had parted company. However, U 460 was still there one week later, although she reported on the 21st that her radar search receiver (W. Anz) had broken down and her new Vierling gun was also damaged.

Doenitz took the opportunity to send out an admonitory message. Boats were reminded again that aircraft might be spotted at any time of the day or night in even the most remote sea areas. Special care was therefore needed when refuelling: 'Waiting boats should no longer form an all-round screen to the limits of visibility, but form an all-round screen at 500 metres for full protection. Strict lookouts are to be kept and are not to be diverted.' Boats should never lie stopped on the surface during daytime; they needed forward momentum so as to be able to dive fast in an emergency. Whenever possible, refuelling was now to be done at night.

U 460 was ordered to refuel further boats for the new *Rossbach* pack after a short move, originally from the 18th. The new rendezvous was reached safely and three U-boats (U 448, U 603 and probably also U 338, but not U 610 as claimed in the U-boat Command war diary) were oiled on 24 September. In addition U 68 supplied a replacement W. Anz apparatus to the U-tanker. As was now common practice, no homing signals were transmitted at any time and the U-boats had received strict orders not to make any wireless transmissions within 250 miles of a refuelling rendezvous in order to protect the surviving milk cows.

Again British Intelligence broke the fuelling orders for the 18th, but could not interpret the disguised rendezvous grid. U-boat Command had finally decided to send the boats to sea with sealed envelopes containing fuelling rendezvous squares. A reminder of the orders by U-boat Command on the 19th sufficed to give the position away, but again the U-tanker had moved on.

A fresh mining effort was also made, this time using some of the purpose-designed Type VIID minelayers. The U-minelayer U220 (Oberleutnant zS Barber), Type XB, was additionally sent out from Germany on her first war cruise on 28 August with orders to lay a mine barrage off St John's, Newfoundland. The original minelaying orders for U220 were dated 11 May 1943 and explained the need to lay mines off St John's, with details of regular ship movements discovered by U-boats already in the vicinity. The orders stated explicitly that the U-minelayer was to serve first as a milk cow, then to proceed to lay mines on the night of a new moon. Further orders detailed the position and grouping of the mines.

The 39-year-old Barber was highly experienced, having served as First Officer on Korth's U93 between July 1940 and October 1941, and as commander of U58 until the end of August 1942. He had then held various shore positions until he had commissioned U220 on 27 March 1943. Five months of training and working up in the Baltic had followed.

After a short stop in Bergen, which she left on 8 September, U220 was at sea again. However, it appears that her orders had been modified so that, in accord with standard practice, she should attend to the minelaying first and then return to the middle Atlantic to serve as a milk cow. As was now commonplace, Barber chose to maintain strict W/T silence and was ordered by U-boat Command to show his position on 21 September. His reply, at AK8345 in the middle of the North Atlantic air gap, prompted a warning from U-boat Command about the danger of Allied escort vessels known to be in the vicinity.

Four days later, U-boat Command again intervened to order U220 to head at once for the badly shot-up U422 north-east of the Azores. Her doctor was required to remain, if necessary, with the patient on U422. But the boats could not find each other in night fog and a further rendezvous was arranged between U422 and U460 (see below).

Now north of the Azores, U220 was ordered to serve as a weather boat, but she made few signals. The delay was doubtless to ensure that the moon was new by the time the mines were to be laid. Then there is a long gap in the reconstructed war diary of U220 as the U-minelayer headed west, before U-boat Command reminded Barber of the need to show the outcome of her minelaying mission. That same night (9/10 October), U220

189

laid sixty-six 'eggs' off St John's, then slipped away. Barber reported 'mission accomplished' on the 11th and received congratulations from Doenitz. U 220 now moved on to her subsequent refuelling mission (see below). The mines sank two small freighters of 3,478 and 3,721 tons on 19 October.

U 214 and U 218, both Type VIID minelayers, steered towards the Caribbean. On 9 September, U 214 was sighted on the surface 92 miles south-south-west of Santa Maria by aircraft from the *Croatan* carrier group. Heavy flak from the U-boat severely damaged the aircraft and the boat escaped, entering the Caribbean at the end of the month. U 214 planted fifteen mines 4 miles off the Panama Canal on the evening of 8 October. The American air search resulted in the inadvertent sinking of the US submarine *Dorado*, while U 214 escaped. The mines were swept within a month, having caused no damage. Meanwhile, U 214 continued an offensive patrol in the Caribbean.

U 218 laid her fourteen mines off Port of Spain (Caribbean) on the night of 26/27 October, having previously beaten off an air attack near Grenada. She then crept away unobserved. Again, good intelligence alerted the Allies and minesweepers swept the area for months, without ever finding anything.

The elderly Type IXB boat U 103 was sent out with orders to lay eight mines as close as possible to the West African port of Takoradi. The mines were of the new TMC type, which became active only after being overrun by a predetermined number of times, making them much harder to sweep. U 103 slipped out in September, refuelled from U 488 on 6 October (see below) and reported on 1 November that she had laid her mines successfully. Her further story will be taken up later.

The *Leuthen* pack was ready to commence operations, after its refuelling, by 16 September. Doenitz had decided that the pack was to concentrate on the ballasted, west-bound convoys, rather than their heavy laden, east-bound counterparts, apparently because the convoy defence was likely to be weaker. B-Dienst had already detected two convoys (ON.202 and ONS.18) moving close together and the pack was ordered to the attack. But British Intelligence had overheard the exchange of signals and an escort group was rushed to the aid of the other escorts of the convoys as they approached the threatened zone. Simultaneously long-range aircraft flew continuous patrols to keep the U-boats down. The U-boats finally located both convoys on the 18th and, after a running battle, the pack reported the sinking of nine merchant ships and twelve escorts. In fact the figures were exaggerated, for the U-boats counted each T-5 explosion as a sunk ship whereas many torpedoes exploded prematurely or in the wake of their target (after the war, it would be estimated that the success rate of the T-5 acoustic torpedo was little better than 10 per cent). The real figures were six merchant ships and three escorts sunk at a cost of three U-boats, with a further six U-boats damaged.

These apparent successes against the convoy defences led Doenitz to co-ordinate the pack for another assault, but three convoys dodged them and aircraft sank three more U-boats. The *Leuthen* group only finally made contact with another convoy on 7 October and this time the ever-present air patrols kept sinkings down to one merchant ship and one escort, while once again three U-boats were sunk.

The U-boats were again sustaining heavy casualties for little return in the vicinity of the convoys, but this was not their only problem for carrier groups were also operating around the Azores and British Intelligence was again able to decipher the instructions telling the U-boats where to go for fuel.

Another blow was dealt by the US Army Air Force when a series of bombing raids on the French ports of Nantes and La Pallice resulted in the sinking of the surface tanker *Ermland* (11,232 tons) on 23 September, together with the blockade runner *Kulmerland* (7,363 tons), the tanker *Monsun* (8,038 tons) and other ships. It may be recalled that the *Ermland* had at one time been assigned to resupplying U-boats, although those days had long gone.

At the end of September, the order telling U-boats to shoot it out with attacking aircraft was finally completely rescinded. U 460 took a wounded sailor off U 422 on 27 September – there were several wounded aboard from an air action requiring a visit from the tanker's doctor. At this stage, Schnoor was moving on the surface during the day, submerged at night, and U 460 had refuelled eight U-boats of the North Atlantic packs, but her new fuelling orders had already been decoded.

U 422 now reported that she was ready for action again so, instead of returning to base, she wanted fuel, and was commanded to join U 455 and U 264 at the planned rendezvous with U 460. On 3 October, U 460 was ordered to supply U 422 at a different rendezvous, still in the same general area. Suddenly she was attacked by nine carrier aircraft. She managed to dive, resurfaced later to charge her batteries and dived again when more aircraft appeared. Yet Schnoor did not find it necessary to mention the proximity of carrier aircraft to U-boat Command.

Next morning, U 460 lay on the surface at the new rendezvous. Also present were U 264, U 455 and U 422. U 264 was oiled first with 15 tons of fuel, but an aircraft searching from the *Card* carrier group sighted the U-boats and attacked out of the sun just as the U-tanker was about to cast off the refuelling lines to U 264.

Schnoor's innovation of sending a doctor and an engineer to different boats at each rendezvous has already been mentioned. The suddenness of the attack left Chief Engineer Conen of U 460 stranded on U 264, unable to return. It is from Conen's subsequent account to U-boat Command that we owe the story of the tanker's movements between Bordeaux and this fateful day.

The U-boats remained on the surface to shoot down their assailant, despite the suggestion from the experienced commander (Kapitaen-leutnant Looks, who survived the war as a prisoner) of U 264 that the milk cow should submerge at once. The first attack by the aircraft missed, bombs falling between U 264 and U 460 and the U-boats remained on the surface, weaving in zigzag patterns while staying close together. The aircraft carried a Fido, but could not use it while the U-boats remained on the surface. The pilot circled, awaiting reinforcements. At this point the U-tanker should have submerged, covered by the fire of the other U-boats, but she failed to do so.

Looks, the senior commander present, signalled urgently to Schnoor to dive, but the tanker manned her 37mm cannon instead. Looks signalled again and one can imagine with what desperation for none of the attack boats was permitted to submerge while the tanker remained on the surface. Crewmen from U 264, including both Looks and Conen, clearly saw Schnoor give shrugs and signals as though he did not know what to do.

After thirty minutes U 455 submerged, despite the standing orders that the cow should do so first. Then three more aircraft from *Card* arrived on the scene. They attacked, but all were beaten off by the heavy volume of anti-aircraft fire.

The U-boats seized the chance to crash-dive and Looks took a last look round as he did so – U 422 and U 460 were still on the surface as U 264 submerged beneath the waves. With all the U-boats underwater, the first aircraft was able to drop its Fido, which was placed in front of the diving swirl of 'a large U-boat'. Within minutes debris and oil came floating to the surface. As the shocked crew of U 264 slipped away underwater, they heard underwater detonations and twice a strong 'swooshing' as though the tanker's crew sought to blow its tanks fully. Thus died Schnoor, probably the best of the tanker commanders, with U 460, on her sixth cruise. There were no survivors from the 62-man crew. But now begins the mystery.

Shortly afterwards, U 264 was severely damaged by a 'bomb' in the stern, but she survived to return to base. At about the same time a U-boat of the group resurfaced only 3 miles away, apparently damaged. She submerged again, chased by a second Fido. It was long believed that this boat was U 422 (Oberleutnant zS Poeschel) and that she had been sunk without survivors. However, in 1993 a German historian (Dr Alex Niestlé) and the Naval Historical Records Division of the British Ministry of Defence reinvestigated all the available evidence. They concluded that it was U 264 that had been hit and damaged by the second Fido. Thus U 422 and U 460 had both apparently been sunk together with just one Fido at the original fuelling rendezvous. Further examination of the records showed that the

Card aircraft had dropped its first Fido into the swirl of a 'large U-boat' and not, as previously had been supposed, into the swirl of the largest boat (the pilot had incorrectly identified the presence of one milk cow, two 'large' U-boats and one smaller boat, instead of the real situation of a cow and three small boats). Thus it was concluded that U 422 had been sunk by Fido at the original rendezvous.

What, then, of U 460? It was widely agreed that she was in no position to dive quickly, but the other boats had abandoned her on the surface as a swarm of fresh carrier aircraft approached. It is reasonable to suppose that Schnoor decided to take the lesser of two evils: he dived while not in a proper condition to do so and the U-tanker sank too quickly for him to change his mind.

According to members of the surviving U-boats, Schnoor of U 460 had complained of being harried daily by carrier aircraft. The rendezvous was changed each time an aircraft was sighted, which necessitated the transmission of wireless signals from U-boat Command, rendering worthless the blanket order of W/T silence around a fuelling rendezvous. All these signals were decoded by British Intelligence. However, for once U-boat Command was up to date with the situation at sea, for on 7 October U 460 was presumed lost as of 4 October, and a planned rendezvous in a new sea area with U 155 was cancelled (as it happened, U 155 had already refuelled from U 488). At the same time, boats at sea were reminded that 'in the case of air attacks, the tanker is to dive at the first opportunity. The remaining boats are to screen her diving with every available means and at full risk to themselves. They may only dive when the tanker has reached a safe depth.'

U 488 (Oberleutnant zS Bartke) had been despatched from Bordeaux on 8 September for the second cruise of both tanker and commander. Her objective was to refuel U-boats heading for remote waters. After her escort had departed, U 488 crossed the Bay of Biscay entirely submerged, other than time needed at night to recharge her batteries. Naturally, this slowed down her rate of progress across the Bay, but this was a fact of life that all U-boats now had to accept.

The Germans had finally cottoned on to the idea of making larger changes of rendezvous, involving movements of hundreds of miles, rather than the 50-mile shifts that had previously been favoured, and which could be covered by a carrier aircraft in half an hour. Now the nightmare began. The first ill omen occurred when one of the crew went down with appendicitis less than one week into the cruise. Bartke took the tanker deep so that the doctor could operate on the patient and the operation was successful. Next day, the tanker reported its position to U-boat Command and immediately deployed two Aphrodite radar decoys. Bartke was ordered to proceed carefully to his fuelling rendezvous in mid-Atlantic, far to the west of the Cape Verde Islands, the plan being to refuel three U-cruisers (U 177, U 181 and U 196) heading from the western Indian

Ocean back to France. En route a British submarine was sighted (the 16th) and Bartke deployed two more Aphrodite decoys, discovering as he did so that the U-tanker was leaving a trail of oil from an unknown cause.

Next day, U 488 sighted an aircraft carrier with its screen of destroyers. The cow went deep, reporting her observation to U-boat Command the following day. Meanwhile, the cause of the oil trail had been located (defective packing material) and fixed.

U-boat Command then cancelled the refuelling of the U-cruisers (the U-cruisers had reported that they retained enough fuel to reach France) and directed U 488 to a position west-south-west of the Azores (22 September), thereby irritating Bartke who had to retrace some of his steps in order to relieve U 460 then positioned north of the islands. Next day, the W. Anz transformer ran hot and the radar receiver was to be of doubtful value for the remainder of U 488's cruise. A carrier aircraft was spotted in broad daylight as the sun flashed off it and the tanker dived quickly.

U 488 still had plenty of time to reach her rendezvous, which she achieved running mostly submerged during the day. On the 27th, she foolishly signalled: 'Will arrive on the 29th', and subsequently had to dive to avoid another aircraft, later releasing two more Aphrodite decoys. Reporting the presence of carrier aircraft, U 488 was moved to a new rendezvous north of the original, now due west of the Azores.

U 488 commenced her refuelling operations, replenishing the U-boats that had been sent to the Caribbean and South Atlantic. On 29 September, U 68 was refuelled with 42 tons of oil, two weeks' provisions, motor oil and some parts; U 488 was then ordered to move a little way to refuel U 155 (Piening) and U 103 (Janssen). After injudicious use by U 488 of homing signals, and then megaphones, U 155 was refuelled with 30 tons of oil on 4 October, and then U 103 on the 6th for her minelaying operation off Takoradi. All these supply operations proceeded without interference, but the W. Anz on U 488 broke down. U 68 and U 155 were returning from missions in remote waters.

By 7 October, U 488 appeared to be going in circles to the west of the Azores and U-boat Command ordered Bartke to move to a position north of the islands to replace the lost U 460. U 488 made the move on the surface at night and received W/T instructions for the repair of her W. Anz radar receiver, although the crew remained doubtful about its usefulness. Further orders arrived on the 9th: U 488 was to refuel five U-boats 600 miles north of the Azores from 11 to 13 October, each with 35 tons of oil. These were some of the mangled survivors of the *Rossbach* pack, which had taken a severe beating without accomplishing much itself. The tanker was then to move south while the attack boats headed north to intercept the North Atlantic convoys.

U-boat Command again became seriously concerned about the safety of their milk cows and issued new standing orders on 11 October:

1. In the areas South, North and West of the Azores our supply groups have recently several times been picked up by carrier-borne aircraft and attacked by surprise. In order to avoid such attacks, the following orders are given:
2. Supply boat and boats about to be supplied are to proceed submerged on the day of the rendezvous and arrange to reach the rendezvous position two hours before sunset. Then surface and contact the tanker in daylight.
3. As a general rule, supply will only be carried out at night. Careful with lights. Morse signalling with blue lamp. Only officers and petty officers detailed by the commanding officer may carry dimmed torches. Boats in waiting should join on, on the side of the tanker from which supply is not being carried out.
4. The tanker will always remain submerged in the area by day and will be at the rendezvous again by sunset.
5. If there is heavy weather, or the night is so dark that distances cannot be safely kept, supply may have to be carried out by day. In these weather conditions carrier-borne aircraft are not on the whole to be expected.

U-boats in the South Atlantic were told not to expect refuelling when they returned, owing to the shortage of tankers, while two more aircraft traps, U 953 and U 256, stood as decoys in the North Atlantic. The latter beat off an aircraft attack on 8 October and was then directed, with another flak boat, U 271, to stand guard over U 488.

As previously, plenty of time was allowed for the cow to make an underwater transition and U 488 arrived in good time on the 12th in heavy weather – U-boat Command had advised that this might delay the arrival of the other boats, and also warned frequently of the threat posed by carrier-borne aircraft.

Between 11 and 12 October, the U-tanker and four U-boats (U 402, U 584, U 731 and U 378) waiting to be refuelled were sighted repeatedly by aircraft from the carrier *Card*. U 488 observed a large land-based bomber over the rendezvous on the 12th and the rendezvous was moved. It was on the 12th that, according to Allied Intelligence sources, U 488 was caught on her own, on the surface, by more aircraft from the carrier group. Allegedly, she fought off four planes for over an hour before finally being able to dive, albeit once again with Fido on her tail, but this time the acoustic torpedo apparently exploded prematurely and the U-boat was not sunk. Yet there is no mention of this attack in the war diary of U 488 and the description closely fits an attack on U 731 which was damaged the same day. Other American sources state that U 488 was sighted by carrier aircraft on the 12th while in the act of surfacing, but dived smartly as the aircraft began a bombing run. Fido was dropped instead, but there was no result. A second Fido attack a few hours later was likewise unsuccessful.

U 488's supply area was moved to the south-east. The following day, U 402 came searching for the U-tanker in her original area, but found only aircraft and she was sunk by a Fido.

U 488 surfaced at the new rendezvous on 14 October to discover two U-boats (U 378 and Manseck's U 758) waiting. The crew of the former attended to the tanker's rudder while receiving 48 tons of oil; U 758 took on 14 tons for her homeward trip. The boats dived at daylight and the crew of U 488 was stunned by the sudden death of watch officer Bergmann, from a heart attack, despite treatment during the day, an event that was doubtless caused by the stress of the tanker's mission. Bergmann was buried at sea late on the 16th.

U 641 was now given 17 tons of oil, just sufficient for the homeward journey. Bartke then asked plaintively of U-boat Command: 'Our position here is very sad. We have supplied two and a half boats and seen a fourth. Where are the others?'

Protection against aircraft was provided by the two aircraft traps U 256 and U 271 which took up station beside U 488. The aircraft traps were similarly armed to U 441, which had decoyed Allied aircraft in the Bay in July. U 256 herself had been severely walloped by an aircraft in the Bay of Biscay in August 1942 while returning to France, the U-boat being so badly damaged that she was out of action for a year, during which time she had been rebuilt for her present task.

Bartke made a determined effort to find some new 'customers' on the 18th, but was frustrated by the weather: 'The weather is always worse, the barometer always lower.' It was not until the 20th that U 731 was located by her homing signals. The damaged U 731 was down to her last 4 tons of fuel and was given 26 tons as a matter of priority early on the 21st. Three more U-boats had been replenished by other attack boats in the new refuelling area before the arrival of the *Core* carrier group on 20 October. On the same day aircraft from *Core* sank U 378 and damaged the AA boat, U 271.

Now the U-minelayer U 220 arrived from her minelaying mission to support the U-tanker. U-boat Command ordered U 220 and U 455 to rendezvous north of the Azores so that the cow could receive surplus fuel from the other boat. The orders were clarified next day: U 220 was to proceed to the same rendezvous to assist U 488 with her fuelling mission. Detailed fuelling instructions followed: four U-boats were to receive large quantities of oil to proceed with their missions; another three boats were to receive barely sufficient fuel to return home. Then U 488 was to say which cow was to remain on station while the other returned home too. U-boat Command was particularly hopeful that U 488 could be rushed home and out again, while U 220 covered her 'customers' in her absence.

196

By 24 October, U 488 and U 220 had met each other far north of the Azores, while the AA boat U 256 (Oberleutnant zS Brauel) stood guard. All the boats dived at daylight and U 488 soon after lost contact with the U-minelayer.

Next day, U 488 was suddenly shelled in the darkness by a fast-closing destroyer, with no warning from W. Anz. The tanker dived at once and went deep. The first depth-charges crashed about as she reached 30 metres, but were poorly placed. The second series was much more accurate, exploding around the U-tanker as she reached 130 metres. The boat took a severe battering, but survived to reach a depth of 180 metres.

The *Block Island* carrier group had been scouring the area trying to run down the sources of the many signals they had detected by H/F D/F, and her destroyer escorts *Parrott* and *Paul Jones* had finally run into the tanker herself. Now a search group of three (according to U 488's war diary) destroyers could clearly be heard overhead. U 488 descended to 235 metres as the depth-charges crashed all around, withstood the water pressure at this depth and managed to creep slowly away. According to the American account of the action, the destroyer attack had been 'poorly organized'.

U 488 surfaced the following day to charge her batteries and the crew discovered shell damage to both hull and bridge. She submerged again after reporting to U-boat Command and effected temporary repairs. The rumble of depth-charges continued all day and well into the next.

Again U-boat Command could not resist providing detailed instructions. On 27 October the rendezvous for U 488 was moved far to the west of the Azores, but the tanker was plagued by a series of problems with her batteries. She sent a plaintive list of her cumulative troubles to U-boat Command, but eventually reached the new rendezvous on 1 November. Also on 27 October, U 220 was ordered to meet U 762, then to proceed in company with U 256 to aid U 584. Clarification was sent two days later. She refuelled U 603 and U 256, but on the 28th aircraft from the *Block Island* carrier group caught U 220 on the surface while she was still connected to U 256.

Both boats lay together, trimmed down and awash, in near perfect visibility, unobservant until the aircraft began strafing. U 220 was the closer to the aircraft, but was not seen to put up any flak, whereas, true to her role, a heavy barrage was put up by U 256. Bombs fell to either side of the conning tower of U 220, which slewed to a halt while describing a circle of 180 degrees, settled in the water, her bow rose to an angle of 45 degrees and then she slid under. There were no survivors from the 51-man crew. The other U-boat managed to dive, but Fido was dropped onto its tail. The torpedo was seen to change course onto the direction of the target, but then disappeared and U 256 escaped despite a determined hunt by other aircraft armed with Fido and sonobuoys (the latter being sensitive sound locators dropped into the sea from an aircraft; they had just come into service).

U 220 was presumed lost by U-boat Command on 31 October, receiving her second star on 5 July 1944.

The above is the conventional account given for the sinking of U 220, but German historian Alex Niestlé has noted that the war diary of U 256 records that, thirty minutes after the air attack which supposedly sank U 220, U 256 and U 220 agreed by underwater signalling to make for a new rendezvous. Eight hours later, the surfaced U 256 observed a series of explosions on the horizon and U 220 failed to keep the revised rendezvous. There was no air attack recorded at this time, so the true story of the end of U 220 will probably never be known.

All attempts at refuelling in the North Atlantic were now abandoned. U-boat Command had always been amazed that the Allies had never attempted to interfere with supply operations north of the Azores during 1942–3, since they must have been apparent if only from the volume of signal traffic. Thus, when American carrier groups started to sweep the areas with decryption information, U-boat Command merely shrugged its shoulders and said, 'Well, that's that then. They finally got round to doing it.' This anticipation of disaster helped to conceal the almost casual use by the Americans of U-boat cipher decryptions.

Meanwhile, U 488 had located U 193 (Pauckstadt) at her new rendezvous far to the west of the Azores and the outward-bound attack boat was given 32 tons of fuel. The Type VIID minelayer U 214 (Stock) had reported that she was also low on fuel in the area, but Bartke felt it prudent to change positions first. U-boat Command at once butted in, ordering U 488 to show her position immediately and to steer at once for U 214. This order to transmit a position jeopardized the rendezvous. Meanwhile, the weather again deteriorated.

U-boat Command sent clarification of orders on 3 November, giving British Intelligence a second bite at the apple if they had missed it the first time. If U 214 was not refuelled by U 488, then two other named boats in the vicinity were to rush to the former's assistance. On the same day, U 488 again provided parts and provisions to the accompanying U 193 – U-boat Command had decided to make the latter boat the escort for the tanker in these dangerous waters – before both boats set out to search for U 214. Meanwhile Bartke took the opportunity to dump 2 tons of ballast – the depth-charging of 25 October appears to have upset her handling at periscope depth.

By 5 November, U 214 had still not been found, but she betrayed the rendezvous by sending out homing signals. U 488 replied in kind, albeit at half normal strength, and the other boat was at last located on the 6th. But as it was now becoming light the boats submerged. At 1028 hrs, Bartke recorded the reverberation of aircraft bombs nearby, followed by more detonations in the afternoon. When the cow surfaced after dark, U 214 was nowhere to be seen.

U 488 cautiously slipped away, deploying Aphrodite decoys. Early on the 7th, Bartke reported his fears about U 214 to U-boat Command, but was directed to search further, albeit without use of homing signals. Battery problems had again begun to trouble the milk cow. U-boat Command then assured Bartke that the supply problem of U 214 'has been taken care of' (U 214 had been supplied by U 193 on the 7th and thus needed more fuel herself, while U 214 survived to return to France) and sent U 488 far to the south-west to a point roughly due south of Newfoundland and due east of Florida, where it was hoped that the carrier groups would not follow – at any rate, not quickly enough to harass the U-tanker. The tanker ran at high speed on the surface at night in an effort to shake off her pursuers, but the order had scarcely been given when a destroyer was sighted. U 488 dived to the alarm and reached a depth of 140 metres, when a second destroyer was heard. Bartke took the boat down to 225 metres and managed to slip away.

U 488 was close to her latest rendezvous by the 10th and sighted U 193 again. But still the roar of depth-charges accompanied the boats as they continued to proceed underwater to where two other boats awaited supply. Now she was able to refuel U 193, U 530 and U 129, all bound for remote waters, between 13 and 14 November. A sick sailor from U 193 was exchanged with one of the cow's crewmen and the three U-boats together received a total of 197 tons of oil as well as thirty-five days of provisions and parts. U 488 dumped much ballast during the rendezvous, which was conducted strictly during the hours of darkness with the boats submerged in daylight.

Bartke signalled to U-boat Command that refuelling was complete, that the tanker was suffering from various mechanical defects, had 102 tons of oil remaining and could he go home now? U-boat Command had planned that U 488 should hand over her remaining fuel to the minelayer U 219 that was passing through the North Atlantic (see below) and might serve as a substitute for her sister ship, the sunken U 220, but 'as it did not seem worthwhile to refuel U 219 as arranged and the tanker would be in too much danger', next day (the 14th) U-boat Command approved the homeward run.

A certain amount of cheer must have been afforded by the report of U 129 (Oberleutnant zS von Harpe) that she had hit an aircraft carrier in the vicinity on the 15th. In fact, U 129 had indeed fired on the *Core*, but the torpedoes had exploded without hitting their target. U 129 at once went deep and managed to slip away.

U 488 started the long cruise back to France to the sound of a constant barrage of underwater detonations. Travelling submerged by day and surfaced at night, she was again west of the Azores on 22 November when the starboard diesel engine broke down. Repairs were effected overnight.

Then came another tragedy. A seaman had fallen ill on the 22nd with a swelling of the neck that grew rapidly worse and threatened his breathing. Despite several incisions, ultimately to insert an air tube into the lungs, Seaman Heinlein died on the 25th. Bartke wrote in the war diary: 'Thus was taken from our midst in a tragic way a good soldier and comrade.' Heinlein was buried at sea early on the 26th.

U 488 continued to handle sluggishly underwater and on the 28th Bartke decided to jettison another 4 tons of ballast. Meanwhile, U-boat Command West had signalled that U 488 could make a free run at the Piening route, close to the Spanish coast, into France.

Now north-east of the Azores, U 488 heard the sound of detonations begin anew, at one point almost every ten minutes, and released another Aphrodite decoy on 1 December. By now, Bartke had some difficult decisions to make. W. Anz had been unreliable since 25 October and he decided to switch off the short-wave receivers in order to prevent any possible radiations. While still heading for home, mostly submerged at 40 metres, the First Officer fell ill on 5 December. Two days later, Cape Finisterre was passed and U 488 entered the Bay of Biscay. She crossed the Bay again almost entirely submerged and took up her escort outside Bordeaux on the 11th. The river Gironde was reached but even so, at this late stage of the war, an air attack in the river estuary was a distinct possibility so U 488 was provided with a strong escort all the way up the river. Her progress was suddenly interrupted when her rudder broke down, but was repaired on the spot overnight, and U 488 finally reached her bunker at Bordeaux on 12 December.

Bartke had done very well to refuel ten U-boats at sea and it is instructive to note that as many as 2,500 miles (16.7 per cent) of her total 15,000-mile cruise had been travelled underwater. Compare this with the 6.1 per cent travelled submerged by U 459 on her first patrol. Moreover, the pace of refuelling had greatly slowed down: only one boat per night could now be supplied – and none in daylight.

Admiral Godt of U-boat Command felt moved to give U 488's war diary a much lengthier review than had hitherto been customary. He expressed sympathy for the deaths of the crew members and Bartke was praised for his care, caution and perseverance. Nevertheless, Bartke did not return to U 488 after his harrowing cruise, although the records do not state the reason why he was transferred to a school for attack commanders. His summary of the patrol did, however, contain one provocative statement: both commander and Chief Engineer wished that the U-tanker could be better rebuilt in Germany.

Bartke was replaced by Oberleutnant zS Studt, twenty-five years old, who had served on the lower deck of U 108 early in the war, been recommended for promotion, served as the watch officer of the U-tanker U 459 until June 1943, and had then spent six months in a shore appointment

200

before taking over command of U 488 (January 1944). Bartke himself did not survive the change of boat. He took command of the attack boat U 1106 and was killed in action north-east of the Faeroe Islands in March 1945.

In October 1943, Portugal agreed to lease air bases in the Azores to the Allies. The first aircraft began operations from these islands on the 19th, closing the Azores air gap and making the surrounding waters so hot for the U-boats that they were soon withdrawn from the area between Portugal and the islands. Refuelling was no longer considered possible in the area that had for so long harboured the milk cows during resupply of the wolf-packs between convoy attacks.

Meanwhile, the dozen or so U-boats in the North Atlantic found themselves in an increasingly precarious position after the loss of U 460 and U 220. U-boat Command realized that U 460 had been sunk by 7 October, and the Type VIIC attack boat U 405 was ordered to the aid of U 762 and U 91 near the Azores, both of which had nearly run out of fuel.

Individual U-boats met north of the Azores to exchange supplies at the end of October, in the absence of any U-tanker in the locality, but the carrier groups that were operating in pairs near the area (relieving each other at regular intervals) made all rendezvous on the surface extremely risky. On 30 October, aircraft from *Card* attacked a U-boat that managed to escape. Next day, U 584 and U 91 were caught together on the surface, with hoses connected, by an aircraft from *Card* as the first boat tried to re-oil the second. The boats put up heavy anti-aircraft fire and the solitary aircraft followed standing orders by circling, awaiting reinforcements. U 91 managed to submerge in time without fuel, but U 584 (Kapitaenleutnant Deecke) continued to sit on the surface, although she ceased firing. As aircraft reinforcements arrived from *Card*, U 584 belatedly submerged and was chased by two Fidos, both of which hit her. Inevitably, there were no survivors.

The Americans believed that U 91 had been the cow and sent the destroyer *Borie* out to chase the escaped boat. Instead, the *Borie* stumbled across U 256 (Brauel) which had moved into the area after her unsuccessful defence of U 220 (see above). U 256 was severely damaged by depth-charges, but managed to limp home to base. On 1 November, U 405, which had originally been scheduled to replenish U 91, was also discovered by the *Borie* and sunk in a gun and torpedo duel that also saw the loss of the US destroyer escort.

The U-minelayer U 219 (Korvettenkapitaen Burghagen) had been despatched from Germany on 5 October for a lengthy minelaying mission off Cape Town and then off Colombo (Ceylon), with its final destination Penang. U 219 had been commissioned on 12 December 1942 by the 52-year-old Burghagen, who had served as a U-boat officer in the First World War and had hitherto held office appointments in the Second World War. It is not enough, opined Napoleon, that a commander should be competent

201

– he should also be lucky. Burghagen was to demonstrate that he possessed both qualities in full measure.

U 219 began her active service with a flak practice with U 967 before both boats departed in the company of a small escort. Two days later, the U-boats arrived together at Kristiansand where the milk cow carried out test-dives and other exercises. Then U 219 departed for the minelaying mission proper on 8 October, but was found to be leaving an oil slick. Next day she dived when a Leigh light bomber appeared and signalled her return to Bergen. She was docked between 10 and 12 October, while her propeller shafts were repaired.

Burghagen departed again on 17 October. U 219 had been fitted with the new W. Anz radar detector and on the 25th it gave a strong alarm in the Northern Transit area. Burghagen dived at once but no air attack ensued. Now heading south-west into the mid-Atlantic, U 219 received coded orders to go to 'Green AC00' (a disguised rendezvous grid) and await new orders. She continued westwards to the thunder of constant detonations and on 1 November gave her position far south-west of Iceland, where heavy weather prevented routine maintenance work. The Naxos receiver gave a shrill alarm during the night, but again the U-minelayer was able to submerge undetected.

U 219 was now in the North Atlantic air gap, conveniently close for any U-boats struggling with insufficient fuel. On 2 November, U-boat Command directed Burghagen to abandon his minelaying mission and to navigate directly at highest speed to the aid of the other boats. The cautious Burghagen interpreted 'highest speed' to mean progress above and (slower) below the water during night and day, as appropriate, but on 4 November he was ordered to head at maximum acceleration to U 91. Matters were complicated for U 219, on her errand of mercy, by strong Naxos warnings that day and the next, but U 91 was located on the 5th at 'Green SP4399' (actually BD2399), north of the Azores. Both boats dived but resurfaced just after midnight to begin the fuelling operation. It took nearly six hours to deliver 31.5 tons of oil, and the wind and sea prevented the transfer of provisions.

The fuel transfer was twice disturbed. Within an hour (0100 hrs, 6 November) U-boat Command had ordered all U-boats to switch off their W. Anz radar detectors, fearing that it still emitted radiations. Wanze was switched off and an entry made in the war diary of U 219. Then a strong radar warning was received from Naxos. The sailors could only man their guns and cross their fingers, but no attack materialized.

Next, U 219 was ordered at full speed to the assistance of the empty U 762 (Kapitaenleutnant Hille) that was now adrift after failing to meet tanker U 488. U 219 searched unsuccessfully for U 762 but abandoned the task on the 7th when she learned that another U-boat (U 343) had refuelled U 762 on 5 November.

U 219 was then commanded to meet U 488 to take on the latter's fuel before the U-tanker returned to France, but the order was countermanded shortly afterwards. Instead, U 219 was directed to support other U-boats at a rendezvous far to the south, west of the Cape Verde Islands. For the next few days, she made steady progress above and below the water surface as she headed south-west, to the west of the Azores. Her continued mission is described below; in the meantime, U-boat Command informed all U-boats in the South Atlantic that they could not expect to be refuelled.

As a result of the difficulties in refuelling in the Central Atlantic, U-boats sent to remote theatres yet again ran the risk of being stranded. Patrols projected for these areas had to be curtailed and only a handful of U-boats maintained the pressure. These were mostly of the Type IX boats that could spend up to four months on patrol without refuelling, although most of the time was spent en route to the operational area. Nevertheless, these U-boats tied down Allied defences out of all proportion to their numbers. U 516 (Kapitaenleutnant Tillessen) did particularly well in the Caribbean, when she sank six ships totalling 25,000 tons and evaded a week-long search with the attendant loss of so much fuel that she had to be refuelled (see Chapter 16).

The Germans never seem to have considered the possibility of a 'pair' system of refuelling and patrol, whereby two U-boats of the same type leave base together; they travel together 30 per cent of the distance to the operational area, U-boat(1) gives up 30 per cent of its fuel to U-boat(2), so that U-boat(1) now has 40 per cent of its remaining fuel, sufficient to return to its base, while U-boat(2) has fully topped-up tanks, sufficient to complete its patrol. This system would have been perfectly viable from late 1943, considering that all the crews had now been trained in refuelling techniques and it was only necessary to maintain a handful of U-boats on patrol in remote waters.

On 15 October, the newly formed *Schlieffen* group attacked convoy ON.206 but sank only one ship from it and the closely following convoy ONS.20. In return, six U-boats were sunk, of which four had fallen foul of radar-fitted bombers. Towards the end of October, Doenitz formed a new patrol line of twenty U-boats, many fresh from their bases since those at sea had had to return for want of fuel. They failed to find any convoys and three were sunk by sea and air escorts.

At the end of October, Doenitz disbanded the wolf-packs, which no longer seemed to be able to overwhelm a convoy's defences but which instead provided concentrated targets for Allied defences. Refuelling at sea had in any case become too hazardous for the packs to be adequately supported. In September and October the packs had sunk only nine merchant ships in the whole of the North Atlantic at a cost of twenty-five U-boats.

From November 1943 to May 1944, small groups of three U-boats continued to operate in the North Atlantic, unsupported by cows. Their normal operational area was now much closer to the Biscay ports in order to cut down the time and fuel spent in transit. The U-boats had originally moved westwards from their bases in an effort to avoid the strong British defences close to the United Kingdom in 1941, but this consideration no longer applied when Allied defences were now effective all over the Atlantic. Their lack of success caused increasing irritation at U-boat Command with their commanders, but the U-boats continued to achieve so little at such a high cost that at the end of March 1944, Doenitz again withdrew them from the North Atlantic, as he had in 'Black May', explaining to Hitler that only the arrival of the eagerly awaited, fast, 'electric' U-boats would induce him to send U-boats back into those waters. Between September 1943 and March 1944, the rate of attrition had been such that no fewer than six U-boats had been lost for every convoyed merchant ship sunk.

Still the orders from U-boat Command were being decoded. The signal 'Kammerarrest' (Stop combing) sent out on 25 November ordered all U-boats in the South Atlantic to cease attacks on single ships – a fresh wave of German blockade runners was expected in the area, en route to France from the Far East. The order was decoded just one day later, alerting the Allies, so that just one of the luckless blockade runners made the run home to a Biscay base. Thereafter, the Germans cancelled all blockade running by surface ships.

Operations in December in remote theatres were supported by the U-minelayer U219, which we last saw west of the Azores. U-boat Command ordered her to rendezvous initially with U170 (Pfeffer) and U510 (Eick) in 'marine quadrant 80 of the big quadrant east of Blue Nanni Jota' (*sic*). This laboured language was obviously intended to mark the rendezvous quadrant by reference to a prearranged fixed point (Blue Nanni Jota). But if any of the U-boats transmitted their current positions while en route, then decryption or H/F D/F would reveal the 'big quadrant' to British Intelligence. U219 now steered south-east to the intended rendezvous, west of the Cape Verde Islands. She arrived finally on 29 November, still bearing her unused mines from her aborted minelaying mission, having suffered some trouble with her electric motors en route. At the rendezvous, the assembled U-boats began a strange courtship ritual of surfacing for one hour at sunrise and sunset to find one another. U170 was supplied with 43 tons of oil and U510 with 46 tons. Both boats received provisions and spare parts, and one sailor was exchanged with U219. The rendezvous was not disturbed.

Now U219 headed south-east again, meeting U103 (Janssen) on 3 December. This worn-out boat received 56 tons of oil as well as provisions, after returning from her minelaying mission off Takoradi. She was now to return directly to Norway, and then to Germany where she would be paid off.

Next day, Burghagen signalled: 'Still have 114 tons' (of oil). U-boat Command directed him on 7 December to make one last rendezvous and then to return home. The outward-bound U 172 (Oberleutnant zS Hoffmann) was to be provided with fuel before she proceeded into the Indian Ocean. After some calculations, Burghagen reckoned that he could not make the rendezvous in time if he travelled underwater. He therefore took U 219 to the surface and steered for the new rendezvous south of the Azores and west of the Cape Verde Islands.

But the orders from U-boat Command had been decoded by the US '10th Fleet'. The *Bogue* carrier group left its convoy (GUS.23) and steered towards the rendezvous. Meanwhile, U 172 was apparently not ready to refuel when U 219 arrived (12 December) and things proceeded very slowly. Burghagen vented his ire in the war diary: 'Boats that must be supplied outward-bound should receive orders to empty first that bunker which can itself be most quickly filled. Boats supplied should have ready for the supplier written, precise demands to be handed over with the first dinghy to reach the supplier.' And so on. According to Burghagen, U 172 also required different parts to those that were supplied, necessitating many return dinghy trips to the cow.

The coding machine of U 172 was repaired on U 219 and Burghagen was concerned when he heard that Hoffmann had come under air attack at night – luckily without damage – with no warning from the boat's Naxos or Borkum radar receivers. In the end U 172 took on a meagre 25 tons of oil, plus provisions, and U 219 steered for home.

She was barely over the horizon and U 172 had dived when aircraft from the *Bogue* carrier group arrived and spotted Hoffmann's boat at periscope depth. Fido was dropped onto the unsuspecting U-boat which was hard hit, but the crew somehow regained control and the boat came to the surface in a welter of oil. The U-boat promptly dived again but was battered by depth-charges from *Bogue*'s destroyer escort. She surfaced after dark, but was at once detected by radar and engaged with gunfire. Again Hoffmann managed to dive his boat but the position was hopeless. Aircraft spotted the moving oil streak at dawn and the destroyers attacked anew with depth-charges, forcing Hoffmann to the surface again. Some of the crew abandoned ship, but others returned the destroyers' fire, causing casualties. But this could not last and U 172 sank under a hail of shells, exploding underwater. Hoffmann and forty-five of his crew were rescued after an heroic 24-hour chase.

This battle may have saved U 219 as she was far away by the time the *Bogue* aircraft resumed the hunt, and evaded all further attacks. U 219 now steered back for France, submerged by day and surfaced at night only long enough to recharge her batteries.

She docked at Bordeaux on New Year's Day 1944. Admiral Godt had little to say, except that Burghagen had done well on his first patrol as commander with a new boat. Burghagen himself had had the wisdom to make very few signals indeed from U 219, which may well have saved him, his boat and his crew.

Anti-aircraft defences finally became very effective for the U-boats towards the end of 1943. In his situation report, Doenitz reviewed the various flak weapons. The Vierling 20mm guns had been fitted to all U-boats by August, but had proved to be too weak in heavy seas, while an aircraft hit by their gunfire was rarely brought down before it had finished its attack. The twin 20mm cannon which had been fitted to all U-boats by October was good, handy and well liked, but was again too light and gun shields had been found necessary resulting in modifications to the gun itself. The new-pattern, automatic, quick-firing 37mm cannon first tried by the flak boat U 441 in July had been fitted to several U-boats after October, and was eventually to be fitted to all. (By the beginning of 1944 80 per cent of U-boats carried the gun, but it was found to have been shoddily built and rusted easily in sea water, although these faults were remedied.) The aircraft decoy boats were to be reconverted to attack U-boats. They had poor seaworthiness, it was too dangerous to use them in the Bay of Biscay, they carried too few torpedoes for use against convoys and ordinary U-boats now carried anti-aircraft armaments that were almost their equal.

The situation with radar was also becoming promising. Towards the end of October, U-boats began to be equipped with the Naxos-U radar search receiver, capable of receiving 10cm radar transmissions. By February 1944, the performance of Naxos had been so improved that it was an effective search receiver for all Allied radar transmissions, including the new 3cm radar that came into service in mid-1944. Doenitz transmitted a rousing message to U-boats at sea on 13 November to the effect that Naxos, Borkum and W. Anz-2 did not emit radiation and were effective. But the damage caused by fears about radiations from Metox and W. Anz could not so easily be undone. Most U-boat crews so feared the possibility that emanations could be detected from their receivers that most of the time the latter were left switched off.

Chapter 16

Maintaining the Pressure
January to May 1944

With the collapse of wolf-pack operations in the Atlantic, it was more important than ever that U-boats should be able to make attacks in as many different places as possible, since merely forcing the Allies to continue the convoy system tied down huge numbers of aircraft and warships, and wasted much valuable shipping space. But the medium-range Type VII boats could not reach distant waters without refuelling, while the longer-range Type IX boats could operate much more effectively if they were replenished at sea. U-boat Command elected to use only Type IX boats for these patrols on account of the danger of Type VII boats being hopelessly stranded if anything should happen to the surviving cows.

At the beginning of 1944 the only cows still available were U 488 (Type XIV) and U 219 (Type XB) at Bordeaux, and U 490 (Type XIV) and U 233 (Type XB) in German waters. All were fitted with the now standard heavy anti-aircraft guns. The last of the Type XB series, U 234, would enter service in March 1944, having been damaged in May 1943 by bombing while being built. The entry of U 490 into service was delayed by two serious accidents. After being commissioned on 27 March 1943, she suffered a battery explosion during trials on 7 May, necessitating a return to Kiel for a month for repairs and extra work. Released again on 23 June, U 490 conducted re-fuelling exercises with the 27th U-boat Flotilla off Gotenhafen in July 1943. She had just surfaced after a practice dive on the 23rd when water poured into the diesel room, apparently through open vents, and the tanker sank to the bottom, 65 metres down. After an anxious three-quarters of an hour of repairs, U 490 managed to regain the surface, but the electric motors, radio communications and rudders had all failed (the signal to this effect, made through the accompanying U 845, was decrypted by British Intelligence). U 490 returned to dockyard hands from 29 July 1943 to 10 February 1944, when training resumed with trials of a new schnorkel. Eight boats were given practice refuellings. Some eight months later than planned, U 490 was ready for operations on 4 May 1944.

An interesting facet of U 490 was that the tanker was strengthened by having her ribs fitted externally, rather than internally. These gave more room within and enabled the tanker to dive safely to 300 metres. She also had a powerful flak defence, comprising two twin 20mm mounts on the upper gun platform and an automatic quick-firing 37mm gun of the new design on the lower platform. There was additionally an automatic 37mm deck gun forward of the conning tower, but U 490 lacked radar which was planned to be fitted at Bordeaux.

Apart from these standard cows, the first of a limited series of Type VIIF torpedo transport U-boats had been completed. Four were built in all, but again bombing delayed the entry of two of the boats (U 1061 and U 1062) into service. Since the stocks of torpedoes in the Indian Ocean were running down and since this was one of the few theatres still capable of providing good results (see Chapter 14), the Germans decided to use two of these transporters to carry torpedoes to the Far East, although their range was not sufficient to enable boats of this class to reach Penang without mid-ocean refuelling.

In order to keep up the pressure in distant waters, it was only necessary for a handful of U-boats to operate. Increasing the number of U-boats would have little effect in terms of Allied ships sunk, while possibly leading to higher losses among the participating boats. The more boats operating in an area, the more likely the Allies were to increase their defences to a level at which no U-boat could expect to survive. For this reason, only one cow was to be sent out at a time, both to conserve stocks and because one cow carried enough fuel for all the U-boats sent to remote theatres. Losses to the long-range Type IXB/IXC U-boats had been so great in March–July 1943 that thereafter there were never enough to maintain more than four on patrol in remote theatres at one time. Inevitably, the strategy of sinking ships faster than they could be built had to give way to the 'inferior' strategy (in Doenitz's eyes) of tying down enemy forces.

U 544 (Type IXC/40) was ordered to refuel U 516 (Tillessen, coming from Panama) and U 129 (commanded by the newly promoted Kapitaenleutnant von Harpe) 500 miles west of the Azores in January 1944; in addition, Naxos would be supplied to both U-boats. These orders were decoded by the American '10th Fleet', so when U 129 arrived at the rendezvous on the 16th she could only hear the sound of destroyers and depth-charges – aircraft from the *Guadalcanal* carrier group had surprised U 516 and U 544 on the surface in broad daylight while both were connected by hoses.

The first aircraft fired rockets in three salvoes, each of two. The first pair of missiles fell short of U 516, the second punched a hole in U 544 and the third pair also hit the supply boat, which was simultaneously straddled by bombs as the aircraft flew over. In the ensuing panic, U 516 submerged stern-first and this unorthodox disappearance led the pilots to believe, incorrectly, that she had been severely damaged. The crew of U 544

208

abandoned ship as their boat sank and between twenty and thirty-five survivors were observed swimming in the water, although they were never seen again, despite the efforts of two American destroyers sent to rescue them.

U-boat Command now arranged a fresh rendezvous between U 516 and the outward-bound U 539. Both boats were attacked at the new rendezvous (the 19th) by carrier aircraft and U 516 had the additional indignity of being depth-charged by a destroyer. Her desire for fuel had only arisen after a long hunt by warships in the Caribbean, causing her to take overlengthy evasive action. After days of cautious searching at dusk, the boats again located one another and U 539 oiled U 516 on 4 February in such heavy seas that the hoses were repeatedly disconnected. As a result, the operational area of U 539 had to be moved from the east coast of the USA to the closer Newfoundland, and she had to abandon her patrol by 5 March due to shortage of fuel.

Kapitaenleutnant Tillessen was an able and intelligent U-boat commander who managed to survive the war after three successful patrols in U 516. He had on his own initiative plotted the position of every fuelling rendezvous that had been attacked by Allied forces and had already concluded that the wise commander did not signal anywhere near a gathering of U-boats. U 129 had arranged the earlier rendezvous by coded transmission from a point remote from the meeting of all three U-boats involved, and the final position had been signalled to all three boats in code from U-boat Command in France. When Tillessen finally reached France on 26 February, he reported to U-boat Command that the naval codes *must* have been broken. He was not believed, although the wireless communications staff felt it necessary to annotate his war diary. It should also be mentioned that the carrier aircrews had been similarly astounded by the accuracy with which they had been vectored across a deserted ocean to a crowded refuelling zone.

U-boat Command was not only blind to the fact that its codes had been broken, it did not even consider the possibility that the capture of a U-boat with its codes intact might lead to a series of planned captures. Yet one of the Atlantic packs, U 744, was forced to surface on 6 March after a thirty-hour hunt by a Canadian escort group (the longest successful U-boat hunt of the war). She was boarded, the codes were seized and the U-boat was then sunk by a torpedo from one of the escorts. As it happened, Allied Intelligence had no need for this new material, but the possibility that the codes might have been used to capture another U-boat remained.

The Type VIID minelayer U 218, which had laid mines in the Caribbean in October 1943, was sent out again in February 1944. She entered the Caribbean in March, but was driven away from the intended target of Trinidad when spotted by aircraft. U 218 then dropped two mines off St Lucia (23 March) followed by the remaining fifteen mines off San Juan de

Puerto Rico on 1 April. U 218 managed to evade the resulting search and returned to France. The mines caused no damage.

U-tanker U 488 (now commanded by Oberleutnant zS Studt) was sent out from France, apparently from Brest, on 22 February into a position west of the Cape Verde Islands. Here she could support U-boats en route to the Indian Ocean, as well as those proceeding to the South Atlantic and Brazilian waters. U 1059, a Type VIIF U-transporter, was sent out from Germany with torpedoes for Penang, departing from Kiel on 4 February and from Bergen on 12 February.

U-boat Command transmitted orders for Operation Maske on 14 March, the supply by U 488 of U 843, U 801 and U 123 in different sea areas on different dates. The tanker herself was to maintain complete radio silence. But there were now sufficient Allied carrier groups that some could operate around the Cape Verde Islands and Canary Islands, as well as around the Azores. On 16 March, U 801 (Type IXC/40), while en route towards West Africa, asked for directions for a new rendezvous with the U-tanker after sustaining casualties in an air attack, but was located by H/F D/F from the *Block Island* carrier force. After a long chase by the destroyer escorts, U 801 was forced to surface with heavy damage caused by Fido and depth-charges, and was then sunk by gunfire and air attack, despite deploying 'Thetis' radar decoys (floating buoys with upright poles bearing radar reflectors). By now, Operation Maske had been extended to include U 1059 with the rendezvous for U 123.

On the 19th, the Type VIIF boat U 1059 (Oberleutnant zS Leupold), outward-bound to the Indian Ocean, was surprised south-west of the Cape Verde Islands as the crew sunned themselves on deck or swam in the sea. According to survivors' accounts, her commander had allowed eighteen members of his crew into the water with the instruction 'Watch out for aircraft in this fine weather'! The sailors manned the guns but the U-transporter was soon sunk by bombs dropped by aircraft from the carrier – apparently the first bombs hit an ammunition locker with catastrophic effect – although an aircraft was shot down. There were initially fifteen survivors in the water, but they lacked lifebelts owing to the suddenness of the attack and only seven men, including the wounded captain, were rescued, together with the sole survivor from the downed aircraft. Both boats (U 801, U 1059) had been close to their refuelling rendezvous with the U-tanker, which had been arranged for the 20th.

These events, coupled with the loss of the surface tankers *Brake* and *Charlotte Schliemann* in the Indian Ocean within a fortnight of each other in late February/early March, and Tillessen's report, gave U-boat Command unpleasant food for thought. The Germans began to use a new cipher for instructions to rendezvous with milk cows at sea. The key for each U-boat was based on its crew list and a large number of rendezvous had to be made so that outgoing boats could present those at sea with the new keys *by hand*. But the job was complete by 11 April.

The new code was broken with difficulty by British Intelligence, although its first use during this period was penetrated readily enough. The German anxieties were apparent to British Intelligence and, in an effort to protect their secret information, the latter warned British warships to lay off their attacks on U-boats at remote rendezvous for a while. But the Americans could not be persuaded of the need for restraint and only the dogged German insistence that their codes were secure protected this valuable secret information for the Allies.

In addition, underwater trials of refuelling were ordered to be tested again in the Baltic. Meanwhile, Doenitz moved the refuelling rendezvous to the west of Madeira – taking the carrier groups with it. The carriers had been able to mount all-night, radar-fitted patrols since February 1944.

On 9 April, U515 was sunk by the *Guadalcanal* carrier group north of Madeira, and U68, which had done so well in these waters from 1941 onwards, was sunk by *Guadalcanal* aircraft in the same area the following day. Again both U-boats had been looking for the cow. On the same day (the 10th), the Type VIID minelayer U214 was bombed on the surface in the same vicinity, but escaped with little damage. When she resurfaced, she signalled to U-boat Command, who changed her rendezvous with U68 for the purpose of receiving new ciphers.

U488 was meanwhile in an area 700 miles west of the Cape Verde Islands. She refuelled two U-boats and on the night of 16/17 April refuelled U129*, which was headed for Brazil, and U537, en route for the Indian Ocean (U537 would be refuelled again as soon as she had reached her theatre of operations – see Chapter 14). Three other U-boats had been sunk before reaching the tanker. Aircraft from the *Tripoli* carrier now attacked U543 as she waited for U488 on the 19th. The U-boat managed to escape both aircraft and destroyers sent after her, and next day U-boat Command again moved the rendezvous. U488 had not herself reported to base since 30 March (and then only to report the status of U123, whose W/T equipment had broken down) – W/T silence at sea had become commonplace among U-boats.

U66 (Oberleutnant zS Seehausen) was returning from the West African coast with successes, but low on fuel and provisions. On the night of 20/21 April, she signalled to U-boat Command relaying her condition and was ordered to make a rendezvous with U488 for the night of 25/26 April, far west of the Cape Verde Islands. This message was intercepted and de-coded by the '10th Fleet', and on the night of 25/26 April aircraft searching for U66 from the *Croatan* carrier group located instead the U-tanker

*U129 would be the first U-boat to operate off Brazil since the area had been abandoned in late 1943 due to strong aerial activity. It was hoped that her new Naxos radar receiver would protect U129, a wish that proved to be well founded.

720 miles north of the Cape Verde Islands. U 488 submerged, and evaded Asdic and sonobuoys for a while, but was relocated by Asdic on the 26th after three of the carrier's escort destroyers had joined the hunt. Three explosions were heard after two 'Hedgehog' attacks (depth-charges that exploded only on contact with a U-boat) and the U-tanker appeared to have become stationary. In the distance, the submerged U 66 recorded that she had heard sinking noises.

An oil slick was seen in the afternoon that got larger over the next two days, but the escorts were uncertain whether they had a confirmed sinking, especially since Asdic contacts were received on and off. The destroyers plastered the oily area with conventional depth-charges during the morning of the 29th, onto an unmoving target at a depth of 170 metres. There was no sign of any effect, but at some time between the 26th and 29th U 488 was sunk without survivors.

There has been some dispute about which U-boats may have been refuelled by U 488 before the tanker was sunk. Key war diaries of U-boats that attended the rendezvous have been lost, because the boats were sunk or headquarters at Penang later destroyed them. The author has re-examined the U-boat Command war diary and also decrypted U-boat messages for the period 13 March to 9 May 1944. The decrypts show that the U-boats involved were ordered to maintain W/T silence until commanded to report by U-boat Command, thus signals from U-boats were very limited. Refuellings were to be carried out at night. The Germans appear to have reverted to the earlier procedure of making short changes to compromised rendezvous and U-boats were directed to the general area before receiving final details. Disguised rendezvous positions were transmitted by U-boat Command, but these must have been betrayed repeatedly by U-boats sending their positions in clear. All the U-boat signals were decrypted within one to two days, giving the Allies plenty of time to react to rendezvous orders given up to a week in advance.

It appears that only five, or perhaps four, refuellings were made by U 488 in all:

U 843 (outward-bound, reported on 25 March that she had been refuelled).

U 123 (homeward-bound, 29 March, reported by U 488 on 30 March).

U 129 (outward-bound, 16/17 April, found in her war diary although there were no signals).

U 537 (outward-bound, 16/17 April – circumstantial evidence only for date. U 537 was ordered to refuel on the same day as U 129, is known to have been in the area on time from a position signal and signalled on 16 May off South Africa that she still had fuel stocks of 174 tons out of a full capacity of 214 tons. There is no signals evidence before 9 May for a refuelling with U 488).

U 543 (outward-bound, survived and probably was refuelled, but made no signals. After the sinking of U 488, U 543 neither requested fuel to continue her patrol nor protested when asked to act as an emergency tanker for another boat – see below. U 543 patrolled the Gulf of Guinea and off Freetown, but was sunk on 2 July during her return to France).

The unfortunate U 66, which had observed the attack on U 488, was now left in mid-ocean without fuel to get home. U-boat Command was brought up to date with the loss of their penultimate U-tanker and the Type IXC/40 boat U 188 (Kapitaenleutnant Luedden), returning from the Indian Ocean and in sore need of a refit, was ordered on 30 April to make fuel available at yet another rendezvous. Two days later, U-boat Command sent revised orders: U 66 and U 188 were to share fuel and provisions, which would last for three weeks, and refuel from U 198 and U 543 which, travelling at full speed, would reach the others within nine days.

Again the signals were intercepted (H/F D/F) and the *Block Island* carrier was ordered to search with her four destroyers. U 66 was driven deep, forced to remain submerged until all her air had been consumed and then, after she had returned to the surface on the night of 6/7 May, her desperate captain made another signal: 'Resupply not possible owing to constant harassment.' This was also intercepted by the carrier group, U 66 was soon located off Cape Verde on the same night by aircraft from the carrier and the destroyer *Buckley* was sent to investigate. As the shadow of the *Buckley* loomed large, the crew of U 66 allegedly sent off three red Very lights in the mistaken belief that U 188 was approaching (it is now thought more likely that U 66 was firing at a persistent night-flying aircraft in the vicinity).

Within five minutes the *Buckley* was on the spot and opened fire. After a brief gun battle, during which Seehausen was badly wounded, *Buckley* turned to ram. Now occurred one of the tragedies of the naval war for, as *Buckley* turned, her stern scraped along the U-boat so close that some of the German sailors tried to jump on board. They intended only to abandon ship and came aboard with their hands up (a fact later censored from the American account of the action), but in the darkness and confusion the American sailors thought that they were being boarded and opened fire with small arms and grenades. Most of the boarders were killed and the U-boat was sprayed with machine-gun fire. (A similar incident occurred off Land's End in April 1945, although this time in broad daylight. The mortally wounded U 1063 surfaced actually under a British sloop so that members of the crew were able to step smartly onto the latter's stern and were taken prisoner.) Engulfed in flames, U 66 staggered on another 100 metres before sinking. Belatedly, the *Buckley* was able to rescue thirty-six crew members from the water. Not rescued were Seehausen and two British POWs, who had been taken from their sinking ship.

U 188 saw the action from afar and ran straight on towards Bordeaux, which she reached on 19 June, wisely keeping radio silence in the meantime.

U 66 had lived a charmed and eventful life. Under the command of the experienced Zapp, she had played a full role in Operation Paukenschlag. Under Markworth and Seehausen, she had been sent on several long patrols during which her fuel supply had run down to dangerous levels and she had been present at the sinkings of two of the cows sent to suckle her (U 117 and U 488). Now her luck had finally run out.

Retaliation came on 29 May, when U 549 torpedoed and sank both the carrier *Block Island* and one of her destroyers. However, she was then herself sunk, without survivors, by the remaining escorts.

This multiple disaster brought Doenitz's efforts in remote waters to a premature end. Very few merchant ships were sunk in exchange for heavy losses, many caused by Allied Intelligence predicting the fuelling rendezvous. U 488 had been written off as sunk, as also had U 66, U 68, U 188, U 198 and U 515. All had failed to report at different rendezvous, although it later transpired that U 188 had simply kept radio silence, while a breakdown in the W/T equipment of U 198 meant that she had failed to hear any of her rendezvous orders. 'Refuelling even in mid-Atlantic will scarcely be possible in future,' wrote Doenitz (U-boat Command war diary). 'This situation will continue until the introduction of submerged refuelling. Until then, refuelling will be carried out only in urgent cases from combatant U-boats. All U-boats have received instructions to begin their homeward passage in good time so they can reach port without refuelling.' U-boats were forced to return to France for want of oil and some of those outward-bound had to be employed to refuel other U-boats returning from American waters. This required the U-boats to rendezvous in mid-ocean, frequently near the Azores, in order to effect the transfer of fuel, which proved to be extremely unpopular with the crews who would do anything to avoid such an occurrence if they could. Indeed, the war diary of U-boat Command indicates that just six U-boats were refuelled by other attack boats in the entire period from September 1943 to May 1944.

Standard procedure was for each U-boat to enter the rendezvous area submerged and then to surface an hour or so before darkness in order to locate one another. Refuelling would then take place during the cover of darkness. Frequently the U-boats found their rendezvous zones patrolled by Allied aircraft as a result of decryption of signals detailing the meeting point, and matters reached the stage where neither U-boat would make a signal even if they could not find one another during the day appointed for the rendezvous.

Although U-boat Command never admitted or realized that its codes had been broken, the U-boat crews had a strong suspicion that all rendez-vous would be known to the Allies and that any wireless signal could give away the location of a U-boat.

U-boat Command could not ignore the fact that refuelling at sea had reached the near suicidal, and the new 'electric' U-boats were designed to operate as far as Cape Town and be able to return to base without the need to refuel. Further, on 12 May, Doenitz directed that Type VIIC boats in the North Atlantic should spend less than eight weeks at sea, to 'lessen sea time and relieve too heavy a burden on the crew'.

Plans for New U-tankers

Plans were made in the middle of 1943 to bring into rapid production the new 'electric' U-boats of Type XXI, through a policy of mass assembly at the dockyards of the various prefabricated U-boat sections. The scheme reduced the requirement for refuelling U-boats since the Type XXI craft possessed their own large fuel supplies, while their unusual design meant that any deviation from the standard construction pattern would require considerable expenditure of labour. As a preliminary step, on 8 October 1943, all outstanding contracts for the remaining Type XIV U-tankers were switched from Deutsche Werke at Kiel (which was now required to pro-duce 'electric' U-boats) to Germania at Kiel, and the series U 491–U 500 was laid down.

By now, U-tanker Types XV (2,500 tons) and XVI (5,000 tons) had been mooted as developments of the Type XIV, but incorporated large work-shops. Both types would be seriously underpowered by their standard diesel engines (taken from the Type VIIC boat, and also used in Type XIV), and were promptly rejected by Doenitz. The 'K' team also proposed the Type XXB that combined elements of the XIV-series tanker and the XX-series U-transporter into a general-purpose U-supplier that could trans-port either oil or rubber in external tanks. The battery size would be larger at the expense of some storage capacity internally and/or externally. This scheme was also rejected on 18 October 1943.

The 'K' team now proposed two schemes at a meeting with the Naval Staff on 8 November:

1. Type XIVB, a development of the standard U-tanker with extra batteries in an extension under the pressure hull. It was agreed that this useful addition would be fitted to the last six U-tankers to be completed by Germania in 1945.
2. A Type XXID modification of the standard attack 'electric' U-boat, with all torpedo tubes and torpedoes removed, the upper deck widened to support fuel transfer, various trimming modifications, the fitting of oil transfer equipment and extra refrigeration added

for food storage. An open bridge, for easy manoeuvring on the surface, and increased flak protection were also to be provided. A Type XXIC U-transporter was also recommended, essentially lacking only the torpedo tubes of the attack version, but both the C and D sub-types would lose half of their battery capacity to create more space.

Again the non-standard requirements of the new types caused difficulties and no construction was ever initiated. On 27 March 1944, Doenitz directed that the new 'electric' boats might take on fuel, but only when submerged, so the changes to the bridge and flak of Type XXID could be dropped, while two torpedo tubes were reintroduced to provide some defensive capability. Again, no work was started before the end of the war. The long-range attack boats always had clear priority of production, but were themselves repeatedly delayed by manufacturing difficulties.

Work was abandoned on the Type XIV tankers U491–493 at Deutsche Werke in June 1944, when the boats were about 75 per cent complete, and never resumed. Other Type XIV U-tankers (U494–500 and U2201–2204) under construction or ordered at Germania Werft were suspended on 3 June and cancelled on 23 September. The Type XB minelayers had not been reordered after the first craft had proved to be unsuccessful for their designed purpose. Since no more Type VIID U-minelayers were being built either, it would appear that the Germans had lost enthusiasm for the SMA-type mine, which could only be laid from a submarine minelayer through purpose-designed shafts.

Chapter 17

The End of the Milk Cows
June 1944 to May 1945

Doenitz sent out another nine U-boats to remote areas at the end of May 1944, and the last U-tanker, U 490, was sent out from Germany in support. By mid-May, U 490 was in the Northern Transit area. Apart from these boats there were only five U-boats in remote theatres (excluding the Indian Ocean) tying down Allied forces, and on 4 June one of these, U 505, was captured by the *Guadalcanal* carrier group off Dakar. The code books were recovered intact, but there was little to be gained from them at this late stage of the war. Indeed, the US '10th Fleet' discovered that the codebooks and other documents on board U 505 were less up-to-date than their own records, since the U-boat had been at sea for some months. Much more useful, however, was the capture of the short-signals books.

On 1 June, Doenitz reviewed the U-boat war in the U-boat Command diary. 'Our efforts to tie down enemy forces have so far been successful,' he wrote. 'The numbers of enemy aircraft and escort vessels, U-boat killer groups and aircraft carriers allotted to anti-U-boat forces, far from decreasing, has increased. For the submariners themselves the task of carrying on the fight solely for the purpose of tying down enemy forces is a particularly hard one.'

At this time Doenitz and all members the armed forces were mostly concerned with the impending Allied invasion of Normandy, with large numbers of U-boats lying in bomb-proof pens along the French and Norwegian coasts with a view to impeding the invasion of either country. The 'electric' U-boats had been held up by Allied bombing and were not expected to enter service until January 1945 (in fact, the first long-range 'electric' U-boat did not commence operations until the last days of the war).

However, there was some hope with the advent of the schnorkel. This originally Dutch invention was essentially an air mast raised to the surface of the sea that enabled a submerged U-boat to run its diesel engines and thereby recharge its batteries without having to come to the surface. The invention was, of course, a major advantage at a time when aircraft were sinking so many surfaced U-boats, and the Germans claimed to have invented it independently of the Dutch. The schnorkel was by no means a cure-all as it emitted a stream of gases in operation that could be seen a long way off, so schnorkelling was conducted at night. Even so, the head of the schnorkel could be detected by the new 3cm radar entering into Allied service. However, the improved Naxos-U radar search receiver could pick up these radar transmissions, enabling the U-boat to submerge again almost instantly. Use of the schnorkel reduced the U-boats' speed to about 5 knots, whereas on the surface they had been accustomed to making 17 knots. Even a slow convoy would leave a schnorkelling U-boat behind, but the the new device proved to be so useful as a defensive measure that on 1 June, Doenitz ordered that no U-boat should proceed on operations without one.

The schnorkel was ideally suited to milk cows, which had no interest in chasing convoys but only wanted to preserve themselves from air attack. But the development was too late for the U-tankers. On 1 June, the last survivor, U 490, was already at sea, cruising through the North Atlantic air gap on a southerly heading. The U-boat Command war diary lists U 490 as one of several boats recalled that day to France for fitting with a schnorkel. Presumably this was a typing error in the diary, for U 490 already possessed the equipment and made no effort to return to France. On the 7th, U-boat Command ordered U 490 to continue southwards as planned.

U 490 was commanded by the experienced Oberleutnant zS Gerlach, and had left Kiel on 4 May with instructions to proceed to the mid-Atlantic where she was to support operations for the remote theatres, before heading on into the Indian Ocean to assist the return of the U-boats remaining there. The 39-year-old Gerlach was another sailor promoted from the lower deck, having served on the successful U 124 between July 1940 and September 1941. He had then been selected for officer training, after which he had returned to U 124 as a watch officer in 1942 before being sent on the commanders' course in 1942–3. He had commissioned U 490 on 27 March 1943 and the boat had remained in the Baltic for correction of bombing damage and subsequent serious flooding (see Chapter 16), and for training until her services were required.

U 490 successfully negotiated the difficult Northern Transit area as she passed from the North Sea into the North Atlantic, and reported a convoy on 4 June. Meanwhile, the crew had difficulty with her schnorkel, which appeared to be usable only in fairly calm seas. U 490 was located by H/F D/F in the middle of the ocean as she made a weather report on the 10th. Gerlach, described by his crew as nervous about Allied air activity, wanted to maintain radio silence, but he could not ignore a direct order requiring him to transmit information about the weather as he passed through the Atlantic. The American escort carriers were at this time making a concerted drive against the handful of U-boats stationed in the Atlantic to provide weather reports. On 11 June, U 490 made another weather transmission, but it was to be her last. She was caught on the surface within hours by aircraft from the *Croatan* carrier group, but managed to submerge and went very deep.

She was then hunted all through the night and the next day by the carrier's destroyer escorts, which dropped 189 depth-charges in all. U 490 carried some experimental guinea pigs aboard. These kept squealing during the attacks and had to be destroyed to reduce the noise. Eventually her air ran out and she was forced to return to the surface. The destroyers in the meantime had played the trick of moving off in opposite directions at decreasing speed (giving the sound effect of a high-speed departure), and then creeping slowly back to the target area. The U-tanker surfaced and when it was at once attacked with heavy gunfire, Gerlach ordered his boat to be scuttled; all sixty crew members were rescued. American interrogators described the crew as 'undistinguished', but remarked on the unusual seniority of the petty officers. The crew volunteered to answer 'honourable questions' provided they were not handed over to the British, but they had little new to report.

As U 490 had not refuelled a single U-boat when she was sunk, this effectively wrecked the last of Doenitz's hopes for overseas operations, and only one or two U-boats were able to patrol in remote waters, with occasional refuelling by fuel sharing with one another. The war diary of U-boat Command shows that just three U-boats were successfully re-fuelled by other attack U-boats in the period June 1944 to May 1945.

However, the loss of U 490 was not immediately appreciated as her crew had been too agitated to remember to send a final distress signal. As late as 27 June, U-boat Command ordered U 490 to make for Penang at high speed, where the boat was to load up with essential war supplies, with a minimum docking time, and return home. While on passage (in either direction), any Type IXC boats in the Indian Ocean (presumed to be U 183, U 510, U 532 and U 843) were to be refuelled for the journey home.

The Type XB minelayer U 233 had been commissioned on 22 September 1943 by the 36-year-old Kapitaenleutnant Steen, who had previously been the First Officer on her sister ship, U 117, from October 1941 to February 1943, and had subsequently attended a commanding officers' course. Most of the crew were new recruits. After the usual working-up exercises in the Baltic, which involved a practice minelaying mission of 132 mines in that sea during the winter of 1943, U 233 received a full overhaul and refitting from February 1944. She left Kiel on 27 May for her first war patrol, with orders to lay sixty-six mines apparently off Halifax, Canada. However the U-boat Command war diary claims that U 233 received 'alternative orders' on 17 June to carry out her minelaying operation off Halifax. She was not fitted with a schnorkel and, according to her crew when later interrogated, there had been no plans to deploy U 233 for refuelling purposes after the minelaying operation, neither did the boat carry spare parts for other U-boats.

Travelling on the surface at night to recharge her batteries, U 233 entered the Northern Transit area, which was then the scene of a massive search by Coastal Command for outward-bound U-boats, but she was one of the few fortunate boats to break through, albeit after many tribulations. On 1 June, U 233 sighted many aircraft and next day was suddenly attacked by a four-engined bomber, too late to dive. U 233 defended herself with her 37mm and two 20mm cannons scoring some hits, but the aircraft still managed to drop five bombs that exploded all around the U-boat, remarkably causing no damage. The U-minelayer seized the chance to dive.

After resurfacing, U 233 was again forced to dive by aircraft combing her likely route and changed course in a successful effort to shake off her aerial pursuers. Steen then steered for the east coast of the USA, surfacing at night just long enough to recharge his batteries. The quick-firing 37mm flak gun had repeatedly jammed during the engagement with the bomber and test-firing two weeks later caused a shell to explode in the barrel, rendering it useless.

Then her luck ran out. Now close to Nova Scotia, Canada, she sent a message by W/T. This was intercepted by H/F D/F, leading to a search by the *Card* carrier group. The carrier aircraft spotted an oil slick on 2 July and dropped sonobuoys, which gave a positive response to underwater sounds, although thick fog interfered with further aerial operations. The US destroyer escort finally gained passive sound contact (i.e. listening only, without using active Asdic) on 5 July. This was not detected by the U-minelayer, which was then floating at a depth of 30 to 50 metres while servicing her stern torpedoes. Suddenly the horrified crew heard the whine of the propellers of the destroyer *Baker*, followed by the shocking impact of depth-charges all around the boat.

U 233 was badly shaken, the lights went out and the boat plunged out of control to 120 metres. Water poured in through a leak in the stern and a heavy aft torpedo was toppled out of its stay, killing a crew member. When a second pattern of depth-charges drove U 233 to 230 metres, a desperate Steen gave the order to 'blow tanks' and surface. The milk cow managed to reach the surface, where she was instantly engaged with a hail of fire at a range of only 500 metres. Two destroyer torpedoes also struck the hapless U-minelayer, but had been fired from so close that they did not have time to arm themselves and bounced off without exploding. Steen gave the order to abandon ship, while the Chief Engineer went below to scuttle the U-boat. Meanwhile, shells continued to land all around as the crew jumped overboard, many losing their lives at this point.

Then another destroyer, the *Thomas*, stormed in and rammed the luck-less U 233 which subsequently sank. Steen himself was severely wounded, but was supported in the sea by one of the surviving crew members. The American destroyers rescued Steen and twenty-nine other survivors from the sixty-man crew. It transpired that so accurate had been the American fire on the conning tower as the U-boat crew tried to abandon ship that virtually all the rescued survivors were those who had escaped from the forward hatch. Steen died of his wounds the following day and was buried at sea from the deck of the carrier *Card*. U 233 had been sunk before she could drop her mines and her loss was not recognized by U-boat Command until 11 August. Interrogation of survivors established that the crew were 'dreadful', almost devoid of experience, except for Steen himself and a few petty officers added to leaven the mixture. Steen had been well liked and the crew were unusually security conscious.

As a result of the early loss of the cows, the U-boats engaged in the remote waters campaign (excluding the Indian Ocean) sank only twenty ships between January and September, while thirteen of the U-boats engaged in this campaign were themselves sunk.

The Allies invaded Europe on 6 June, and by August the Biscay bases were in such danger of capture, and escort groups in the Bay posed such a threat, that all the U-boats within their pens were despatched either to Norway or, in the case of a few long-range boats, to the Indian Ocean. U-boat Command had already warned boats at sea, on 12 June, that they should retain enough fuel to reach Bergen, if necessary, rather than a French port. Some other U-boats were in no fit state to be sent out to sea and had to be scuttled in the French ports. Among them were: U 129, Type IXC, which we have encountered frequently at fuelling rendezvous and which had returned safely from her last aggressive patrol off Brazil; the U-cruiser U 178, returned from Penang; and U 188, Type IXC/40, returned from the Indian Ocean after an eventful journey (see Chapter 16). All were scuttled between 18 to 20 August. Kapitaenleutnant von Harpe of U 129 had performed an extraordinary job in keeping the boat operating successfully during his tenure (July 1943 to July 1944) while so many were being sunk around him. He would be rewarded with command of one of the brand-new 'electric' U-boats, U 3519, in January 1945, but boat and commander were lost off Warnemuende (Germany) in March 1945 after an air attack.

By 25 August, there remained no serviceable U-boats at Bordeaux, and the boatless crews, dockyard workers, army troops and German civilians reassembled at La Rochelle, from where 20,000 would attempt to make the journey back across France to Germany. The unwanted ex-Italian UIT 21 had been one of those scuttled at Bordeaux on 25 August and her former crew, including Wilhelm Kraus, now set out for Germany on bicycles. Many of them were captured in mid-France by partisans and Kraus was not released until the end of 1946.

The general chaos, with U-boats attempting to redeploy to Norway from France, resulted in complications for boats returning from remote waters. The homeward-bound U 516 (Kapitaenleutnant Tillessen), low on fuel, was unexpectedly required to steer for Norway instead of her closer French base. She signalled her predicament on 16 August and was ordered to meet a U-boat giving weather reports south-west of Iceland. On the 25th, U 858, the weather boat, reported that she had refuelled U 539 at the rendezvous (AK1832), but had not seen U 516. U 855 was appointed as replacement weather boat while a fresh rendezvous between U 855 and U 516 was fixed for the same area on 3 September. Tillessen waited two days for U 855 at her rendezvous south of Iceland before signalling to U-boat Command that the supply boat had failed to appear. The Type VIIC boat U 245 was at once directed at full speed to her aid, but on the 9th U 516 was able to report that she had been refuelled by U 855 after all. Both boats returned to Norway.

After her return from the North Atlantic in January 1944, U 219 (Korvettenkapitaen Burghagen) had been prepared for a special cruise, as the first blockade runner of her class to the Far East. The minelayer was to be fitted out with supplies, rather than mines (the mineshafts had a huge capacity), but eight torpedoes would also be taken on board to retain some offensive capability from her two stern torpedo tubes. Planning for the event took three to four months, during which time radio equipment was loaded for Japan (the port of Kobe), also substitute machine parts, torpedo parts, medical supplies, operational orders, spare parts for the Arado196 seaplane at Penang (a parting gift, long before, from a German auxiliary cruiser), duraluminium, mercury and optical items for the Japanese. However, contrary to recent reports, there were no parts for a putative Japanese atomic bomb, nor any foreign personnel aboard.

No one knew how the U-minelayer would behave with such a loading, so the first test cruise of U 219 in April was, to say the least, fraught with interest. Senior engineers from the 12th U-boat Flotilla went on board to give what aid they could. During the first trim-dive U 219 sank like a stone, but the engineers managed to recover her poise. After return to her bunker, as much as possible was done to save weight, including the removal of the large 105mm gun on deck and all its ammunition.

Schnorkel trials began on 1 May. When the Allied invasion began, the bunkers suffered constant air attack but U 219 remained safe in hers, although shortage of supplies caused a long delay in equipping the U-minelayer, which was also fitted with one of the new high-pressure designs of lavatory. This could expel its contents when at great depth, but required careful operation – faulty manipulation was to cause the accidental flooding and loss of one U-boat later in the war.

The two Type IXD1 U-transporters, U 180 (Oberleutnant zS Reisen) and U 195 (Oberleutnant zS Steinfeldt), were recommissioned at Bordeaux as the other two blockade runners planned to sail to the Indian Ocean. Both had needed replacement diesel engines to permit this trip and were to be joined by U 219.

The former U-boat bases on the west coast of France were declared by Hitler to be 'fortresses', to be fought to the last man, but this meant that munitions had somehow to be ferried to them. U-boats were the vessels of choice, two small attack boats had already carried out a ferry operation, and U 180 and U 195 seemed to the Army to be especially good candidates. They were loaded with dynamite and ammunition for a planned operation to St Malo and Lorient, but the naval staff were singularly unenthusiastic – not to mention the crews – and finally seized on the shortage of supplies at Bordeaux as the excuse not to send the U-transporters out on this mission.

U 219 finally left her bunker on 20 August. It took until the 23rd to reach Le Verdon at the mouth of the River Gironde where she had to wait for U 195 and U 180, which had also sailed on the 20th. (According to a decrypted W/T message, U 219 had attempted to sail from Le Verdon on the 23rd, but an air attack on the escort had caused a withdrawal.) As this valuable assembly of blockade runners waited for a propitious moment to break into the heavily patrolled Bay of Biscay, the crews saw the destroyers Z 24 and T 24 attacked by a cloud of some forty Mosquito fighter-bombers. Both ships would be sunk by air attack at Le Verdon, respectively on the 25th and 24th. The signal announcing the imminent departures of U 180, U 195 and U 219 was decrypted by British Intelligence but, owing to a shortage of suitable escorts, U 219 did not enter the Bay of Biscay until the 24th. Finally the U-boat group emerged in the evening and put to sea with orders to sail to the Far East (Penang), with a paltry escort of only two M-boats. Evidence of heavy Allied aerial activity caused the boats to dive in only 50 metres of water, instead of the more common 200 metres.

It would have been at this time that U 180 disappeared without trace. She is commonly supposed to have hit a mine and sank, the sinking generally being listed as having occurred on 22 August, but this does not fit the information given above, derived from decrypts and survivors of U 219. Meanwhile, U-boat Command continued to give estimates of her supposed position until 3 October, when U 180 was presumed lost. The historian Alex Niestlé has discovered that the escort left U 180 in deep water late on 23 August, so that a mine sinking is most unlikely. A more probable explanation for the loss, in the view of the author, is a schnorkel defect (compare the troubles experienced by U 219 at the same time, below). Experiences from other U-boats make it clear that a sufficiently serious schnorkel failure could poleaxe an entire crew within sixty seconds.

U 219 began to use her schnorkel on the 26th, despite her lack of experience. The next few days were spent acquiring better knowledge of the schnorkel as the boat headed west. By 2 September, U 219 had reached the Atlantic, and surfaced briefly to clear the air in the boat and to determine her position. Then she began schnorkelling again. But on the 15th the device suddenly failed and could not be repaired, jammed at an angle of 45 degrees. U 219 ran thereafter on the surface at night for the minimum length of time needed to recharge her batteries; otherwise she remained submerged.

Meanwhile, the homeward-bound torpedo transport U 1062 required more fuel if she was to reach Norway. U 1062 was returning from Penang with a cargo of rubber and other strategic materials and had already had an eventful ride (see Chapter 14). But now she had been diverted from her originally intended French base owing to the Allied advance towards the Biscay ports. U 219 was conveniently close and U-boat Command radioed orders on 21 September for her to supply U 1062 at sundown south-west of the Cape Verde Islands, at a position of about 11.30N 34.30W.

But the rendezvous had already been revealed when the exchange of signals between U-boat Command and U 1062 on the 18th had been decoded, after the disguised grid reference had been cracked by local H/F D/F indicating the location of U 1062. The *Mission Bay* and *Tripoli* carrier groups were moved to the area and they mounted continuous air patrols looking for the U-boats. Arriving at the rendezvous in good time on 28 September, U 219 was alarmed to hear far-off explosions. She surfaced at dusk and the crew manned the anti-aircraft guns. Unknown to her crew, the U-minelayer had been detected by the large radar on the *Mission Bay* carrier.

Suddenly, in darkness, a carrier aircraft flew over at an altitude of only 70 metres. It saw the cow too late, circled and attacked. Heavy flak from the cow's 20mm and 37mm guns shot the aircraft down, but not before it had dropped several bombs which exploded all around the boat. As the spray fell away, the stunned crew of U 219 found that their boat had stopped dead in the water, although there appeared to be no serious damage. A second aircraft saw the gunfire and closed, firing rockets that all missed. U 219 remained on the surface and was harried with guns and bombs before diving. Burghagen debated what to do. He thought it prudent to abandon the rendezvous, but U-boat Command ordered him to remain searching. All night the crew could hear the sound of distant explosions, blissfully ignorant of the fact that U 219 had just been chased by a Fido that had failed to make contact, and was even now being hunted with sonobuoys.

At light next day (the 29th), Burghagen sighted searching destroyers but still continued to wait hopefully for U 1062. U 219 surfaced on the 30th to recharge her batteries and then dived again to the constant thud of distant bombs and depth-charges.

Meanwhile, U 1062 had been located by sonobuoys on 30 September, chased repeatedly and unsuccessfully with Fidos, and finally sunk by hedgehog and depth-charge attacks by destroyers of the *Mission Bay* carrier group while close to the rendezvous, south-west of the Cape Verde Islands. There were no survivors.

On the first day of October another Allied search group was heard at the rendezvous by U 219, looking for the cow whose presence was still suspected. Next day the batteries were again depleted and U-boat Command had made no further pronouncement (the reason for which is unknown. U-boat Command did not recognize that U 1062 had been sunk until 2 December, by which time the staff claimed to have had no word from U 219 either.) U 219 drifted underwater at creeping speed for several days – so many that her crew became ill and it became necessary on 4 October to surface again to vent the boat. She was promptly located by an aircraft from the persistent *Mission Bay* group, but the intended bombs fell short. Sonobuoys were deployed and another Fido was dropped after a few hours. An explosion was heard but U 219 was unharmed.

On the following day, Asdic echoes came too close for comfort and Burghagen finally abandoned the rendezvous, heading south. The *Tripoli* carrier group did not, however, abandon the hunt for this valuable U-minelayer. U 219 had crossed the equator by the 11th, submerged but with due ceremony, and thereafter she ran mostly on the surface at night, albeit with constant dives before radar alarms. Unknown to Burghagen, the *Tripoli* was still in pursuit. On 30 October, aircraft from the *Tripoli* carrier group finally relocated U 219 with sonobuoys off South Africa and attacked the sound location with depth-charges. Underwater explosions were heard, but U 219 escaped (her crew seems to have been oblivious to this attack).

U 219 finally reached her most southerly point on 11 November, having at last thrown off her tenacious pursuer. Here she had to wrestle with some engine trouble before steering north-east, into the Indian Ocean and towards Penang. U-boat Command altered the destination base to Djakarta on the 20th, citing the new proximity of Allied bombers to Penang as the reason for the change.

When masts were seen well into the Indian Ocean on 26 November, Burghagen made a submerged attack, firing two torpedoes. One detonation was heard but, on coming to the surface, nothing could be seen of the target. U 219 claimed a sinking on the basis of this flimsy evidence, but in fact no merchant ship had been sunk; evidently Burghagen lacked confidence in the claim too, since he did not repeat it to U-boat Command after arrival at base.

U 219 at last reached the rendezvous for her Japanese escort in the Sunda Strait, punctually on 12 December. She hung around nervously, all crew on deck for fear of an attack by an Allied submarine in these infested waters. Burghagen's fears were not eased when the 'escort' proved to be a Japanese fishing cutter that proceeded casually to Djakarta with the helpless U-minelayer tagging slowly along behind. However, she reached port without mishap.

U 195 had enjoyed a fairly uneventful cruise from Bordeaux to Djakarta. She left Bordeaux with a 250-ton cargo comprising optical instruments, mercury, dismantled V-weapons, torpedoes, blueprints, radar sets and a Japanese technical officer. After departing in company with U 180 and U 219, as described above, on the night of 23/24 August, she had been attacked almost at once by small patrol craft (probably MTBs) and chased with the use of hydrophones. The boat had escaped by lying on the sea bottom at 100 metres. Subsequently U 195 had schnorkelled to the Spanish coast to fix minor damage and the crew had repaired the boat on the surface in Spanish waters. Thereafter the boat sailed without difficulty all the way into the Indian Ocean, presumably using her schnorkel through the North Atlantic. Her daily distance travelled at sea near the Azores was around 100 miles. The boat claimed that she had suffered fuel losses, forcing a slower passage at most economical speed, and she was ordered to refuel from U 181 if necessary. U 181 (Kapitaen zS Freiwald) had started on 19 October on the return trip from Djakarta to Norway, sinking a large American merchant ship (2 November) en route, but had suffered near Cape Town from 'badly burnt bearings' and was commanded on the 26th to return to Djakarta. U-boat Command prepared a fuelling rendezvous in the south-western Indian Ocean between U 195 and U 181, but the boats failed to locate one another at their joint rendezvous in square KT90 on 12 December, and both continued independently to Djakarta.

U 181 was instead commanded to meet the homeward-bound U 843 at dusk on 20 December in KL6555, and to refuel the smaller boat 'fully'. By 1 January, U 181 could inform U-boat Command that she had refuelled U 843 and was returning to Djakarta where she arrived on the 6th. On the 11th, the report was amplified: U 181 had supplied U 843 with 60 tons of fuel and 2 tons of lubricating oil in an operation hampered by bad weather and poor equipment. U 181 had sailed from Djakarta with ten cases of acute malaria, three of dysentery and seven of severe boils or skin troubles, and the commander had suffered from diphtheria. However, the crew had returned to base 'in better shape'. U 195 docked safely at Djakarta on 29 December and two U-cruisers also arrived. The commander's report (used above) was transmitted to Berlin, together with his favourable opinion on the deployment of the Type IXD1 boat as a transport, while the cargo was removed for transhipment to Japan.

The arrival of U 219 and U 195 sufficed to provide new radar detector equipment (Borkum and Tunis) for all the U-boats then based in the Far East. The signal to this effect from the German radio station at Penang (17 January 1945) was intercepted and decoded by the Australian Defense Agency, but nothing could be done. However, both boats were suffering from numerous mechanical defects, as well as only two-thirds of expected battery capacity. The intention was that both U 219 and U 195 should load up with a cargo of rubber, tin, wolfram and other commodities obtainable with difficulty in Germany, and then return home. But the planned move of U 219 to Surabaya, like Djakarta on the coast of Java, for the purpose of loading up with these strategic materials, was rudely interrupted on 27 December. A large Japanese ammunition ship, the *Taicho Maru*, suddenly exploded in Djakarta harbour – apparently she had been torpedoed – the blast rocking the port and damaging U 219, whose crew observed the many floating corpses in the harbour – and the sharks. U 532 and U 510, also moored in the port, suffered no damage. Specialists were summoned to the stricken U-minelayer and were commanded to prepare the boat for her return to Germany in February 1945. Meanwhile, her crew enjoyed a lengthened stay at the Tjikopo rest home, high in the mountains, while U 219 was placed in dry dock in January. Djakarta was now abandoned by the Germans as a U-boat base.

In December, U-boat Command ordered all U-boats in the Indian Ocean to return to Germany, filled with such cargoes as they could manage. They were expected to carry the barest minimum of torpedoes home in order to maintain a slight offensive capability against undefended targets. In this connection, U 510 sailed from Djakarta on 11 January 1945, U 532 on the 13th and the U-cruiser U 861 (Korvettenkapitaen Oesten) on the 14th. Since the two Type IXC/40 boats lacked sufficient fuel to reach Norway, the U-cruiser was needed to replenish them in the west Indian Ocean, while U 195 was to sail as a back-up (or, if possible, as another homeward-bound boat). U 195 had arrived at Djakarta after the 27 December explosion. Having been offloaded, she set out on her way back on 19 January 1945, although in urgent need of a refit. Her principal mission was to refuel the returning U 532 as she was carrying no fewer than 437 tons of fuel, 17 tons of lubricating oil and twelve weeks of supplies.

A joint rendezvous was arranged between U 861, U 532, U 195 and U 510 about 900 miles south of Madagascar. The rendezvous position seems to have been agreed verbally among the commanders before departing from base, a wise, albeit very late, innovation. Even so, the rendezvous might have been compromised when U 861 wanted a change of date for the replenishment to 7 February. All four boats met together on 8 February 1945, when U 195 refuelled U 532 with 100 tons of oil and U 861 replenished U 510. Surprisingly this left the U-cruiser short of fuel, since part of her fuel capacity had been used to store rubber. Then U 195 returned to Djakarta with diesel defects and her putative return to France abandoned, arriving on 5 March before moving next day to Surabaya.

The other boats then headed into the Atlantic, having begged U-boat Command successfully, with a joint request, that they should not be required to make frequent tell-tale progress reports while en route. U 861 would subsequently arrive safely in Norway just before the end of the war.

U 532 would surrender at sea in the North Atlantic after Germany's surrender, having sunk two single ships in the South Atlantic. U 510 remained short of fuel and was forced to make for St Nazaire in France, which was still in German hands, on 23 April 1945 in search of more fuel, repairs and a schnorkel. All three boats had been advised by U-boat Command on 25 March to put into St Nazaire for schnorkels. Later decrypted messages from the German Navy coastal service show the difficulty of arranging schnorkels for St Nazaire, requiring either hazardous flights by the Luftwaffe or a round trip from Norway by a transport U-boat. U 510 was still there when the European war ended, having sunk one ship in the South Atlantic.

The returning *Monsun* boats had at any rate escaped the massive Allied aerial minelaying operation that fouled the entire 'Southern Area' command on 23 January 1945. Penang, Djakarta, Surabaya and the Malacca Strait were all listed as having been paralysed by mines and the sea lanes were not cleared until 7 February. Burghagen expected U 219 to be ready for sea by March 1945, but battery and other defects caused further delays and a move to Surabaya. Likewise, U 195 was kept waiting until she could have her batteries replaced in a dry dock, which was scheduled for mid-May. The deteriorating situation in Europe caused increasing alarm to the crews of U 219, U 195 and the handful of U-cruisers still present. They feared that any day the war might end, they would be arrested and imprisoned by the Japanese. Those boats with defects were attended to without stint of labour. Then the blow fell. In April, U-boat Command ordered U 219, U 195 and the surviving UIT boats to remain in the Far East for the benefit of the Japanese.

U 183 (Kapitaenleutnant Schneewind) had been sent to Kobe for replacement of her batteries in November 1944. However, her planned January return had to be put back to allow the keel ballast to be changed and diesel defects to be corrected. Finally, on 22 February 1945, U 183 left Kobe for Djakarta, arriving on 9 March. The Japanese and local German commands had decided in January that U 183 was to patrol the southern approaches to the Philippines in order to intercept American landing craft, while Japanese submarines patrolled the northern approaches. U-boat Command objected strenuously to the original plan, stating that anti-submarine defences were likely to be weak and U 183 should close right up to the invasion area.

It was not until 21 April that Schneewind could report (in a decrypted signal) that he had departed Djakarta for an operational area south of the Philippines as far east as 122 degrees, the operational area to be reached on 29 April. Two days later (the 23rd), the forewarned US submarine *Besugo* located U 183 still on the surface and fired a six-torpedo spread. One of the torpedoes struck U 183, sinking her with only one survivor remaining to be picked up by the *Besugo*. The loss of U 183 would not be recognized by

U-boat Command until after the end of the war, when she failed either to return to base or to signal her surrender.

The Japanese finally seem to have appreciated the contribution of the U-boats in the Indian Ocean, and proposed in March and April 1945 that more be sent. Doenitz rejected the request on the grounds of lack of fuelling facilities en route, but the Japanese offered to send up to six of their submarines to refuel the U-boats in the Indian Ocean. Again the offer was rejected, to the embarrassment of the German naval staff in Tokyo, who reported that the Japanese believed them to have the authority to make such decisions. Consequently the Germans in Tokyo had lost face. On 3 April, Doenitz also rejected Japanese suggestions that U-boats could be used to land Japanese agents on Allied-occupied islands.

No further refuelling missions had been carried out in the Atlantic by appointed cows after the failure of U 219 with U 1062. U-boats were now being deployed in coastal waters around Britain and the sinking of U 1062 was to be the last by the American Atlantic carrier groups until April 1945. No U-tankers remained and the last Type XB U-boat outside the Indian Ocean, U 234 (Kapitaenleutnant Fehler), remained in German waters.

Fehler had previously been an officer on the auxiliary cruiser *Atlantis*. After the latter ship had been sunk, he volunteered for the U-boat service and commissioned U 234 on 2 March 1944. U 234 was especially well equipped in anti-aircraft armament, for she was fortunate enough to have an extraordinarily competent black market 'fixer' as one of her officers. Originally fitted with three 20mm anti-aircraft guns, he managed to get it augmented by official and unofficial means to two 37mm guns of the new automatic design (see Chapter 15), a Vierling mounting and two twin 20mm cannon. Later still, a twin 37mm cannon replaced the Vierling. When she finally put sea on active service, U 234 carried a twin 37mm cannon on the aft bandstand behind the conning tower and two single 37mm cannon on the tower itself.

For the remainder of the year, U 234 carried out her working-up exercises and then other trials in the Baltic while others pondered her fate. Now carrying a schnorkel, she was converted in September 1944 into a submarine blockade runner between Germany and the Far East, but experienced considerable difficulty in the Baltic with her schnorkel trials. The trials were carried out under the supervision of an old First World War U-boat ace, Kapitaen zS Valentiner, who imparted this pearl of wisdom: 'We used to say, he who schnorkels well lives longer. Now we say, he who schnorkels wrongly dies quicker.'

With no more time for trials, U 234 was ordered to practise more with her schnorkel off Norway. Owing to difficulties in equipping her, she did not leave Kiel until 25 March 1945, by which time she was furnished with an active radar mattress, a Kurier flash signal transmitter and a large range of materials amounting to some 240 tons to take to Japan, as well as several important passengers. U234 also carried seven torpedoes, to maintain some offensive capability, and written orders for two minelaying operations: twenty-one mines were to be laid off Cape Town and twenty-one mines off the port of Colombo, Ceylon. The commander was told to be particularly sure that he noted that the mines off Cape Town should have settings for the southern hemisphere, while those planted off Colombo were required to have settings for the northern hemisphere. However, it was conceded that the mines should be laid only if it was 'safe'. She then proceeded to Kristiansand, Norway, and started her schnorkel trials again in Hortenfjord on 28 March. Three days later, U234 was rammed in the stern, while at schnorkel depth, by U1301. An oil bunker and a diving cell were dented, while the torpedo tubes of U1301 were so damaged that she took no further part in the war. U234 was repaired back in Kristiansand.

Departing again on 24 April, U234 proceeded into the Atlantic, initially using the schnorkel but later, during a strong storm, mostly on the surface through heavy seas (after further schnorkel difficulties), Fehler having decided that he would try to outrun any destroyers that located him rather than be caught at a slow speed underwater. U234 had orders to schnorkel to the equator and then proceed to Japan, relying on radio signals transmitted from Norway and Spain to fix her position (the Elektra-Sonne radio navigation system). This system did in fact work quite well while the U-minelayer made her way between Iceland and the Faeroes 'Northern Transit route'. Her total absence from German waters was expected to be about a year, so at least one of the German naval staff must still have been quite an optimist.

U234 surrendered at sea on 14 May, six days after the cessation of hostilities in May 1945. The crew had lost contact with Germany after radio frequencies had had to be changed as the Russians closed in on Berlin, and it was not until 10 May that orders were heard in English commanding all U-boats to surrender. This had resulted in a long discussion about what to do next. The two Japanese passengers she was carrying committed suicide. When her 163-ton cargo was offloaded in the USA, ten cases of 'uranium oxide' for 'the Japanese Army' were found aboard in heavy, lead-lined containers. These were found to be so radioactive (unlike ordinary uranium oxide) that one of the German officers was forced to handle the cases. The nature of the contents was finally disclosed as recently as 1995 from American records. Among other items, U234 was carrying enriched uranium to assist the Japanese with the development of an atomic bomb. Instead, the material was offloaded in the USA and, almost certainly although this has never been confirmed, used to make up the shortfall in enriched uranium required for the bombs dropped by the Americans on Japan.

U 218 had some further minelaying operations to come, in the English Channel on 2 July 1944 and again on 18 August 1944. She had been fitted with a schnorkel prior to these hazardous operations. This Type VIID U-minelayer was then withdrawn from service for refit in German waters between October 1944 and March 1945. She was at sea on her way back to Norway after a final mining operation in the Clyde when the war ended in May 1945. U 218 surrendered at Bergen and was the only one of the five Type VIID U-minelayers to survive the war.

The two surviving Type VIIF torpedo transporters, U 1060 (Oberleutnant zS Brammer) and U 1061 (Oberleutnant zS Hinrichs) had been commissioned respectively on 5 May and 25 August in 1943. After the usual trials and working up, both had been used to operate a shuttle service between Kiel and the U-boat base at Narvik, with intermediate stops at Kristiansand, Bergen, Trondheim and other ports, from December 1943 to July 1944. By then, each boat had completed four round trips and had returned to Kiel. Both boats were then re-equipped, the schnorkel being the most important new item, and in October both were sent, separately, to Horten for schnorkel training.

On 27 October 1944, U 1060 was being escorted by the minesweeper M 433 as she headed southwards back to Norway, after she had picked up survivors from a previously attacked U-boat, when she was herself attacked by carrier aircraft operating in the North Sea. During the assault M 433 caught fire and one of the aircraft was shot down, the pilot being rescued by the U-boat. After a second aircraft attack, M 433 was abandoned and another aircraft was shot down, while the U-boat lost twelve men including her commander. The damaged U-boat was beached by her crew, then destroyed on the 29th by rockets and depth-charges from other aircraft. The last torpedo-transporter, U 1061, was damaged by a bomber while en route to Bergen on 30 October. She returned in stages to Trondheim where repairs took until 29 January 1945. She put to sea again, but was forced to return to Bergen for further repairs, where she remained until 26 April. Now with a new commander (Oberleutnant zS Jaeger), U 1061 moved southwards to Kristiansand with U 991 and U 1307 but, with the end of the war imminent, returned again to Bergen on 4 May where she surrendered. The former Dutch boat, UD 5, had also escaped the holocaust in the Baltic and similarly surrendered at Bergen.

The German Naval Command ordered in April 1945 that all war diaries that could not safely be returned to Germany should be destroyed rather than risk capture. This applied especially to war diaries of U-boats sent to the Far East, all of which were destroyed. Thus there are no original records for operations by U-boats in the Far East, excepting those such as U 178 that had returned to Europe before the end of the war.

When the European war ended on 8 May 1945, the remaining U-boats in the Far East were taken over by Japan, although none was used operationally. U 219 (Type XB) and U 195 (Type IXD1) were among those that shared this fate (the others being UIT 24, UIT 25 and the U-cruisers U 181 and U 862). All were in a poor state of repair one way or another. Admiral Wenneker, in charge of the German Tokyo office, sent out two signals on 6 May. One was to the U-boat crews in the Far East, and may be summarized thus: 'U-boats must surrender. Uncertain fate in Far East. Regrettable, but necessary; hope the Japanese will understand your plight. Thanks for loyalty and hope to greet you in the hope of a reunion at home.' The second was to the German naval staff at Kobe: 'Carry out "Luebeck" order [general surrender] at 11.00 Tokyo Time and report.' Next day U-boat Command sent a message to the Southern Command: 'All U-boats, except Freiwald (U 181), to be handed to Japan. Ask if they want them as free gift or will pay. Crews to be disembarked. Freiwald is to return – in own boat, or a substitute.'

The crew of U 219 (Korvettenkapitaen Burghagen) was, as usual, working on board when Japanese soldiers marched in, saying that the Japanese Navy had taken over the boat as I.505. The German crew was required to leave at once and be interned. However, a 'gentlemen's agreement' was speedily reached, whereby the German crews were permitted to stay on their boats as volunteers to aid the Japanese in putting the boats into good order. Surplus crew members could remain at the Tjikopo rest home. The crews ignored an order from U-boat Command on 16 May (sic) to surrender to the Allies – they were requested to leave their harbours, report to an Allied radio station and head for the nearest Allied harbour – together with the admonition: 'The Grand Admiral [Doenitz] expects it of you.' Discipline remained until the Japanese surrender in August, although the crews were now neither POWs nor sailors. U 219 was made fully operational, but was never deployed for use.

U 219 and the other U-boats still at Djakarta surrendered to the cruiser HMS *Cumberland* on 10 September. Tjikopo was occupied by British sailors on 2 November, where Burghagen negotiated for the Germans. All the U-boat crews remained as prisoners until 1946.

All the U-boats that had been requisitioned by the Japanese had survived until the end of the Pacific war, in August 1945. UIT 24 and UIT 25 both surrendered in August from the Japanese port of Kobe. The crews of both boats had been required to train replacement crews for the Japanese, after the German surrender, and it appears that each boat made one transport mission under Japanese command between Japan and the oil terminal in Borneo. Payments by the Japanese to the Kriegsmarine (now under Allied control) for these operations allowed the former crews to live fairly comfortably within a small Japanese hotel until the end of the war with Japan. Subsequently, every one of the requisitioned U-boats was scrapped in 1946.

Epilogue

The milk cows had served to replenish other U-boats during the most decisive phases of the naval war, from the 'Paukenschlag' against America, through 'Black May' and the Bay of Biscay offensive mounted by Coastal Command, until the final stages where they were used to support operations in remote waters to tie down Allied forces.

Estimates as to how many U-boats they supplied are difficult to establish, since some boats were replenished more than once in a single patrol, others needed only medical aid and not fuel or provisions, and the records become chaotic from mid-1943 when so many boats were sunk without returning to base (so accurate figures cannot be ascertained by reading their war diaries). However, it can be said that roughly 500 boats were supplied between March 1942 and June 1944, of which about 400 had been handled by the U-tankers. The Type XB U-minelayers accounted for the balance, although U A contributed three boats refuelled. This tally does not include refuellings made by boats appointed as emergency tankers when the milk cows had been sunk or were overburdened.

It has been alleged that the morale of the U-tanker crews was inferior to that of the attack boats. This is hard to substantiate, but all the U-boat crews were volunteers and it must have taken a special breed of crewman to serve in a milk cow during the latter part of the war, under constant air attack but with no hope of dishing it out yourself. The casualty rate among the milk cow crews was frightful, with none of the associated glory of sinking enemy ships. The average life expectancy of the cow was only three war patrols and there were few survivors from the sinking U-boats. After May 1943, few of the cows survived even one patrol and three of the ten U-tankers were sunk before they had made a single refuelling. The breaking of German ciphers was the primary reason for this disaster.

Every one of the custom-built U-tankers was sunk, as were all but one of the Type XB minelayers used in a refuelling capacity. But without the cows the wolf-packs would not have been able to operate for as long as they did at sea, and U-boats would not have been able to remain so long in areas where Allied defences were weak.

Although it is impossible to quantify accurately the contribution of the milk cows to the onslaught of U-boats on Allied merchant shipping, there can be no doubt that they were indirectly responsible for a considerable proportion of the 14 million tons of Allied shipping sunk by U-boats in the course of the Second World War.

The results that the milk cows achieved as a direct contribution to U-boat successes are listed in Appendix 1. An estimate of sinkings attributable indirectly to the milk cows can be made in the following manner. There were sufficient cows at sea to influence the number of U-boats operating between June 1942 and December 1943. In this period, U-boats sank 4,845,000 tons of Allied shipping in the North Atlantic alone. According to Doenitz, refuelling at sea doubled the length of time that a U-boat could remain on patrol; assuming that half of the attack U-boats were supplied, then milk cows were responsible for one quarter of this total, say some 1,200,000 tons. In addition, 250,000 tons of the 635,000 tons of shipping sunk off Cape Town and in the Indian Ocean during this period were accounted for by the *Eisbaer* and *Seehund* groups comprising U-boats which could only reach the operational area if supplied by cows. Thus the milk cows were indirectly responsible for the sinking of some 1,400,000 tons of shipping, or about 10 per cent of total shipping losses caused by U-boats throughout the war. There were only eighteen cows (2.4 per cent) out of a deployed U-boat force of some 750 boats. To put it another way, with the benefit of hindsight we can see that one milk cow possessed the approximate value to U-boat Command of four attack boats. This rough figure takes no account of the strategic value of the milk cows in tying down enemy forces, by permitting U-boats to attack areas that normally they could not reach.

It is unlikely that there is any lesson to be learned from the refuelling operations themselves. Modern submarines have much longer ranges than the U-boat of 1939–45 – almost infinite range in the case of nuclear-powered boats – although the large reduction in the number of ship targets does mean that modern submarines might have to patrol for much lengthier periods (merchant ships today are larger, but fewer in number). In particular, the submarines of NATO countries are always likely to have surface tankers or land bases available.

For a time there was considered to be a serious threat to North Atlantic shipping from the large Russian submarine fleet, but again the Soviet Navy never felt it necessary to provide submersible tankers to supply their submarines.

The other side of the coin is that aircraft ranges and detection systems – particularly those carried by satellites – are such that refuelling by a minor power of its submarines in NATO-controlled seas would easily be detected. Thus any future refuelling of attack submarines by submersible tankers would certainly best be carried out wholly underwater. It is surprising now that German U-boats did not make more use of this strategy; the milk cows were at their most vulnerable while cow and suckler had hoses connected as both boats travelled slowly on the surface.

The real lesson from the story of the milk cows is the folly of over-reliance on any code or cipher system that an enemy can overhear, and it is perhaps significant that modern military communications systems rely heavily on tightly focused beams sent to a satellite and then onto the recipient. These cannot be so easily intercepted.

The U-boat skippers who survived the war were not those who said, 'We'll refuel in square XYZ'. The survivors were those who said, 'We'll refuel in that square I told you about just before we sailed' (or who, indeed, ignored instructions from U-boat Command altogether). The 'square I told you about' represents an example of the 'one-time' code system, still widely believed to provide the only absolutely secure form of code. Just two parties are involved and both make reference to a source (more commonly a book or manual) known only to them for translating different words. A typical example might be for one party to tell the other to find the seventh word on the eighth page, the twentieth word on the fifteenth page, and so on. A different book is used for each message, so that code-breakers can never find a pattern by repetition of common words between messages. The big problem with the one-time system is that it cannot address all the units of an army, navy or air force at once, although it was used to transfer knowledge of German Enigma messages between Allied sites.

The increasing use of the Internet for computer communications brings its own security fears. The original rationale for the Internet was to provide a telephone line-based communications system in the USA in the event of a general disruption of other communications as might have occurred in a nuclear war. By definition, then, the Internet is easily accessible to any-one with a telephone line and the right computer equipment. The idea of carrying out any kind of secure or confidential transaction over the Internet seems to be fraught with danger, yet increasingly users are being invited to carry out financial transactions in this way using computer encryption technology that is unlikely to have been licensed unless governments can break the code used. Far too many hackers have broken far too many computer encryption schemes. As has already been explained, decryption in principle comprises only systematic trial and error against messages of known content, although greatly accelerated by the acquisition of some clues. Thus anyone who knows that an Internet line is being used to pay, say, a gas account by credit card has a big start in being able to discover your credit card number. The reader's attention is also drawn to another very common security flaw: there is absolutely no point in having state-of-the-art encryption for your personal details sent over the Internet if the business concerned then dumps the decrypted data all over its website for any hacker to see. This elementary security blunder has caught out very many companies doing business over the Internet, including many household names.

The author would never conduct any confidential business over the Internet, nor with a mobile telephone. Telephones using land lines are safer, but can be tapped. It was announced around three decades ago that bored telephone operators amused themselves by listening in to phone conversations.

The moral of the story of the milk cows is this: always assume that others can read and decipher your messages, whether actual or electronic. Just make sure that, even after being read, your message still conveys nothing except to the intended recipient.

Appendix 1

Results Achieved by the Milk Cows

Since the cows were intended only to refuel other U-boats, and not to make any attacks, any results which they achieved were an added bonus to U-boat Command. These were as follows:

1. Ships sunk by gun or torpedo

U-boat	Type	Sunk (tons)	Damaged (tons)
U 116	XB	2 (11,377)	–
U 180	IXD1	2 (13,298)	–
U 195	IXD1	2 (14,391)	1 (6,797)

2. Aircraft shot down or forced to crash

U-boat	Type	Aircraft	U-boat	Type	Aircraft
U 219	XB	1	U 487	XIV	1
U 459	XIV	2	U 489	XIV	1
U 461	XIV	½	U 1059	VIIF	1
U 462	XIV	1½	U 1060	VIIF	2

3. Ships sunk or damaged by mines laid by U-minelayers (Type XB)

Date	U-boat	Location	Sunk (tons)	Damaged (tons)
10.42	U 117	N.E. Iceland	0	0
2.43	U 118	Straits of Gibraltar	3 (14,064) + 1 corvette	2 (11,269) + 1 destroyer
2.43	U 119	Reykjavik	0	0
4.43	U 117	Casablanca	1 (3,777)	2 (14,269)
6.43	U 119	Halifax	1 (2,937)	1 (7,176)
9.43	U 220	St John's	2 (7,199)	0

Note: mines laid by other types of U-boat are not included in the above tally.
Totals: Thirteen merchant ships sunk (67,043 tons) together with one corvette. Six merchant ships (39,511 tons) and one destroyer damaged. Ten aircraft shot down.

Appendix 2

Spanish Co-operation 1940–2

Four German tankers lying in Spanish ports were used to provide fuel and provisions for U-boats during the early part of the war, with the connivance of the Spanish authorities. The U-boats concerned crept in at dead of night, and then slipped away again before the following morning. According to U-boat war diaries, the following refuellings took place:

Tanker *Bessel*, Code 'Bernado' lying at Vigo (north-west Spain): U 43, 19.6.40; U 29, 21.6.40; U 52, 1–2.7.40; U 77, 8.11.41; U 96, 27–28.11.41; U 574, 11–12.12.41; U 575, 12–13.12.41; U 434, 15.12.41.

Tanker *Thalia*, Code 'Gata' lying at Cadiz (south-west Spain): U 25, 30.1.40; U 109, 22.7.41; U 331, 1–2.8.41; U 564, 14–15.10.41; U 204, 16.10.41; U 652, 27–28.11.41 (Out of supplies).

Tanker *Corrientes*, Code 'Culebra' lying at Las Palmas (Canary Islands): U 124, 4.3.41; U 105, 5.3.41; U 106, 6.3.41; U 123, 25.6.41; U 69, 30.6.41; U 103, 6.7.41.

Repairs only: tanker *Max Albrecht*, lying at El Ferrol (north-west Spain): U 30, 25.6.40; U 68, 17.5.42; U 105, 12–28.6.42; U 66, 25.9.42; U 193, 10–20.2.44.

British diplomatic pressure ended the use of the *Corrientes* in July 1941. After the end of 1941, U-tankers were sufficiently available to make the use of 'neutral' ports less attractive. Three of the U-boats calling at El Ferrol did so for repairs after air attack. U 66 had to make an emergency visit for fuel after being inadvertently supplied with water as well as oil by U 460. On 9 July 1942, arrangements were made with the Spanish Navy to assist a U-boat in trouble, since British destroyers deliberately barred the route to El Ferrol.

U 760 entered Vigo on 7 September 1943 as both diesels had failed. Diplomacy was begun and spare parts were sent, but Germany's fortunes in the war were fading and the Spanish interned the U-boat. Thereafter, damaged U-boats in a similar situation were ordered to scuttle off the coast of Spain, but to tell the Spanish authorities that they had been sunk by enemy action. Under international law, the crews were then less likely to be interned. U-boats were also reminded that they could use international law to seek time for repairs (normally twenty-four hours) in a neutral port.

Spain also co-operated with Germany by the installation and operation of radio beacons, used to aid position fixing by vessels and aircraft in the Atlantic and Bay of Biscay. This was known as the 'Elektra-Sonne' system.

Appendix 3

Known War Cruises

The average cruise lasted two to three months, followed by one month in port. The dates given below are taken from the U-boat war diaries. Those published in the BdU (U-boat Command) war diary generally lag by one day, presumably owing to the time needed to send the information from the boat's harbour. A few dates in the BdU war diary differ substantially from those given in the boat's war diary.

Type XB (U-Minelayers)
Type XB minelayers normally carried a crew of five officers and forty-seven men, including a medical officer, total fifty-two. The numerical order shown is the approximate order in which the U-minelayers entered service in their refuelling capacity, from April 1942 to October 1943.

U 116 (Korvkpt von Schmidt; Kptlt Grimme) War diaries 26.7.41–22.9.42.
  1. 4.4.42–5.5.42 to Lorient via Bergen (10 days) ex Kiel.
  2. 16.5.42–9.6.42 Bermuda ex Lorient; cow.
  3. 27.6.42–23.8.42 Cape Verde Is ex Lorient; cow.
  4. 22.9.42–15.10.42 N. Atlantic air gap ex Lorient; cow.
  SUNK Unknown causes 15.10.42 Atlantic.
  Grimme+ (No survivors)
U 117 (Korvkpt Neumann) War diaries 25.10.41–13.8.43.
  1. 6.10.42–22.11.42 N. Azores ex Kiel; minelayer, cow.
  2. 24.12.42–7.2.43 NW Azores ex Lorient; cow.
  3(i). 8.2.43–8.2.43 Direct to Brest ex Lorient.
  3(ii). 31.3.43–14.5.43 Canary Is. ex Brest; cow, minelayer.
  4. 22.7.43–7.8.43 n. & w. Azores ex Bordeaux; cow.
  SUNK 7.8.43 *Card* a/c (FIDO) 39.32N 38.21W (off Azores).
  Neumann+ (No survivors)
U 118 (Korvkpt Czygan) War diaries 6.12.41–27.2.43.
  1. 19.9.42–16.10.42 Madeira ex Kiel; cow.
  2. 12.11.42–13.12.42 Canary Is ex Lorient; cow.
  3(i). 7.1.43–8.1.43 Direct to Brest ex Lorient.
  3(ii). 26.1.43–27.2.43 Madeira ex Brest; minelayer, cow.

4. 27.5.43–12.6.43 Azores ex France; cow.

SUNK 12.6.43 *Bogue* a/c 30.49N 33.49W (west of Canary Is.).

Czygan+ (16 survivors)

U 119 (Kptlt Zech; Kptlt von Kameke) War diaries 1.8.42–27.6.43 (no diary entries from 9.8.42–31.1.43).

1. 4.8.42–10.8.42 Skagerrak ex Kiel; minelayer.

2. 6.2.43–1.4.43 Iceland, air gap ex Kiel; minelayer, cow.

3. 25.4.43–24.6.43 Halifax, Canada ex Bordeaux; minelayer, cow.

SUNK 24.6.43 HMS *Starling* (2nd Escort Grp) 45.00N 11.59W (west of Bay of Biscay).

von Kameke+ (No survivors)

U 219 (Korvkpt Burghagen) War diaries 5.10.43–1.1.44.

1. 5.10.43–1.1.44 Cape Verde Is. ex Kiel; cow (minelaying mission abandoned).

2. 23.8.44–11.12.44 to Indian Ocean ex Bordeaux; transporter.

Taken over by Japan at Djakarta as I.505 in May 1945. Survived war.

U 220 (Oblt z.S. Barber) War diaries 27.3.43–29.10.43

1. 8.9.43–27.10.43 USA, then mid-Atlantic ex Bergen; minelayer, cow.

SUNK 27.10.43 *Block Island* a/c 48.53N 33.30W (north of Azores).

Barber+ (No survivors)

U 233 (Kptlt Steen) War diaries 22.9.43–27.5.44.

1. 28.5.44–6.7.44 Halifax, Canada ex Germany; minelayer (sunk en route).

SUNK 6.7.44 *Card* DEs + a/c 42.16N 59.49W (off Halifax).

Steen+ (29 survivors)

U 234 (Kptlt Fehler) War diaries 2.3.44–17.4.45.

1. 18.4.45–5.45 to Japan ex Germany; transporter.

May 1945 SURRENDERED USA (mid-Atlantic).

Fehler —

Type XIV (U-Tankers)

Normal crew carried was six officers and forty-seven men; total fifty-three. Extra crew members were sometimes carried as replacements for other U-boats. The numerical order shown is the approximate order in which the U-tankers entered service. The first series of six boats was ready for operations in 1942 and all were in service by August. The second series of four boats entered service in mid-1943.

U 459 (Kptlt → Korvkpt von Wilamowitz-Moellendorf) War diaries 15.11.41–27.7.43.

1. 22.3.42–15.5.42 Bermuda ex Kiel.

2. 6.6.42–19.7.42 N. Azores ex St Nazaire.

3. 18.8.42–4.11.42 S. Atlantic ex St Nazaire.

4. 19.12.42–7.3.43 S. Atlantic ex St Nazaire.

5. 20.4.43–3.6.43 N. Azores ex Bordeaux.

6. 22.7.43–24.7.43 mid-Atlantic ex Bordeaux.

SUNK 24.7.43 Bomber 45.53N 10.38W (west of Bay of Biscay).

v. Wilamowitz-Moellendorf+ (44 survivors).

U 460 (Kptlt Schaefer; Oblt z.S. → Kptlt Schnoor) War diaries 24.12.41–4.10.43.

1. 7.6.42–31.7.42 Bermuda ex Kiel.

2(i). 27.8.42–29.8.42 Cape Verde Is. ex St Nazaire.

2(ii). 1.9.42–12.10.42 Cape Verde Is. ex St Nazaire.

3. 11.11.42–19.12.42 W. Canary Is. ex St Nazaire.

4(i). 26.1.43–29.1.43 N. Azores ex St Nazaire.

4(ii). 31.1.43–5.3.43 N. Azores ex St Nazaire.

5. 24.4.43–25.6.43 Central Atlantic ex Bordeaux.

6. 30.8.43–4.10.43 NW. Azores ex Bordeaux.

SUNK 4.10.43 *Card* a/c (caused marine accident) 43.13N 28.58W off Azores.

Schnoor+ (No survivors)

U 461 (Kptlt → Korvkpt Stiebler) War diaries 21.6.42–1.8.43.

1. 21.6.42–16.8.42 N. Atlantic ex Kiel (special mission).

2. 7.9.42–17.10.42 E. St John's ex St Nazaire.

3. 19.11.42–3.1.43 Cape Verde Is. ex St Nazaire.

4. 13.2.43–22.3.43 Azores ex St Nazaire.

5. 20.4.43–30.5.43 N. Atlantic ex St Nazaire.

6. 27.7.43–30.7.43 Central Atlantic ex Bordeaux.

SUNK 30.7.43 Bomber 45.42N 11W (Bay of Biscay).

Stiebler− (15 survivors)

U 462 (Oblt z.S. → Kptlt Vowe) War diaries 5.3.42–1.8.43.

1. 23.7.42–21.9.42 SE. St John's ex Kiel.

2. 18.10.42–7.12.42 Cape Verde Is. ex St Nazaire.

3(i). 20.1.43–22.1.43 N. Azores ex St Nazaire.

3(ii). 19.2.43–11.3.43 N. Azores ex St Nazaire.

4. 1.4.43–24.4.43 N. Azores ex Bordeaux.

5(i). 17.6.43–17.6.43 Direct to La Pallice ex Bordeaux.

5(ii). 19.6.43–23.6.43 Central Atlantic ex La Pallice.

5(iii). 28.6.43–6.7.43 Central Atlantic ex Bordeaux.

5(iv). 27.7.43–30.7.43 Central Atlantic ex Bordeaux.

SUNK 30.7.43 Bomber 45.08N 10.57W (Bay of Biscay; scuttled after heavy damage).

Vowe− (64 survivors)

U 463 (Korvkpt Wolfbauer) War diaries 2.4.42–18.5.43

1. 11.7.42–3.9.42 mid-Atlantic ex Kiel.

2. 28.9.42–11.11.42 N. Azores ex St Nazaire.

3. 6.12.42–26.1.43 SW. Azores ex Brest.

4. 4.3.43–17.4.43 N. Azores ex St Nazaire.

5. 12.5.43–15.5.43 N. Azores ex St Nazaire.

SUNK 15.5.43 Bomber 45.57N 11.40W (Bay of Biscay).

Wolfbauer+ (No survivors)

U 464 (Kptlt Harms) War diaries 30.4.42–24.8.42.

1. 4.8.42–20.8.42 N. Atlantic ex Kiel, via Bergen.

SUNK 20.8.42 Bomber 61.25N 14.40W (south of Iceland).

Harms– (53 survivors)

U 487 (Oblt z.S. Metz) War diaries 21.12.42–18.7.43.

1. 27.3.43–12.5.43 N. Azores ex Kiel.

2. 15.6.43–13.7.43 SW. Azores ex Bordeaux.

SUNK 13.7.43 *Core* a/c 27.15N 34.18W (off Azores).

Metz+ (32 survivors)

U 488 (Oblt z.S. Bartke; Oblt z.S. Studt) War diaries 18.5.43–12.12.43.

1. 18.5.43–10.7.43 SW. Azores ex Kiel.

2. 8.9.43–12.12.43 Azores ex Bordeaux.

3. 26.2.44–26.4.44 Cape Verde Is. ex Bordeaux.

SUNK 26.4.44 US DEs (*Croatan* Grp) 17.54N 38.05W (off Cape Verde Is.).

Studt+ (No survivors)

U 489 (Oblt z.S. Schmandt) War diaries 8.3.43–5.8.43

1. 22.7.43–4.8.43 N. Azores ex Kiel

SUNK 4.8.43 Bomber 61.11N 14.38W (west of Faeroes, south of Iceland)

Schmandt– (53 survivors and 3 rescued German fliers)

U 490 (Oblt z.S. Gerlach) War diaries 27.3.43–4.5.44.

1. 4.5.44–12.6.44 Cape Verde Is. ex Kiel

SUNK 12.6.44 US DEs + a/c (*Croatan* Grp) 42.47N 40.08W (mid-Atlantic).

Gerlach– (60 survivors)

Summary for the Milk Cows

Approximately 50 completed cruises; 18 cows.

Note: Commander +/–: +, commander died; –, commander survived.

Source: *US Submarine Losses World War II*, Naval Historical Division, Office of Chief of Naval Operations, Washington, 1963. Quoted in Cremer 1984.

Type IXD1 (U-transporters)

U 180 (Korvkpt Musenberg; Oblt z.S. Steinfeldt) War diaries 16.5.42–30.9.43.

1. 9.2.43–2.7.43 Indian Ocean ex Kiel. Decommissioned 30.9.43.

2. 20.8.44–23?.8.44 Indian Ocean ex Bordeaux.

SUNK, probably mine or marine accident in Bay of Biscay on or after 23.8.44.

Steinfeldt+ (No survivors)

U 195 (Korvkpt Buchholz; Oblt z.S. Reisen) War diaries 5.9.42–23.7.43.

1. 20.3.43–23.7.43 Indian Ocean ex Kiel. Decommissioned 30.9.43.
2. 20.8.44–28.12.44 Indian Ocean ex Bordeaux.
3. 26.1.45–4.3.45 Norway ex Penang. Returned to Penang with defect. Taken over by Japan at Djakarta as I.506 in May 1945. Survived war.

Type VIIF (torpedo transport)
U 1059 19.3.44 Leupold- SUNK *Block Is* a/c 13.10N 33.44W.
U 1060 27.10.44 Brammer+ SUNK *Implacable* a/c 65.24N 12E.
U 1061 May 1945 Hinrichs, Jaeger. Scuttled by Allies (Operation Deadlight).
U 1062 30.9.44 Albrecht+ SUNK *Mission Bay* DEs 11.36N 34.44W.

Type VIID (minelayer)
U 213 31.7.42 v. Varendorff+ SUNK DEs 36.45N 22.50W.
U 214 26.7.44 Conrad+ SUNK HMS *Cooke* 49.55N 03.31W.
U 215 3.7.42 Hoeckner+ SUNK HMS *Le Tiger* 48N 66.38W.
U 216 20.10.42 Schulz+ SUNK Bomber 48.21N 19.25W.
U 217 5.6.43 Reichenberg-Klinke+ SUNK *Bogue* a/c 30.18N 42.50W.
U 218 May 1945 Becker, Stock. Scuttled by Allies (Operation Deadlight).

Foreign captured submarines
UIT 22 11.3.44 Wunderlich+ SUNK Bomber 41.28S 17.40E.
UIT 23 14.2.44 Striegler- SUNK HMS *Tallyho* 04.25N 100.09E.

U A (ex Turkish) (Kptlt Cohausz 21.9.39–29.8.40) (Korvkpt Eckermann 30.8.40–16.2.42) (Korvkpt Cohausz 16.2.42–24.4.42).
0. 27.4.40–10.5.40 Supplies to Norway ex Kiel, transporter.
1. 2.6.40–30.8.40 Freetown ex Kiel, patrol.
2. 25.2.41–18.3.41 N. Atlantic ex Kiel, patrol.
3(i). 14.4.41–26.4.41 Freetown ex Lorient, patrol.
3(ii). 4.5.41–30.7.41 Freetown ex Lorient, patrol.
4. 7.10.41–25.12.41 S. Atlantic ex Lorient, patrol.
5(i). 21.2.42–22.2.42 Abandoned with engine trouble.
5(ii). 14.3.42–24.4.42 Bermuda ex Lorient, cow (followed by return to Germany).

UD 3 (ex Dutch) (Fregkpt Rigele) War diaries 8.6.41–3.3.43.
1. 3.10.42–22.10.42 Kiel to Lorient, transit.
2. 3.11.42–6.1.43 Cape Verde Is. ex Lorient, torpedo transport.
3. 10.2.43–3.3.43 Gotenhafen ex Lorient, transit.

UD 5 (ex Dutch) (Kpt z.S. Mahn; Oblt z.S. Koenig from 21.12.42) War diaries 1.11.41–9.1.43.
1. 27.8.42–12.11.42 Cape Verde Is. ex Kiel, patrol.
2. 21.12.42–9.1.43 Germany ex Lorient, transit.

The Principal U-boat Types in this Book

Type	Comments	Displacement (Surfaced at full load; tons)	Max. speed (knots)	Max. cruising range (miles)	Guns (not AA)	Torpedo-tubes (cm)
IIC	Coastal	341	12	3,800	–	3 × 53.3
VIIC	Seagoing	769	18	8,500	1 × 88mm	5 × 53.3
VIID	Small minelayer	965	17	11,200	–	5 × 53.3
VIIF	Small transporter	1,181	18	14,700	–	5 × 53.3
IXC	Ocean-going	1,120	18	13,450	1 × 105mm	6 × 53.3
IXC/40	Improved IXC	1,144	18	13,850	1 × 105mm	6 × 53.3
IXD1	U-transporter	1,610	16	12,750	–	–
IXD2	U-cruiser	1,616	19	31,500	1 × 105mm	6 × 53.3
XB	U-minelayer	1,763	17	18,450	1 × 105mm	2 × 53.3
XIV	U-tanker	1,688	15	12,350	–	–

Appendix 5

U-boat Quadrant Map

Each lettered square was divided into nine sub-squares, and each sub-square into nine smaller squares. The smaller squares would themselves be divided into eighty-one lesser squares. Thus a rendezvous point might be referred to as 'Quadrant BD7434'.

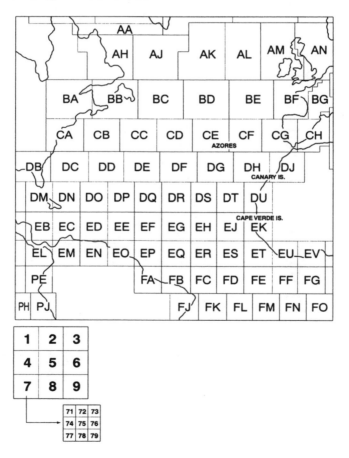

Appendix 6

German Naval Ranks

The Germans had a slightly larger number of ranks available to junior officers at sea than was the case with the British Navy; thus there are no direct British equivalents for intermediate grades. These are the common ranks found among officers at sea, in declining order:

Kpt zS	Kapitaen zur See; captain
Fregkpt	Fregattenkapitaen; commander
Korvkpt	Korvettenkapitaen; lieutenant commander
Kptlt	Kapitaenleutnant; lieutenant
Oblt zS	Oberleutnant zur See; sub lieutenant
Lt zS	Leutnant zur See; junior sub lieutenant

Bibliography

The bulk of the general material cited in this book was derived from the author's private database: a compilation of German Navy operations between 1926 and 1945. Other general data were obtained from the following sources:

Boeddeker, G. and Luebbe, B., *Die Boote im Netz*, Bergisch Gladbach, 1994.

Busch, R. and Roell, H.J., *Der U-Boot Krieg 1939–1945. Die Deutschen U-Boot Kommandenten*, Verlag Mittler & Sohn, 1996 (lists German U-boat commanders).

Doenitz, K., *Memoirs: Ten Years and Twenty Days*, Lionel Leventhal Ltd, 1990.

Frank, W., *The Sea Wolves*, George Mann (Maidstone), 1973 (English revised edition).

'Fuehrer Conferences on Naval Affairs', *Brassey's Naval Annual* (1948), William Clowes & Sons Ltd.

Jones, G., *Autumn of the U-boats*, William Kimber, 1984.

Kuenne, R.E., *The Attack Submarine: a Study in Strategy*, Yale University Press, 1965.

Mielke, O., *Tankmotorschiff 'Charlotte Schliemann'*, Schicksale Deutscher Schiffe Nr. 68 (1955).

MOD Naval Historical Branch, *War with Japan*, vol. IV, HMSO, 1995 (contains some information about the role of the U-boats in the Far East).

Morison, S.E., *History of United States Naval Operations in World War II*, vol. X, 'The Atlantic Battle Won', Little, Brown & Co., Boston, USA, 1990 reprint.

Niestlé, A., *German U-boat Losses in World War II*, Greenhill, 1998.

Robertson, T., *Walker RN*, Pan Books, 1956.

Roessler, E., *The U-boat – The Evolution and Technical History of German Submarines*, Arms and Armour Press Ltd, 1981.

Rohwer, J., *Axis Submarine Successes of World War Two*, Greenhill, 1999.

Rohwer, J., *U-Boote*, Gerhard Stalling Verlag, 1962.

Rohwer, J. and Huemmelchen, G., *Chronology of the War at Sea*, Parts I and II, Ian Allan.

Roskill, Captain S.W., *The War at Sea*, vols. 2 and 3 (Part I), HMSO, 1954–61.

Taylor, J.C., *German Warships of World War II*, Ian Allan, 1966.

Excellent descriptions of life aboard U-boats can be found in:

Brennecke, J., *The Hunters and the Hunted*, Corgi paperbacks, 1960.

Cremer, P., *U 333*, Bodley Head, 1984.

Sellwood, A.V., *The Warring Seas* (about U 234), Universal-Tandem Publishing Co., 1972.

Werner, H.A., *Iron Coffins*, Pan Books, 1972.

The constant battle between aircraft and U-boat is graphically conveyed in:

Poolman, K., *The Sea Hunters*, Sphere Books, 1982.

Price, A., *Aircraft versus Submarine*, William Kimber, 1973.

Y'Blood, W.T., *Hunter-Killer*, Naval Institute Press, USA, 1983.

The intelligence battle is described in:

Beesly, P., *Very Special Intelligence*, Sphere books, 1978.

Hinsley, F.H., *British Intelligence in the Second World War* (3 vols), HMSO, 1979–88.

HyperWar Foundation, *Ultra in the Atlantic*, vols II and IV. An account of American decryptions with Ultra, containing much information hard to obtain elsewhere. Available at www.ibiblio.org/hyperwar. Transcribed and formatted for HTML by Chuck Roberts and Ian Williams.

The National Archives at Kew (London, England) contains many valuable documents from British Intelligence. A high proportion of the original transcripts was destroyed after the war, but summary data are available from the RAF, Coastal Command and the Admiralty. Some of the most useful are outlined below:

Coastal Command Reviews, vols I–IV AIR.15.

U-boat Dispositions 9.39 to 5.45 AIR.15. 861.

Air Historical Branch – *The RAF in Maritime War*, vols III–V AIR.14. 47, 48, 74.

Admiralty Intelligence summaries ADM.223. 15, 16, 17.

Raw Ultra B transcripts are held in DEFE3.

The war diaries (KTBs) of the U-boats are available from a number of sources. They are, of course, written in German. The original copies were held by the British Admiralty for a long time, but were released for public perusal in 1977. It is not clear why they were deemed to be so secret for so long; there is nothing in them that could not have been guessed from Roskill's *War at Sea* in the mid-1950s. The microfilm copies made during that time may be consulted by arrangement at Naval Historical Branch (Foreign Documents Section), Ministry of Defence, 24 Store, PP20, Main Road, HM Naval Base, Portsmouth, Hants, PO1 3LU. However, the documents cannot be copied. Copies on microfilm may be obtained from NARA, Washington, USA, but their service can be slow to a foreign requester. Copies may also be obtained from the original documents which are now held at Freiberg, Germany. Copies may be consulted at the U-boat Museum in Cuxhaven, Germany: Traditionsarchiv Unterseeboote, Bahnhofstrasse, D-27478 Cuxhaven, Germany. The U-boat Command war diaries – known as the BdU war diaries – are also available from the above sources on microfilm. English translations of the war diaries may be consulted at the office of the Naval Historical Branch, address above. *The U-boat War in the Atlantic 1939–1945*, MOD (Navy), HMSO, 1989 is actually the annotated history prepared for the Admiralty by Fregattenkapitaen Hessler immediately after the war from the BdU war diaries, and kept secret long after the war diaries had themselves been released.

Horst Bredow's U-Boot Archiv additionally contains many personal accounts from U-boat survivors that cannot be found elsewhere. The details of the cruise of U 219 to the Far East were taken from this source.

The *Schaltung Kueste* is the magazine for ex-U-boatmen and contains many survivors' stories. They are written in German. Contact Fregatten-kapitaen Guenther Hartmann, Neugartenstr. 36, 88709 Hagnau a.B., Germany.

Index

251

Brauel, Oblt z.S., 197, 201
Brazil, operational area, 37, 41–3, 92, 108, 150, 211
Brest, U-boat base, see French bases
British Intelligence, 13–14, 16–19, 24, 28, 43, 45, 52, 60, 66–7, 73, 77, 94–8, 100–2, 105, 109, 111–12, 132–5, 145, 153, 155, 157, 160, 166, 168–9, 171, 173, 176, 188–91, 193, 195, 204, 211, 223
Buchholz, Korvkpt, 152, 164–5
Bullaren (T), 22
Burggraf, U-boat group, 103
Burghagen, Korvkpt, 201–2, 205, 222, 224–5, 228, 232

Cagni, Italian submarine, 95, 106
Cape Town, operational area, 17, 23, 26, 43, 45, 86–92, 94, 120, 163–4, 166
Cappellini, Italian submarine, see also UIT 24, 88, 165, 174
Caribbean, operational area, 30, 32, 34, 37, 41–2, 45, 77, 166
Carls, Admiral, 6
Chandra Bose, Indian Nationalist Leader, 164
Charlotte Schliemann (T), 10, 27, 92–3, 110, 164, 166, 169–71, 210
Checkmate, 25, 43
Chop zone (German/Japanese), 168
Churchill, Winston, 9
Ciphers, Allied, 65, 97, 105
Ciphers, German, viii, 12 *et seq.*, 22, 24, 27, 105, 148, 172, 198, 209–10, 215, 217, 233
Clausen, Kptlt, 23
Coastal Command, 27, 64, 110–11, 117, 122–3, 134, 137–45, 220
Cohausz, Kptlt, 9, 31
Colossus, computer, 19–20
Constanza, U-boat base, 185
Convoy system, 9, 31–2, 37, 172, 177, 181
Convoys
DN.21, 106
GUS.23, 205
HX.126, 12
HX.209, 77
HX.228, 104
HX.229, 104–5
HX.230, 107
ON.113, 70
ON.131, 77
ON.166, 103

ON.202, 190
ON.206, 203
ONS.18, 190
ONS.20, 203
ONS.122, 71
ONS.144, 81
ONS.165, 103
ONS.167, 103
OS.33, 68
PQ.17, 81
SC.95, 71
SC.118, 101
SC.121, 104
SC.122, 104–5
SC.126, 107
SL.119, 76
TM.1, 97
TS.37, 116
UGS.4, 97
UGS.9, 149
Corrientes (T), 10–11, 16–17, 21, 92, 110, 238
Crash-dive, 54
Creeping attack, 127, 144
Cremer, Kptlt, 33, 89–90, 95, 159, 161
Crew rotation, 59
Czygan, Korvkpt, 74, 77, 82–3, 98–9, 149–50

Deecke, Kptlt, 201
Delphin, U-boat group, 97–8
Deutsche Werke, 7, 44, 215
Deutschland, see also *Luetzow*, 3
Dinghies, rubber, 47
Diving times, 46, 50, 53, 55, 65, 84, 124
Djakarta, U-boat base, 163, 172–3, 176–8, 227–8
Do217, long-range bomber, 186
Doenitz, Admiral, see U-boat Command
Doggerbank (T), 43
Dommes, Korvkpt, 172
Dora, active radar, 115
Drewitz, Kptlt, 158

Eckermann, Korvkpt, 11
Egerland (T), 11, 15–16
Eick, Kptlt, 169, 204
Eisbaer, U-boat group, 87–91, 234
Elbe, blockade runner, 16
'Electric' U-boat, see Type XXI
Elektra-Sonne, navigational aid, 230, 239
Emmerman, Kptlt, 87, 150, 161

Italian U-boats, see also UIT-boats, 36, 41–2, 62, 85, 88, 95, 99, 108, 128, 163–6, 169, 173

Jaeger, Oblt z.S., 231
Jaguar, light destroyer, 56, 127, 129, 134–5
Janssen, Oblt z.S., 194, 204
Japanese submarines, 169, 176, 179, 228–9
Junker, Fregkpt, 116, 170–2
Ju88, long-range aircraft, 27, 123, 126, 129–30, 138, 144, 186

'K' design team, 4–6, 215
Kapstadt, U-boat group, 23–4
Kentrat, Korvkpt, 177
KG40 (V) Group, 123
King, US Admiral, 149
Koch, Oblt z.S., 125–6, 152
Kondor, light destroyer, 56, 127, 134
Koppenhagen, Korvkpt, 134–5
Kormoran, auxiliary cruiser, 11
Korth, Kptlt, 15
Kota Pinang (T), 12, 17, 22–3, 28
Kulmerland, German blockade runner, 191
Kuppisch, Kptlt, 159–61
Kurier, flash transmitter, 229

Laconia, liner, 88
Lange, Kptlt, 121, 151
Lassen, Kptlt, 83, 105–6
Lavatory, high-pressure, 222
Lech, blockade runner, 16
Leigh Light, 64
Lemp, Kptlt, 14
Leupold, Oblt z.S., 210
Leuthen, U-boat group, 187–8, 190–1
Loewenherz, U-boat group, 107
Lohs, U-boat group, 71, 74
Long Lance, Japanese torpedo, 164
Looks, Kptlt, 192
Lorient, U-boat base, see French bases
Lothringen (T), 12, 15–17
Luchs, U-boat group, 77
Luedden, Kptlt, 109, 171, 213
Lueders, Kpt, 23
Luetzow, pocket battleship, 3, 182
Luftwaffe, 7, 14, 19, 26–7, 58, 118, 122–3, 130, 135, 138, 144, 181, 186, 228
Luis, Kptlt, 133

M 403, minesweeper, 175
M 433, minesweeper, 231
M 1101, minesweeper, 38
M-boats (minesweepers), 56
Mahn, Kpt z.S., 76, 84–5
Maintenance, U-boat, 7, 49, 57–8
Manseck, Kptlt, 123, 149, 196
Mark 24 Mine, see Fido
Markworth, Kptlt, 75, 157, 214
Max Albrecht (T), 238
Me 410, German long-range fighter, 123
Mechanism of refuelling, 9, 15, 33–4, 46–7, 151, 195
Mediterranean Sea, operational area, 18, 23, 165, 183
Meier, Oblt z.S., 177–8
Meise, U-boat group, 107, 109
'Mercator' boats, 173, 177
Merchant aircraft carriers (MACs), 118
Merten, Korvkpt, 87
Metox, radar receiver, 51, 53, 64–5, 76, 101–2, 105, 110–11, 113, 130, 145, 206
Metz, Oblt z.S., 48, 85, 109, 112, 116, 127, 152–4
Metzler, Kptlt, 159
Michel, auxiliary cruiser, 93
Minelaying, Allied, 38, 56, 90, 108, 178, 223, 228
Minelaying, German, 4, 8, 11, 35, 43, 52, 62–3, 69, 75, 99–100, 107–8, 117, 120–1, 130, 147–9, 155, 189–90, 194, 201, 209, 219, 230–1, 237
Missing U-boats, 60
Moewe, light destroyer, 56, 127, 129, 134–5
Mohr, Kptlt, 83, 116
Monsun (T), 191
Monsun, U-boat group, 152–5, 159, 167–70, 172, 228
Monsun, 2nd U-boat group, 169
Morale, of U-tanker crews, 59, 112, 124, 188, 233
Muenchen, weathership, 14
Muetzelburg, Kptlt, 38, 71
Musenberg, Korvkpt, 164
Mussolini, Benito, 23

Napoleon, 201
NATO, 234
Naval Command, German, 5–6, 9, 14, 22, 24, 31, 43, 73, 87, 132
Naval Group North, 100

255

258

260